THE SYMBOL OF TAOISM

THE YELLOW EMPEROR

LAO TSE

Shen Nung the Emperor of
Shen Nung Dynasty
(3494 B.C.)
He and his administration
tested all kinds of herbs to
ascertain their healing
effects. People honored
him as the God of herbolism.

THE GREAT TAO

DR. STEPHEN T. CHANG

Tao Publishing

Copyright © 1985 by Stephen T. Chang

Published by Tao Publishing

Tao Longevity LLC
P.O. Box 33910   , U.S.A.
Reno, NV 89533

First Printing 1985
Second Printing 1986
Third Printing 1987
Fourth Printing 1992
Fifth Printing 1994
Sixth Printing 1998

Typeset by Rex Ramseyer, The Ruling Arm, San Francisco

Printed by Edwards Brothers, Inc., Ann Arbor, Michigan, U.S.A.

Library of Congress Cataloging in Publication Data

Chang, Stephen Thomas, Date
    The great Tao.

    "A Tao Institute book."
    Bibliography: p.
    Includes index.
    1. Taoism.   I. Title.
BL1920.C44   1985   299'.514   85-4722
ISBN 0-942196-01-5

ABOUT THE AUTHOR

Dr. Stephen T. Chang is an internationally well-known scholar. His grandmother was a master-physician, while her father was both personal physician to Empress Tse Shi and the first Chinese ambassador to the United Kingdom. Dr. Chang has been trained in both Chinese and Western medicine, and in addition to his medical doctor degree, he holds doctor degrees in philosophy and theology. He also holds two law degrees. He lectures worldwide on various aspects of Taoism, and he is the author of the following books:

The Complete Book of Acupuncture
The Great Tao
The Complete System of Self-Healing: Internal Exercises
Tao of Healing Diet: Secrets of a Thin Body
The Tao of Sexology
The Forgotten Food Diet—Herbology and Health, and
The Tao of Management.

Several books—university and hospital textbooks—have been translated into ten languages. Dr. Chang is now chairman of the Foundation of Tao.

ACKNOWLEDGEMENTS

The author gratefully acknowledges the support and help of:

Helene Chang

Kate Leffler

Sam Matthews

Stephen Soja

James Sykes

Leonard Worthington

Nancy Worthington

PREFACE

I, Stephen Thomas Chang, the humble servant of Tao, pray that grace and peace surround those, who have great fortune and who have done many good deeds in the past, in their entrance into the Kingdom of God by means of the perfect knowledge of Tao.

Any form of life that exists in the universe is a meld of three states of being: the past, present, and future. The present is the result of past actions, and the future is the result of present actions.

Therefore, anything which exists has a purpose, a meaning, and anything with purpose exists.

The purpose of life is evolution. In the cycle of evolution, no form of life is excluded. Everything, from minerals to plants to animals to human beings, must evolve until it reaches everlasting peace, happiness, and existence in the Kingdom of God.

Everybody enters the Kingdom of God through his or her own efforts; one who sows goodness reaps goodness, and one who sows evil reaps evil. Those who sow goodness are closest to the shores of happiness, and those who sow evil are drowning in the ocean of suffering. To enter the Kingdom of God, one must evaluate one's physical consciousness, mental consciousness, and spiritual consciousness. Elevating the physical consciousness confers upon a person the power to liberate himself or herself from suffering, disease, and death; to correct mistakes or wrongdoing that may result in failure of the bodily functions; and to utilize knowledge and techniques that correct mistakes and wrongdoing. Elevating the mental consciousness confers upon a person the power to disseminate wisdom to overcome evil, sorrow, cruelty, stress, tension, anxiety, greed, and ignorance; to "live divinely" according to the laws of the universe; and to recognize the best course toward a better future. Elevating the spiritual consciousness confers upon a person the power to unite microcosm and macrocosm—human beings and God, to spiritualize his or her entire body to achieve immortality.

Dear friend, I urge you to seriously consider the precious teachings of the Holy masters: to make kindness and leniency the priority of life. Those who are kind will not be selfish, envious, critical, malicious, and impatient, but they will be generous, helpful, and charitable. Few Taoist teachings encourage "love," for love connotes desire, possession, and great egotism. In the name of love, countries are divided, people are killed, families are destroyed. The greater the love, the more attachment there is; the greater the attachment, the more Karma there is. Love embroils people in bitter suffering, and it pulls more souls downward than it pushes upward. Life is difficult, but it can be made easier if everyone were more lenient towards each other. When one person is lenient, that person starts a chain reaction of goodwill. Chain reactions always come full circle, and those who initiate goodwill receive goodwill.

Taoism is a very simple and easy science. That is why it is still strong after more than 6,000 years. It is strong because it benefits people easily, and people keep it strong. Life is simple and easy if one is a Taoist. It is also abundant, rewarding, and successful, because whatever one sows one reaps.

Let all of the negativities die with yesterday, and let all of the positivities be born anew today. May pleasure and honor be with you now and forevermore.

October 10, 1984
San Francisco, California U.S.A.

CONTENTS

INTRODUCTION

THE TAO

I

Tao is God, according to the Chinese, who translate Gospel John 1:1 thus: "In the beginning was the Tao, and the Tao was with God, and the Tao was God." According to the English translation of the Bible, the Word is God. And according to the original Greek version of the Bible, Logos is God. The word *Logos* generally connotes life, light, creation, power, wisdom, love, healing, spirit, force, knowledge, rational, logic, reality, and method. The Chinese word *Tao* has the same connotations as the word *Logos.* That is why the word *Tao* was used in the Chinese Biblical translation.

The ancient masters did not evision Tao as an old man who, seated above the clouds, struck people with a bolt of lightning when they transgressed. Since Tao is life, light, . . . , it is everything and everywhere. Since Tao is omnipresent, it is in you and me as long as we are alive; therefore, God can be experienced in our daily living.

Once, a request was put to the Taoist master Chuan Tse by his disciples.

"All-knowing master, please show us God," said they.

Chuan Tse replied, "God is omnipresent. He is in the table, in you, in me, . . . He is even in excrement."

"Oh master! How could God be there?!"

Chuan Tse replied, "If God were not in our bowel movement, we would all be in big trouble!"

Mankind's concern since the beginning has been and is that of survival. To survive one must learn to understand oneself, one's needs, one's functions, and one's goals. Mankind is prone to experiment. Experimenting wisely with knowledge and understanding of *cause and effect* is progress. Without awareness mankind faces sickness, disease and oftentimes sudden death. Subconsciously we all realize sickness is a road to death. No one wants or cares to be ill in any degree however small, for to suffer discomfort or pain detracts from the joy of living. To suffer is to die a thousand deaths.

Throughout the Bible we read of the sick being healed and the dying being brought back to life. Many philosophies and religions preach of health and immortality. In the New Testament, Jesus said, "Whosoever believeth in me should not perish, but have everlasting life." (Meaning you shall not die more than once.) Also, according to Genesis 5:24 "Enoch walked with God, and he was not, for God took him." He didn't die. All the generations of Adam recorded in the book of Genesis had a time of birth and a time of death except for Enoch. He walked with God, and God took him. "Everybody must die" is a universal principle; but where there is a principle, there are exceptions to it. Besides Enoch, those who have attained immortality include Elijah and the Taoists of China. How and why these individuals were able to accomplish this feat is simple. They walked with God. How does one walk with God—experience Tao? Can we, can you and I, learn to walk with God?

Many important religions and philosophies of the world have taught that the consciousness, spirit, or soul cannot die and that there are specific ways to prepare the consciousness for an after-life. Buddhism teaches people to prepare for their next life by undergoing asceticism.

Among all of these teachings we find no mention of how to prepare for the immortalization of the present physical body. It is really unnecessary to teach the preparing, or knowing, of the undying consciousness, for the spirit is not limited by space and time (it cannot cease to exist). The spirit is not limited by space and time because it is formless. Our bodies are physical forms, which are limited by birth and death. Since the spirit has no beginning or ending, it is infinite. We are wasting precious time when we sacrifice our present life—subjecting our physical bodies to renunciation or asceticism, for example—to prolong something that is everlasting.

There was a naive beggar who thought that everybody led lives tormented by starvation. He noticed that one man never came out of his house to beg.

He said to himself, "His life must be harder than mine. I will help him by giving him some of my food."

So the beggar ate half of his meager meal and offered the other half to the man, not realizing that he was a millionaire. The millionaire had no use for the dirty food and refused it.

16

"How kind he is to save this food for me and not take it for himself." thought the beggar.

From then on, the beggar always saved half of his food and left it on the millionaire's doorstep. Eventually the beggar starved himself to death, unknown to the millionaire, whose fortunes were too vast to be benefited from the beggar's contributions.

The truly important thing is to teach people to prepare for the immortalization of their physical bodies. Our life is short and fraught with problems; therefore, we should not increase the aggravation. The purpose of Taoism is to immortalize the present physical body by providing techniques that are practiced by human beings to promote a longer, healthier, happier, and wiser life. That is Taoism.

According to the Bible Jesus retained his physical body after resurrection. He continued to eat, preach, and travel until he was finally lifted. He is the quintessential Taoist adept because he had a spiritualized (a taoist term meaning immortalized), or transformed body.

But his disciples, Peter, John or Paul—none of them had a resurrection or immortalization. Why? And what about the multitudinous followers of Jesus?

Records show that Jesus had been in the East. Then he returned to Israel to teach "everlasting life," terms that are very Taoist in nature. He called himself the son of God. The people had never heard of these concepts, which caused great confusion amongst them. Perhaps they were not ready to accept these concepts. Perhaps three and a half years did not provide Jesus with enough time to share the technical information dealing with immortality with the people. In the Bible there are no records of teachings that explain the technical aspects of "everlasting life." The Bible does mention faith, but faith is a mental attitude, not a technique. Faith only leads to salvation, not immortalization. In James 2:17, it is stated that "Faith, if it hath not works, is dead, being alone." So faith without action— physical work—is dead. But biblical records indicate that no physical works were devised to help mankind achieve "everlasting life."

Jesus' disciples followed him for less than three and a half years, for they were mostly preoccupied with preaching, teaching, traveling, and working. In the book of Acts, it is evident that their religious pursuits were hurried. Furthermore, Paul did not even see Jesus personally. Their learning was incomplete, so they were not resurrected.

In China, Taoists have practiced walking with God, or Taoism, for at least six thousand years. About two thousand famous Taoists have attained immortality. Their personal histories can be found within the historical records.

What is "WALK WITH GOD?"
The human being follows (the laws of) the earth,
the earth follows the heavens,
the heavens follow God (Tao),
and God must follow nature.

Tao Te Ching

When we live according to the natural law, we walk with God. How do we live by the natural law? This is revealed by Taoism, the oldest religion, philosophy, and science in the world.

Taoism is a science because it is based upon a detailed understanding of underlying physical, chemical, biological, mathematical, psychological, and political theories and laws. Science rests on the assumption that all events of the entire universe can be described by physical theories and laws. But the sciences studied in our universsities deal with the material universe; they cannot deal with the spiritual or immaterial universes, which cannot be observed directly or indirectly through our senses. Taoism acknowledges that all elements of the universe are subject to the same physical theories and laws; therefore, the physical theories and laws of the material universe are applied to the spiritual universe. Taoism is a complete science, and an understanding of Taoism results in the complete understanding of the entire (material and immaterial) universe.

Taoism consists of many scientific techniques or methods that help immortalize the physical body. These techniques have endured over six thousand years of continuous testing; and the passage of time has increased their value, so greatly that Asians believe that Sakyamuni Buddha is the transformation of Lao-Tze, who was a grand master of Taoism. Even in the twentieth century, the teachings of Taoism are continuously being proven effective with scientific means. Valued preciously in the twentieth century, the Eight Great Systems of Taoism, which will be explained later, are tremendously beneficial for people of all walks of life and of all ages.

For thousands of years, these teachings have been kept beyond all possibilities of the attainment of complete knowledge. But I do have the feeling that this is the time for the secret to be unveiled to the world.

II

How the ancient Taoists incorporated the principles of philosophy, chemistry, physics, biology, mathematics, etc. into a system called Taoism can be summarized by the principles of Yin and Yang and the evolution of these principles into the sixty-four hexagrams.

The Nei Ching states that "The entire universe is an oscillation of the forces Yin and Yang." While many people who have given much time to the study of Eastern philosophies totally accept this statement as fact, very few have subjectively experienced or understand the elements by which it can be proven valid.

To explain Yin and Yang as they apply to the universe, it is necessary to imagine that state of pure being that preceded the creation of the cosmos. The ancient, sacred manuscripts that talk about the creation of the material universe begin with the question, "What thought could be the only thought that could possibly arise in that infinite state of omnipresence that preceded the creation of the cosmos?" We know that a thought is the result of perceiving an object in the world, but what would be the nature of a thought if the world of objects had not yet been created? The only thought that could possibly arise in that initial state of being would have to be one of self-awareness—there would be no other object in the world for that being to focus its attention on other than on itself. In other words, that initial state of omnipresence became aware of itself as being omnipresent. The first thought then was the exclamation, "I am omnipresent!" It's the same thing that happens when we reflect upon ourselves in a mirror and suddenly become aware of a particular physical characteristic that had been present all the while but which we had taken for granted only because our gaze was always directed outward. A logical second thought was, "Since I am omnipresent, I am all-powerful and can give birth (create) to anything I imagine!" As each thought "died" and another thought was "born," the high intensity energy of each of those thoughts began to vibrate less and less until solid matter, which any scientist will tell you is really energy, resulted. Thus the material world was created by the "birth and death" of thought that "molded" the energy from the initial, infinite source. Many wise men in history, after a sudden flash of illumination have exclaimed, "Why! The whole universe is nothing but a mass of thoughts!" *Yang* is the causative, active, creative principle—life; *Yin* is the resultant, passive, destructive principle—death. The universe is an oscillation of the forces commonly referred to as Yin and Yang.

Figure 1

The relationship of Yin and Yang to that of the world is often illustrated in another way by equating them to the negative and positive poles within a galvanic current flow; each is separate and distinct in expression, but both are an integral part of the same current. The current could not possibly exist without the bipolarity of its Yin and Yang elements and hence Yin and Yang are distinct and individual but they are also inseparable. Within every object in the universe is the constant, dynamic interaction of these two polar opposites.

Consideration of the principles regarding the natures of Yin and Yang has led Taoists to conclude that the feminine is Yin and the masculine is Yang.

Also, God, life, goodness, justice, righteousness, light, peace, sun, heat, wealth, happiness, heaven, risings. . . the active, that which is on the surface, is Yang.

And Satan, death, evil, injustice, unrighteousness, darkness, war, moon, cold, poverty, unhappiness, earth, sinkings. . . the passive, that which is deep or hidden, is Yin.

Just as we cannot know what heat is if we've never been cold, or what happiness is if we've never been sad, so too Yin and Yang can never exist in total isolation from one another—each is a different side of the same coin; both are constantly interacting and changing. This inseparable dualism persists through all things: food, attitudes, personal characteristics, thoughts, etc.

Yin and Yang represent every conceivable pair of opposites: birth and death, growth and decay, health and illness, etc. Everything that is born must die, and everything that grows will one day decay, and we can assume that what is Yin today is destined to become Yang in the future, and vice-versa. The relativity of Yin and Yang and the dynamic tension of their interaction are the basis of thought and expression in Taoism. Maintaining a balance between Yin and Yang results in perfect health of body, mind and soul.

The Taoists simplified the Yin and Yang symbol into a digram thus:

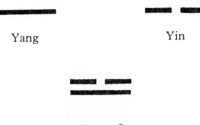

Figure 2

The Yin and Yang digram is called *Liang Yi,* and through "evolution" it gives rise to complex symbols (trigrams and hexagrams) that embody a profound explanation of the nature of the universe and of the life contained within it.

The *Liang Yi* can be equated to the atom. Just as the atom is composed of protons (which possess positive charges) and electrons (which possess negative charges), the *Liang Yi* is composed of positive and negative charges. The atom can be composed of one or many protons and electrons. To the *Liang Yi* many Yin and Yang (negative and positive) symbols may be added. Unlike the atom, the *Liang Yi* symbolizes spiritual insights into the basic nature of the universe.

Scientists have traced the complex organization of atoms into material objects. Taoists have traced the "evolution" of the *Liang Yi* into a "blueprint" of the universe, describing all levels of transmutation in the universe; from creation through growth, maturity, decline, dissolution, and re-creation. The "evolution" into the universal blueprint is a three-step process.

The first step involves the application of an algebraic formula, $(a + b)^3 = a^3 + 3a^2b + 3ab^2 + b^3$, to the *Liang Yi:*

Given a and b
Let a represent Yang ────
Let b represent Yin ── ──
then,

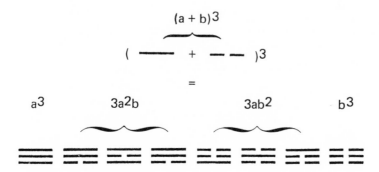

Eight trigrams are produced, and Taoists have assigned manifold attributes to each trigram to reflect such phenomena as: familial relations, cosmic phenomena, directional phenomena, and the Eight Pillars of Taoism.

Familial Relations

To each of the trigrams was assigned a familial title:

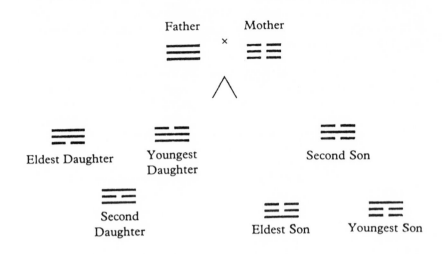

Father   Mother

Eldest Daughter   Youngest Daughter   Second Son

Second Daughter   Eldest Son   Youngest Son

Figure 3

You may have noticed that two Yin symbols are found in the "Son" trigrams and that two Yang symbols are found in the "Daughter" trigram. These trigrams reflect the patterns of parental trait domination discovered through genetic research. Boys possess more maternal traits than their sisters, and girls possess more paternal traits than their brothers.

Cosmic Phenomena

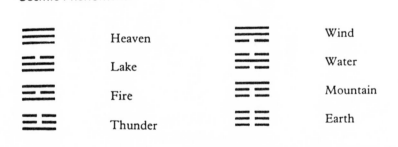

Heaven   Wind

Lake   Water

Fire   Mountain

Thunder   Earth

Figure 4

22

Directional Phenomena

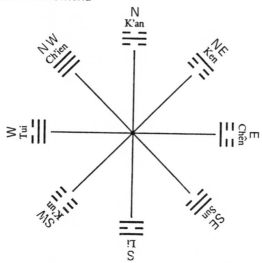

Figure 5

On earth, we orient ourselves according to the points of the compass. According to Taoism the directions are divided into nine basic directions: North, South, East, West, Northeast, Northwest, Southeast, Southwest, and the Middle Direction. When the trigrams are arranged specifically in their appointed positions around the Yin and Yang symbol, which occupies the Middle Direction, a *Pa-Kua* is formed and an energy pattern is developed.

Figure 6

23

This sign, hung on walls, will confer upon people a peaceful, balanced, and healing vibration; because the sign represents peace, healing, balance, love, and power. A similar sign can be found in western civilization:

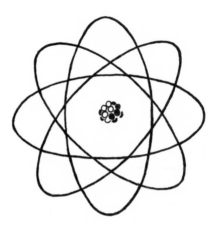

Figure 7

The person who does the right thing while following a path in the right direction, at the right time, will meet with longevity, peace, and success; if not, the outcome of the future will be completely reversed. This is a subject covered by Taoist Directionology, which will be discussed later.

Eight Pillars of Taoism

▬▬ represents the Tao of Philosophy, which comprise political, family, military, economic, business, amour, and many other philosophies.

▬ ▬ represents the Tao of Revitalization.

▬▬ represents the Tao of Balanced Diet (regular or daily food diet).

▬ ▬ represents the Tao of Forgotten Food Diet (Taoist Herbology).

24

☲ represents the Tao of Healing Art (acupuncture, acupressure, and other spiritual healing methods).

☵ represents the Tao of Sex Wisdom (Taoist Sexology).

☶ represents the Tao of Mastery (Personology, Fingerprint System, Numerology, Astrology, Directionology, and Symbology).

☳ represents the Tao of Success.

The principles of the Eight Pillars of Taoism will be explained in this book.

The second step of the "evolution" involves transforming the eight trigrams into eight hexagrams, by applying a mathematical formula, C x 2 = 2C (C = trigram), to every trigram. These are the results:

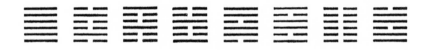

Figure 8

Each hexagram then gives rise to seven more hexagrams, resulting in eight groups of eight hexagrams, or sixty-four hexagrams total.

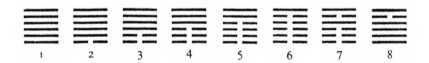

Figure 9

Each new hexagram is derived from the "movement" of Yin and Yang lines of the previous hexagram. "Movement" is the conversion from Yin to Yang and Yang to Yin, and it begins from the bottom of a hexagram and progresses upwards. This pattern of change is illustrated in Figure 9.

25

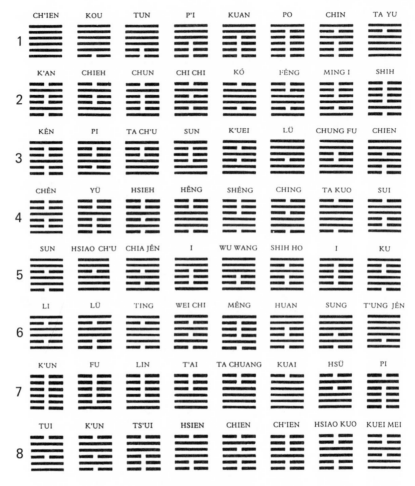

Figure 9 (Cont'd.)

The eight groups of eight hexagrams were designed to reflect all levels of the process of transmutation in the universe and the nature of all the elements of the universe, and it was designed to help mankind lead successful lives. The secrets of success were hidden within the groups of eight hexagrams. The first group, called Heaven, describes the nature of success, creation, leadership, power, and social position. It also describes the problems associated with these phenomena and the best way to face and solve these problems. The second group, called Water, deals with danger, risk, challenge, death, the military, and the associated problems and solutions. Mountain, the third group, describes the phenomena of stability, retreat, tolerance, aggregation, wealth, and their associated problems and solutions. Thunder, the fourth group, deals with stimulation, commencement, establishment, and the problems and solutions associated with these phenomena. The fifth group Wind deals with choice, discipline, adversity, stress, healing, fate, external and internal pressure, politics, finance, education, and instincts. Also described are the associated problems and solutions. Fire, the sixth group, describes the phenomena of brightness, charm, desire, sex, relationships, jubilation, connection, groupment, rigidity, strength, and legal battles. The associated problems and solutions are also described. The seventh group Earth deals with competition, disaster, suffering, rebellion, overcoming, recovery, patience, subjugation, and the associated problems and solutions. Lake, the eighth and last group, deals with the phenomena of happiness, surroundings, finance, emotional connection, modesty, poverty, entertainment, overflow, and inertia. The associated problems and solutions are also described.

Moreover, the sixty-four hexagrams can be arranged in many forms. These arrangements are used for astronomy, geomancy, construction, and other special purposes. Because these subjects have no bearing upon daily living, details of the arrangements will not be given—it will be of little or no interest to many people.

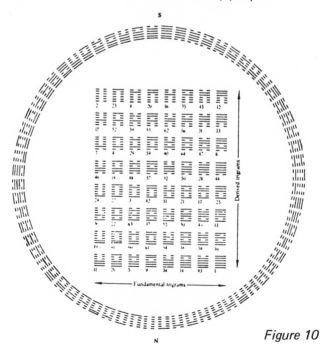

Figure 10

27

In the following chapters, the secrets contained within the Eight Pillars of Taoism will be disclosed in the order defined by the *Pa-Kua*. On the *Pa-Kua* the universe is divided into heaven and earth. The boundaries of heaven begin with the Heaven trigram and end with the Thunder trigram. The boundaries of earth begin with the Wind trigram and end with the Lake trigram. Earth is depicted as forming a slanted horizon with heaven, because the axis of earth the planet is slanted:

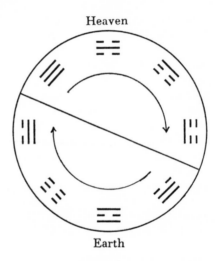

Heaven

Earth

Figure 11

The order of the universe is read as follows: one begins at the Heaven trigram and reads across the heavens toward the right until one reaches the Thunder trigram. Then one begins to read across the earth by starting at the Wind trigram and moving left until one reaches the Lake trigram. Therefore, the first secret to be unveiled must be the Tao of Philosophy, symbolized by the Heaven trigram.

1

THE TAO OF PHILOSOPHY

I

*LIFE IS LIKE THE HARVEST. THE WHEAT WILL BE
GATHERED. THE WEEDS WILL BE LEFT TO BURN.*

Life is to live. Life is also to evolve. Anything that takes form in this universe has a purpose, that of using space and time to improve itself and to evolve into a higher form.

There are four kingdoms in this universe: the Kingdom of Vegetation, the Kingdom of Animals, the Kingdom of Humankind, and the Kingdom of God. The members of each kingdom exist to improve themselves, to evolve into a higher kingdom.

1. The members of the Kingdom of Vegetation, which includes bacteria and protozoa, have only physical bodies and physical feelings. Their sole purpose is to reproduce. They possess no creativity and never benefit each other in any way. Any physical body that has feelings also has a right to live.

2. The members of the Kingdom of Animals have, in addition to a physical body, a mental body. Possessing a mind, a dog is trainable. Animals always reproduce according to a certain timetable, they have no comprehension of disatisfaction, and they have no creative abilities. They mechanically follow universal laws, with no will or desire to change their position in life.

3. The members of the Kingdom of Humankind possess physical, mental, and spiritual bodies. The spirit imbues human beings with the ability and desire to create—the development of science results from creativity. God gave mankind His spirit and His desires. Therefore man's basic desire is to be immortal. God gave man this desire so that he will improve himself, so that one day he may enter the Kingdom of God. However, man has reversed this desire into a desire to create material things. Man has hope, but this hope is never satisfied by material things. This creates frustration.

4. The members of the Kingdom of God are spiritual beings. They possess spiritualized bodies and have access to all corners of the universe. This being is immortal and experiences total happiness and tranquility. And this being is in unity with Tao and the universe.

Not all human beings can evolve into the Kingdom of God. According to Taoism there are four kinds of human beings in the Kingdom of Humankind, and they are (in ascending order) evil men, little men, gentlemen, and sages. Only those who are sages are qualified to evolve into the Kingdom of the Divine. There are three kinds of *hsiens,* or immortals, and they are (in ascending order) *Jen Shien* (Transformed Immortal), *Ti Shien* (Terrestrial Immortal), and *Tien Shien* (Celestial Immortal). So there must first be "promotion among the ranks" before there is evolution to a higher kingdom.

Evil men are only human in form, for they are still animalistic in nature. Their evolution from the animal kingdom is not complete, for they do not understand or apppreciate culture, morality, or propriety. Entertainment, contention, consumption, and reproduction, the four basic instincts, preoccupy their daily lives. In most societies this group is controlled by force, because they are capable of murder, rape, and other acts of evil.

Little men are ignorant, unwise, and limited in abilities. Everything done by these people are done for short-sighted gains. Members of this group are capable of scheming and cheating for useless, unimportant things—they are too cowardly to commit crimes or help society in a grand way. Their concerns and their lives are petty. This group is effectively controlled by laws in most societies.

Gentlemen understand and pursue morality, culture, and propriety. They desire enlightenment for themselves and other human beings. When the members of this group increase in number, society flourishes. When their numbers decrease, society suffers. Gentlemen are guided by propriety.

Sages are those who truly understand and pursue righteousness. These individuals work to improve and enlighten all human beings, and create a peaceful world through spreading peace. This group is guided by righteousness.

Transformed Immortal is a cultivator of Taoism. Being extremely wise, holy, and kind, this person is involved in improving world affairs. After death, this person will be resurrected, leaving no corpse behind. Frequently and unexpectedly, this immortal will materialize to help more human beings. (Jesus is considered to be a Transformed Immortal.) Love is the guiding force of these immortals.

The Terrestrial Immortal is a Taoist who, being extremely wise, holy, and ego-less, has left behind all human characteristics. The immortal dwells deep within the mountains for centuries and occasionally leaves his home to help a needy mortal. Perfect virtue is his guiding force.

A Celestial Immortal is a Taoist who has survived for thousands of years and has accomplished a great number of good deeds. The body of the Celestial Immortal is completely spiritualized (not limited by space or time). The Celestial Immortal and God are one. Tao is the guiding force.

The members of all these groups have physical, mental, and spiritual bodies. The differences between the groups are due to the degree of dominance of one body over the others. In evil men the physical body dominates the mental and spiritual bodies. In sages the mental body dominates the other bodies. In Celestial Immortals the spiritual body dominates the other bodies.

The physical body is governed by four basic instincts: entertainment, consumption, contention, and reproduction. Therefore, the physical body can be represented by a square:

Figure 12

The mental body can be represented by a triangle, because of three faculties: thinking, experiencing emotion, and exercising the will.

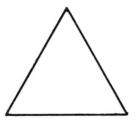

Figure 13

The spiritual body can be represented by a circle, because it is not limited by space or time. It is capable of communicating with God, it has a conscience, and it possesses flawless intuition.

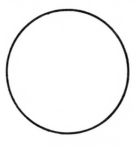

Figure 14

Ideally the physical and mental bodies should be subservient to the spiritual body. The spiritual body should send orders to the mental body, which determines the proper method of bringing these orders into fruition. The mental body then guides the physical body in carrying out these plans. Every activity is based on foresight, wisdom, and conscience and every activity conforms to the ways of Taoism. We are essentially chiseling out a circle with the teachings of Taoism.

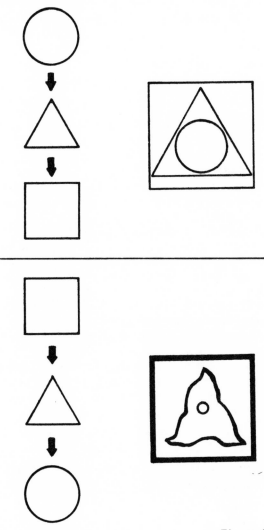

Figure 15

Unfortunately this is rare. We find instead repressed spiritual bodies and enslavement of the mental bodies by the physical bodies. Mankind's need for entertainment, lust for sex, thirst for violence, and need for food forces the mental body to contrive ways to satisfy and sanctify these primal needs. There is a complete reversal of the true order, resulting in all the miseries of this world.

Lao Tse has said that when Tao is lost, human beings take up virtue; then virtue is lost, human beings insist on love; when love is lost, people demand righteousness; when righteousness is lost, people rely on propriety; when propriety is lost, law is sought; when law is lost, force is sought; when force is sought, all traces of civilization is lost.

What are the prerequisites for evolutionary advancement?

The practice of Taoism that culminates in the accomplishment of many good deeds.

According to Pao Piao Tse, 200 good deeds are required to become a Transformed Immortal, 300 good deeds are required to become a Terrestrial Immortal, and 1200 good deeds are required to become a Celestial Immortal.

With one transgression, all of the good deeds that were accumulated will be nullified. According to Lao Tse, our every action is recorded and computed by the stars, which are governed by the North Star.

Evolution without Taoism is a painfully slow process—it has taken us millions of years of evolution to become what we are. Practicing Taoism speeds up the evolutionary advancement by helping mankind accumulate good deeds in the most efficient way possible: contributing to society without martyrdom. A long-lived and properly functioning physical body allows more good deeds to be accomplished. Martyrdom cuts off the flow of benefits to society and retards one's evolutionary advancement.

Good deeds are defined as actions that benefit oneself as well as others. Actions that hurt one party while benefiting another are undesirable. Actions that hurt both parties are least desirable as they are mistakes that can nullify all of the accumulated good deeds and reverse one's evolutionary progress.

Without the practice of Taoism, there will be no salvation.
Without Taoist evolution, there will be no Kingdom of God.

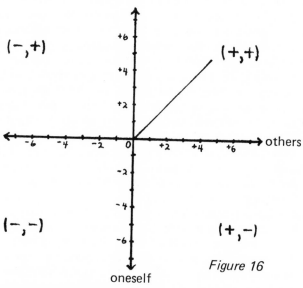

Figure 16

+, + = Good deeds (everyone benefits)
−, − = Harmful deeds (everyone is hurt)
+, − = Partially good deeds (others benefit; the self is sacrificed)
−, + = Partially harmful deeds (others are hurt; the self benefits)

II

When the caliber of the subjects improve, the caliber of politics will improve. The type of government ascends until it attains Tao. And the caliber of the subjects ascends until they reach celestial immortality. Then eternal peace will be achieved—heaven on earth.

Seven Levels of Humankind	Seven Types of Government
Celestial Immortal	Tao
Terrestrial Immortal	Perfect Virtue
Transformed Immortal	Love
Sages	Righteousness
Gentlemen	Propriety
Little Men	Law
Evil Men	Force

In the entire history of China only two dynasties, the Han and Tang Dynasties, observed the philosophies of Taoism. These empires were the wealthiest, happiest, and the most advanced of all the earthly civilizations. The prisons were empty. Any valuable object left on the streets remained on the streets. All the subjects had self-esteem. This is because the governments of these two dynasties had attained the Righteous and Propriety levels of government. Historians refer to these dynasties as the Golden Ages of China.

The fall of these dynasties began when Confucianism was adopted as the philosophy of government by selfish emperors. Confucianism demanded complete obedience to one's ruler or other figures of authority. Confucianism in the extreme allowed the father to order his son to die just to demonstrate their faith in Confucianism. Obedience at all levels of society results in repression of free thought. Conservatism, unchallenged by free thought, halts progress and the society plunges into backwardness. Everybody becomes the prisoner of the state and the family. There is no escape from either one of these prisons, except through death. The rich will capitalize on this state of society, making life a playground for the few and a torment for the majority. Such deterioration of society resulted in the fall of the Han and Tang empires.

Unfortunately, the dynasties that followed also observed Confucianism for selfish reasons. No other empire equaled those of the Han and Tang Dynasties, which created the highest forms of government in history.

The universal principles of government or private organizations in Taoism should be as follows:

A. The size of government must be small.
B. Laws and regulations must be simple and few.
C. Policies must be honest.
D. Economic system must be fair.
E. Taxes must be low.
F. Population growth must be controlled.
G. Individual freedom must be protected.
H. Education must be a priority.
I. Military expenditures must be limited.
J. The leader must voluntarily retire.

In the following paragraphs, the word government represents both government and private organizations.

A
Small Government

Lao Tse insisted that the size of government must be small, so that power may be distributed in favor of the people. A big government deprives the people of freedom, and a strong government weakens the people. When power is placed in the hands of the government officials, who will use this power to expand their own power, heavier taxes, huge government deficits, and administrative inefficiency will only be a few of the many problems plaguing the country. Since the balance of power between the people and the government is inherently unbalanced and power in the hands of government officials tends to expand unjustly, the freedom of the people is best secured by limiting the size of the government.

B
Laws and Regulations

According to Lao Tse, laws and regulations breed evil. Saint Paul said almost the same thing: "While we were living in the flesh, our sinful passions, aroused by the law . . . If it had not been for laws . . . I should not have known sin."

When a government imposes laws and regulations upon its subjects, it becomes its subjects' worst enemy. A government that produces excessive numbers of laws and regulations (fascist and military governments) tend to be short-lived. This is because the merciless and continuous oppression of the people heighten their endurance to the point that death becomes appealing. Lao Tse said that when people take death lightly, nothing can hold them back. In revolution there is everything to gain and nothing to lose. So the wisest form of government is that which forms a peaceful alliance with its subjects. Peace is insured.

Another argument against laws and regulations is that they produce more problems than they solve. Laws and regulations need enforcement, which requires police officers, judges, lawyers, and hundreds of other people. This escalates government expenses and results in higher taxes. Furthermore, other laws and regulations must be made to enforce the original laws and regulations. Then other laws and regulations must be made to enforce the new ones. An endless chain reaction results, and government expenses are multiplied a million times. The endless chain reaction also results in confusion, which causes early laws and regulations to be forgotten.

Too many regulations = No regulation

Nothing is accomplished, yet the confusion and expenses grow.

During the Ch'in Dynasty, China was ruled by tyrants and the laws and regulations were said to be as numerous as the hairs on a cow. This dynasty was overthrown and was replaced by the Han Dynasty. The Han Dynasty, a Golden Age of China, began with the nullification of these laws and regulations. Only three simple laws were made, but everybody remembered and obeyed them enthusiastically.

C
Honest Policy

The government should treat its subjects with honesty, to create a bond of trust between its subjects and itself. The policies of the government, by reflecting the moral wishes of the larger portion of the population, should protect the people from oppression in any way, form, or means. The government is not allowed to grant any wish of the majority that may cause any short term or long term discomfort or harm to any individual.

Government officials must serve the people and represent their moral wishes. Lao Tse said that politicians should not form their own opinions. They must regard the mind of the people as their own. On the contrary, in Romans 13:1, Saint Paul said, "Let every person be subject to the governing authorities. For there is no authority except from God and those that exist have been instituted by God." But entrusting a ruthless politician with one's well-being is not wise, especially when his policies reverse one's evolutionary progress. The succession of abuses of power must be halted by selecting government officials for their integrity toward the people. Otherwise "the politicians who are not benevolent treat people like dogs," according to Lao Tse.

When a government engages in cheating games with its subjects, it weakens the state. No matter what ruses it uses against its subjects, its subjects will always outwit it, because they outnumber the government workers. Such games create an unbridgeable rift between the subjects and the government; nothing will prevent a revolution from toppling this government. Lao Tse said, "Rulers who try to use cleverness cheat the country. Those who rule without cleverness are a blessing to the land."

D
Economic System

Lao Tse said, "The tao is nameless because it is in everything and yet is is formless. Its simplicity and minuteness is unmatched by all the power of the alliance of all the world's nations. When the leaders are able to utilize it, everything comes to an equilibrium and heaven and earth will be unified."

Lao Tse also said, "A balanced universe is one in which the rich are denied and the poor are supplemented. However human beings defy the Tao and exploit the poor to perpetuate the rich. Violent confrontations will result and all human beings suffer" and "The Tao of heaven is found in the aiming of the bow and arrow. That which is too high must be brought down and that which is too low must be brought up."

According to Lao Tse, "the sweet dew of heaven nourishes all. All peoples are self-sufficient." Everybody must have an equal share of opportunities to improve themselves, for "the multiplication of prohibitive enactments increases the poverty of the people."

Taoism teaches free enterprise and economic equality—social capitalism. The government is discouraged from interfering in the business ventures of its subjects. Taxation of businesses and other acts of interference complicates and worsens the economy. But it is responsible for guiding the direction of the economy and keeping and enforcing strict standards of moral and fair business practices. Social capitalism is the fusion of the best theories of capitalism and socialism.

E

Taxation

Lao Tse said, "People suffer from poverty because of excessive taxes."

The taxation policies of a government determine whether it is a benevolent or tyrannical government. A benevolent government is one that fixes the tax rate at 3%. A tyrannical government imposes a tax rate of 10% or more on its subjects.

During the Golden Ages of China, the Han and Tang Dynasties, the tax rates were 3%. The subjects prospered because of this low tax rate, and anti-social activities were almost non-existent.

When the later Han rulers raised the tax rate to 10% or more, revolution followed as surely as the shadow accompanies the body.

The Old Testament proposed a 10% tax rate. (This might have begun as a settlement between Jacob and God.) The fact most people neglect is that during the age described by the Old Testament, church and state were not separated. The taxes collected were for the church and the state. In reality, only 5% of the income was collected for the government. During the Roman occupancy of Israel, the Israelis were forced to pay the original 10%, in addition to the payments to Caesar. The taxes were doubled and life was insufferable for the Israelis. That is why Caesar's tax collectors were called sinners by the Israelis.

When a government increases taxes, it is drinking poison to

relieve its thirst.

Why does a government suffer from thirst, or deficits?

(1) War and weapons.
(2) Squandering and extravagance.
(3) Oversize.
(4) Scandal and corruption.

These four problems make government deficits a chronic disease.

This "disease" may be treated by a good "physician." More often than not, a great "surgeon" better suits this purpose.

The cure is moral adjustment rather than economic adjustment. The cure should be administered to the ruler himself. As the person who serves as a model to his subjects, the leader should reverse his selfishness and corrupt behavior. If reversing a leader's character becomes impossible, then healing of the nation is virtually impossible.

F
Population

Lao Tse insisted upon small governments. He also insisted upon small populations.

It is impossible to achieve peace and happiness if population growth is not firmly controlled. Overpopulation causes hunger, hunger leads to war, and war results in death, the greatest transgression from the viewpoint of Taoism. These are only a few natural elementary or birth-control responses triggered by overpopulation, others include natural disasters and killing diseases.

Over-reproduction takes place among people who cannot discipline their lust, a result of poor education. To prevent over-reproduction, people must be taught that sex should not be limited to mere physical interactions. Sex should be an act of intimacy, love, understanding, helping, and caring. Taoist teachings also provide techniques that separate sex and reproduction. As discussed in Chapter 6, sexual activity can be utilized to improve one's health and elevate one's spirituality. Practicing Taoism will help people discipline their lust and further social progress.

Population control is not empty conjecture, political opinion, or philosophical belief that can never be practiced. It is vital to the advancement of society and the effectiveness of small governments.

G
Individual Freedom

Taoism values and respects life. That is why it places great emphasis upon protecting life. According to the Taoist theory of evolution, all humans arise from other forms of life and are dependent upon other forms of life; therefore, Taoists do not deny plants, animals, or humans the right to live. Life, longevity, and happiness are sacred rights.

Nobody has the right to violate the rights of others. Nevertheless, people and other organisms are intentionally slain or hurt for money, privilege, and other petty reasons. These perpetrators will never escape punishment, even if they escape earthly laws. No one escapes the Law of Cause and Effect, or Karma, the unseen but omnipresent protector of life. Lao Tse has said (in reference to Karma), "The meshes of the net of heaven are large and far apart, but it never allows anything to escape." Any act that denies life will cause the perpetrator perpetual torment in his present and future lives.

Greed causes transgressions; therefore, it must be eliminated. Lao Tse said, "There is a time to be born and a time to die. Three out of ten are spent ministering life, another three are spent ministering death, and another three are spent perpetuating life through excessive endeavors, which only result in death" and "There is no fault greater than greed and no fault greater than furthering one's gains. People who recognize contentment are always wealthy."

The government has a very important duty, that of discouraging the egoism and ambition of its people, especially those of the leaders. Excessive efforts, extravagance, and self-indulgence are symptoms of egoism and ambition, and these must be discouraged. Lao Tse said, "Too much color makes people blind. Too much music makes people deaf. Too many flavors dulls the palate. Too much entertainment maddens the mind. Too many precious things leads one astray." To maintain peace, "the leaders must repress selfishness and evil, like lust." Lao Tse also said, "Not exalting the superior genius prevents rivalry. Devaluing treasures prevents robbery. Not seeing desirable things prevents false illusions and desires from confusing the mind." By diminishing the occurances of anti-social activities through the practice of Taoism, the rights of all organisms are protected and the nation is strengthened.

H
Education

Improving the educational system must be a priority in any government agenda. Education, Taoist education, directly affects an individual's satisfaction with life. A wrong educational approach increases disatisfaction, which can surface as antisocial activities, divorces, child abuse, etc.

Many systems of education exist, but few are successful—history books and newspapers are ample evidence of educational failure. Children are taught mathematics, chemistry, physics, literature,

sports, etc. These are called, in Taoist terms, *Dead Knowledge.*
Dead Knowledge encourages egoism and ambition, it is irrelevant
to everyday life, and it distinguishes enthusiasm for learning. Children are led to believe that identities and satisfaction can be found
in material possessions and material success. That is why nuclear
bombs, crime, chemicals, madness, and other abnormalities exist.
Material possessions and material success never provide satisfaction
in life, they provide only frustration and rage, which will surface in
antisocial activities and the invention of other abnormalities. Generations of people have lived their lives blindly, without any understanding about the true meaning of life.

Students should first be taught how to live, how to live better,
and how to live longer. The knowledge they learn can be applied to
their life immediately and will be useful to them for the rest of their
lives. They will see immediate results and interest in learning will be
stimulated.

With a preliminary education in the meaning of life, the students
will be able to apply themselves and their secondary education,
mathematics, literature, etc., in ways that speed up the evolution
of man and protect the natural ways of the universe.

The success of fair government policies depends on the cooperation of the people. Without Taoist education, nothing can succeed
because the majority of the subjects will be evil or little men, who
will, because of their selfishness and ignorance, block any attempt
to better the world. Through Taoist education evil and little men
are lifted to higher levels; when gentlemen outnumber evil and little
men, the world will become a better place in which to live.

I

Warfare

Warfare is not limited to the human kingdom, it is also a characteristic of the animal and vegetable kingdoms. Therefore desiring to
throw away weapons is being unrealistic. Human beings find it
necessary to protect their right of life, as long as those uneducated
in Taoist theories exist; therefore, theories concerning warfare,
called the Tao of Abnormality, are a necessary part of life.

Sun Tse, the disciple of the famous immortal Quei Ku Tse,
wrote a book called "The Art of the Military," 3000 years ago.
"The tao of abnormality" is the first verse in that book. In the book,
Sun Tse states that conquering the enemies' hearts is better than
occupying their cities. In other words he is saying that psychological
warfare is more effective and more important than combat. Sun Tse
wrote, "battles need not be fought, for a three-inch tongue is
mightier than the cannon."

Human beings are the only organisms who use weapons in warfare. The need for weapons results in the invention of complex and destructive weapons which produce an aura of hostility, or abnormality. When the state of abnormality becomes uncontrollable, an entire planet could be destroyed. Lao Tse said, "Advanced weapons are better instruments of evil Karma . . . [they] do not belong to gentlemen" and "Whenever the army has passed, briars and thorns spring up. Years of hunger follow in the wake of a great war."

Lao Tse said, "Those who assist the leaders must suggest Taoism." They must never suggest military solutions [because] the army shall be the very last resort, as its success is uncertain." History has shown that weapons alone can never win the war. The economy, education, the leader, the spirit of the people, all contribute to victory. The government may do everything necessary to strengthen the country except engage in a competition of weapons with potential enemies. Weapons do not guarantee victories, but they do empty the state treasury. Furthermore, weapons which bear evil Karma, bring the state misfortune.

J
Leader

A nation's leader is a leader because of his accomplishments, which suit the will of heaven. The leader is a leader because his thoughts, actions, wisdom, Karma, ability to ignore criticism, and good or bad deeds perfectly suit the conditions of a particular period in time. His mission is to carry out the will of heaven.

When that leader has accomplished his mission, he must voluntarily step down from office, for his policies will not suit a new time period. If he persists, he will block the mission of another person, reverse all progress made, and incur the people's wrath. He can never finish or hope to finish the projects he began, because the universe is always in a state of flux. If he does not realize this, he will be terminated and his credits taken away.

Tao is change and the needs of the time always change. When the leader follows the Tao, he has accomplished a good deed. When he goes against the Tao, he has done a great wrong. Lao Tse said:

The utility of Spring is the renewal of life.
The utility of Summer is the growth of life.
The utility of Autumn is the harvest of life.
And the utility of Winter is the storage of life.

If, for example, the Spring season were to continue, the arrival of Summer and the other seasons will be delayed and the order of the universe muddled. Any blockage is a disease to be removed.

When a leader clings desparately to his post, he will be removed in three ways:

1. When he has accumulated good Karma during office, he will be removed by death, a benign method of allowing the successor to fulfill his destiny.

2. When he has accumulated both good and bad Karma, he will be assassinated.

3. When he has accumulated bad Karma, he will be forced off his post through shame and public humiliation. He may suffer a violent death or his name will be associated with evil and filth.

The pages of history provide ample evidence for these three universal principles. For example, George Washington would not be respected if his ambitions provoked him to declare himself a king.

III

Taoism must be practiced. You cannot enter the Kingdom of God by paying somebody to pray for you. Take the simple example of a plane flight. Think of the amount of energy that goes into a takeoff. Then think of the amount of energy needed to sustain the plane in flight—there is no string holding the plane up. Now think of the amount of energy you spend in trying to enter the Kingdom of God. Can you trust something as important as your entrance into the Kingdom of God to a simple prayer? You must walk with God yourself. You must practice Taoism step by step. Not only will you eventually enter the Kingdom of God, but you will gain immediate benefits.

The entire universe is governed by the Cause and Effect Law (Karma), and this law determines whether you move upward or downward on the Taoist evolutionary scale. No one escapes judgement by this law, not even suicides (in fact, suicides face greater punishments because they have taken a life). When one learns one's lessons well and uses one's knowledge only for magnanimous purposes, one progresses into a higher state of consciousness. When one's knowledge is used for devious purposes, one will be slapped back into a lower evolutionary level. This is best summarized by this saying:

Plant melons, reap melons
Plant beans, reap beans

What you do in this life will determine your fate in the next life, and what you have done in your past life has determined your present fate. Tai Shan Tractate said, "There are no special doors for calamity and happiness. They come as men themselves call them. Their recompenses follow good and evil as the shadow follows the substance." and "Accordingly, there are stars that record and compute men's transgressions, and, according to the lightness or gravity of their offenses, take away from their term of life or sentence them to bitter sufferings."

No other story captures the essence of Karma as the following story told by a Taoist master. There once was a wicked man who stole, cheated, and oppressed other people to make himself rich. At an old age, he had everything: countless possessions and three grown sons who had just gotten married. He was looking forward to having grandchildren.

Then one day he thought to himself, "I'm so happy! I do not have to continue doing all the cruel things I have done in the past. Now I want to make up for what I have done. From this day on I shall repay those I have ruined and help others in need."

He became a good man. Then one month later, his eldest son suddenly became ill and died. The widow married another man. This turn of events left the old man extremely sad. Then a month later, his second son died and his widow also left to marry another man. This left the old man very shaken. Then a month later, his beloved third son died.

"There is no justice in this world!" he cried in anguish.

"When I was wicked I had everything. I almost held a grandchild in my arms! From the day I converted to Taoism and began doing good deeds, all these calamities befell me. What hope do I have? My dear sons, for whom I have slaved for, are all dead! There is nobody to inherit the products of my labors."

He became a madman. He hated everything and everybody. One day, in the midst of a fit, he was interrupted by a servant, who said that a Taoist master came to visit him.

"Bring him to me!" roared the old man, "I want to rub his nose in his ragged teachings! I will show him how wrong he is!"

When the master was shown in, the old man treated him with utmost cruelty. But the master, calm as ever, asked, "Do you know why?"

"That is what I want to know. Why?"

"Do you remember how, 25 years ago, you and your friend fought for a property? Violence erupted and your friend was killed and you obtained the property. You knew this man very well. You knew all the characteristics of his personality. Now think about your eldest son. Do they not display exactly the same characteristics?"

"Yes." said the old man, "they are very much alike."

"Your friend has reincarnated as your son. He has come to recover what he has lost to you."

"Do you remember cheating another man," continued the master. ". . . That man has reincarnated as your second son. And he has come back to claim his property. And do you remember hurting another man? . . . He has come back as your third son. Your sons were not your sons. They were your "enemies" and they came with the blessings of the universe to claim your debt to them. They were here to collect interest from you too. They were to waste all of your money and treat you with utmost cruelty. For the last part of your life, you were to suffer as if you were boiling in oil. Finally you were to kill yourself. But when you converted and did many good deeds, you automatically paid off your debt. The higher beings in the universe found that your good deeds balanced your debts. They found no necessity for your "sons" to claim your debts. So they were removed painlessly. You have not lost your sons, you have only lost your enemies. Since your good deeds have paid off your debt, you will not be denied a grandson. The wife of your third son is now pregnant. She will give you a grandson who will cherish you, respect you, and love you. You will be extremely happy and you will enjoy the rest of your life."

The old man, enlightened, cried with tears of gratitude.

Christianity is taught in many churches, wherein Jesus is described as the lamb of God, the sacrifice that would serve as payment for everybody's sins. In these churches one is also taught that whoever believes in Jesus will never be condemned, be guaranteed a place in heaven, and have everlasting life. The Crucifixion has been called the Mercy of God by theologians; with the Crucifixion, all of God's demands for justice will be satisfied and no one will have to be responsible for their actions, since all bad Karma has been dissolved. But from the Taoist view of Christianity, Christian teachings still hold a person responsible for his actions, even if he has faith in Jesus. A detailed study of the New Testament will uncover the truth, that everyone is not forgiven for their sins and that faith without deeds will incur the denial of Jesus and the exclusion from heaven.

Jesus died on the cross to pay for man's sins, or bad Karma, so that man will not have to suffer the consequences of his sins. Now whenever a transgression is made, Jesus is supposed to take the transgressors place and bear the punishment intended for the transgressor. Every time a transgression is committed, the transgressor just opens his mouth and calls Jesus by name to summon Jesus to bear his punishment. Or the transgressor may confess to a priest to wash away the sins. A simple act of repentance is supposed to unfailingly set the transgressor free. Does this seem logical? If paying for a car is so hard, how could payments for one's sins be made so easily?

Although some parts of the Bible extoll the virtues of calling upon Jesus' name, other parts of the Bible do otherwise. A story in the Old Testament describes the futility of repentance: when King David abducted the wife of his friend, the punishments he and his family suffered from continued to plague them, although David repented. (Knife and sword never left his house). In Hebrews 6:6-8, it is clearly stated that those who call upon Jesus' name to crucify him again and again will sin even more.

This passage reads as follows:

> If they shall fall away, to renew them again unto repentance; seeing they crucify to themselves the Son of God afresh, and put him to an open shame.
> For the earth which drinketh in the rain that cometh oft upon it, and bringeth forth herbs meet for them be whom it is dressed, receiveth blessing from God:
> But that which beareth thorns and briers *is* rejected, and *is* nigh unto cursing: whose end *is* to be burned.

According to Hebrews 4:3, a sinner is punished by being excluded from the Kingdom of God, called "rest" in this passage, which reads as follows:

> For we which have believed do enter into rest, as he said, As I have sworn in my wrath, if they shall enter into my rest: although the works were finished from the foundation of the world.

Entrance into the Kingdom of God is described as the fruits of one's labors in James 1:25 and 2:14-26, which read as follows:

> But who so looketh into the perfect law of liberty, and continueth *therein,* he being not a forgetful hearer, but a doer of the work, this man shall be blessed in his deed.

and

> What *doth it* profit, my brethren, though a man say he hath faith, and have not works? can faith save him?
> If a brother or sister be naked, and destitute of daily food.
> And one of you say unto them, Depart in peaced, be *ye* warmed and filled; notwithstanding ye give them not those things which are needful to the body; what *doth it* profit?
> Even so faith, if it hath not works, is dead, being alone.
> Yea, a man may say, Thou has faith, and I have works: show my faith without thy works, and I will show thee my faith by my works.
> Thou believest that there is one God; thou doest well: the devils also believe, and tremble.

But wilt thou know, O vain man, that faith without works is dead?

Was not Abraham our father justified by works, when he had offered Isaac his son upon the altar?

Seest thou how faith wrought with his works, and by works was faith made perfect?

And the scripture was fulfilled which saith, Abraham believed God, and it was imputed unto him for righteousness: and he was called the Friend of God.

Ye see then how that by works a man is justified, and not by faith only.

Likewise also was not Rahab the harlot justified by works, when she had received the messengers, and had sent *them* out another way?

For as the body without the spirit is dead, so faith without works is dead also.

In Matthew 7:21-23, Jesus placed our entrance into the Kingdom of God in our own hands. He said:

Not every one that saith unto me, Lord, Lord, shall enter into the kingdom of heaven; but he that doeth the will of my Father which is in heaven.

Many will say to me in that day, Lord, Lord, have we not prophesied in thy name? and in thy name have cast out devils? and in thy name done many wonderful works?

And then will I profess unto them, I never knew you: depart from me, ye that work iniquity.

In Romans 12:19, God is described as being subject to the Law of Cause and Effect. This passage reads as follows:

Dearly beloved, avenge not yourselves, but *rather* give peace unto wrath: for it is written, Vengeance *is* mine; I will repay, saith the Lord.

Some Christian churches place great emphasis upon the crucifixion of Jesus, thinking that calling upon Jesus' name saves a person and guarantees his entrance into heaven. Concerning the Crucifixion, it is based on the ancient practice, described in the Old Testament, of sacrificing animals to appease God. By sacrificing innocent creatures and shedding their blood, the ancients hoped to wash away their sins and seek forgiveness from God. Since sins cannot be washed away this easily, these practices seem silly and inhumane. Theoretically speaking, one cannot help thinking that if there is such a God, he would double the sacrificers' sins — the sacrificers not only killed innocent creatures for selfish purposes, they also did nothing to pay for their original sins. Examining the crucifixion from the modern man's viewpoint brings to mind a question: How could civilized people still glorify such cruel and barbaric behavior?

Human beings are born with spiritual, mental, and physical bodies. They are capable of exercising wisdom in order to evolve to a higher evolutionary level. This innate ability should be used and it should not be abused or buried because of laziness or bad deeds. How quickly one attains immortality depends on how hard one works. Eventually, everyone will complete their evolution and enter the Kingdom of God, for the universe is eternal.

Taoism is also very different from Buddhism. Unlike Buddhism, which emphasizes the ugliness and bitterness of life, Taoism emphasizes the beauty of life.

According to true Buddhist teachings, all that is within the universe is a cause for suffering. There are eight causes for bitter suffering: birth, aging, sickness, death, not getting the things you desire, getting the things you do not desire, not being loved by the one you love, and a loving relationship that cannot last.

The Buddhists found relief from pain in the avoidance of the human pattern of life and in death. Since human beings are more often than not tortured by their emotions, they must cease to feel. Since human beings suffer from indigestion after feasting, they must cease to feast. And so on. Thus enlightened Buddhists deny all mundane matters, including the existence of the universe. Buddhist teachings forbid participation in world affairs, for all must await death, through which the soul is emancipated from earthly sufferings.

However, Buddhists do not realize that, in seeking true happiness, they have caused themselves more pain. If a Buddhist adept shuns intercourse, he or she would have to fight sexual urges and temptations for fifty years or more. If the Buddhist adept shuns delicious foods, he or she would have to fight cravings for food throughout their lives. So suffering cannot be avoided; human matters are more complex than what Buddhists have anticipated.

Buddhist classics group human beings into three groups, according to their understanding of the above concepts, and they are: 1) the Multitude, 2) the Associates, and 3) the Buddhists. The first group comprises unenlightened people who drown in a sea of bitterness (suffering). The second group comprises those who are sympathetic to Buddhist teachings and who support Buddhist monks and temples with monetary offerings. These people are called good men or good women. The third group comprises Buddhist monks or nuns. To become a real Buddhist, a person must break all worldly relationships (called *leaving the family*); then accept lessons in the various forbiddens (sex, wine, meat, fighting, lying, etc.) from an advanced monk; and then attend Buddhist lectures, read Buddhist classics, meditate, and practice isolation until death elevates the Buddhist to the level of Buddha. In death the "dirty bag", or physical body is kicked off, and the Buddhist has achieved the highest state of being. (Some divergent groups of Buddhists even deny the existence of Buddha, regarding Buddha as empty or vain.)

In direct contrast, Taoists acknowledge the existence of the universe and seek a thorough understanding of the universe. According to Taoist teachings, life is not fraught with misery nor is it replete with bliss. The universe is in a state of flux; therefore, misery is always succeeded by bliss and bliss is always succeeded by misery. Knowing this, one will never be too sad or too happy, one will comprehend the underlying forces of this universe, and one's eyes will be opened to the good in everything. The knowledge Taoists seek increases enjoyment of life, extends happiness, increases longevity, and helps mankind achieve immortality. Thus, Taoists are able to praise human relationships, feast without indigestion, engage in world affairs, and so on. Anybody who practices Taoism can experience heaven on earth.

Buddhism survived into the twentieth century in the Far East because of three reasons. Buddhist monks first changed their masks superficially by adopting some Taoist teachings, to escape political persecution. Statues of Taoists were made and placed in Buddhist temples, although true Taoists never favored idolatry. And some Buddhists became I-Ching scholars, herbalists, acupuncturists, personoligists, directionologists, etc. The second reason was that Buddhists willingly changed their religion because Taoist-Buddhism was easily accepted by the public and because Buddhists themselves experienced a greater degree of freedom with the change. The third reason was that, over a period of time in an environment of different values, Buddhism itself was completely and permanently changed, into Taoist-Buddhism. The change was too complete: Taoism and Buddhism were thought of as sister religions, and Buddha was thought to be the transformation of Lao Tse.

These changes benefited Buddhism. Taoist-Buddhism was not a negative religion. Instead of encouraging estrangement of mankind, it encouraged a helpful attitude toward mankind.

These changes, however, reduced Taoism to a religion maintained by superstition.

Buddhist concepts, such as idolatry, burning of incense, construction of temples and participation in other religious rituals, were adopted by Pseudo-Taoists, those who were unable to understand the teachings of Taoism. Much of these concepts are still retained today. So there are two Taoistic traditions: that embraced by scholars and that embraced by uneducated temple worshippers. The scholars walk with God. The common people use Taoism to tell fortunes, cast spells, chase spirits, and so on.

This book introduces the entire spectrum of Taoistic, scholarly teachings.

In China, Buddhism developed another branch, called Zen Buddhism, which deals strictly with dialogue. Zen Buddhism was founded 2,500 years ago by a scholar named Kung Sun Lung when he developed theories of word play. These theories are represented by the following phrases: "hard stone is not stone", "white horse is not horse", etc. When these phrases were incorporated in a dialogue between the famous monk Huei Nen and his master, Zen Buddhism was born. An excerpt of such a dialogue is as follows:

Master: The body is the Buddhi tree,

His mind is a mirror on its stand.

Thou shalt always keep them clean and

shalt never let them be covered by dust.

Huei Nen: Buddhi never existed as a tree.

The mirror never existed on its stand.

If there has never been such a thing,

How could they be covered by dust?

The dialogues always dealt with the non-existence of something. Poetry and literature lovers were fond of these and devoted tremendous amounts of time to composing them. The futility of Zen Buddhism made it the favorite status indicator for the relatively upper classes.

Taoism must not be mistaken for Buddhism or Zen Buddhism, or anything else that may borrow from Taoist teachings. (Because of the expansiveness of Taoist teachings, Taoism is often mistaken for many things to which it is not even remotely related. For instance, it is often mistaken for medicine, since its teachings include many healing techniques. But, medicine only emphasizes diagnosis and the cure of *diseases*. In contrast, the methods, tools, and knowledge set down thousands of years ago by Taoists are for helping mankind complete their evolution into the Kingdom of God.)

The tremendous efficacy of Taoist methods and techniques attracted many people who "borrowed" bits and pieces of information to become geomancers, politicians, martial arts instructors, dieticians, exercise instructors, acupuncturists, etc. But these people do not realize that these bits and pieces of information, when isolated from other Taoist teachings, can not help mankind enter the Kingdom of God. These bits and pieces are branches without roots and, in the words of Jesus, can not bear fruit.

For example, when people discovered the healing potentials of some Taoist methods and techniques, they isolated these and called them medicine. When one branch of Tuei-Na was converted into medicine and was given the name *Acupuncture,* it was mechanized and altered by the incorporation of lasers, soundwaves, lights, and electronic machinery into its original procedure. As a branch without its root, acupuncture is less effective than Tuei-Na. That is why the AMA claims that acupuncture has only 18% effectiveness and that it is not worth the title of medicine. There is a great gap between Taoist Tuei-Na and medicinal acupuncture.

IV

Taoism instructs mankind to lead lives that follow God's ways. These teachings are best summarized by the following passage from the Ching Chin Ching, or The Classic of Purity. The passage, from the translation by James Legge, is as follows:

1. Lao the Master said, The Great Tao has no bodily form, but It produced and nourishes heaven and earth. The Great Tao has no passions, but It causes the sun and moon to revolve as they do.

The Great Tao has no name, but It effects the growth and maintenance of all things.

I do not know its name, but I make an effort, and call It the Tao.

2. Now, the Tao (shows itself in two forms); the Pure and the Turbid, and has (the two conditions of) Motion and Rest. Heaven is pure and earth is turbid; heaven moves and earth is at rest. The masculine moves and the feminine is still. The radical (Purity) descended, and the (turbid) issue flowed abroad; and thus all things were produced.

The pure is the source of the turbid, and motion is the foundation of rest.

If man could always be pure and still, heaven and earth would both revert (to true-existence).

3. Now the spirit of man loves Purity, but his mind disturbs it. The mind of man loves stillness, but his bodily desires draw it away. If he could always send his desires away, his mind would of itself become still. Let his mind be made clean, and his

spirit will of itself become pure.

As a matter of course the six desires will not arise, and the three poisons will be taken away and disappear.

4.   The reason why men are not able to attain to this, is because their minds have not been cleansed, and their desires have not been sent away.

If one is able to send the desires away, when he then looks in at his body, it is no longer his; and when he looks farther off at external things, they are things which he has nothing to do with. When he understands these three things, there will appear to him only vacancy.

The idea of vacuous space having vanished, that of nothingness itself also disappears; and when the idea of nothingness has disappeared, there ensues serenely the condition of constant stillness.

5.   In that condition of rest independently of place how can any desire arise? And when no desire any longer arises, there is the True stillness and rest.

That True (stillness) becomes (a) constant quality, and responds to external things (without error); yea, that True and Constant quality holds possession of the nature.

In such constant response and constant stillness there is the constant Purity and Rest.

He who has this absolute Purity enters gradually into the (inspiration of the) True Tao. And having entered thereinto, he is styled Possessor of the Tao.

Although he is styled Possessor of the Tao, in reality he does not think he has become possessed of anything. It is as accomplishing the transformation of all living things, that he is styled Possessor of the Tao.

He who is able to understand this may transmit to others the Sacred Tao.

2   1.   Lao the Master said, Scholars of the highest class do not strive (for anything); those of the lowest class are fond of striving. Those who possess in the highest degree the attributes (of the Tao) do not show them; those who possess them in a low degree hold them fast (and display them). Those who so hold them fast and display them are not styled (Possessors of) the Tao and Its attributes.

2.   The reason why all men do not obtain the True Tao is because their minds are perverted. Their minds being perverted, their spirits become perturbed. Their minds being perturbed, they are attracted towards external things. Being attracted

towards external things, they begin to seek for them greedily. This greedy quest leads to perplexities and annoyances; and these again result in disordered thoughts, which cause anxiety and trouble to both body and mind. The parties then meet with foul disgraces, flow wildly on through the phases of life and death, are liable constantly to sink in the sea of sufferings, and forever lose the True Tao.

    3.   The True and Abiding Tao! They who understand it naturally obtain it. And they who come to understand the Tao abide in Purity and Stillness.

The task that lies ahead of you can be made simpler by using the Three Treasures, which were given to us by Lao Tse. They are: 1) Be kind to all people and all other organisms. 2) Be thrifty. And 3) Be humble. Lao Tse said that being kind encourages one to be brave, that being thrifty helps one to be liberal, and that being humble allows one to be the vessel of the highest honor. Regular people will shun kindness while being brave, regular people will forget thriftiness while being liberal, regular people will shun humility while seeking to be foremost. Anyone able to possess these treasures will be saved, for these treasures offer protection against all adversities.

In the entire history of earth, only those selected were allowed to enter the Kingdom of God. Those selected spent many lives in the pursuit of comprehending and cultivating Taoism.

2

THE TAO OF REVITALIZATION

INTERNAL EXERCISES

I

Life is to live. We expend great amounts of energy combatting life-endangering forces of the microenvironment and macroenvironment, e.g., bacteria, viruses, radiation, and natural disasters. We spend our lives fulfilling two basic physical needs to maintain, nourish, revitalize, and prolong our lives. These are:

1. Consumption (eating, drinking, etc.)
2. Motion
    a. Mind "movement" (thinking)
    b. Body "movement" (breathing and other functions of the internal organs and external limbs)
    c. Sex

Life will cease if either of the two basic conditions is not fully or properly satisfied. Without consumption of nutrients, life will normally cease within ten days. Without *proper* consumption of nutrients, life will be shortened. Without motion, the body will atrophy. Without *proper* motion, the body will weaken. The effects of inactivity are immediately obvious, unlike those of starvation. When breathing, made possible by diaphram contraction and expansion, ceases, death results within minutes. If the heart stops beating, death will result within seconds. Any variation in the motions of other organs, like intestinal peristalsis, will also lead to complications. The delicate functions of the body can be improved by the Tao of Revitalization, the philosophy and method of thinking, breathing, and movement.

The method for prolonging and protecting life involves the utilization of a system of correct and balanced mental and physical movements. These movements are unlike the known forms of exercises (aerobics, Tai Chi, sports, etc.). The creator of this system was the Yellow Emperor, who was also the father of Taoism, the science and philosophy of life and longevity. He called this system the *Yang Sheng Shu,* which translates directly to Tao of Revitalization. Tao of Revitalization is the achievement of a happy, healthy, and long life through the utilization of a single or a group of mental and physical movements to prevent and correct all ailments, reverse the aging process, and improve all functions of the body.

Tao of Revitalization has a long history — six thousand years — of success. Realizing its enormous medicinal potential, the Yellow Emperor called it the foremost of therapies. In the Tao Te Ching, Lao-Tse called it the best therapeutic method for promoting and prolonging life. Its reverent and faithful practitioners are multitudinous. It was effective even when its expansive teachings were fragmented and reorganized.

Many versions of Tao of Revitalization exist, each with appropriately descriptive names. These names, however, do not reflect the true meaning and function of Tao of Revitalization. One version is *Tao-Yin*, which means the utilization of thought, tools, and certain body movements to guide the flow of energy to heal ailments of all kinds. Presently, Tao of Revitalization is immensely popular in Japan. *Do-in*, as it is called in Japan, is taught in clubs organized in every city, village, and neighborhood. Club members meet once or many times a week to help and encourage each other in the practice of selected methods of *Do-in*; thusly, the club members prevent and treat diseases. The form of Tao of Revitalization that is popular in China is *Chi-Kung*, also called *Nei-Kung*. The term *Nei-Kung* translates to Internal Exercises. The term *Chi-Kung* translates to Breathing or Energizing Exercises.

A scientific study was conducted on *Chi-Kung* therapy by Dr. Pao Ling, in China. His work, published in Guolin Research Report, involved 2,873 terminal cancer patients who took part in an experiment wherein *Chi-Kung* therapy was used as treatment for their afflictions. Within a six-month period, 12% of the patients were cured and 47% showed significant improvements in their conditions. 41% showed no improvement. Another experiment involving school children was conducted to test one part of *Chi-Kung*, the eye exercises. They were accompanied by music and instructional intercom announcements. As results of the exercises, farsightedness, nearsightedness, and other eye problems became a rare affliction. Other experiments conducted with *Chi-Kung* therapy demonstrated the tremendous and rapid efficaciousness toward sinus allergies, hemorrhoids, prostate gland problems, and aging. In the hospitals, clinics, and health organizations of China, *Chi-Kung* therapy is chief among the other treatments, such as chemical therapy, surgery, and acupuncture. *Chi-Kung* therapy cures and *prevents* diseases, whereas the other treatments only treat diseases.

In the U.S., a scientific study was conducted on the Internal Exercise by Dr. Cecilia Rosenfeld. After practising the Internal Exercises and experiencing an immediate improvement in health, Dr. Rosenfeld decided to prescribe Internal Exercises to her patients. Internal Exercises were taught to her patients, and within one week, about 80% of the patients showed positive results. Then eight nurses were hired, they were taught the Internal Exercises, and they were trained in the instruction and supervision of patients. Several patients were assigned to each nurse after the patients were diagnosed and specific Internal Exercises were prescribed to them. Most patients reported experiencing immediate improvement in health without feeling pain or discomfort, and the nurses themselves reported experiencing boundless energy after a day of performing and demonstrating the exercises. One nurse explains, "It used to be that a nurse's life was miserable. Every day all we saw was sickness, suffering, pain, and death. All we heard was complaints. The patient never calls the nurse to say 'It's a nice day!' After working eight hours on our feet, we felt as if we were ready to die. But now, since we started using these exercises—a hundred times a day—we feel as if we're ready to jump through the roof at the end of the day. We have so much energy we can't stand it anymore!"

As a result of this study, the Internal Exercises became a subject of study at many universities, colleges, medical schools, and hospitals. Also, over a million copies of the book on Internal Exercises were bought by the general public.

The healing powers of Tao of Revitalization are scientifically proven.

II

Tao of Revitalization is an incorporation of many mental and physical movements called Internal Exercises. The Internal Exercises bear no resemblance in form or function to the "external exercises" (sports, martial arts, body building, Hatha yoga, and dancing). The "external exercises" primarily emphasize the external figure, because its creators gave less consideration to all of the internal organs of the body. Building strong external muscles is now impractical. Our society no longer requires hunting skills or the ability to excel at physical combat. And strong muscles do not provide protection against new forms of disease-causing agents. Moreover, the stress, strain, pain, and contortions associated with the external exercises deplete the body of its energy; in a weakened condition, the body cannot fight off invasion by viruses and other disease-causing agents. Tao of Revitalization is not composed of motions that are foreign to the natural inclinations of the body. Deceleration, smoothness, quietude, precision, and naturalness—the properties of the Internal Exercises — energize the entire body.

Energy is a dynamic force in constant flux that circulates throughout the body. Many people plausibly substitute the word *life* for the word *energy* since the essential difference between the two words is so subtle that it eludes all but semanticists. Each term is vital to developing an accurate understanding of the energy theory as it applies to the body.

For all practical purposes, it can be stated that life is an *indication* of energy within the body. All that comes to mind on hearing the word *life*—breathing, talking, sleeping, eating, even the ability to read, think, and hear—all these can be achieved only because of the energy within the body. This invariably applies to those functions or activities that are not conspicuously perceptible: the metabolic processes within each single cell could not be accomplished without energy to sustain those functions. Energy is the basis for the apparent solid structures of the body also, for solid structures, such as bones, are really a mass of living cells. All forms and activities of life, both anatomical and physiological, are supported by, and simultaneously depleted by the energy within the body.

Although most people assume that inert matter is completely solid or dense, it is energy that binds the protons, electrons, and neutrons within each individual atom. Inanimate matter, then, is simply energy at a different rate of vibration than most of other forms of life. *Energy therefore is the absolute basis for all forms of life and matter in the universe.*

Since energy supports all vital functions associated with the body, adjusting that energy through Internal Exercises enables one to regulate those functions which that energy supports. If, for example, one strengthens the immune system, one improves one's immunity to disease.

Of equal importance to the health of the body is energy balance. Energy imbalance among the organs (functionally interlocked like clockwork) is another source of illness. The energy within an organ is determined by the vigor and regularity of its pulsations. The normal heart rate is 72-78 beats per minute. If this rate increases to or beyond 80 beats/minute, a fever or high energy is indicated. The normal rate of kidney pulsation is 36 pulsations per minute. We have two kidneys, so the total rate is 72 pulsations/minute. The heart and kidneys are in balance. Now if the person owning these organs takes diuretic pills, that person is beating more pulsations into the kidneys. What happens to the heart? The heart, in order to maintain balance, pumps faster, and this results in high blood pressure and copious blood flow to the kidneys. The kidneys are then forced to work harder. That person has created a vicious cycle between his heart and kidneys. Imagine the effects upon the rest of the body. If one cogwheel of an intricate clockwork speeds up, all the other cogwheels must speed up or all the springs and wheels will jam, bringing all activity to a stop. When we are in disharmony with the universe, we are in grave danger. But the properties of the Internal Exercises can correct and prevent imbalance among the organs.

The principle of energy equilibration serves as a foundation of a theory that can help us understand the circulatory system, a vital link to life. This theory is the Circulation Theory.

The circulatory system of the human anatomy is in many respects a transportation system. Oxygen, fixated upon red blood cells in the lungs, is transported in the bloodstream to every cell in the body. The wastes eliminated by cells are conveyed through the bloodstream to the excretory system, which excretes the wastes but saves the blood cells for further utilization. Nutrients are also conveyed from the intestine to the cells, through the bloodstream.

When circulation of the blood is impeded, the body is besieged by problems. Upon the delay of nutrients or oxygen, cells die from the lack of sustenance. Upon the impediment of blood flow, efficiency of cellular waste elimination is greatly reduced. Upon the accumulation of waste matter due to cellular dysfunction, health problems develop.

This would lead some people to conclude that increasing the rate of circulation will decrease the chances of problems developing inside the body. The method that comes to most people's minds as appropriate for accelerating the circulation is exercise (external exercises). Accelerating the circulation through the acceleration of the heart by exercise seems logical, because of two widely known facts: blood vessels are connected to the heart, and the rate of blood flow is synchronized with the heart rate.

Consequently, the ideal heart rate *during* exercise was determined for different ages. The determination process follows this rule:

220 beats/minute - # of years = maximum heart
(constant)   (age)   (rate)

The maximum heart rate for a person at forty years of age would be 180 beats/minute. This is the ideal rate. If that person were to elevate his/her current rate to 80% of the ideal rate during exercise, then that person will be in the normal category. The rates achieved by normal people of different ages are as follows:

Table 1.

Age	Beats/minute
20	160
30	156
40	144
50	136
60	128
70	120
80	112

According to Table 1, the capacity of the heart deteriorates as age increases. The deterioration increases until the heart ceases to function — death.

Many exercise books advise that one should try to meet the rates specified in Table 1 for a certain length of time—one hour weekly or more—to maintain good health.

Does forcing the heart to increase its rate really improve the circulation and benefit the heart?

Not necessarily. In the hospital, one often sees a patient who suffers from poor circulation with a very high heart rate. Although this person lies in bed with cold hands and feet, his heart beats continuously at a rate of 160 beats per minute. Circulation does not depend entirely upon the heart rate, for it is also dependent upon the blood vessels. Artery disease, injury, stress, strain, tension, etc. can block the blood vessel and cause the blood supply to diminish. The body has an inherent ability to correct malfunctions, and it will respond to the obstruction of the blood vessel by accelerating the heart rate. However, the supply of blood will remain diminished, for the blockage that is the cause of the problem still remains. The heart will exhaust itself in the attempt to correct the malfunctions of its connecting structures. The heart also suffers from imbalances in nervous stimulation. The heart is controlled by the autonomic nervous system, which requires no conscious effort on the part of the person to operate. The system is composed of two parts: the vagus nerve, which slows the heart rate; and the sympathetic nervous system, which increases the heart rate. The vagus nerve originates in the hindbrain and the sympathetic nervous system originates in the spinal cord. Due to the control of the autonomic nervous system, the heart pumps involuntarily and continuously from the moment it appears two weeks after conception to the moment death is officially announced. Throughout its lifetime, the heart is stimulated more by the sympathetic nervous system than by the vagus nerve. Anger, smoking, coffee drinking, ball-game watching, horror-movie watching, lovemaking, stair climbing, etc. are common causes of the exhaustion of the heart, for they accelerate the heart rate through stimulation of the sympathetic nervous system. If exercise is added to the burdens of the heart, its chances of resting and assimilating nutrients necessary to its tissues are greatly diminished. Can the heart, in its weakened condition, continue under so much stress and strain? No, the heart will fail.

Is there a better method for improving the circulation without adding more burden to the heart?

The Tao of Revitalization, special in characteristics, is uniquely qualified for solving delicate problems. The objective of the many Internal Exercises is different from that of the regular exercises;

the main purpose of the Internal Exercises is to relax the entire body, so that the afflicted part can receive nourishment and heal itself. Heart exhaustion can be prevented by utilization of certain exercises of the Tao of Revitalization to train or direct the brain to stimulate the vagus nerve to slow the heart rate, for the vagus nerve originates in the brain. Local circulation can be improved through utilization of, for example, the Crane Exercise, which does not afflict the heart.

In addition, stress, strain, tension, and hypertension can be relieved through the practice of Meridian Visualization and Concentration, Crane Exercise (wisdom of the Crane), etc. Tao of Revitalization gives total consideration to all factors involved in an ailment, because it was created for healing purposes. In contrast, the regular or external, exercises were created from the need for play, contest, and combat training.

Within the past seventeen years in the Bay Area, 863 persons from my audience have sought my help for heart problems and circulatory problems. Most of their ages range from 35 years to 93 years. There were, however, two persons in their 20s. All of them began practicing Tao of Revitalization instead of "cardiovascular exercises." These were the results: 761 persons led completely healthy lives; 72 persons did very well after combining their practice with light dosages of medications prescribed by physicians; 27 persons remained unchanged; 1 person, a 93 year old lady, died from an accidental fall; another person, a 56 year old man, died after having two surgeries within five months; and another person, a 72 year old man, died from a stroke after a family argument.

I am so confident that Tao of Revitalization is the best answer for the problems or potential problems of the cardiacvascular system that, for the past 8 years, I have discoursed on this subject in colleges, universities, private groups, and television and radio programs throughout the world.

The importance of prevention, a principle of Tao of Revitalization, can never be overemphasized. If minor health problems do not develop, major health problems do not develop, and if major health problems do not develop, we will not die. The primary purpose of Tao of Revitalization is to help people increase their lifespan.

Therefore, Tao of Revitalization is not a sport; it is not designed to provoke competition, require strenuous movements, increase stress or tension, or deplete energy. It is not designed to reduce one's lifespan. It keeps the body fully charged with energy. Tao of Revitalization is not a form of martial art. Unlike Kung Fu, Karate, etc., it involves neither strenuous movements nor tension. Although the movements in T'ai Chi appear slow, they actually build tension, for T'ai Chi was originally designed for combat. However, one aspect of T'ai Chi, that of the unification of mind and body, is similar to that of the Tao of Revitalization. Tao of Revitalization is not Hatha Yoga, for it does not overwhelm the body with a series of twisting, bending, or stretching poses and motions. Lastly, Tao of Revitalization is not another form of meditation, because the objective of the most popular forms of meditation is to "empty" the mind—inactivate the mind. The mind cannot be emptied, for directing the brain to empty itself is itself an activation of the mind. Anything that does not meet the above principles is not Tao of Revitalization.

In the Tao of Revitalization, the emphasis is upon internal, rather than external, development. Initially Tao of Revitalization involves physical movement, but as one's practice gradually becomes refined, one's concentration upon physical movement will be reduced and one's concentration upon internal movement will be increased. One will become still externally, but alive and active internally.

The very important quality of the Tao of Revitalization is flexibility. Anybody, regardless of age, health, or condition, can practice the exercises of his or her choice any time, anywhere. No equipment is necessary. The most basic of metabolic processes, breathing, can be transformed by the associated Tao of Revitalization techniques into a powerful therapy. The conscious state of mind and body movement are also potential therapies. Thus, sexual problems, aging, chronic diseases, and many "incurable" diseases will be remedied.

The heartwarming benefits so immediately reaped from a sincere and selfless application of any of the exercises are enough to instill within us a kind of fervor which of itself will move us forward along the path of greater understanding, longevity, and spiritual development.

When you do external exercises,
you must do internal exercises.
When you do internal exercises,
you may forget to do external exercises.

III

The Five Animal Exercises

Tao of Revitalization is a vast system comprising many exercises.

The exercises are grouped under five categories:

Hormone Exercises:
*Deer Exercise
etc.

Healing Exercises:
Zodiac Exercises
Crane Exercise
*Stomach Rubbing Exercise
etc.

Mental and Physical Exercises:
*Pa-Kua Exercise
*Five Animal Exercises
etc.

Energizing Exercises:
Meridian Exercise
Eye Exercise
etc.

Nerve Exercises:
*Dharma Forms
Turtle Exercise
etc.

Only those asterisked will be discussed at length in this book, because one chapter cannot do justice to hundreds of Internal Exercises. Developing a comprehension of the asterisked exercises necessitates acquisition of theoretical and practical knowledge; therefore each exercise will be accompanied by an explanation of the underlying theory.

Five Elements Theory

The ancient Taoists, by observing and contemplating the workings of the universe, devised a theory to explain the balance of the complimentary and antagonistic units of which it is composed. The characteristics and relationships of these dynamic units are explained in the Theory of Five Elements.

In this theory, the life force in all of its myriad manifestations comes into and goes out of existence through the interplay of the Five Elements: fire, earth, metal, water, and wood. This five-element model is unique to Taoism, because ancient Western and Indian philosophy used a four element model, which consists of the elements earth, air, water, and fire. In Taoism, air is included in the concept of fire, for without air, fire would not burn.

There are two cycles that illustrate the interaction between these elements. In the first cycle—the cycle of generation—each element generates or produces the succeeding element: thus wood produces fire, fire produces earth, earth produces metal, metal produces water, water produces wood—the cycle begins again. In

64

the second cycle—the cycle of destruction—each element destroys or absorbs the succeeding element: thus fire destroys metal, metal destroys wood, wood absorbs water, water absorbs fire, fire destroys metal—the cycle begins again.

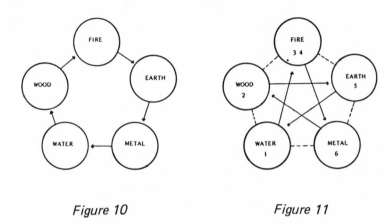

Figure 10   Figure 11

Because the universe maintains balance through the interplay of the Five Elements, our bodies, a microcosm of the universe, are thought to achieve mental and physical harmony in the same way. Energy flows through the body via the meridians and their respective organs and bowels in well-defined cycles. The cycles depicting the flow of energy within the body mirror the two cycles that depict the interaction between the five elements. Taoism identifies each of the viscera with one of the elements in the following manner:

fire — heart   metal — lungs
   small intestine   large intestine
   triple heater   skin
   (Endocrine glands)
   heart constrictor   water — kidneys
   (Blood vessels)   bladder
      bones
earth — spleen-pancreas   wood — liver
   stomach   gallbladder
   muscle   nerves

The elements as assigned to the Organs and Bowels are:

Table 2

	Wood	Fire (Prince)	Earth	Metal	Water	Fire (Minister)
TSANG— Organ	Liver	Heart	Spleen	Lungs	Kidneys	Heart Constrictor
FU— Bowel	Gallbladder	Small Intestine	Stomach	Large Intestine	Bladder	Triple Heater

Identifying each of the organs with its respective element in the first cycle results in: the heart (fire) supporting the spleen-pancreas (earth); the spleen-pancreas (earth), the lungs (metal); the lungs (metal), the kidneys (water); the kidneys (water), the liver (wood); the liver (wood), the heart (fire). The bowels also follow the same cycle: the small intestine (fire) supports the stomach (earth); the stomach (earth), the large intestine (metal); the large intestine (metal), the bladder (water); the bladder (water), the gallbladder (wood).

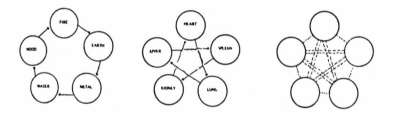

Figure 12

If the energy within an organ is not balanced, that organ, rather than being able to effectively support the organ succeeding it on the meridian circuit, will adversely affect, or will be adversely affected by, another organ; this pattern has been depicted in the second cycle on the interaction between the elements in which each element destroys or absorbes the other. Thus, when the energy within the heart (fire) is imbalanced, it (heart, fire) will adversely affect the lungs (metal); the lungs (metal), the liver (wood); the liver (wood), the spleen-pancreas (earth); the spleen-pancreas (earth), the kidneys (water); the kidneys (water), the heart (fire). The second also applies to the bowels: imbalanced energy within the small intestine (fire) will cause it to adversely affect the large intestine (metal); the large intestine (metal), the gallbladder (wood); the gallbladder (wood), the stomach (earth); the stomach (earth), the bladder (water); the bladder (water), the small intestine (fire).

In showing that the cyclic interaction between the organs and bowels is identical to the interaction between the elements, the Taoists not only provided a means by which the sayings, "That which is above is the same as that which is below" and "The microcosm reflects the macrocosm," can be realized and understood, but they also provide a means whereby the interaction of energy between the organs and bowels can be accepted as fact in that the basis for that interaction is founded upon the very same logic whereby the interaction of the five elements is instinctively realized to be true.

Five Animal Exercises

The Taoist modeled five exercises after five animals. The animals' characteristic movements are imitated by human beings, to alleviate the imbalanced functioning of human organs: the five organs and the related minor organs. The exercises were named after the five animals, which were the dragon, tiger, bear, eagle, and monkey. The movements of a particular animal stimulate a particular five element organ.

Table 3

Ele-ments	Wood	Fire (Prince)	Earth	Metal	Water	Fire (Minister)
Ex-ercise	Tiger	Dragon	Bear	Eagle	Monkey	Dragon
TSANG-Organ	Liver	Heart	Spleen	Lungs	Kidneys	Heart Constrictor
FU-Bowel	Gall-Bladder	Small Intestine	Stomach	Large Intestine	Bladder	Triple Heater

In addition to healing and balancing the organs, these exercises also effectively remove tension, stress, anger, and anxiety. According to Tao of Revitalization theories, tension and stress are detrimental to health. Taoists believe all health problems can be traced to tension and stress. Even with the best foods and medications, tension and stress can so restrict the functions of the organs that none of the nutrients necessary for health can be absorbed.

The proper use of thought, imagination, and visualization plays an important part in each of the Five Animal Exercises. It has been recognized for centuries that a thought is as much a reality as a material object, and in fact, that they are one and the same. They are both forms of energy. These ancient theories have been confirmed by the work of Dr. Karl Pribram, a Stanford University neurosurgeon and psychologist. Imagination and visualization are used, then, to bring together the mind and the body so that they function as a unit. Unifying the image of a particular animal with that of one's body strengthens a person psychologically and physically.

When one performs the exercises, one's thoughts must be fixed upon the image of the animals. The exercise must stop the moment the mind wanders. Also, the miming of the animals' movements must be executed in a free, flowing manner.

Figure 13. Dragon

THE DRAGON EXERCISE

For the ancient Chinese, the dragon was a mythical creature which symbolized the Yang force of the Creative; that dynamic electrically charged energy manifested in the thunderstorm. The flying dragon was always portrayed as being accompanied by rain, winds, clouds, and lightening.

See *Figure 13*

The use of its image was reserved for personal use by the Emperor, the Son of Heaven, as the dragon represented supreme wisdom, power, control, and social effectiveness.

The purpose of the Dragon Exercise is to instill the characteristics of the dragon into the mind and body of the practitioner. This exercise affects the mind by helping to overcome feelings of depression, anger, hostility, and all the anxieties brought on by being overwhelmed by adverse circumstances, for the dragon, flying through the heavens, is above all mundane concerns.

In some ancient Chinese texts, the Dragon Exercise appeared under other names. This was a precautionary measure taken to avoid political repercussions or death penalties. The emperors have forbidden the common people from picturing themselves as dragons.

The dragon represents the Fire Element, and the physical effect of this exercise is to bring equilibrium to the heart, blood vessels, and absorption in the small intestines.

Begin the exercise by standing still. Then, take a few deep breaths while imagining as vividly as possible that you are a dragon with glowing eyes, open mouth with fangs, glistening emerald scales, curling tail, paws splayed showing long claws. Then, raising one foot, assume the pose and character of a dragon. While imagining that your hands are claws, hold one arm up with claws down and hold the other arm down with claws up. As this is not a formalized pose, a certain degree of freedom of expression is allowed within the confines of the image. Hold the pose as long as you can hold the image without straining. Repeat as many times as is comfortable.

See *Figure 14*

The most important aspect of this and all the other exercises is the union of the body and the mind. If the image fades or the mind wanders during the pose, stop and begin again. No benefit will be obtained unless the body and the mind are in union.

Figure 14

THE TIGER EXERCISE

While the dragon symbolizes the Emperor, the Supreme, the tiger represents the General: a military leader with ambition, knowledge, power and physical effectiveness who protects the Imperial Throne and enforces the wishes of the Emperor.

The tiger corresponds to the Wood Element, so the Tiger Exercise affects the liver and nerves. The Taoists believe the structure of the nervous system is like a potted plant which sprouts from the liver.

The Tiger Exercise is useful in overcoming the adverse mental states of anxiety or hostility, ineffectualness, and lack of ambition. These adverse mental attitudes are believed to result from metabolic imbalances caused by liver dysfunction.

This exercise is recommended for healing and detoxifying the liver, to sooth inflamed nerves, to balance gall bladder functioning, and to detoxify the brain cells.

The tiger demonstrates its power in its ability to capture something by leaping over it and grabbing it. The tiger pose is an imitation of this "leaping over" movement.

70

Begin by standing still. Take a few deep breaths while imagining yourself to be a tiger. When the visualization is complete, bend your knees slightly and rise up on your toes while reaching up and out until your arms are straight. Keep the claws down, as if you have reached over and out to grab something. Maintain this position as long as you can hold the image without straining the body. Repeat as many times as is comfortable.

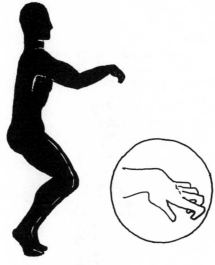

Figure 15

THE BEAR EXERCISE

The bear is also a very powerful animal, but it is a leisurely animal as well. Bears eat well, sleep well, wander about slowly, and are rather lazy and unaggressive. Bears are left alone and are not teased because they have the strength, courage, and prowess to deal with any potential adversary. The bear represents those who have attained a high degree of physical and material comfort. They can be successful business executives sitting behind large desks.

The Bear Exercise is recommended to aid the thought processes, to aid conceptualization, and to instill decisiveness into decision making.

The bear is associated with the Earth Element, and so this exercise affects the enzyme production of the spleen-pancreas and the functioning of the stomach muscle. This exercise is therefore

71

recommended for bad digestion, hyper- and hypoglycemia, and diabetes.

The power and strength of the bear becomes evident when it stands and walks on its hind legs. In this position, the most prominent physical feature of the bear also becomes obvious: its stomach, which protrudes outward and prevents the bear from walking straight.

Begin this exercise by standing still. Take a few deep breaths while visualizing yourself as a bear. Then with legs stiff, stomach pushed out, arms sloping out in front, walk slowly forward. As you do this, you will feel the movement of your abdomen and the stimulation of the area of the spleen-pancreas.

Continue walking this way as long as the image remains fixed in your mind. Repeat as many times as is convenient.

Figure 16

THE EAGLE EXERCISE

To the ancient Taoists, the flying eagle represented the spirit because of its holy, god-like qualities: silence, serenity, and invisibility. The eagle is also an accomplished hunter. It soars effortlessly to great heights, and its sharp eyes are alert to all details of the landscape below. The eagle manifests its attributes of intelligence, alertness, and ease when it hunts.

72

The eagle is associated with the Metal Element, so the Eagle Exercise stimulates the lungs, skin, and the large intestine.

This exercise is useful in overcoming feelings of melancholy, forlornness, and depression, which can result from or cause lung problems. (It is no coincidence that so many of the romantic poets and writers of western literature suffered from tuberculosis.) This exercise is recommended for the treatment of emphysema, asthma, as well as skin problems. The Taoists consider the skin to be the "third lung."

Outstretched wings effortlessly holding the eagle aloft and when it is flying, its eyes are open and it sees everything.

Begin the Eagle Exercise by standing still. Take a few deep breaths while imagining yourself to be an eagle.

When the visualization is complete, begin to walk slowly with your arms held out to the side in a slant, or with your hands gently clasped behind you. As you walk, imagine you are an eagle, effortlessly floating through the blue sky, untouchable, holy. Your body should be very relaxed, but your mind and eyes should be very alert, noticing everything without focusing on any one thing in particular.

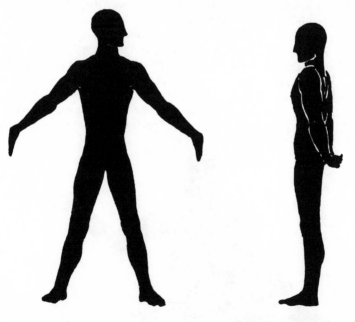

EAGLE EXERCISE (1)   EAGLE EXERCISE (2)

Figure 17

Continue the exercise as long as the mind does not wander. If it does, stop and begin again. Though this exercise can be performed anytime, anywhere, it is especially effective if done outdoors, after the evening meal.

THE MONKEY EXERCISE

For the Taoist, the monkey (or ape) epitomized boundless activity, curiosity, and the exercise of free will. The monkey is constantly active, whether on the ground, swinging in the trees, or leaping playfully about, uninhibited by any cultural conventions.

The monkey is associated with the Water Element, so the Monkey Exercise stimulates the functions of the kidneys and bladder. This exercise is recommended for those feeling confined or restricted by circumstances in which there is a lack of freedom. To the Taoists, the will power resides in the kidneys. The Monkey Exercise is also recommended for any problems involving the kidneys, bladder and/or urinary tract.

As the embodiment of free will, the Monkey inspires an exercise that is free-style in the broadest sense. This exercise is best done in private as the presence of others might be inhibiting.

Begin by standing or sitting. Take a few deep breaths while imagining yourself to be a monkey. When the visualization is complete, kick off your shoes, throw off your clothes, and begin to act like a little monkey. Sit on the floor, crouch in a chair, leap about, bounce up and down, hang upside down or by one arm, whatever is physically possible to do without strain or exertion.

Figure 18

This exercise is completely free-style; all the movements and actions should act out impulses and whims as they occur to you. Monkeys also rub and scratch themselves a great deal; you may do this also, especially in the area of the kidneys.

For anyone who is basically healthy, any of the Five Animal Exercises can be used whenever circumstances permit to maintain a balanced physical and emotional state. If a specific problem exists, then one may choose the exercise that deals with the affected organ group or apply what in Taoism is called the Mother and Child Law.

The Mother and Child Law, as it applies to the human body, is based upon the interaction between the Five Elements. Each element is the "mother" of the succeeding element and, at the same time, the "child" of the element that precedes it in the cycle depicting the flow of energy throughout the elements. For instance, earth is the mother of metal and also the child of fire.

As energy circulates throughout the body, it passes through each organ and bowel in a well-defined cycle. Each organ or bowel is the "mother" of the organ or bowel succeeding it on the circuit; this phenomenon is based on the law of the Five Elements. For example, the lungs support the kidneys and therefore the lungs are said to be the "mother" of the kidneys. If the energy within the kidneys (child) is deficient, according to the Mother and Child Law, by stimulating the energy within the lungs (mother) with the Eagle Exercise, the kidneys will automatically receive an increase of energy. Here, one is treating two organs with one exercise. By consulting the diagram of influences (figures 10 and 11), an exercise or a group of exercises can be selected to suit any need.

Never over do one exercise. If one concentrates too much on the Eagle Exercise (metal), for example, one could decrease the liver function (wood). If you become too relaxed, the nerves will become dulled. But if the liver is overactive — having an augmented energy level, it could be calmed by the Eagle exercise. So, the key word is balance.

IV

Pa-Kua Exercises

All the elements of the universe occupy space and time and are therefore directional. Since we are a microcosm of the universe, we are influenced by space and time and are therefore directional. Directionality arises whenever electric forces are present — and electric forces are everywhere because they are a property of matter. The electric forces are the means whereby two magnets, or other substances are drawn together or repelled apart. These forces are also the means whereby a weak magnet, for example, is made more powerful. This "recharging" of electrical forces involves correct orientation of a body, or "rechargee", with respect to the "recharger." For example, the north pole of a magnet must be placed against the south pole of another magnet, in order for magnetic induction to take place. So directionality plays an important role in the energizing of mankind.

After repeated experimentation, Taoists developed eight directional exercises for energizing mankind, a process that requires the execution of correct actions in the correct directions. The forms of these exercises were modeled after the forms of the *Pa-Kua,* or eight trigrams. Its efficaciousness earned it the name *Pa Tuan Chin,* or "Eight Brocade Pieces." The word "brocade" was used to express its preciousness to generations of people. These exercises can also be called The Eight Directional Exercises or The Eight Energizing Exercises.

The exercises are as follows:

Northwest   For the Northwestern Exercise, orient the front of the body toward the Northwest. Stand with the feet shoulder-width apart. Point the toes inward. This takes the pressure off the nerve endings in your heels and prevents imbalance in pressure.

Now pretend you are lifting a barbell of medium weight (to prevent too much straining). While keeping the legs straight, bend down to pick up an imaginary barbell. Lift the barbell to waist level. Then lift the barbell as high as possible above your head. Really visualize that you are lifting a barbell. Then reverse this procedure. Do the exercise as many times as you want.

This exercise helps increase one's strength. It is also good for the lungs and large intestines.

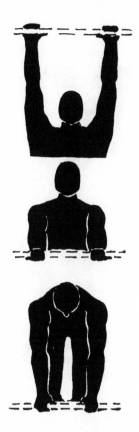

Figure 19

North

For the Northern Exercise, have your torso oriented in the Northerly direction. Spread the feet widely apart. Pretend you are shooting an arrow from a bow. Shoot to your right and shoot to your left. Your head, arms, and torso change positions, but your feet remain stationary. Really visualize that you are pulling a taut bowstring and shooting an arrow. Do this exercise as many times as you wish.

This exercise is good for the lungs, kidneys, large intestines, bladder, skin, and bones.

Figure 20

Northeast

Facing Northeast, bend down and touch the toes with your fingertips. Keep the legs straight. Bend as much as possible. Imagine that you are a mountain. You may hold this position as long as you wish.

This exercise is good for the spleen-pancreas, muscle, and digestion.

Figure 21

East

In the morning, stand under the sunlight and face East. Place your feet shoulder-width apart. Point the toes inward and close your eyes. With your arms hanging at your sides, turn the *upper body* to the sides. Let your head turn with the torso. Let the eyeballs trace the source of radiant heat emitted by the sun. Never move your feet. Your mind should follow these movements—never let it wander. Do this as long as you like.

This exercise is good for the nerves, liver, eyes, gall bladder, and weight reduction.

Figure 22

Southeast

Facing Southeast, stand with your feet shoulder-width apart. Point your toes inward and raise yourself on your toes. Lower yourself. Do this seven times as a set. If you wish, you may do more. Do not let your mind wander from your actions.

This exercise benefits the nerves, liver, gall bladder, and heart.

Figure 23

79

South

Facing South, rotate your hips as if you had a hoola-hoop around you. You may change the direction of the rotation. Never let your mind wander onto other subjects. Do this as long as you like.

This exercise is good for the sexual organs.

Figure 24

Southwest

Facing Southwest, pose as if you were about to fight. Bend the knees slightly. Bend the arms slightly and clench the fists. Make your eyes bulge out with rage. Your mind must be with your body. Hold this pose as long as you wish.

This exercise benefits the digestive system, lungs, and nerves.

Figure 25

80

West Facing West, stand with your feet shoulder-width apart. Point the toes slightly inward. Raise one hand up in the air. Bring the hand down and raise the other hand. Try to keep your abdomen still. Your mind must follow these actions. Do this exercise as many times as you wish.

This exercise benefits lower back pain, shoulder pain, kidney problems, and spinal problems.

Figure 26

These exercises are extremely versatile as they can be done anywhere and anytime. In two minutes, an executive, soldier, athlete, or anyone else can energize their tired bodies and minds. When the body is energized, business problems are solved easily, durability of the body is increased — anything is made easier.

V

Life is to live. Living is a function. This function is described by a Taoistic formula, which is as follows:

Let f = function
    o = organ
    e = energy

$$f = o + e$$

In order to function, one must have both organ and energy. An organ without energy is dead. Pure energy without an organ is a ghost. Life will be meaningful — have a function — only when organ and energy are together. Energy, within the organs, can be present at excessive or insufficient levels, but this imbalance can be adjusted by either dispersing (weakening energy) or tonifying (strengthening energy). Organs must be maintained by nutrients, and the subject of consumption will be discussed later. The subject of energy is discussed in the present chapter, which deals with movement.

Many methods of harnessing and utilizing energy to balance our organ systems have been discussed, e.g., utilization of space for energy balance. Now I will discuss energy balance of specific organs utilizing time measured by the biological clock.

Biorhythm—often referred to as the biological clock—is the regulation of the flow of energy within the body in relation to both solar and lunar time measurement. The word "biorhythm" encompasses all those concepts that denote the natural, inherent pulse underlying all functional aspects of life. In many ways this rhythm is taken for granted because being aware of it would, in a sense, be the same as being constantly aware of the rhythmical basis of one's own breathing. Because it has such a subtle and elusive nature, biorhythm is best exemplified when it is disrupted.

Jet-fatigue—the consequence of suddenly traveling from one time zone to another—is a perfect example of how the body's natural rhythm is disrupted as a result of long-distance travel in a short period of time. It is sometimes difficult to conceive of the body functioning on a strict time schedule until one is abruptly placed in an environment regulated by a *different* schedule. The stress of having to readjust to an environment in relation to time makes one intensely aware of how rigidly scheduled *are* the bodily functions.

Taoists, after observing the circulation of energy throughout the body, formulated biorhythm cycles that precisely account for the energy flow along the meridian circuit during every second of the day. Meridians are minute pathways along which energy circulates throughout the body. (More will be said about the meridians in Chapter 5.) It was discovered that each of the main meridians has two-hour periods, called "watches," during which energy has a maximum intensity of circulation. For example, between 9 and 11 a.m. energy is at its peak in the spleen-pancreas meridian. It is during this time interval that the spleen-pancreas works the hardest. Between 11 a.m. and 1 p.m. when the energy activates the heart meridian, it is simultaneously at a minimum intensity in the spleen-pancreas meridian. There are twelve "watches" in a day and they correspond to the twelve houses of the Zodiac. The following chart lists the "watches" and the hours during which energy reaches its peak in each of the organs and bowels and their respective meridians.

1–3 A.M.	Liver
3–5 A.M.	Lung
5–7 A.M.	Large Intestine
7–9 A.M.	Stomach
9–11 A.M.	Spleen-Pancreas
11–1 P.M.	Heart
1–3 P.M.	Small Intestine
3–5 P.M.	Bladder
5–7 P.M.	Kidney
7–9 P.M.	Heart Constrictor
9–11 P.M.	Triple Heater
11–1 A.M.	Gallbladder

Chart 1

Utilizing the biorhythm chart will prove to be especially beneficial in pinpointing the specific organic causes of discomfort and balancing the energy level of that organ through the application of exercises that will either disperse or intromit energy, according to the needs of the organ. For example, if insomnia causes you to wake up between 1 and 3 o'clock in the morning regularly, a look at the chart will tell you that the cause of the insomnia is a disorderly liver or nervous system. The aftereffects of insomnia—poor performance at work, tiredness, feeling of guilt, etc.—can be eliminated by applying the exercise appropriated for the 1 to 3 o'clock time interval. If you are constipated, the cause can be traced to untimely bowel movements. The recommended and biorhythmically determined time for bowel movements is from 5 to 7 o'clock in the morning. If you follow this schedule for bowel movements, you will not have to suffer from drugs, colonics, enemas, etc.

The exercises for these and other problems are called Zodiac Exercises and they are listed in the order of the "watches" they correspond to. They are:

Watch A
(1-3 a.m.)

If ever you are awake during this time interval, you should sit with your legs crossed and try to see the tip of your nose. Drop your eyelids halfway to do this. Repeated attempts will enable you to see the tip of your nose. Also wrap the fingers around the thumb to make a closed fist and rest the fists on your knees. Breathe deeply and relax. Do this exercise for 5 to 30 minutes—the length of time is determined by you.

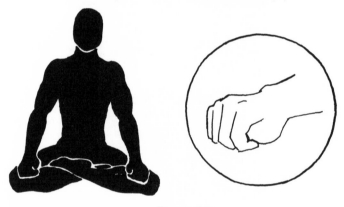

Figure 27

Watch B
(3-5 a.m.)

If ever you are awake during this time interval, sit with your legs crossed or in a position most comfortable to you. Close your eyes halfway and look at your nose. Hold your head by lacing your fingers behind the head and supporting with your palms. Click your teeth. Deeply and slowly inhale and exhale nine times. Do this for 5 to 30 minutes.

Figure 28

Watch C
(5-7 a.m.)

Cover the ears with the palms of your hands. Tap on the back of your head with your middle or index fingers so that a drum-like sound is made. This is called Playing the Heavenly Drum. Count your breaths. Inhale and count "one." Exhale and count "two." Inhale and count "three." And so on. Do this very slowly until you have reached the count of nine.

Figure 29

Watch D
(7-9 a.m.)

Sit with legs crossed. Use your hands to hold the shins of your legs and move your upper body around in circles. Make the circles as large as you can. Move freely. Reverse directions now and then to prevent dizziness. Do this exercise several times.

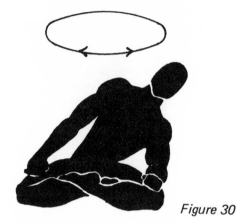

Figure 30

Watch E
(9-11 a.m.)

Brush your teeth with your tongue. This creates saliva. Save the saliva until you have a mouthful. Then rinse your mouth with the saliva by swishing the saliva around in your mouth as if it were mouthwash. Swallow the saliva slowly by dividing the mouthful of saliva into three swallows. Do this exercise several times.

Figure 31

Watch F
(11 a.m. to
1 p.m.)

Remove clothing. Sit in a comfortable position. Inhale and hold your breath. Rub your hands together very hard and place them on your back in the area of the kidneys and rub until you cannot hold your breath any more. Breathe and relax. Repeat the exercise.

Figure 32

Watch G
(1-3 p.m.)

Sit comfortably. Inhale as deeply as you can. Imagine the air coming into your solar plexus—your abdominal area. Use the navel as a center of focus. Then hold your breath to keep the air inside. Then imagine a fire burning in the area. Concentrating on the fire will enable you to feel heat. Then exhale. This exercise is difficult to do, but repeated attempts will enable you to do it well.

Figure 33

Watch H
(3-5 p.m.)

Pretend you are turning the handle of a manual meat grinder. Turn in such a way that your hand moves away from you on the downstroke. Alternate between the right and left hands. Both hands should turn eighteen times. This is one set. You may repeat the exercise.

Figure 34

Watch I
(5-7 p.m.)

Sit on the floor or the bed with your legs outstretched flat. Then lace your fingers and—palms up—reach for the ceiling, as far as you can go. Feel your back and side muscles stretch. When tired, rest hands on your head. Then lift them up again. Breathe normally. The exercises may be repeated as many times as you wish.

Figure 35

Watch J
(7-9 p.m.)

Sit on the floor with your legs outstretched. Reach forward and try to touch your toes. Then try to touch the soles of your feet. If you cannot reach your toes, do not force yourself. Then relax. Assume the initial sitting position. Pat your upper legs, lower legs, and thighs. Relax. Then repeat the exercise as many times as you can. Gradually, you will be able to grab the soles of your feet. Hold this position until you can no longer hold it. Release and relax.

Figure 36

Watch K
(9-11 p.m.)

Follow the procedures for Watch E.

Figure 37

Watch L
(11 p.m. to
1 a.m.)

Follow the procedures for Watch G, but as you hold your breath tighten the muscles of your rectum as much as possible and as long as possible. Imagine that a tingling sensation is shooting up your spine. Release, relax, and exhale slowly. Repeat this exercise several times. This is also a difficult exercise that can be mastered after continuous practice.

Figure 38

VI

Dharma Forms

2,000 years ago during the Han Dynasty, a man from the west went to China and devoted his entire life to the study and practice of Taoism and a form of Buddhism. His name was Dharma and he resided in the White Horse Temple in the capital of the Han Empire.

His book, *The Text of Altering Nerves* was the result of his lifework. It contains only a few pages of complex verses, which were frequently used to discourage those who laugh at knowledge. Hidden within the verses is information that can increase our longevity. In his book, Dharma stated that all human problems are caused by problems within the nervous system and that human beings could live longer if they alter, or renew, their nervous system.

Developing a comprehension of Dharma's theories introduces an understanding of the nervous system. The nerves are an intricate and elaborate network of "communication cables" connecting our brain to our organs and our organs to our organs. One break in your "cable" will cause your body to suffer. For example, if tension chokes a nerve in your finger, your finger will soon atrophy and you will be forced to cut it off. Nerve cells need chemicals produced by interaction with other cells to survive, and the functions of other cells are dependent upon the nerves. Moreover, our nerves shrink and become hardened after we have reached twenty years of age. When nerves deteriorate, impulses are conducted at slower rates. When nerve impulses are slow, mental and physical processes are slow. This is aging. Young people below twenty years of age have nerves that are soft and expandable.

To remain youthful, we must exercise our nerves to reverse deterioration and to preserve softness and expansibility. Dharma developed twelve exercises called Dharma Forms that soften and expand our nervous system. The exercises resemble the exercises of Tai Chi Chuan in form, but not in theory. Tai Chi Chuan was developed for combat, whereas Dharma Forms were developed for removing stress and tension and preserving the nervous system.

Dharma Forms unite the mind and body in order to bring about relaxation. If you have ever tried to relax your entire body with your mind, a concept employed by biofeedback machines, you will find that relaxation of the body is impossible to achieve. Relaxing the body with the mind involves clearing your mind of all thoughts. This is a difficult feat because your mind is always cluttered with thoughts. Dharma, acknowledging the fact that the mind is always active, made the mind follow a series of body movements that will lead both mind and body to a state of relaxation. Relaxation is the first step to preservation. Thus, if we can preserve our nervous system, i.e., altering the deteriorating nervous system, we can live longer and preserve our youth.

Each exercise leads to the next exercise; therefore, all twelve exercises must be done in their proper order. The exercises, in their original order, are as follows:

1. Stand with your feet shoulder-width apart. Direct toes inward. Do not face south when doing the exercise. Place palms on breasts so that the middle three fingers of each hand meet over the thymus gland. Feel the heart beat. Smile and imagine you are humble and polite. (This induces relaxation by removing the spirit of contention.)

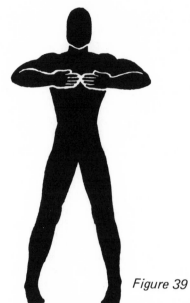

Figure 39

2. While holding the first pose, spread your toes and dig them into the ground as if they were claws clutching at something. Open your mouth and look blankly ahead, as if you are a fool. (A fool does not seek knowledge and is therefore re-

Figure 40

laxed.) Then move the hands outward with palms downward and fingers bent loosely. Hold it there.

3. While holding the second pose, stand on your toes. Then
clench your teeth. Then lace your fingers and lift them,
palms up, as high as you can stretch. Then lower yourself
until you are standing with your feet flat on the ground.

Figure 41

4. While holding the third pose, put one hand on your head to
prevent it from moving (keep other hand up) while the eyes
move forcefully from side to side. Now repeat this exercise
using the other hand to prevent the head from moving.

Figure 42

5. If the hand held straight is the right hand, move the right leg forward; if the hand held straight is the left hand, move the left leg forward. The hand held straight moves down and makes an overhand fist. (All fists should be made with the thumb hidden under the fingers). The hand from on top of the head moves to the side and makes an underhand fist (while doing so, bend elbows). Your eyes should be on the overhand fist. Reverse positions of the limbs. Change positions back and forth in a karate-like movement.

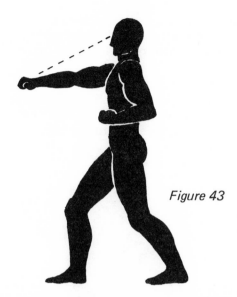

Figure 43

6. Adopt the original position and make underhand fists at your side. Bulge out your eyes as if you are angry. Bring the fists up. Now they are in an overhand position. Push, but slowly as if you are pushing somebody. Your right eye should be fixed upon the right fist and the left eye should be fixed

Figure 44

upon the left fist. Then quickly and forcefully, pull the arms back so that fists are underhand again. Then repeat exercise seven times. Then relax the entire body, including the eyes.

7. Put one hand under your chin and one hand over your head and turn your head to the right and left sides. Reverse positions of hands and turn the head again. Do this three or four times.

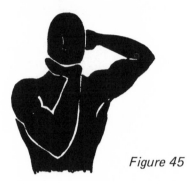

Figure 45

8. Adopt the original pose. Now stoop down, while pretending your arms are pushing something down. As you sink, pretend you are pushing yourself down. Stand up and sink again. Do so seven times.

Figure 46

9. Adopt the original pose. Follow the instructions for exercise number five, only this time the fingers are rounded (no fists), and the arms are close together. Move the arms out and in and feel the effects on the arm and back muscles. Then relax. Repeat exercise.

Figure 47

10. While in the original position, relax. Bend over and walk forward on your fingers until you are on your toes. If you cannot do this, walk on your hands. Hold this position until you can no longer hold it. Later, you may try walking on your middle three fingers.

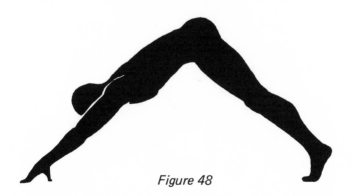

Figure 48

97

11. Move to the original position. Lace your fingers and place them behind your head and bend down. Close your eyes while doing this. Then raise your upper body to return to the original position.

Figure 49

12. Keep holding your hands behind your head and bend the upper body forward, pushing one leg back. Keep one leg forward and bent. Then return to center position. Repeat except push the other leg back. Then return to center position and adopt the original pose. After you have placed your hands in the heart position, you will have finished the exercises.

Figure 50

VII

Stomach Rubbing Exercise

The Five Animal Exercises, Pa-Kua Exercises, Zodiac Exercises, and Dharma Forms are for general healing. In addition to these, the Tao of Revitalization offers approximately a thousand other exercises that energize and strengthen individual parts of the body. These exercises deal with specific health problems. An example of these exercises is the Stomach Rubbing Exercise (similar to the Crane Exercise).

If one is to live a long and healthy life, it is necessary to build a strong internal system with stomach, abdominal muscles, internal organs, lungs, and circulatory system. Historically, as well as in modern times, man has suffered from obesity and many acute and chronic problems of the abdomen including constipation, diarrhea, ulcers, diverticulitis, and cancers of the stomach and intestines. All of these diseases are caused by a similar problem—imbalance in one or more parts of the digestive tract. When a tissue or an organ is imbalanced, it is more susceptible to disease, and the greater the imbalance, the more intense the symptoms. The Stomach Rubbing Exercise was developed by Taoists to energize and strengthen the digestive, respiratory and circulatory systems.

Obesity is a disease because it is dangerous to one's health. When a person becomes excessively overweight, the whole body is burdened. For every inch you gain in girth, the body grows approximately *four miles* of blood vessels to nourish the extra tissues. Blood which would normally be sent to the head and brain remains in the abdominal cavity, aiding the digestive organs with their increased work load. The heart must work harder due to the increase of fatty tissue. Because of this undue strain, the heart gradually becomes critically weakened and more likely to collapse. The excessive fats and lipids (which, along with carbohydrates and proteins, constitute the principal structural material of living cells) in the bloodstream obstructs the circulation in the arteries and veins. This obstruction in the circulatory system contributes directly to high blood pressure. Excessive weight brings on mental as well as physical fatigue, and the shift of weight to the lower front of the body puts stress on the spine, often causing lower back pain.

So there is not much to recommend in being overweight. But the conventional methods for losing weight and inches are quite often not only very difficult, but also very expensive. Also, as a person ages, exercising the stomach and abdominal area becomes increasingly difficult. It is not a very good idea to be doing sit ups after the age of forty, unless you are now, and have been, engaged in a regular exercise program for some time. The problem is that, unlike most of the other bodily extremities, the abdominal area cannot be directly controlled. (There are, however, thoroughly documented cases of advanced yogis who have perfect control over even these so-called "involuntary muscles.") Such men are the exceptions to the rule. For the rest of us, fatty tissue accumulate there very easily.

The exercise that meets these conditions is the Stomach Rubbing Exercise. It is the simplest and most natural method for losing weight. Begin by lying down flat on your back. Relax. Put the palm of your hand on your navel. (If you are right handed, use your right hand; if left handed, use your left hand.) Then start to rub clockwise from the center (that is, from right to left), first in small circles and then gradually expand the movement until the upper and lower limits of the stomach and abdomen are being rubbed (see Figures 51, 52). When you have completed the first movement, then reverse it, rubbing counterclockwise in smaller and smaller circles until you are back to the center of the navel. You need not press down with any force. Apply a slight pressure as you rub slowly. Repeat this clockwise and counterclockwise motion as many times as you wish.

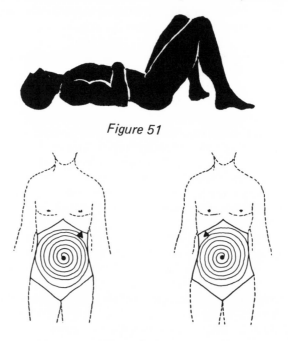

Figure 51

Figure 52

Fatty accumulations and deposits are disturbed from their resting place and eventually broken up. They are then passed into the eliminatory system and out of the body. By such apparently simple means, the superfluous areas of the stomach and abdomen are literally rubbed away.

When you rub in a clockwise direction (which again, is from your right to your left in gradually widening circles), you are encouraging proper and easeful bowel movement. Quite often constipation is a symptom indicating that the large intestine is overfunctioning. The large intestine is absorbing too much water from the waste matter as it passes through on its way to the rectum. This causes the waste matter to be compacted to the point where the normal peristaltic activity of the large intestine is not sufficient to expel the waste matter. Constipation results and fecal material that would normally have been passed on through the anus are stored in the body. The clockwise motion augments the peristaltic activity and slows down the water removal process to normal levels.

One young woman I taught this exercise to told me she had suffered from constipation most of her life. She was only 23 years old, but she had been suffering from constipation for 15 years. She had tried drugs, laxatives, and enemas. But nothing she did eliminated the problem. And yet, from the first week she began doing this exercise, she ceased to have problems with bowel movements. She felt, by her own admission, like a new person. She told me later that after three months of doing the exercise, her whole digestive system evened out and she never had the same problem again.

Rubbing in a counterclockwise motion has the opposite effect—that of helping to solidify fecal material as it passes through the intestine (see figure 52). It does this by stimulating the passage of water from the large intestine to the kidneys. An extreme case of chronic diarrhea which was corrected with this simple technique was recently brought to my attention. One of my students told me that ten years ago his mother had been operated on for cancer of the colon. Since that time, she has had absolutely no control over her bowel movements. She could not even go out for fear she would suddenly find she had to use the bathroom and not have access to one. Her son taught this technique to his mother. She had tried every other remedy by that time and was ready for anything that held some promise of helping her. After a few days of practicing the exercise, her stools formed for the first time in ten years. Since then she has been able to normalize her life and the problem has ceased to plague her.

Rubbing the abdomen in both the clockwise and counterclockwise directions will help stomach ulcers. One case demonstrating the efficaciousness of the exercise is that of a ninety-six year old Chinese senator. He tackles his duties with more enthusiasm and energy than people one-fourth his age. He is also actively involved in many different activities. Yet, he is never sick. His blood pressure, checked every morning by the government-appointed nurse, is always normal. When admirers asked about his secret of youth, he told them a story about a youthful experience. As a young man, he suffered from painful stomach ulcers, tuberculosis, and other diseases. When he served in the army, he sought medical help from doctors wherever he was stationed. Then one day, someone told him about a famous, aged healer who lived deep in the mountains. He made an appointment to see the healer and struggled over the rocky terrain to see the healer. The old man meditated through the young man's introduction and presentation of his problem. The old man did not open his eyes or speak. Finally, the healer uttered, "Go home and rub your stomach." Further questioning drew no replies. Back home, disappointment, exhaustion, and anger caused the ulcer to flare up again. Left with no alternative, the young man rubbed his stomach. Immediately the pain faded away. Thereafter, he faithfully rubbed his stomach. A few months later, the ulcer completely disappeared. Gradually the tuberculosis disappeared also. His health improved daily. He now rubs his stomach daily, after every meal and whenever he feels uncomfortable.

The second, and equally important facet of the Stomach Rubbing Exercise, involves the use of your imaginative powers. When you are performing the exercise, you should visualize that energy is coming from your hand and penetrating into the skin and the organs beneath. You should also visualize that the energy is being retained and that it is heating up your abdominal tissues. As more energy penetrates your body, the area around your navel will begin to burn as if a fire had been started within your tissues.

The distinction between the psychological and physiological basis for disease is starting to blur. But what is becoming increasingly clear is that the way a person thinks, believes, and sees the world affects his or her physiological processes.

The man who has contributed significantly to making visualization healing techniques accepted in professional medical circles is Dr. Carl Simonton. Dr. Simonton directs the Cancer Counseling and Research Center in Fort Worth, Texas. He has produced a startling body of work which points to a strong psychological basis for the healing processes in the body. Even the powerful malignancy of cancer can in some cases be brought to heel with the use of intensive visualization techniques. Once again, it is a matter of cooperating with the body's natural wisdom in allowing the body and mind to heal themselves.

The first year I was invited to lecture at the University of Oslo in Norway, one of the subjects I dwelt on was the Stomach Rubbing Exercise. The following year, I was invited back to lecture before an overcrowded audience again. After lecture coordinator Dr. Bjorn Overbye introduced me, I began to speak, but an old man in the audience interrupted me. His request for permission to speak was granted, and he told the audience to listen to me because whatever I said would be beneficial. Then he told everybody a story. He said that he attended my first lecture with a distended abdomen full of water because he was suffering from terminal liver cancer. He was in terrible pain and the doctors gave him only a few weeks to live. Every week he had to go to the hospital to have his abdomon pumped to remove the water. When he learned about the stomach rubbing technique, he went home and rubbed his stomach. The pain went away and water never collected in his stomach again. One week later, he went to see his doctor and astonished him. His doctor exclaimed, "This is a miracle! I can't believe it! What did you do?" He replied, "I didn't do anything. I just rubbed my stomach." Thereafter, he faithfully rubbed his stomach. His liver did not bother him anymore, though it was still cancerous. He was able to discontinue chemotherapy; he had become "healthy," and he was able to go back to work. When I returned to Norway in the third year, the man was still around.

The efficaciousness of the exercise is explained by the penetration of energy from the hand into the abdominal tissues. Kirlian Photography, a recent technological development, has produced graphic proof that the body itself is permeated and surrounded by a field of energy. (Kirlian Photography is also called "high voltage photography.") The photographs produced from research done with this technique show that the energy field is most intense around the head and hands and that energy shoots out from our hands like the rays of the sun.

To augment the energy penetration and make the exercise fully effective, you must use your imaginative powers to visualize the energy coming from your hand and penetrating into the skin and organs underneath. You should also visualize that the energy is being retained and that it is heating up your abdominal tissues. As more energy penetrates your body, the area around your navel will begin to burn as if a fire had been started within. This visualization requires a great deal of concentration and patience, and it should be done every time you do the exercise.

Other Exercises

103

Here is a list of other Tao of Revitalization exercises:

The Male Deer	Rubbing the Arms and Legs: Meridian Massage
The Female Deer	Upward Massage
The Prone Deer	Downward Massage
The Crane	Weight Reduction
The Turtle	The Lower Back
The Sitting Positon	Healing the Stomach
The Standing Position	Heart Exercise
The Standing Crane	Energizing the Heart
Walking	The Abdomen
Sleeping	The Lungs
Bone Breathing for Complete Relaxation	Sexual Glands and the Lower Body
Toe Wiggling and Body Stretching	Pain Relief
Internal Organ Relaxation	The Hands, Arms and Upper Body
Eye Exercise	Meridian Meditation
The Nose, Lungs and Sinuses Exercise	Contemplative Exercises for Practical Purposes
Beating the Heavenly Drum	Sunlight Contemplation
Mouth Exercises: Tongue, Saliva and Teeth Clicking	The North Star Contemplation
Rubbing the Face	Candlelight, Sunlight and Moonlight Contemplations
Stimulating the Kidneys	Brain Cleansing Breathing
Liver Exercise	Brain Cleansing One
Bringing Fire into the Stove	Brain Cleansing Two
Small Heavenly Cycle	Large Heavenly Cycle

If you wish to learn more about these exercises, please refer to *The Complete System of Self-Healing: Internal Exercises* (Tao Publishing).

VIII

By practicing the Tao of Revitalization, one forgets oneself and the ego becomes smaller, while the spirit of God within becomes larger. Mankind has a higher purpose than merely to exist. This is exemplified in man's pursuit of his material life — he always wants something more than he has. We also have a desire to improve ourselves. Why? Because we have a spiritual need to improve ourselves into the Kingdom of God. To be religious means to find a way to get into the divine Kingdom of God — to become immortal. The ancient Taoists recognized this primal urge of mankind and through their knowledge of the natural laws perfected this system of exercises as a means whereby — with daily practice — man could realize his birthright, his divine self. The system is meant to provide each of us with the opportunity to unify our bodies with our minds and our spiritual selves. Only then can we realize the Tao and enter into the Kingdom of God.

3

THE TAO OF BALANCED DIET

I

All human beings need food, enjoy food, and crave food, but
most do not know how to consume it, i.e., most human beings do
not know how to balance, select, avoid, or prepare food. This

chapter will deal with the regular food diet and the theories and principles of consumption. Regular food diet is represented by the letter o in the equation $f = o + e$. (The letter e has already been explained in the previous chapter.)

The Taoist studies on consumption resulted in teachings that help mankind achieve fulfillment in life through the preparation of foods that satisfy four criteria:

1. Pleasing in aroma
2. Pleasing in taste
3. Pleasing to the eyes
4. Beneficial to the body

The preparation of these foods (recipes) will be explained in the third part of this chapter, since the first two parts will deal with Taoist Theories of Health and Nutrition and Dietary Do's and Don't's.

Taoist Theories of Health and Nutrition

Health, in Taoist terms, is synonymous with what you eat, what you metabolize, and how you balance your diet. What you put in your body becomes part of your body. If you put in healthy food, your body becomes healthy. If you put in "garbage," your body becomes "garbage." What you metabolize ultimately decides how that food will be used. If your body can digest and absorb what it needs and eliminate what it does not need, your body will be healthy. If your body cannot take what it needs from the food you eat, if it eliminates what it needs, or if it cannot eliminate what is toxic, your body will become weak and unhealthy. A balanced diet is also essential for good health, because it helps balance the body. A truly well-balanced body, one in which all the organs and glands are functioning properly and regularly, is self-supporting and self-regulating. It is less likely to be ill or weak. These relations between food and health will be explained in the following paragraphs.

The "Five Tastes"

Since the "Five Elements Theory" applies to every facet of existence, it also applies to all types of food. In this case, the five elements are represented by the Five Tastes. Any food will fall into one of these five groups. Food is divided in this way because each group (taste) of food affects the organs it is related to within the

Five Elements Theory. For example, foods with a bitter taste will be guided to the heart, so bitter food nourishes the heart. The nutrients and vital energy in a bitter food will enable the heart to build more tissues, thereby strengthening itself and improving its function. Anyone who has drunk two or three cups of strong coffee within a brief period may have experienced an acceleration in heartbeat. Coffee is bitter in taste and therefore directly affects the heart. Unfortunately it gives little or nothing in the way of nutritional help to the heart, it simply stimulates it to beat faster.

The following is a chart of the Five Elements along with their related Organs/Bowels, Superficial Organs, Organ Opening, and Taste.

Table 4

Element	Taste	Organ/Bowel	Superficial Organ	Organ Opening
Metal	Spicy	Lung/Large Intestine	Skin	Nose
Wood	Sour	Liver/Gall Bladder	Nerves	Eyes
Earth	Sweet	Spleen/Pancreas/Stomach	Muscles	Mouth
Water	Salt	Kidney/Bladder	Bones	Ears
Fire	Bitter	Heart/Small Intestine	Blood Vessels	Tongue

In other words, you can say that spicy or piquant food is food for the lungs and large intestine. As an example, cinnamon, pepper, chili, and curry are good for colds and coughing, and, in fact, they are the basis for many home remedies for this type of illness.

Sour food is food for the liver. Apples, grapefruit, and something known in Chinese cooking as Yellow Flower are examples of sour foods.

Sweet food is food for the pancreas. String beans are considered food for the pancreas.

Salt is food for the kidneys. Salt stimulates the kidney and makes it work. Too much salt, however, over-works the kidney and weakens it. A weakened kidney, as in the case of people who retain water, needs to rest; it does not need more stimulation of the type it receives from diuretics.

Table 5
The Five Tastes of Food

Sweet		Sour	Bitter	Salty	Spicy
Almonds	Pancreas	Barbecue	Artichokes	Beef	Chili
Beans	(any type)	Sauce	Asparagus	(prepared)	Curry
Black Eye	Pastry	Beets	Avocados	Bones	Garlic
Peas	Peanuts	Breads	Bamboo	Butter	Ginger
Bran	(Raw)	Buttermilk	Shoots	Canned	Liquor
Brazil Nuts	Peas	Chicken	Black	Foods	Lung
Cabbage	Pecans	Collards	Fungus	Cheese	(any type)
Cakes	Pies	Fish	Bitter	Egg	Mustard
Candy	Pudding	(Fresh-	Melon	Fish	Onions
Canned	Pumpkin	water)	Bock Choy	(Saltwater)	Parsley
Fruits	Rice	Fruitjuices	Broccoli	Frozen	Pepper
Carrots	Sherbet	(most)	Cauliflower	Foods	Rhubarb
Cereals	Snow Peas	Fruit (raw)	Celery	Ham	Vanilla
Coconut	Soft Drinks	Liver	Chard	Kidneys	Wine
Corn	Sorghum	(any type)	Chinese	(any type)	
Cream	Squash	Mayonnaise	Mustard	Margarine	
Cucumber	Starch	Meats (red)	Chocolate	Processed	
Dried Fruit	String Beans	Pickles	Cocoa	Foods	
Eggplant	Sugar	Salad	Coffee	(most)	
Eggnog	Sun Flower	Dressings	Endive/	Salt	
Fova Beans	Seeds	Salami	Escarole	Saltwater	
Honey	Sweet	Sausages	Gelatin	Fish	
Ice Cream	Potatoes	Sour Cream	Green	Shellfish	
Jicama	Sweetened	Sprouts	Vegetables	Soy Sauce	
Juice	Fruit	Tartar	Heart	Tofu	
Kale	Syrup	Sauce	(any type)		
Kentucky	Walnuts	Tomatoes	Leeks		
Wonder	Wheat	Turkey	Mushrooms		
Beans		Vinegar	Mustard		
Lettuce		Yeast	Greens		
Molasses		Yogurt	Napa Cabbage		
Milk			Rutabagas		
Milk			Spirulina		
Beverages			Tea		
Oatmeal			Turnips		
			Vegetables		
			(greens)		

Table 6
Five Tastes Balanced Diet

To maintain a balanced diet, according to the Five Tastes Theory, over each twenty-four hour period food intake should be as follows:

SWEET	20%
SOUR	20%
BITTER	20%
SPICY	20%
SALTY	20%

Table 7
Excessive Sweet Taste Diet

If a person does not follow this dietary balance, illness and health problems will develop. For example, if a person's food intake followed these percentages:

SWEET	50%
SOUR	30%
SPICY	10%
BITTER	5%
SALTY	5%

the following health problems would be liable to occur: hypoglycemia, diabetes, heartburn, indigestion, constipation, water retention.

Table 8
Excessive Sour and Salty Taste Diet

If the percentages were:

SWEET	20%
SOUR	30%
SPICY	10%
BITTER	10%
SALTY	35%

there is a strong likelihood of developing kidney weakness and disease, heart ailments, and high blood pressure.

The key criterion here is balance. If an organ is too weak, you cannot overstimulate the organ without making it weaker in the long run. For instance, too many apples a day (sour) would further fatigue a weak liver eventually, even if it is activated and appears stronger temporarily. In this case the Taoist science of nutrition

111

would balance the equilibrium in the body in order to deal more completely and delicately with the liver. According to the Five Elements Theory, the five elements (as well as the organs they represent) support and control each other mutually, according to a pre-established order (see figures 10 and 11).

In the generative cycle, each element strengthens the successive one through a generative process and each element becomes stronger and stronger along this wheel of creation.

In the destructive cycle, the elements mutually reduce the strength of each other and compensate for the generating process taking place in the generating cycle. These balancing equilibriums are used in Taoism to "tune up" the functioning and health of individual body parts. For instance, by strengthening the kidney (water) you indirectly strengthen the liver (wood), as water generates wood according to the Five Elements Theory. By calming or regulating the lungs' overfunctioning (metal) you also release the burden on the liver (wood), as metal controls or destroys wood. Thus, a weak liver can be brought to normal functioning by tuning up the organs interrelated with it. The applications of these interrelationships also apply to various levels in the body from the organs (the deepest), to the bowels, the superficial organs, and the organ openings (the most superficial). For instance, someone with weak kidneys is prone to ear aches, ringing ears, and ear infections; stronger lungs (metal) will strengthen the kidneys (water) (metal generates water) and will indirectly remove the susceptibility to ear aches.

The key to stimulation and the provision of nutrition for tissue build-up of these various parts of the body by our food is dictated by its taste, as explained before. This idea applies to *all* foods — the kind we buy at the grocery store as well as herbs.

Energy Level of Food

The regulation, or "tune up" of the body's general functions, must also consider the energy level provided to the different body parts by the food eaten.

Cool or cold foods are "yin." If the body is tense and congested, cool or cold foods can be used to release the blocked energy. As a rule, cold and cool foods such as fish should be cooked with a little bit of hot food to balance the energy in order to prevent losing too much energy.

112

Table 9

Energy Level	Energy Characteristic	
hot	very energizing	
warm	mildly energizing	yang
neutral	neither adds nor reduces energy	
cool	mildly reducing energy	yin
cold	very energy reducing	

Below are listed most of our commonly eaten foods according to where they belong in terms of hot, cold, warm, cool and neutral energy characteristics.

Table 10

Cold	Cool	Neutral	Warm	Hot
Celery	Algae	Eggs	Beans	Chili
Freshwater	(Spirulina)	Grains	Beef	Cinnamon
Fish	Butter	Tea	Coffee	Garlic
Shellfish	Dairy products	Tofu	Poultry	Ginger
	Fruit (most)		Root	Lamb
	Green vegetables		vegetables	Pepper
	Mushrooms		Vegetable	Wild game
	Oils		flowers	
	Pork			
	Processed or			
	frozen foods			
	Seafood			
	Sprouts			
	Sugar			

This intrinsic balance at the organ level should also be inter-related at the body's overall functioning level, i.e., according to the Five Element Theory. A liver (wood) weakened by excess alcohol intake (and therefore having a low energy level) will break the stand-off or controlling balance it has with the stomach (earth). Being free from control, the stomach will then begin to overwork. Part of this over-functioning results in an excess of acidic secretions by the stomach which creates heartburn sensations.

The Taoist energy theory applied to nutrition unveils a whole dimension neglected in Western dietetic science. For example, lamb, which is hot, will contribute additional energy, while pork, which is cool, will reduce that energy level. (Pork is helpful in times of congestion, but has an adverse effect in the case of weakness.)

Energy Balance of Food

The energy or vital force must be balanced between the organs for smooth functioning and perfect digestion and metabolism. Each food provides its own level of energy, and the energy intake as a whole must match the body's needs and compensate for the imbalances which may already exist in the body.

The energy referred to here is the vital force which keeps our blood circulating and our organs functioning. Without that energy our body would be like a perfect machine without the force or fuel to make it run. This energy represents the essence of life, and contributes to the natural functioning of our body's growth, repair, and response to disease and infection. This energy should not be confused with the calories identified in medical science. The latter represents the fuel consumed in muscular efforts.

Each food has a different energy level from "cold" to "hot." A food with warm or hot energy will bring vital energy to the organ affected, according to the corresponding taste. A food with cool or cold energy will reduce the vital energy level of the organ affected, according to the corresponding taste. A weak organ (i.e., one lacking energy) needs food with warm or hot energy in order to be revitalized. It is the opposite with an inflamed organ which needs to be fed cool or cold foods to reduce the inflammation (energy level). Neutral foods neither adds to nor drains energy from the body.

Hot and warm foods are considered to be "yang," that is, positive and energizing. Hot foods are too energizing to eat a lot of. Ginger, for example, is a very "yang" food, and while safe in small quantities and mixed with other, balancing foods, it can be very harmful if used in large quantities or by itself.

If you are weak, you need warm food. Many people practicing a vegetarian diet will add fish to their regimen hoping that the additional protein will give their overall energy level a boost. Instead, the fish, which is cool, weakens or lowers their energy level even further, by taking even more energy out of their bodies.

Similarily, high calorie foods may deplete the level of vital energy in the body. For instance, sugar, while high in calories, also has a cool energy level. Excessive consumption of sugar will deplete the vital energy lodged in the pancreas (related to the sweet taste by the Five Elements Theory) and weaken its functions. The weak pancreas will then "leak" excessive insulin into the blood and neutralize the blood sugar.

114

Forgotten Foods

It is important to have a balanced diet, as already defined, in order to maintain good health, or not to aggravate an existing bodily imbalance. However, some imbalances, created by serious disease (such as hepatitis) or serious abuse cannot be corrected by the food encountered in our regular food markets, despite use of the Taoist knowledge of common diet. For example, an imbalance resulting from damage to the liver tissues can only be perfectly healed through the implementation of foods or herbs called "Forgotten Foods." These foods, such as the bupleurum tree for the healing of the liver, have been neglected down through the centuries as our ancestors gradually limited their diet to foods of pleasing taste or easy commercialization. The science of Forgotten Food Diet represents a separate and complex knowledge of its own and is explained in the next chapter.

pH Balance of Food

When people hear the term "balanced diet," they think of the generally accepted idea of eating food belonging to all of the "Basic Five Food Groups" so often discussed by Western nutritionists.

There is another aspect of "balance" in the diet which is essential to our health. This balance has to do with the levels of acids and alkali in the food we eat. If the food in our stomachs is too acid or too alkaline, it is not properly assimilated by our bodies. In addition, food with poor pH (acid-alkaline) balance is digested too slowly, giving it a chance to decompose in our digestive tract. When this happens, this decomposing food becomes a welcome home for germs and parasites which enter our bodies through our food. The pH balance in the stomach keeps germs away while the body metabolizes the food. If the pH balance is missing, the food is corrupted immediately by the germs and parasites in the body.

If our food is balanced, it passes quickly and efficiently through our digestive tract, and the waste passes out of our bodies in the form of stools. This all happens before the food has an opportunity to become a home for unwanted organisms.

The typical American diet contains an abundance of acids and very little alkali, which explains the success of antacid tablets (which are alkaline) in this country. When consumed, these alkaline pills neutralize the acid in the stomach. This brings temporary relief (just as the television commercials say). What they neglect to say is that the stomach *needs* acid in order to digest our food. Neutralizing our stomach acid with pills results in food remaining in our stomachs.

115

Eventually the stomach must produce more acid in order to digest it, this produces heartburn and we again have to take antiacid pills. Thus a cycle is established of alternating between heartburn and the ingestion of antiacid pills.

A look at a typical menu will give you a clearer idea of just how much acid is in our diet:

Table 11

Acid	Alkaline
1. Pre-dinner cocktail, tea or fruit juice (all alcohol is acid)	1. Small portion of green vegetables
2. Soup (if tomato based)	2. Baked potato
3. Bread (or croutons)	
4. Salad dressing	
5. Meat, fish or cheese entree	
6. Wine	
7. Dessert	
8. Coffee, tea or juice	

Acid foods outweigh alkaline foods 40 to 1! Not only that, but to properly balance the servings of meat and vegetables, you should eat an equal amount of vegetables as meat, so your meal should consist of 50% meat and 50% vegetables. The only way to be sure of getting the right pH balance in your meals is to be aware of what you need, and to plan your meals accordingly.

Table 12
Acid/Alkaline Balance of Foods

The following chart shows which foods are acid and which are alkaline.

Acid	Alkaline
Alcohol (All)	Cooked vegetables
Bread (or Croutons)	Grains (including rice)
Cheese	Green vegetables
Coffee	Potatoes (baked or boiled)
Deep fried foods (All)	Sprouts
Desserts	
Fish	
Fruit Juices	
Meat	
Salad Dressings	
Soups (if tomato based)	
Tea	

116

Nutritional Balance

It is said that we should have nutritionally "balanced" meals, such and such an amount each day of proteins, vitamins, minerals and other "foods." If you ask me whether or not you need these, my answer would be "What are vitamins? What are minerals? What are proteins?" And "How much knowledge do we really have about them?"

The point is that "proteins," "vitamins," and "minerals" are just terms developed by scientists who study foods in order to determine what kind of effective composition they contain. Each time scientists discover new components, they invent new names to "explain" what these components are. They also attempt to explain a food by the components they have isolated within that food. For example, scientists have found Vitamins A, C, Fructose, Pectin and Laetrile in apples. So they say an apple will supply these nutritional components. Or, worse yet, they say if you take these components individually, you can substitute them for an apple.

Well, even non-scientists know that an apple is not only composed of Vitamin A, C, Fructose, Pectin and Laetrile. Most scientists recognize that there are probably two thousand additional components in an apple which are still unknown at this time. For this reason, if we consumed an apple in order to obtain just those known components—or if we separated those components from the apple and took them by themselves—we would be fools. We would be misusing our scientific knowledge (or scientific superstition).

I respect the known scientific knowledge, but it is incomplete, and I do not feel we should be overly attached to the theories of an area which is not yet fully known. Food *components* are not sufficient for good health. We should eat whole foods, in as natural a state as possible. There have been instances of hunger strikers who have been given "perfectly balanced nutrition" injections—and then died from malnutrition. Their bodies were not capable of surviving on "solid" scientific principles of nutrition. They needed whole food.

The conclusion is that in the near future it is unlikely science will have a complete understanding of what a true "nutritional balance" is. But that need not deter you. Because if you follow the principles of this book you will be eating whole, healthy foods—not vitamins, proteins and minerals. You will be secure in the knowledge that every component of that food—whether it be called vitamin, protein, mineral or whatever—is in just the right amounts, and in perfect proportion and balance to all other components of that food. Indeed it is a law of nature that were they not in balance, it would not be possible for that food to even exist, for balance is a basic foundation of the reality of nature.

II

Dietary Do's and Don't's

There are a number of dietary do's and don't's which are necessary to follow if we are to maintain a balance in the functioning of our bodies.

Meat

DO eat meat. We need to eat animal protein, because our bodies need the high energy level that only animal tissues can supply. (Assuming, of course, that you have not avoided our high-pressure society and are simply sitting and meditating all day long in some isolated mountain retreat.)

However, there are problems connected with eating animal protein these days because of the stimulants and growth hormones which are so widely used by the growers and producers of the meats we buy in our stores. Also, individual animals carry various diseases, especially tuberculosis in beef, in their blood streams. These unnatural additives and disease organisms can have detrimental effects on our own health if we consume them.

Therefore it is a "must" that the meat we eat be treated, and prepared in such a way as to cleanse it of its harmful components, leaving only the beneficial body tissue of the animal for our consumption. Treating the meat correctly does not lessen its nutritive value. The protein and tissues remain intact; only the harmful parts are disposed of.

Here is the correct method for preparing meat for cooking:
1. Place the meat in a shallow dish and cover it with water.
2. Soak the meat for several hours, changing the water frequently as the blood is soaked out of the tissues. (The harmful toxins and the germs are only in the blood, not the tissues themselves)
3. When all the blood is soaked out of the meat (when the soaking water no longer turns pink) drain the water off the meat.
4. Slice the meat very thinly.

118

5. Return the meat to the shallow dish for a second soaking period. This time cover the slices of meat with any strong alcoholic beverage such as whisky, gin, vodka, or brandy. (This will kill any remaining germs or parasites in the meat. Many of these organisms resist heat well and are not killed by ordinary cooking.) A little soy sauce and "Five Spices" (a blend of spices available at specialty stores and Chinese markets) may be added to the marinade. This marinade will give lots of flavor to the meat as well as treat it.
6. Marinate the meat for about 30 minutes.
7. Cook the meat quickly at high temperatures, without burning it, until it is completely well-done (no pink color left).

DO NOT EAT animal fat. Any type of animal fat, including dairy products such as butter and cheese, contains high levels of cholesterol. This cholesterol clogs the honeycomb structures in the liver, interfering with or blocking the organ's functions, which can lead to serious liver diseases. The reason is that the animal has already converted its food into fat, and this fat will not melt once it is in our bodies. Instead it collects in the liver. In addition, cholesterol collects in the blood vessels where it can create dangerous problems for the heart.

Beef fat is the worst kind of fat. It will only melt or break down when heated to temperatures over 600°. That is why it is used in heavy industries to grease machines.

Beef must be sliced thin, cooked well-done over high heat, and the fat must be allowed to drain off as it cooks. Of course, when choosing meat, pick the leanest possible and trim off all fat before cooking.

Pork fat is the animal fat which is easiest for humans to consume because it breaks down or melts very easily inside the body. Unfortunately, pork is very toxic because pigs do not perspire and cannot rid their bodies of toxins, and these toxins collect in the body tissues of the pig.

We do need fat in our diet. Its purpose is to clean and lubricate the liver, kidneys, and lungs—the three filters of the body—but it must not clog them, as we have mentioned before. The best fat for this purpose is cold-pressed sesame oil. It is the lighest of all vegetable oils; it is even water-soluble. Some people object to the heavy, pervasive tastes and odors of vegetable oils. These can be eliminated by browning a few slices of fresh ginger root in the oil before cooking. This will purify the oil, and also rid the oil of most of the odor and flavor.

Vegetables

Do cook all vegetables at least briefly. Cooked food is easier for the body to digest and assimiliate because the chemical changes that take place during cooking assists the body in its digestive processes. Raw food tends to overstimulate the small intestine. Moreover, there are many harmful organisms residing in the vegetables and fruits we eat, as well as in meat.

By simply parboiling most vegetables very briefly (less than one minute) in boiling water, most of the organisms are killed. This way very little nutrition is lost and the color of the vegetable or fruit remains attractive.

Some strong vegetables (green beans, for example) need to be chopped and stir-fried for a few minutes in a small amount of oil. This will draw out the water in the vegetable, thereby killing the organisms in that water. This method is also more tasty than the parboiling method.

Some weak vegetables, such as lettuce can be eaten raw by most people, although everyone has a different tolerance for such food. If you experience heartburn after eating a salad, this is a signal that raw vegetables are not for you. Even these weak vegetables contain unfriendly organisms. By soaking the vegetable in vinegar and water for a few minutes, then rinsing with cold water, these unwelcome guests will be taken care of.

Fruits

DO EAT fruits raw when they are fruits which have skins. First, however, the fruit should be peeled—even apples—because worms live under the thin skins of fruits such as these. In addition, the skin of anything is hard to digest.

The seeds of the fruit should also be eaten. The body can benefit greatly from the contents of the seeds as well as the "heart"—the center of the fruit nearest the seeds, such as an apple core. The heart and seeds contain laetrile (as well as countless other as-yet-unidentified things) which cleanses the liver and detoxifies the body.

In ancient times in China, a person exposed to too much smoke was given apples to eat as a way of detoxifying the liver. (The liver is the body's filter for all solid substances.) These days apples can be used in the same way when a person is exposed to air pollution or smoke inhalation.

Any type of smoke is poisonous to the body, including tobacco and marijuana smoke. Marijuana is especially toxic because of the way it is smoked: the smoke is drawn into the lungs and held there until it is completely absorbed into the blood stream. After five minutes of marijuana smoking the liver is overloaded with toxins and can not handle them anymore. If a person is a heavy user of marijuana, within one month 10% of the liver will be permanently damaged. Smoking marijuana is, therefore, definitely not recommended.

Whole Food

Do eat whole food. Follow God's wisdom and eat the *original* food. Believing that vitamin tablets can make up for the vital food missed in a reducing diet is a mistake. Our bodies have the knowledge they need to deal with food in its original form. Highly concentrated vitamin pills are foreign to the make-up and inner workings of the body, and pass through, largely unassimilated, into the urine.

Variety

DO eat a diversity of food. In so doing, you will satisfy your appetite in a way that can not be done with limited eating habits. Your appetite will normalize itself and any desire to binge or overeat will dissipate.

Also, by eating a variety of foods—that is foods representing all of the Five Tastes—your body will receive the balanced nutrition and energy it needs to function well. In addition, if you avoid a particular food, your body will suffer from some kind of shortage. In the long run, it will reject that particular food if it is ever eaten again because it is not used to or is estranged from the chemical elements in the food. This can lead to atrophy in some organs and possible death.

Fasting

DO NOT fast, because fasting can atrophy the entire body. Many cases show that after fasting for a long period of time, people are not able to digest *any* food. The final result is death.

The universe is the macrocosm, the body is the microcosm. In other words, the human body represents all the elements of the universe. So we should eat a diversity of all universal substances. God intended it that way. He gave us the different flavors of food for our mental and spiritual pleasure, and for our physical needs. We need to nourish all three parts of ourselves—the mental, the spiritual and the physical.

Fiber

DO include fiber in your diet. It is essential for the health of the large intestine. To function properly, the large intestine has to be filled up firmly, like a sausage, on a regular basis. The large intestine is very soft, and without anything to fill it, it shrinks, and the sides of the intestinal wall rub against each other, which can lead to ulcerations of the colon. This condition can gradually lead to cancer of the colon, as dirty waste deposits build, aggravating the condition further. Also, lack of fiber can be the cause of both chronic diarrhea and chronic constipation, which can lead to cancer because of chronic inflammation in the colon area.

Over one thousand years ago, the Taoists recognized the importance of fiber and decided that nothing in their daily diet included enough of it. That is why they added bamboo shoots to their diet. Today, bamboo shoots remain the best souce of fiber, and can be found in most Chinese recipes.

Bamboo shoots are good for both chronic diarrhea and chronic constipation. I once treated a woman who had suffered from alternating constipation and diarrhea for twenty years through improper eating habits and the use of laxatives. I advised her to include bamboo shoots in her diet and to eat as many as possible in soups, salads, and other foods. The results were practically immediate, and she felt better than she had felt in twenty years. "What's in those bamboo shoots?" she asked. "Nothing," I replied. "They just fill up your intestines so they can work!" Bamboo shoots have no nutritional value—no vitamins, minerals, proteins, or acids.

Carrots are also a good source of fiber. However, since the nutrients of *raw* carrots or carrot juice are not absorbed by the body, it is recommended that they be cooked in order to get the full benefit. Heat changes the chemistry of carrots, making the nutrients available to the body.

Bran is a good source of fiber. But do not eat it raw. It may scratch the wall of the stomach or intestine. Bran becomes gentle with cooking, and then can be eaten safely. (Bamboo shoots and carrots are naturally soft and act gently to stretch the intestines.)

Tofu

DO include tofu (soybean curd) in your daily diet. Tofu is an excellent source of lecithin, which has the ability to clean out the cholesterol that has collected in our blood vessels. It is also an excellent source of protein, fiber, and calcium. Under normal circumstances, tofu sits for days in water where germs may have a chance to establish themselves. For this reason, always cook tofu before eating it. If tofu is sour, it is spoiled. Do not eat it. Tofu has a very bland taste and texture, and combines well with a variety of dishes.

Skin Mushroom

Another ingredient used in Chinese cooking deserves special mention. It is a fungus, known as the skin mushroom or "cloud ears" which grows on pine trees. Being bitter, according to the Five Element Theory the benefit of its nutrients goes to the heart. And it too cleans up the wastes and cholesterol that collect in the blood stream. If included in the daily diet, as it is in China, it can prevent heart disease—which is virtually non-existent in China.

An equally important role the skin mushroom plays is that of a cleansing agent for the small intestine. There are tiny microvilli in the walls of the small intestine where nutrients are absorbed. Over time, these microvilli can become blocked by various things such as tiny hair off the poultry and fowl we eat. (Hair is never digested. When preparing poultry, wash it well and inspect it carefully for any hairs. A pair of tweezers works well in removing these hairs.)

When it is digested, part of the skin mushroom is absorbed (which goes to cleanse the blood stream, as mentioned before) and the rest passes through the small intestine in a sticky, gelatinous state, molding itself into the folds and curves of the intestine. As it passes through the small intestine, it picks up the little hairs and germs, and carries them out in the stools, thereby unblocking the pores. The skin mushroom is the only food that has this ability, making this a very important part of our diet.

Food Combinations

DO combine your food wisely, taking into consideration the Five Tastes, the Energy Levels, and the Acid-Alkaline balance of the food you eat.

It will come as a surprise to many people that some foods become mildly toxic in our bodies when eaten in certain combinations. These toxic combinations are: beef eaten with onion; banana with sweet potato, which produces dizziness; and crab with persimmon, which poisons the intestines.

Body Signals

DO listen to your body and pay attention to its signals. Each person has a different system and reacts differently to each individual food. If you notice signs of mucus, pimples, diarrhea or constipation after the consumption of certain foods, this is an indication that your system cannot assimilate the food properly, and that the food is irritating or poisoning your body in some way. This type of condition is commonly called food allergy. If a certain food affects you in one or more of these ways, avoid it.

Cravings

Food cravings indicate an imbalance in the body which can lead to food allergy. If you crave a particular food, this is an indication that your body has already had too much of it. Try to leave it alone —your body really does not need more of what it craves. Giving in to the craving can only lead to health problems in the long run.

Please note that we say DO listen to *certain things*—gas, indigestion, etc.—but NOT to *cravings* of any kind, whether they be sugar, water, meats, or whatever.

Shellfish

DO NOT EAT shellfish in warm weather. Some foods are toxic even when eaten alone. For example, shellfish is very toxic when eaten in warm weather. (For some people, a particular shellfish can be toxic to their systems *any* time of the year.) This is because shellfish, such as clams and oysters, like cold water. When the water warms up in the summer, these animals are sick and suffering, and their bodies have to fight back, and to do this they produce a hormone which helps them relieve the effects of the heat.

While this hormone is good for the shellfish, it is harmful to our bodies. This hormone aggravates the hidden trouble spots in our bodies, such as acne, neuritis and infections. For this reason, it makes good sense to avoid these foods in the summer and whenever you are already sick.

Again, and we continue to repeat this because it is the single most important point in this book, DO LIMIT YOUR INTAKE OF LIQUIDS. Healthy human kidneys can comfortably filter six cups of liquid a day. Any more is stored in the body tissues, causing water retention. If water retention is allowed to persist, this water in the body becomes jelly-like and collects the wastes and bacteria in the body, poisoning the tissues of the body in turn. The nerves are particularly affected. Not only are they squeezed under the pressure of the water retained under the skin, but they are also attacked by the germs and poisons existing in that stagnant water. This is why people who suffer chronic water retention also feel nervous and edgy.

Natural Food

DO eat food in its natural state. Chemically processed foods cannot be metabolized properly by the body, and the toxins from the food remain in the system. Our bodies know how to use only whole, natural foods. Chemical additives and preservatives are not God-given; they are man-made. Avoid MSG, commercially processed sugar (raw, untreated sugar is a good food and contains many necessary nutrients), and decaffeinated coffee (the chemicals used in the decaffeinating process make it even worse than plain coffee)!

Margarine

DO NOT eat margarine. As we said before, it is even worse than butter for our system. As a result of the process by which it is produced, margarine remains the same under any circumstances. It even remains unaltered when it is placed in the sunlight to melt.

Time To Eat

Again, DO eat on time. And DO eat when you are in a peaceful, loving state of mind. Eating when we are angry can have harmful effects on our well being, because when we are angry the liver releases real poisons into our system.

DO NOT eat when you are extremely tired. There will be a lack of energy to digest food, and eating will result in undigested food and the restulting putrefaction and food poisoning. For this reason DO NOT eat immediately after sexual intercourse. Nor should you eat immediately before intercourse for the same reason. Speaking of sex, if you engage in oral sex you should not consume semen if you are interested in losing weight. Semen, although small in quantity, is tremendously nutritious and could negate the efforts you make to lose weight.

White and Brown Rice

DO eat white rice and in general grains which have been milled to remove the shell around the seed. The shell of brown rice and wheat is very hard to digest, with the result that the vitamin B and other nutrients are not assimilated by the body. The brown grains remain in the stomach and ferment, causing self-poisoning. You can obtain the nutrients you might miss by following this guideline if you eat meals balanced in the Five Tastes as previously discussed.

Water or Liquid With Meal

Do not drink liquids with your meals. To drink too much liquid of any kind with food is in effect to wash the food down. This prevents the mixing of saliva with the food during the chewing process. Saliva is a natural regulator of the acidity (pH) of the stomach. Without its being mixed into each bite of food, the acidity or pH of the stomach can be upset thus interfering with digestion. Often gas or belching during or after a meal is a result of too much liquid with the food causing an improper pH in the stomach.

DO drink a small glass of wine with your daily meals if you wish as this aids in the digestion of the food.

III

Recipes For Full Nutrition

Every one of the recipes in this section exactly follows the Taoist principle and theory of nutrition and balance, including the "Five Elements," the "Five Tastes," energy (hot/cold) balance, pH balance, and the proper preparation and combination of foods. As you eat and enjoy these meals, you will have the full assurance and satisfaction that you are eating food that will help you lose weight at the same time it provides full, balanced nutrition. You will literally be eating your way to health, energy, and a more vigorous and enjoyable life. Good Eating!!

The Four Principles of a Healthful Meal

There are four basic principles for recipes:
1. Good taste
2. Good smell
3. Good appearance
4. Good nutrition

Every dish must meet these four principles. If any recipe is lacking in any of these requirements, it is not a good recipe.

There is a universal principle for eating. Let's refer to Genesis—after man was created. The first order of God to man is the principle of eating: "Of every tree in the garden thou mayest freely eat." But in consideration of one tree, called the "tree of knowledge," God said "You shall not eat of it, for in the day that thou eatest thereof thou shalt surely die."

God's command may be interpreted as an order to eat every tree, not to stick to one. If man eats only one type of food, he will die, because man needs everything to support his body, and one food cannot cover the needs of man. The human body is the microcosm and the universe is the macrocosm. Of course, after the flood, God added animals to man's nutritional list.

Eve chose to use her own concept of the universal principle, which is against the true principle. When she saw that the tree of knowledge was good for food, "that it was pleasant to the eyes, and a tree to be desired to make one wise, she took of the fruit thereof, and did eat, and gave also unto her husband with her, and he did eat." The human concept—Eve's concept—is that one tree covers everything. The universal principle is eating everything but one thing. These recipes follow the universal principle. I shall enlarge upon the food territory as much as possible, so we may use the true wisdom to eat them properly in order to prolong life. I hope the readers are always aware of this principle, for there are many diet plans on the market that go against the true principle. Therefore the diets are not beneficial for longevity or balance of health.

General Comments

All broths can be used in all recipes. For instance, they can be used as sauces, soups, etc. The flavor and nutritive value of any recipe is improved thus. One special use: freeze the broth, cut the jelly-like broth into cubes and use them in salads.

Always when cooking chicken broth, you are better off buying chicken that has been raised without chemical stimulants. When cooking chicken, the fat under the skin (yellow and rubbery) must be removed, because the fat is very abundant.

Bones can be obtained from butchers. Usually they are just thrown away. When you ask for bones you can get many of them for a very cheap price. Bones must be very, very soft because nutrition from bones is difficult to retrieve.

Fish. Catfish contains the most nutrition, but all fishes provide adequate amounts. If you prefer shellfish to other fish, by all means use shellfish. Be sure to remove all sand from clams, mussels, and other shellfish. For shrimp make an incision along the entire back of the shrimp. Remove the dark artery of the shrimp which contains waste products. Note: Use no shellfish with surface blemishes.

Vegetables. Seaweeds are very important for the thyroid gland. Mushrooms are equally important as a cleansing food.

Always eat three meals a day. Keep in mind to eat like a *king* for breakfast, a *queen* for lunch, and a *prince* for dinner.

127

Soak and prepare all meat according to instructions on page 118.

Use raw sugar whenever possible when sugar is called for. Raw sugar is in a natural state and is therefore free of chemicals, making it easier for the body to assimilate.

Sample Daily Diet Plan For 100 Day Diet

You can choose your breakfast, lunch and dinner by following these recipes. All dishes can be combined with rice, bread, rolls, etc. Be sure to eat, everyday, 1 apple and 2 oranges or 1/2 to 1 grapefruit and 1 banana, or other seasonal fruits (8 oz.), cherries, melon, etc.

For example:
Breakfast: Mushroom and Egg
              Toast
              1 cup nonfat milk
              1 orange
              1 banana
              1 cup Long Life Tea
Lunch: Sandwich with barbecued beef tongue
              1 cup Long Life Tea
Dinner: 1 cup/bowl fish soup
              1 cucumber salad
              Wine Vinegar Chicken
              1 cup Long Life Tea
              1 bowl rice

This is just one day's suggestion. I have listed recipes that, with imagination, can make up a 100-day diet plan.

Eating is the most important part of life for healing and maintenance. It is also the most important and best way to enjoy life. One must spend as much time as possible for eating. After your meal has been prepared, sit down, relax, and slowly enjoy your meal.

I repeat.
> *Eat on time.*
> *Eat well.*
> *Eat slowly.*
> *Eat balanced meals.*

And enjoy. Eating is the biggest blessing from God.

BROTH BASE FOR ALL DISHES

There are three soup bases:
> Chicken broth
> Bone broth
> Fish broth

Chicken Broth

> 1 chicken, whole
> 1 green onion
> 2 Tbs. cooking wine
> 2 slices ginger
> 1 Tbs. salt

Chop whole chicken into about 2" squares. Mix it in a bowl with the onion, ginger, salt and wine. Let it sit 20-30 minutes. Put 10 cups of water in a pot and bring it to a boil. Add the chicken and other ingredients to the water, bring to boil. Reduce heat and simmer for 8 hours until the bones are soft. Cool for 1 hour. Strain the broth through a strainer, removing all large, solid particles. Refrigerate overnight. Remove the layer of hardened fat which has collected on top of the broth. The broth is of a jellylike consistency. It can be reheated and added to all recipes to improve taste.

Bone Broth

> 3 lbs. pork or beef bones (never chicken)
> 1 Tbs. salt
> 1 green onion
> 4 Tbs. wine

Follow Chicken Broth instructions. Simmer till bones are soft. Then mash the bones and strain.

Fish Broth

> 2 lbs. catfish (whole, scaled, gutted)
> 1/4 tsp. pepper
> 3 slices ginger
> 1 green onion (omit when using shellfish)
> 4 Tbs. cooking wine

To cook, follow Chicken Broth instructions.

SOUPS

All recipes serve 4 people

Seaweed Soup

1/2 cup chicken broth
3 cups water
2 sheets seaweed, dried
2 oz. pork, thinly sliced
1 Tbs. green onion, chopped
1 slice ginger
1/2 tsp. wine
1/2 tsp. cornstarch
1 tsp. salt, or to taste

Combine pork, onion, ginger, wine and cornstarch in a bowl. Mix well.

Let sit 15 minutes.

Combine broth and water and bring to boil in pot. While boiling, add salt and pork mixture.

Tear seaweed and add to pot.

Boil for a few more minutes. Serve.

Benefits

This soup is a tonic for the thyroid. It is good for the metabolism, cleanses the blood, and purifies and adjusts hormones.

Fish Soup

1/2 cup fish broth
3 cups water
4-5 oz. fish fillet, sliced
1 tsp. cornstarch
1/2 tsp. salt, or to taste
1/2 tsp. green onion, minced
1 Tbs. wine
1/4 cup bamboo shoots, or cucumbers, sliced
2 Tbs. cornstarch
1 Tbs. water
1/2 tsp. salt, or to taste
1/4 Tbs. sesame oil, hot pressed
pepper to taste

Combine fish, 1 tsp. cornstarch, salt, onion, and wine in bowl and mix well, let sit.

Combine broth and 3 cups water, bring to boil, then add above mixture, bamboo and salt.

130

Mix 2 Tbs. cornstarch with 1 Tbs. water in a small dish, then add to soup, stirring slightly.

Sprinkle on sesame oil and pepper and serve.

Benefits

This soup is rich in protein and vitamins. It also rejuvenates, and fights cancer. It builds the body as well as beautifies.

Hot and Sour Soup

2/3 package tofu, rinsed and cubed
1 egg, beaten
1 green onion, finely chopped
6 pieces skin mushrooms (black fungus) from Oriental
    food store
10 pieces lily flowers, dried, from Oriental food store
1 oz. shrimp
1/2 cup chicken broth
3 cups water
10 thin slices, lean pork
1/2 tsp. pepper, or to taste
1/3 Tbs. vinegar, to taste
1/2 tsp. sesame oil, hot pressed
1-1/2 Tbs. cornstarch
1 Tbs. water
1/4 cup bamboo shoots, sliced
1 tsp. salt, or to taste

Soak mushrooms and lily flowers in water until they are soft. Remove hard parts of mushrooms and slice. Cut lily flowers into half length. Combine chicken broth and 3 cups water in a pot. Bring to boil. Add all other ingredients except egg, vinegar and cornstarch. Check taste. Then add vinegar. Stir soup in clockwise direction. While stirring, slowly and sparingly pour in egg. The egg will form ribbons. Finally, mix cornstarch with 1 Tbs. water. Add to the soup. Keep stirring until soup thickens.

Serve hot.

Benefits

This soup is excellent for common colds, coughing, poor circulation, bronchitis, arthritis, sluggish liver, indigestion, hormone imbalance, and toxic blood. It also fights cholesterol.

Corn and Chicken Soup

1 egg, beaten
2 chicken breasts, ground

4 oz. can cream of corn, unsweetened
3 cups water
1/2 cup bone broth
1 tsp. salt, or to taste
1-1/2 Tbs. cornstarch
1 Tbs. water
2 Tbs. milk, lowfat or nonfat

Mix egg and chicken well in bowl. Set aside.

Combine 3 cups water and broth in pot. Add corn and salt and stir.

Bring to boil.

Mix cornstarch mixture to pot and stir. While stirring in clockwise direction, add chicken mixture. Bring to boil again.

Remove from heat. Serve.

Benefits

This soup is rich in Vitamin E. It increases sexual energy. It also strengthens the heart and is rich in all other nutrients.

Tofu and Spinach Soup

3 cups water
1/2 cup vegetable broth
1 package tofu, rinsed and cubed
1/2 bunch spinach, cleaned and chopped
1 tomato, peeled, sliced and seeds removed
1 tsp. salt, or to taste
1/4 tsp. sesame oil, hot pressed
pepper to taste

Combine water and broth in a pot. Bring to boil.

Add to pot tofu, spinach, tomato, and salt.

Add sesame oil and sprinkle on pepper. Serve.

Benefits

This soup is a brain food. It nourishes the brain as well as soothes the heart, and fights cholesterol as well as cleans the blood vessels. The soup is rich in protein and other nutrients.

SALAD DRESSINGS

Spicy Oil with Lemon

1/4 cup sesame oil, cold pressed
1/4 cup fresh lemon juice
1/2 - 3/4 tsp. salt (to taste)

1/4 tsp. gound black pepper

Combine oil, lemon juice, salt and pepper. Shake vigorously.
Refrigerate. Shake well before serving.

Spicy Vinegar and Oil

1 tsp. Dijon style mustard
1/4 cup sesame oil, cold pressed
1/4 cup white wine vinegar
3/4 tsp. dill
3/4 tsp. thyme
1/2 tsp. raw sugar
1 tsp. garlic, minced
3/4 tsp. chives
1/2 - 3/4 tsp. salt (to taste)

Combine all ingredients. Shake vigorously.
Refrigerate. Shake well before serving.

Cucumber/Lemon Yogurt

1/4 cup plain yogurt
2 Tbs. sesame oil
2 Tbs. fresh lemon juice
2 Tbs. cucumber, pureed
2 Tbs. onion, minced
1 tsp. fresh mint, minced
1 tsp. fresh parsley, minced
1/2 - 3/4 tsp. salt (to taste)
1/2 tsp. black pepper, ground

Combine all ingredients. Shake vigorously. Let set 6 hours.
Refrigerate. Dressing can last 1 week.

Blue Cheese

1/4 cup sesame oil, cold pressed
2 tsp. white wine vinegar
2 oz. blue cheese
6 Tbs. heavy cream
1 tsp. Worcestershire sauce
1 tsp. onion, minced
1/4 tsp. black pepper, ground
1/2 - 3/4 tsp. salt (to taste)

Combine all ingredients. Mix well. Refrigerate.

Egg and Oil

1 egg yolk
1/2 tsp. mustard powder
1/2 - 3/4 tsp. salt (to taste)
2 tsp. fresh lemon juice
3/4 cup sesame oil, cold pressed
1 tsp. white pepper
1 tsp. cinnamon (optional)

Beat egg yolk for 2 minutes. Blend in mustard powder, salt and lemon juice. Continue mixing for 1 minute. While mixing, add sesame oil, a little at a time. Add white pepper and cinnamon (optional).

Sour Cream with Spices

1/4 cup sour cream
2 Tbs. Egg & Oil dressing (without cinnamon)
1 Tbs. tarragon white wine vinegar
2 tsp. fresh lemon juice
1 tsp. garlic, minced
1 Tbs. parsley, minced
1 tsp. chives
2 tsp. green onion, finely chopped
2 tsp. anchovy paste
1/2 - 3/4 tsp. salt (to taste)
1 tsp. white pepper

Combine all ingredients. Blend well. Refrigerate.

Oil and Vinegar with Soy

6 Tbs. sesame oil
1-1/2 Tbs. soy sauce
3 Tbs. white wine vinegar
1 tsp. white pepper
1 tsp. garlic, minced
1/2 - 3/4 tsp. salt (to taste)

Combine all ingredients well. Refrigerate. Shake before serving.

BREAKFAST DISHES

All recipes serve 4 people.
Many of these recipes can be prepared the night before, making

cooking the following morning much more simple. All breakfast recipes given here are intended to satisfy full nutritional needs, and are excellent energizers. Green onion does not affect the breath.

Toast with Cheese

    8 slices bread
    8 oz. cheddar cheese, shredded
    4 Tbs. vegetable oil
    4 eggs, beaten
    2 cups skim or low fat milk
    1 Tbs. green onion, chopped
    1/2 tsp. salt
    4 oz. clam, shrimp, or lean meat

Cube bread, place in 13"x 9" baking tray. Spread vegetable oil evenly on tray. Place bread in tray, and sprinkle on shredded cheese.

Combine beaten eggs, milk, green onion, and salt and pour over bread.

Spread meat over top of mixture.

Bake at 350° for 45-60 minutes. Check doneness and serve.

Dish can be wrapped in aluminum foil for overnight refrigeration and reheating the next morning.

Fish with Egg

    4 oz. fish
    1/2 tsp. salt
    1 Tbs. cornstarch
    1 Tbs. wine
    1 tsp. soy sauce
    1/8 tsp. black pepper
    1 green onion, chopped
    1/2 tsp. salt
    1/2 cup fish broth
    1/2 tsp. sesame oil, hot pressed
    4 eggs

Combine fish, 1/2 tsp. salt, cornstarch, wine, soy sauce, pepper and fish broth in bowl and set aside.

Beat eggs and add other 1/2 tsp. salt.

Combine eggs with fish mixture. Add green onion.

Put in double broiler, steam 15 minutes and serve.

Mushrooms and Eggs

4 eggs, well beaten
12 fresh mushrooms, sliced or chopped, medium sized
12 skin mushrooms (black mushrooms), soaked, drained
    and chopped
1 Tbs. green onion chopped
1 slice ginger, finely chopped
3/4 tsp. garlic, minced
1 Tbs. soy sauce
1 tsp. sugar
1 tsp. vinegar
4 Tbs. vegetable oil

Slice all mushrooms and stir them with 1 Tbs. of vegetable oil. Set aside in bowl.

In pan, heat rest of vegetable oil, add onion, ginger, and garlic. Then add mushrooms, soy sauce, sugar and vinegar and stir fry.

At last minute, add eggs, stir and serve.

Bamboo, Beef and Eggs

8 oz. lean beef, sliced
1 Tbs. wine
1 Tbs. cornstarch, dried
2 Tbs. soy sauce
1/4 tsp. salt
1 tsp. sugar
1 green onion, cut into 1'' lengths
4 eggs
2 slices ginger, very finely chopped
4 Tbs. vegetable oil
1 small can bamboo shoots, sliced

Combine beef, wine, cornstarch, soy sauce, salt and sugar. Mix in ginger and bamboo shoots.

In pan, heat 2 Tbs. vegetable oil, add beef mixture and stir fry until beef is well done.

In pan, heat 2 Tbs. vegetable oil, stir fry onion, add eggs and scramble until done.

Combine eggs with beef and serve. Or stir fry onions, add to beef mixture and scramble eggs with beef mixture.

Chicken Breakfast

2 chicken breasts, sliced into 4 pieces

4 Tbs. soy sauce
2 Tbs. wine
1/2 Tbs. sugar
1 Tbs. cornstarch, dried
1 Tbs. sesame oil, hot pressed
4 eggs
8 Tbs. vegetable oil
1 green onion, cut into 1'' lengths
2 slices ginger, chopped

Combine chicken, soy sauce, wine, sugar, cornstarch and sesame oil.
Mix well in bowl and set aside for 20 minutes. Then separate chicken from juice.

In pan, heat 4 Tbs. of vegetable oil, sautee onion and ginger, and fry chicken until done.

In another pan, heat 4 Tbs. of vegetable oil, drop in 1 egg and fry.

Transfer 1 piece of chicken to top of fried egg. Do the same with the other three eggs and pieces of chicken.

Heat juice you have earlier separated from chicken. Pour juice over chicken and serve.

Fried Rice with Eggs

4 cups cooked rice
4 eggs, beaten
4 Tbs. vegetable oil
1 tsp. salt
1 green onion, minced
1 Tbs. bacon, granules

In pan, heat vegetable oil and scramble eggs. Add rice. Then add salt and bacon. Taste. Add more salt if needed. Add green onion.

Stir fry for 3-4 minutes. Serve.

Special Benefit

This breakfast is highly recommended for those who do heavy physical work and need solid food to fill up the stomach in the morning.

Spinach and Egg Puff

1/2 lb. spinach, cleaned and chopped
4 eggs, beaten
1 tsp. salt
1 cup chicken broth
1 tsp. vegetable oil

Combine egg, salt and chicken broth and mix well.

Grease a large bowl with vegetable oil.

Combine spinach with egg mixture and pour into bowl.

Place in top section of the double boiler, steam 18 minutes and serve.

Meat and Egg Pie

1/2 lb. lean beef
1 tsp. salt
1/4 tsp. ginger, powdered
1 Tbs. wine
1 Tbs. cornstarch, dried
1 green onion, chopped
4 eggs
1 tsp. sesame oil, hot pressed

Combine beef, salt, ginger, wine and cornstarch in bowl. Mix well.

Drop eggs on beef mixture.

Place mixture in top part of double boiler and steam for 30 minutes in double boiler.

Check for doneness. Garnish with green onion and sesame oil. Serve.

Egg Roll with Fish

1/2 lb. filet rock cod, ground
4 eggs, each beaten separately
1/4 tsp. black pepper
1 tsp. wine
1 Tbs. cornstarch, dried
4 Tbs. vegetable oil
1 carrot, quartered lengthwise
1 tsp. salt

Combine cod, pepper, wine, cornstarch and salt in bowl. Mix well and let sit.

In pan, heat 1 Tbs. vegetable oil, stir fry cod mixture 5 minutes, drain and set aside.

In another pan, heat 1 tsp. of oil, add 1 beaten egg and spread over bottom of pan to form a crepe-like omelette.

Fill with 1/4 of cod mixture and roll up. Then insert carrot in the middle of the roll. Repeat process with remaining eggs and fish mixture.

Refrigerate rolls overnight.

Next day heat by baking at 325° for 15 minutes.

Serves 4.

LUNCH DISHES

Lunches should be accompanied by fruit and vegetables.   All recipes serve 4 people.

Barbecued Tongue (see dinner recipe).
Barbecued Beef Shank (see dinner recipe).
Barbecued Cha Shao

4 lb. pork
1/2 cup soy sauce
1/4 cup ketchup
1/4 tsp. ground cinnamon
1 Tbs. salt
1 Tbs. sugar
1 whole garlic, minced
1 stick ginger
1 green onion, quartered
2 Tbs. wine
3 Tbs. vegetable oil

Cut pork to 2'' thick.

Combine soy sauce, ketchup, cinnamon, salt, sugar, garlic, ginger, onion and wine. Add pork and soak for 3 hours, turning pork occasionally.

Cook for 1/2 hour, then separate meat from juices. Cool.

In pan, heat vegetable oil, and fry pork until golden brown. Combine with juice. Cool and thinly slice. Serve.

Benefits

This dish supplies energy and nutrients. It is also a decongestant and detoxifier.

Rice with Meat

2 cups rice, uncooked
1/2 lb. ground meat, lamb, etc. or shrimp (completely lean) (soak in boiling water twice, drain and let sit 10 minutes before cooking)
1 carrot, peeled and diced
1 onion, diced
6 Tbs. ketchup
2 Tbs. vegetable oil
1 tsp. salt
3-1/2 cups water

Wash rice. In pan, heat oil, sautee carrot and onion, and add rice, meat, ketchup, salt and water. Bring to boil, reduce to low heat, cover and cook for 1/2 hour, stirring occasionally.

Benefits

This dish is an overall energizer and detoxifier. It is also suitable for dinner.

Spaghetti

    1/2 lb. spaghetti
    4 oz. meat, ground (lean) (soak in hot water twice, drain, let sit 10 minutes before cooking)
    1 tsp. salt
    1 Tbs. wine
    1 Tbs. cornstarch in 2 Tbs. water
    4 oz. fresh mushrooms (chopped)
    4 oz. shrimp
    2 oz. peanuts, unsalted, roasted and chopped
    1 red pepper, small, dried
    3 Tbs. peanut butter
    1 Tbs. vinegar
    1/2 tsp. sugar
    1 green onion, chopped
    1 Tbs. sesame oil (hot pressed)
    2 Tbs. vegetable oil
    1 cup water or chicken stock

Soak shrimp in water, drain, chop.

Cook spaghetti, mix with sesame oil, toss well.

In pan, heat vegetable oil, add shrimp, ground meat, salt, wine, and mushrooms and stir fry for 1-2 minutes or until meat is brown. Add peanuts, red pepper, peanut butter, vinegar, sugar and green onion. Add 1 cup of water or chicken stock and cornstarch. Stir well. Combine with spaghetti and serve.

Benefits

This dish is an overall energy supplier and detoxifier. It is also suitable for dinner.

Curry Pie

    1 box pie crust mix (follow mixing instructions on box)
    1/4 cup water
    10-12 oz. lean pork or beef
    1 Tbs. wine
    1 Tbs. cornstarch

1 tsp. salt
1 Tbs. green onion, chopped
2-3 Tbs. curry powder
4 Tbs. vegetable oil
2 onions, diced
2 egg yolks
1 Tbs. water

Combine meat with wine, starch, salt, green onion. Let sit ten minutes.

In pan, heat 2 Tbs. vegetable oil, and stir fry meat mixture. Add curry powder, stir fry 5 minutes. Drain on paper towel. In pan, heat 2 Tbs. vegetable oil, sautee diced onion and drain. Combine onions with meat mixture.

Roll mixed pie crust into a long "bar." Quarter. Pull each section into a long strand. Cut each section into tenths. Using a rolling pin, roll sections into round "tortillas."

Wrap enough of filling in two tortillas to make "pie." Pinch to seal edges. Make twenty "pies" this way.

Mix egg yolk and 1 Tbs. water well. Grease baking pan.

Brush surface of pies with egg yolk mixture. Place on pan with edges not touching.

Bake 15 minutes at 400°, then 10-15 minutes at 375° till golden brown. Serve.

Benefits

This dish is a stimulant. It is nutritious and energizing.

Living Salad

1 potato (cooked), skin removed, mashed
1 egg boiled
1/2 cup macaroni, cooked
1/2 carrot, peeled, diced, and steamed 3 minutes
1 apple, peeled and diced
1/2 cucumber, peeled and diced
1/2 tsp. salt
1/4 - 1/2 tsp. pepper (to taste)
1 tsp. sesame oil (hot pressed) to taste
1 Tbs. sesame oil (cold pressed)
1 Tbs. mayonnaise

Separate the white and yolk of the egg. Dice the egg white.

Mash the yolk with sesame oil and mayonnaise.

Mix yolk mixture, diced egg white, potato, macaroni, carrot, apple, cucumber, salt and pepper. Serve.

Benefits

This salad provides many nutrients. It is both energizing and cleansing.

DINNER MEAT DISHES

All recipes serve 4 people.

Sesame oil used in recipes should be hot pressed for taste, except where noted. The amount of salt can be adjusted to one's taste in all recipes.

Barbecued Beef Shank

1 lb. beef shank
1/4 cup soy sauce
2 cups water
2 tsp. salt
2 green onions, diced
2 slices ginger
1 stick cinnamon
1/4 cup wine
hot pressed sesame oil

Clean beef and put in pot along with soy sauce, water, salt, onions, ginger, cinnamon and wine. Bring to boil.

Reduce to simmer, and simmer for 3 hours, stirring occasionally. Cool and slice beef thinly.

Sprinkle sesame oil over sliced meat and serve.

Can be eaten for lunch in a sandwich.

Benefits

This dish strengthens the nerves because it is rich in the appropriate nutrients. It supplies energy and contains hardly any fatty tissues.

Spicy Chicken

2 lbs. chicken
3 Tbs. soy sauce
1 Tbs. wine
1 Tbs. vinegar
1 Tbs. green onion (chopped)
1 Tbs. garlic, finely diced
1/4 tsp. chili powder (optional)
2 Tbs. hot pressed sesame oil (to taste)
1 tsp. salt

1 tsp. sugar
1 tsp. cornstarch
2 Tbs. sesame seeds

Roast sesame seeds.

Put enough water in pot to cover chicken, but do *not* add the chicken. Bring to boil. Put chicken in pot. Bring to boil again. Reduce heat and simmer for 25 minutes or until done. Test for doneness by poking into flesh, making sure there is no blood. Cool. Remove skin and fat from chicken. Cut chicken into 2" x 1" pieces and put on plates.

Combine seasonings (soy sauce, wine, vinegar, onion, garlic, chili powder, sesame oil, salt, sugar, and cornstarch) and add to chicken. Heat and serve. Sprinkle with sesame seeds.

Benefits

This dish is rich in nutrients. It strengthens and cleanses the lungs, and stimulates the large intestines and helps in elimination.

Sweet and Sour Pork Loin

1 lb. pork loin, cut into small pieces
2 Tbs. cornstarch
1 Tbs. wine
1/4 tsp. salt
1 green onion, chopped
2 slices ginger
2 cups vegetable oil
2-1/2 Tbs. vinegar
1 tsp. salt
5-1/2 Tbs. sugar
2 Tbs. tomato sauce
2 Tbs. cornstarch
1/2 cup water
1 tsp. soy sauce
1/2 cup green pepper, diced
1/2 cup carrot, diced
1/6 cup pineapple, diced—or pineapple juice

Combine pork, 2 Tbs. cornstarch, wine, salt, onion and ginger. Let sit in bowl 30 minutes.

Put oil in pan on high heat. Fry 2 pieces of pork at a time for 2-3 minutes. Drain on paper towel.

Combine vinegar, salt, sugar, tomato sauce, 2 Tbs. cornstarch, water, soy sauce, green pepper, carrot and pineapple in saucepan. Cook, while constantly stirring, until sauce thickens.

Pour sauce over pork. Serve.

Benefits

This dish soothes the liver and pancreas. It nourishes as well as cleanses these organs.

Steamed Salmon

4 fresh salmon steaks
1 green onion, chopped
2 slices ginger
2 Tbs. wine
1 tsp. salt
1 Tbs. cornstarch
4 oz. ground pork
1/2 tsp. salt
1 tsp. wine
1/2 tsp. cornstarch
1/2 cup bamboo shoots, diced
3 tsp. hot pressed sesame oil (or to taste)
2 tsp. pepper
pine leaves (optional)

Combine salmon, onion, ginger, 2 Tbs. wine, 1 tsp. salt and 1 Tbs. cornstarch in bowl, mix well and set aside. Combine pork, 1/2 tsp. salt, 1 tsp. wine, and 1/2 tsp. cornstarch in bowl, mix well and set aside. Let both bowls set for 30 minutes. Press down salmon mixture, cover with layer of 1/2 cup bamboo. Put pork mixture on top of bamboo, spread out evenly.

Place bowl in top section of double boiler, the bottom of which may be layered with pine leaves. Bring to boil for 3 minutes. Reduce to low heat and let steam for 30 minutes.

Garnish with sesame oil and pepper. Serve.

Benefits

This dish is a decongestant, and is anti-inflammatory. It soothes and cleans the digestive system. The steam enhances flavor because it locks in flavor. When pine leaves are added to the boiling water, the resultant steam promotes longevity, enhances flavor, and increases nutrition.

Coconut Chicken

2 lb. chicken breasts or drumsticks
1 lb. potatoes
2 green onions, diced
1 cup milk
1 cup chicken broth

1-1/2 Tbs. salt
3 cloves garlic, minced
1 Tbs. curry
1 cup flour
2 Tbs. vegetable oil
2 Tbs. coconut juice
6 Tbs. vegetable oil

Heat 6 Tbs. vegetable oil in pan.

Roll chicken in flour until covered. Fry until golden brown. Drain on paper towel.

Mix curry powder with 2 Tbs. oil. Combine onions and garlic and sautee in curry/oil.

Remove skins from potatoes and cube. Fry in oil (from chicken frying) until golden brown. Drain on paper towel. Pour remaining oil from pan and return chicken and onions and garlic to the pan with the potatoes.

Combine milk, broth, salt and coconut juice, and pour over chicken mixture. Cover and simmer for 35-40 minutes. Serve.

Benefits

This dish is rich in protein. It is good for the spleen-pancreas and digestion. It is especially nourishing for the kidneys and sexual organs.

Sweet and Sour Shrimp

1 lb. shrimp
2 green onions, minced
2 slices ginger, minced
6 Tbs. ketchup
2 Tbs. raw sugar
1 Tbs. wine
1 tsp. salt
2 Tbs. cornstarch
1 Tbs. water
6 Tbs. vegetable oil
1/2 cup green peas

Remove epidermis and vein on back of shrimp. Rinse. Drain on paper towel.

Mix ketchup, raw sugar, wine, salt, cornstarch and water in bowl.

In pan, heat oil and sautee onions and ginger for two minutes. Add shrimp and stir fry for 3 minutes. Pour oil out, letting shrimp remain in pan. Add mixture from bowl to shrimp, cook and stir 2 minutes. Put in serving dish.

Cook peas slightly, keeping green color. Add to shrimp mixture

and serve.
Benefits

This dish is an overall energy food. People who have skin conditi—ditions should avoid it, however.

Tofu and Oyster Dish

4 oz. oysters or 4 oysters (washed thoroughly and chopped in small pieces)
1 Tbs. cornstarch
1 tsp. wine
2 packages tofu, cubed and rinsed
1 Tbs. garlic, minced
1 Tbs. green onion, minced
1/4 tsp. ginger, powdered
2 tsp. soy sauce
2 tsp. hot pressed sesame oil (to taste)
1 tsp. salt
2 Tbs. cornstarch
1 Tbs. water
2 Tbs. vegetable oil

Combine oysters, 1 Tbs. cornstarch and wine in bowl and set aside.

In pan, heat vegetable oil and sautee garlic and onion for 2 minutes. Add oysters and fry 3 minutes. Add tofu and gently stir fry for 5 minutes. Mix 2 Tbs. cornstarch with water in bowl, and add to oysters and tofu while still frying. Add ginger, soy sauce and salt. Stir.

Remove from heat, garnish with sesame oil and serve.
Benefits

This dish is a brain and sexual energy food. It helps dissolve tumors.

Family Style Tofu

1 package tofu, sliced to 1-1/2 x 1/2 x 1/2"
1/2 lb. pork, thinly sliced
1/2 tsp. salt
1 Tbs. wine
1 Tbs. cornstarch
2 green onions, cut to 1" long
2 Tbs. soy sauce
1 tsp. brown sugar
2 Tbs. vegetable oil
3 Tbs. vegetable oil

1/4 cup bamboo shoots, diced

2 pieces black mushroom, dried

Combine pork, salt, wine and cornstarch in bowl. Set aside for 30 minutes.

Soak mushrooms in warm water thoroughly. Then slice.

In pan, heat 3 Tbs. oil and fry tofu until golden brown, then remove.

In 2 Tbs. oil sautee onions and bamboo, being careful not to burn them; Then add mushrooms and pork mixture and stir fry for 5 minutes. Add tofu, soy sauce and brown sugar, simmer until hot and blended. Serve.

Benefits

This dish helps the body fight cancer and cholesterol.

Wine Vinegar Chicken

1 cut-up chicken

1-1/2 tsp. salt

1/3 cup wine vinegar

3/4 tsp. black pepper

1 Tbs. garlic, minced

1/4 cup wine

1/3 cup fresh lemon juice

1 Tbs. ketchup

1 Tbs. parsley, minced

1 Tbs. vegetable oil

1 Tbs. cornstarch

Salt and pepper the chicken.

Place oil in pan, heat and fry chicken until golden brown on all sides. Add garlic, 1/4 cup wine vinegar, lemon juice, 4 Tbs. water and ketchup to chicken. Cover and cook over low heat for 15-20 minutes. Add cornstarch to thicken sauce.

Sprinkle parsley on top for garnish and serve.

Benefits

This dish soothes and cleans the gall bladder, liver and nerves. It is good for the eyesight.

Roast in Peanut Butter Sauce

2 lb. English cut roast

1/2 tsp. salt

1 Tbs. wine

1 Tbs. cornstarch

1 green onion, chopped

1 slice ginger
1 tsp. garlic, powdered
1/2 lemon, juiced
3 oz. peanut butter
1 dried red pepper
1 Tbs. garlic, minced
1 onion, cubed
1 Tbs. soy sauce
2 Tbs. vegetable oil

Combine roast, salt, wine, cornstarch, green onion, ginger, and 1 tsp. garlic powder in bowl. Let sit 30 minutes.

In saucepan, heat vegetable oil and sautee minced garlic, onion and pepper.

Mix peanut butter well with a little water. Add to saucepan, bring to boil. Then add lemon juice.

Cut roast to 1/2" thick. Pour sauce from saucepan on roast. Let sit 30 minutes.

Bake roast in oven at 325° for 30 minutes, or until well done.

Serve with juices. If there is not enough sauce, more can be made.

Benefits

This dish is a decongestant. It is also anti-inflammatory.

Beef Tripe

10-16 oz. tripe
1 onion, diced
1 stalk celery, chopped
1 tsp. salt
1 green onion, diced
1/2 tsp. pepper
1 Tbs. vinegar
2 Tbs. cornstarch
1-1/2 cup bone broth
1 tsp. hot pressed sesame oil (or to taste)

Clean tripe. Place in a pot and add enough water to cover. Bring to a boil. Reduce to simmer. Cook 30 minutes.

Cool tripe, then slice.

In pan, sautee diced onion and celery. Add salt, pepper, cornstarch and broth. Then add vinegar.

Pour sauce on tripe. Garnish with green onion and sesame oil. Serve.

Benefits

This dish is good for the stomach, aiding in digestion. It strengthens the stomach tissue and duodenum.

Barbecued Tongue

2-3 lb. beef tongue
1 onion, cubed
1/2 cup ketchup
2 tsp. salt
1 Tbs. soy sauce
1 Tbs. vinegar
2 Tbs. wine
2 Tbs. vegetable oil
water
2 tsp. sesame oil

Clean beef tongue. Place in pot with enough water to cover. Bring to boil for 10 minutes. Skin should be white. Cool in a pan of cold water. Then, using knife, scrape off white skin. Then drain off water.

In pan, heat vegetable oil and sautee onion. Add ketchup, salt, soy sauce, vinegar and wine. Let cook 2 minutes. Add tongue. Then add water. Cook for 3 hours over low heat. Check for doneness, then cool. Slice tongue to thin pieces.

Garnish with sesame oil and serve. Can be eaten for lunch in a sandwich.

Benefits

This dish is a heart food. It is good for strengthening the heart muscles and blood vessels.

DINNER VEGETABLE DISHES

All recipes serve 4 people.

String Bean Saute

1 lb. string beans (ends removed, cleaned and dried)
4 green onions, chopped
2 slices ginger
1 Tbs. garlic, minced
4 Tbs. soy sauce
1 Tbs. wine
1 tsp. sugar
salt to taste
1 cup vegetable oil
3 Tbs. vegetable oil

In pan, heat 1 cup vegetable oil. Over medium heat fry beans till crinkly and brown. Drain on paper towel.

Slice long beans into thirds, short beans into halves.

In pan, heat 3 Tbs. vegetable oil and sautee onions, ginger and garlic. Add beans, soy sauce, wine, sugar, and salt. Stir fry 1-2 minutes. Serve.

Benefits

This dish soothes the pancreas and helps in digestion and balance of blood sugar.

Soybean Dish

4 oz. soybeans
2 carrots, diced
2 sprigs parsley
1 Tbs. hot pressed sesame oil (to taste)
1/2 Tbs. salt

Soak soybeans in water for 2 hours. Clean. Put in pot with enough water to cover. Add salt. Bring to boil, reduce heat and simmer for 2 hours. Drain.

Remove leaves on parsley. Remove skins of carrots.

Dip parsley and carrots in boiling water and remove immediately.

Combine carrots and parsley with beans and add sesame oil. Taste. Make adjustments. Serve.

Benefits

This dish reduces blood pressure, and cleans the blood stream. It is detoxifying. It cleans the kidneys and reduces the amount of water in the body.

Eggplant with Mushrooms

10 oz. eggplant
10-15 small pieces skin mushroom or black mushroom
1 small can water chestnuts, sliced
1 Tbs. green onion, diced
1 Tbs. ginger, diced
1 Tbs. garlic, diced
1/2 red pepper, dried or fresh, diced
2 Tbs. soy sauce
1 Tbs. sugar
2 Tbs. vinegar
1/2 tsp. salt
1/8 tsp. white pepper
1 tsp. hot pressed sesame oil (to taste)

2 Tbs. cornstarch, mixed in water
1/2 cup vegetable oil
3 Tbs. vegetable oil

Clean eggplant, cut in half lengthwise, remove seeds, cut into 1" cubes. Soak mushrooms in warm water for 30 minutes. Slice.

In pan, heat 1/2 cup vegetable oil and fry eggplant for about 5 minutes until they show signs of browning. Drain on paper towel.

In pan, heat 3 Tbs. vegetable oil and over low heat stir fry mushrooms, water chestnuts, green onion, ginger, garlic and red pepper; be careful not to burn. Combine with eggplant and add soy sauce, sugar, vinegar and salt. Then add cornstarch. Over medium heat, cover and cook for 5-6 minutes. Garnish with white pepper and sesame oil. Serve.

Benefits

This dish is good for overall detoxification and thyroid function.

Tofu Salad

1 package tofu, rinsed and cubed
1 big or 2 small tomatoes
1/2 Tbs. salt or to taste
1/2 Tbs. hot pressed sesame oil
1 Tbs. soy sauce

Soak tomatoes in hot, almost boiling water, for 1 minute. Peel and remove seeds. Dice.

Boil tofu in water for 5 minutes. Drain. Dry and sparingly salt. Drain again.

Add tomato to tofu. Add salt, sesame oil and soy sauce. Serve.

Benefits

This dish is good for cleansing blood vessels and the brain, and it fights cholesterol.

Cucumber Salad

1 whole cucumber, peeled and rinsed very clean
4 Tbs. vinegar
4 Tbs. sugar
1/2 tsp. salt
1 tsp. soy sauce
2 Tbs. hot pressed sesame oil
4 Tbs. water

Slice cucumber lengthwise into halves. Bring water to boil, dip cucumber in water, remove seeds and drain. Slice cucumber.

Combine vinegar, sugar, salt, soy sauce and sesame oil, pour on

cucumber, refrigerate one hour and serve.
Benefits
  This dish is good for cleansing the blood vessels.

Cauliflower in Milk

    1 cauliflower
    1 tsp. salt
    2 Tbs. vegetable oil
    1 Tbs. water
    1 cup milk
    1 Tbs. cornstarch
    1 Tbs. flour
    4 oz. cheddar cheese, shredded
    1 Tbs. Parmesan cheese, shredded
    1/2 cup vegetable broth
    1/4 tsp. salt
    1 green onion
    1/4 cup vegetable broth

Separate cauliflower into individual sprigs. Clean. Peal skin off of stalks.
  Sautee green onion in vegetable oil. Add cauliflower,1 Tbs. of water, 1 tsp. salt, and bring to boil. Reduce to simmer. Cover and cook for 3-5 minutes, or until *almost* done. Transfer to baking tray.
  In pan, heat milk, cornstarch, flour, 1/4 tsp. salt, and broth until thick. Pour over cauliflower. Sprinkle cheddar and parmesan over dish.
  Bake at 325° for 5 minutes or until cheese melts.
Benefits
  This dish provides protection from heat. It is a good hot weather food.

Asparagus in Milk

    1 lb. asparagus, cleaned, white stalk removed
    1/2 cup vegetable broth
    2 Tbs. vegetable oil
    2 tsp. salt
    1 cup milk
    2 Tbs. flour
    1 tomato

Put 6 cups of water into pot. Bring to boil. Add asparagus and boil for 2 minutes. Drain, transfer to plates.
  Combine broth, salt and flour in milk.

In pan, heat vegetable oil and add milk mixture. Bring to boil while constantly stirring until thick, and pour over asparagus.

Soak tomato in hot, almost boiling water for 1 minute. Peel, dice, add to asparagus and serve.

Benefits

This dish soothes the lungs, reduces mucus, decongests, and reduces water retention.

Silver and Gold Mushrooms

8 dried Chinese (Tentious edodes) mushrooms
4 oz. fresh mushrooms
1 small can bamboo shoots, sliced
2 oz. water chestnuts
1 tsp. ginger, minced
3 Tbs. vegetable oil
1 tsp. salt
1 tsp. hot pressed sesame oil
1 cup vegetable broth
2 Tbs. soy sauce
2 Tbs. cornstarch mixed with a little water
1 tsp. wine
1/8 tsp. pepper

Soak dried mushrooms in water, discard stem, and quarter each one.

Clean fresh mushrooms.

In pan, heat 1 Tbs. vegetable oil, sautee 1/2 tsp. ginger, bamboo shoots and Chinese mushrooms. Add 1 Tbs. soy sauce, 1/2 tsp. wine, a little salt, 1/2 cup vegetable broth, and cook 3 minutes. Add 1 Tbs. cornstarch and rest of soy sauce. Set on one side of plate.

In pan, heat 2 Tbs. vegetable oil, add 1/2 tsp. ginger, fresh mushrooms, water chestnuts, salt, 1/2 Tbs. cornstarch and cook until thick. Place on other side of plate.

Garnish both with sesame oil and pepper and serve.

Benefits

This dish is an overall body builder and cancer fighter. Beautifies.

Plain Rice

2 cups rice (white), uncooked
water to cover rice 1"

Clean rice in pot by rinsing 3-4 times and churning with hand. (Most chemicals will be removed, including the whitener). Drain.

Add water to rice. Cover. Bring to boil. Reduce to simmer and cook for 30 minutes, stirring occasionally.

Benefits

Steamed rice is a neutral food. It can balance all dishes. It is naturally acid and alkaline balanced. White rice is recommended since brown rice is indigestible because of the shell. The Vitamin B in brown rice is therefore not assimilated.

Rice Soup

1 cup rice, uncooked (white)
5 cups water

Wash rice, add water and bring to boil. Reduce to low heat and cook for one hour.

Combine with any dish and serve.

Benefits

Rice soup soothes the internal organs. It is good for people who have weak stomachs. It is also good for indigestion, fermentation and extreme fatigue. It aids in absorption. It can be combined with any dish to soothe and relax the body.

DESSERTS

Peaches with Almonds

4 peach halves
1/3 tsp. lemon rind, grated
4 Tbs. honey
1-1/2 Tbs. lemon juice
1/2 cup almonds, slivered
1 cup water
1/4 tsp. cinnamon

Place peach halves open side up in casserole dish.

Combine lemon rind, honey, lemon juice, almonds and water. Cover peach halves with mixture. Sprinkle with cinnamon.

Bake for 30 minutes at 325°F. Serve hot or cold.

Orange Pudding

1 package unflavored gelatin (3 oz.)
1-1/2 cup hot water
2 whole oranges
juice of 1 lemon
1/4 cup raw sugar
pinch salt

1/4 cup powdered skim milk
1/4 cup cold water
1/4 tsp. vanilla extract

Clean (brush) 1 orange very well, being sure to remove wax on skin. With a grater, grate only the thin orange-colored layer of skin. Set aside.

Slice orange and juice. Combine peel and juice. Set aside. Peel other orange. Remove skin from orange slices. Keep orange pulp only. Refrigerate.

Combine gelatin and hot water, add sugar and salt. Then add 1 Tbs. lemon juice. Add orange peel and juice. When cool, refrigerate till solid. Combine powdered milk and cold water. Whip until thick and creamy, and add vanilla and 1/2 tsp. lemon juice. Continue whipping. Pour over gelatin mixture. Refrigerate again. Garnish with grated orange skin, slice into cubes and serve.

Banana Cream Pudding

5 Tbs. powdered skim milk
2-1/2 Tbs. flour
2-1/2 cups water
2-1/2 Tbs. raw sugar
2-1/2 lb. bananas, blended until creamy

Combine powdered milk and flour with 2 Tbs. water. Blend until creamy.

Pour rest of water into small pot, bring to boil. Add milk/flour mixture, and add sugar and banana.

Almond Pudding

10 Tbs. powdered skim milk
2 packages unflavored gelatin
2 tsp. almond extract
1/2 cup roasted almonds, finely chopped
3-1/2 cups hot water
1/3 cup raw sugar
1 cup melted chocolate (optional)

Melt gelatin in hot water, add powdered milk, almond extract and sugar. Cool. Refrigerate. Sprinkle with roasted almonds and melted chocolate (optional) and serve.

Bean Pudding

1/2 lb. red beans (from Oriental food store)

155

2 packages unflavored gelatin
3/4 cup raw sugar
5 cups water
Pinch salt

Put water in pot, add beans, sugar and salt. Bring to boil, then reduce to simmer. Cook for at least 4 hours. When almost done, add gelatin. Cool. Refrigerate.

Silver Skin Mushroom Soup Dessert

4 oz. silver skin mushrooms (from Chinese grocery store)
2 cups water
2 Tbs. raw sugar
1 tsp. almond or cinnamon extract

Place mushrooms in a bowl with enough warm water to cover. Soak for 5 minutes, then clean very well.

Place water and sugar in pan. Bring to boil and add mushrooms. Reduce to simmer to cook for 5 minutes.

Add almond or cinnamon extract and serve.

Apple Honey Tea

4 cups apple juice
1 tsp. honey
1 stick cinnamon
4 cloves (whole)
2 black tea bags or Lipton tea bags
rum (optional)

Combine apple juice, honey, cinnamon and cloves in pot. Bring to boil.

Remove from heat. Add tea bags, cover and let sit 10 minutes. Add rum (optional). Serve with any cake or with nuts.

IV

Obesity

There is no need for anyone to be overweight. Nor is there a need to be underweight. In fact, from the point of view of Taoism—the 6,000 year old Chinese philosophy and science of life—there is basically no difference between being overweight or underweight. Both reflect a lack of balance in the human being. In Taoism, every being in the universe is considered to have its own center, and all parts of the being should be in balance with this center. In a human being weight is one aspect of this balance. Each person has a proper weight depending on his or her height, bone structure, shape and other factors. If you are over or under your proper weight, you are out of balance. And because a human being is more than just a physical body, weight imbalance indicates that your spiritual and mental bodies are imbalanced also.

Because of the diet and lifestyle in the Western world, obesity is the major weight imbalance in our society. It is present in all degrees, from extreme obesity to "slightly overweight." You might think that a few extra pounds make no difference. But those few pounds appear different when we realize that for every inch of excess fatty tissue on our bodies, we need an additional *four miles* of blood vessels to support that tissue. And that requires your heart to work harder, pumping blood through that four miles of blood vessels. Two inches of excess tissue require eight miles of blood vessels, three inches need twelve miles. Twelve more miles through which your heart has to pump blood. That is a lot of extra work for your heart. And that extra strain is going to weaken your heart, and eventually cause it to break down.

It's no different than with an automobile. If you load your car too heavily and use it for a long time under the additional strain, the engine will break down. As the heart—your engine—is overworked, it becomes enlarged. The muscles soften and loosen. It no longer has the strength it formerly had. As it deteriorates, it becomes more susceptible to germs, viruses, bacteria and other organisms which can attack weak muscles of the heart and cause inflammation. When a heart attack occurs, even if not fatal, it results in one area of the heart tissue being literally "dead"—it is no longer capable of functioning. A second heart attack results in another area of the heart not functioning. This increases the strain on the still-functioning parts of the heart, which must work harder to maintain the activity of the circulatory system. Fortunately, from a thousand year study we know there are herbs which can provide the right type of nutrition to regenerate new heart cells. But there is no reason for you to need them in the first place. Because there is no reason to be overweight.

Another result of obesity—and its resulting hardening of the arteries and weakened heart—is high blood pressure. Standard medical procedure is for a doctor to prescribe pills to reduce your blood pressure. These pills do reduce your blood pressure. They do this by opening your arteries and allowing your blood to flow more freely. But your heart will continue to work as hard as ever—*undetected* by the blood pressure monitor—because the basic cause, water retention, is unresolved. The pills satisfy the machine, not the body. In addition, blood pressure pills weaken the kidneys. This results in water retention which leads to blocked circulation, which again results in a weakened heart and blood vessels, which cause more high blood pressure. To assit the kidneys, your doctor will prescribe diuretics. Unfortunately, diuretics have the opposite effect than that which doctors hope for; they further weaken the kidneys, lead to increased water retention and shortage of potassium, which results in high blood pressure. It becomes a vicious circle, with one "cure" causing another problem, eventually worsening the illness the medicine was supposed to cure. And all of this is taking place in your body, at the expense of your health.

Gallstones are another result of obesity. Composed of hard, dried fat—almost like rubber—they are very hard to dissolve. You can also find yourself more susceptible to hypoglycemia or diabetes, both results of a weak pancreas, an organ weakened by obesity.

But these problems are not necessary. It is possible to live in a society such as ours, enjoy its benefits, and still avoid the diseases which its excesses lead to. To do this we must first know exactly what causes excessive weight. Then we must know how to reduce it.

First, if the food you eat does not have the proper pH balance— that is, its acid-alkaline balance—it can putrefy in your stomach before your body gets a chance to digest it and absorb its nutrition. In other words, before you eat it, the harmful organisms in your stomach get it first. *They* digest it, and leave you their wastes. The wastes include gas—which you'll notice through bad breath, belching, flatulence or stomach pains—and solids, which are of no nutritional value to your body. They don't provide the nutrition your cells need and your cells become weaker as a result. These waste products—literally poisons—cannot be eliminated, resulting in the cells of your entire body being poisoned. The only way to prevent this type of self-poisoning is through a properly balanced diet, because the proper pH balance works as a natural preservative in your stomach.

Secondly, one of the major causes of obesity is water retention. The kidneys are the filters that separate waste water from the blood. So the amount of water filtered out depends on how well your kidneys are functioning. Normal kidneys can filter approximately six cups of water in twenty-four hours. (It is possible for them to filter a larger volume but this requires them to work harder and the increased strain eventually weakens them.)

So if your kidneys are normal, you can drink six cups of water a day and you will break even. But, if you drink *more* than your kidneys can handle—and remember: for most people the limit is six cups a day!—this water will remain in your body. It will travel back into the blood steam to be eliminated through the skin by perspiration. However, if you have few opportunities to perspire (hot weather, exercise), the water will be retained in your skin. As more and more waste water comes to the area of your skin where water is already being retained, the tissue in that area bloats up to receive the incoming water. Only "fresh" water is eliminated through perspiration. The "stagnant" water remains, receiving even more wastes. This accumulated waste water—and we can consider it *urine*—may stay in this area for day, a month, even a year or more. After a period of time, this water becomes mucus. This mucus is still waste water, only it is in a more solid form. You may think you have added fat. But it is simply mucus which is imbedded between the tissues. When this gelatin-type substance hardens sufficiently, we call it *cellulite.* Animal fats such as butter and fatty meat are particular components of cellulite formation. *And you will not get rid of cellulite by exercise.* The only way is by:

1) Drinking less—limiting your daily liquid intake to less than 6 cups—this is very important.
2) Manipulating the cellulite deposits, preferably in a sauna or hot tub.

The secret of cellulite manipulation is to "heat up and break up" the deposits. The more you deeply massage these deposits, the more they can break up and be eliminated. The heat also causes the pores to open which allows increased perspiration.

When we talk about a limit of six cups of liquid in twenty-four hours, we mean *all* liquids, including soup, vegetables, beverages and fruit. You cannot eat two big bowls of soup and say that you did not drink any water. You can still retain water from that soup, so it must be acknowledged.

For example, one acquaintance of mine was overweight. He ate only one actual meal a day. The rest of the time he drank fruit juices. He had no idea how many gallons of liquids he actually poured into his body. Because he lived on almost nothing but fruit juice, he received almost no nutrition. Because of this lack of nutrition, he was very weak, constantly fainted, had palpitations of the heart, was short of breath, and had gout! (Taoism indicates that gout is a symptom of kidney problems.) He also had high blood pressure. He

159

had these problems for years, and never made the connection between his symptoms and his "healthful" fruit juice diet.

Often people will go to a restaurant, order a *large* salad and a glass of water, and congratulate themselves on their self-discipline. They think they are losing weight. All they are doing is cheating themselves. Chances are that their kidneys are not functioning 100%, so the more water they drink, the more will be retained in their bodies. So the more liquids they take in—even in that salad—the more weight they gain.

How to tell how well your kidneys are functioning:

1. If your body has cellulite, there is no doubt that your kidneys are not functioning 100% because you are retaining water. To check for cellulite, check the areas around the buttocks, thighs, belly and upper arms for flabby or jellylike tissues under the skin.

2. If you experience rapid weight changes—that is gaining or losing as much as five pounds in a period of a day or two—these weight changes are definitely retained water, not fat. No fatty tissues can come and go that quickly.

3. If when you press down with your finger on your arm or leg for a moment, then withdraw it, you see a white impression on your skin which remains briefly, you have water retention. If no water is being retained, there is either no white mark, or it disappears immediately. The longer it stays, the greater the water retention problem.

4. If your physician diagnoses your weight problem as water retention, unfortunately the standard medical cure for water retention is diuretic pills. I call these "beat your tired horse" pills. Why? Because your horse (your kidneys) is already "tired"—that's why you're retaining water. Taking these pills makes your "horse" run even harder. Overnight you may lose 10 pounds. The problem is that when you take these pills, you have to drink more water to wash them down. In fact, your doctor will tell you to drink lots of water in order to lubricate and "flush out" your kidneys. So you end up taking in (and eventually retaining) as much or more water than you eliminate. And during the process you work your kidneys even harder, making them weaker and less capable of functioning properly. Ultimately, overworking your kidneys this way will cause kidney disease or even total failure. We live in a "drinking country." Most people have a high daily intake of liquids, so it is not surprising that we also have a high incidence of kidney disease. But now that you know better, you can escape the norm—and stay healthy by decreasing the

amount of liquids you drink.

Thirdly, accumulating fat will be another reason for obesity. Fats are related to the pancreas and liver functions, and also to the gall bladder function. The liver is the main organ of the body for filtering out solid wastes. Since the poisons and toxins in our bodies are in solid form, we need lubrication to carry them out. Fats provide this lubrication. So it is necessary for us to eat fat.

The problem occurs once the fat is absorbed into the blood stream and carried to the liver. If the amount of fat is excessive, or the structure of the fat is such that it cannot be easily broken down by the body, it will clog the liver tissues, blocking part of the liver's proper functioning. Since the liver's functioning has been partially blocked, more of the wastes cannot be filtered out. This eventually leads to poisoning of the brain and nerve cells by toxins in the blood stream, leading to disorders we call nervous and mental problems—just some of the many detrimental effects of a poorly functioning liver.

Fats can also accumulate in certain parts of the body which are seldom exercised, such as the stomach and hips. When this happens a person begins to accumulate more and more fat. As a result it becomes harder to breathe, and breathing may become quite short and shallow. This also affects the heart, causing palpitations (rapid and irregular heartbeat), fibrillation (uneven contraction of the heart), or skipping pulses. Skipping pulses occur when the heart muscles are loaded down with fat, when the blood vessel walls are clogged with fat, or when the blood is too thick to flow smoothly. All of these problems are caused by accumulated fats. Since we do need fats in our diet, what kinds of fats should we eat? Animal fat is the most difficult for our liver to deal with. This is particularly true of beef fat, including butter, because it cannot be metabolized by our bodies. Few people realize that margarine is even worse. In the process of making margarine it is heated to a very high temperature, making its chemical structure very strong and very difficult for the body temperature to break down.

The best type of fat to use is vegetable oil. And the best type of vegetable oil is sesame oil (cold pressed), or any other oil which you can rinse off your fingers without using a detergent.

In case you have no choice and must consume more fat (animal *and* vegetable) than necessary, you can alleviate problems by drinking strong tea.

A weak nervous system can induce obesity. Allergies result when the nerve endings cannot tolerate a particular food or substance in a food. If you are allergic to some type of food, you cannot digest it. If you cannot digest it, it becomes "poisonous" to you. This toxic (to you) food then adds to your weight problem.

Another cause of obesity is improper eating habits resulting from nervousness. One problem involves the person who has become lazy. He or she just sits and thinks about things that need to be done. Of course, they never do them. They then become guilty about not doing what needs to be done and become even more nervous. So they get no exercise, and eat continually to try to forget their guilt about their inactivity. It is a vicious circle. The worse they feel, the more they eat; the harder it is to do anything, the worse they feel. The only solution is to do something. Anything. Some activity which will keep them busy. But of course they have to first overcome all of the excuses they created about why they can't do anything. It is not an easy position to be in. Or get out of.

These neurotic manifestations can result from psychological programming in childhood. Most adults, when they were children, were encouraged—or even told—to eat "more" or drink "more" by their parents, because their parents "loved them" and wanted them to grow "big and healthy." The beliefs and opinions of the parents gradually sank into the child's subconscious. As the child grew up, he felt guilty when he did not eat or consume enough. So he developed an unconscious habit to eat, eat, eat, or drink, drink, drink. The result—obesity.

With women, sexual satisfaction depends on the man. Despite all the theories (and validity) of women's liberation, a woman's real sexual satisfaction physiologically relies on the man. If a man cannot satisfy a woman, she cannot satisfy herself. If she is not satisfied, she becomes nervous. The more nervous she is, the more she eats.

Finally, heart disease, thyroid dysfunction, pancreas disorder, adrenal and thymus gland disorders can lead to obesity. These problems and diseases must be treated first before any attempt can be made to reduce weight.

Also people who suffer from rheumatism, bronchitis and asthma use cortisone, aspirin, and other drugs to relieve the pain of these disorders. But these can lead to obesity. In fact, obesity is a common side effect of the use of these drugs. In the first place drugs such as aspirin are acidic in themselves. Secondly, they cause the stomach to secrete more acid. Because the sensation of hunger occurs when the stomach acids have dissolved all the food in the stomach, more acid causes more hunger pangs. The more hunger there is, the more a person eats in an attempt to satisfy this hunger. And gradually the eating itself becomes a habit.

There are two basic proverbs to follow regarding diet:

a) *You are what you eat.* In other words, what you put in your body becomes part of your body. If you put in healthy food, your body becomes healthy. If you put in garbage, your body becomes garbage. If you eat "cold food" you become cold. If you eat balanced food, you become balanced.

b) You are what you metabolize. What you eat is the basic foundation. But what you metabolize ultimately decides how that food will be used. If your body can digest and absorb what it needs, and eliminate what it doesn't, your body will be healthy. If your body cannot take what it needs from the food you eat, or if it eliminates what it needs, or cannot eliminate what is toxic, your body will become weak, unhealthy, and eventually overweight.

From the viewpoint of Taoists, a balanced diet is an essential pillar of good health, and that good health will support a life of longevity and happiness. With its 6000 years of experience, Taoism provides a complete and proven system to help people maintain healthy, well-balanced bodies.

V

You can eat everything, but everything may not benefit you. To determine how one must eat, begin with the basic formula for regulating the diet, 50% vegetable and 50% meat, and then adjust the formula according to one's individual needs. If you have little physical work, reduce animal products and supplement with Forgotten Foods (discussed in detail in the next chapter). Never become a strict vegetarian unless you are meditating sixteen hours a day in the mountains or are at a level of cultivation that allows you to live on Forgotten Foods.

Once you become proficient at breathing exercises that allow you to consume energy directly from the universe instead of indirectly from the regular foods, you may not need food at all.

There are basically two kinds of foods. One kind consists of foods with much body and little energy (most regular foods found in the groceries, especially processed foods). The other kind consists of little body and much energy (pure foods and Forgotten Foods).

Taoists train themselves to upgrade their diet from foods with less energy and more body to foods with more energy and less body.

A true cultivator must obey rules regarding the drinking of water. Only pure spring or snow water are suitable for drinking. Too much

163

water must not be drunk. Too little water must not be drunk. Water must be drunk in the following fashion, to derive countless benefits from it: drink a mouthful but retain liquid in the mouth, then extend the neck and gulp water down little by little.

The best liquids to be drunk are not beverages (coffee, soft drinks—the worst, etc.). The caffeine they contain causes troubles.

Taoists prefer to drink a liquid called Long Life Tea. Long Life Tea is a sweet herbal combination without sugar, artificial sweeteners, or caffeine. The formula has been the property of my family for more than four hundred years. One hundred years ago, the tea was served to the royal family, especially to the Empress Tse-shi. Occasionally, the empress might honor a special person with a cup of Long Life Tea.

Long Life Tea contains peppermint, honeysuckle, chrysanthemum, cinnamon, licorice, ginseng, and poria.

Its nutritional values and effective properties are as follows: protein, gelatin, alkaloids, glycogen, calcium, phosphonium, magnesium, iron, potassium, manganese, folic acid, oxalic acid, phobatannin, Vitamins A, B, C, D, E, K, and P, resin, asparagin, saponin, etc. This tea supplies natural oil-removing properties and natural hormones.

4

THE TAO OF
FORGOTTEN FOOD DIET

TAOIST HERBOLOGY

I

If you want to live, you must eat wisely. But eating wisely in the manner described in the previous chapter may not prevent you from becoming sick. Something is missing from the grocery-bought, or common, regular foods. Yet if these inadequate, or "weak," foods can support life, then "strong" foods must be able to strengthen and protect life. This kind of reasoning has driven Taoists to investigate the jungles, mountains, flatlands, and bodies of water and to test every plant, animal, and mineral for properties that will benefit mankind. Their findings produced other dietary wisdom teachings which became the right arm of Taoists. Taoism exists because of herbs. All Taoists depend on herbs, just as we depend on food.

Magnoliae Flos
Uses: To disperse heat on the head and face. To help headache and nasal problems.

Figure 53

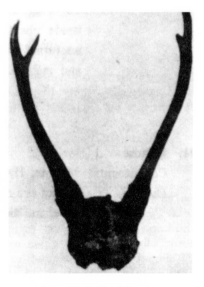

An animal: Cervi Corus
Constituents: Protein, Calcium phosphate, etc.
Uses: To treat phthisis, pain the the flank, lower abdomen, and spine; abscess, ulcers, and carbuncle.

Figure 54

166

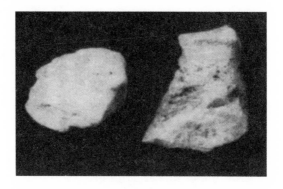

A mineral: Draconis Os

Constituents: Calcium carbonate, Calcium-phostate, etc.
Uses: To stabilize anxiety, and improve muscle function and
ulcers. To treat general distress, nightmares, nocturnal
emissions, sweating, leucorrhea, rectocele, hemoptysis,
umbilical abscess, and scrotal ulcers and pruritus.

Figure 55

Herbs are plants, animals, and minerals that are ingested or applied externally to the human body to prevent and heal physical illnesses by adjusting the flow of vital energy and supplying the better materials for regeneration of body cells or tissues.

Herbs are really our forgotten foods. Because of their often disagreeable taste or smell and our lack of knowledge concerning their utilization, our forefathers eliminated them as food and later generations ignored them. Our forefathers, in search of food, tasted many plants, such as carrots and ginseng. They took the better tasting carrots back to their farms and then passed the knowledge of farming, eating, and selling carrots on to their progeny. All regular foods sold in markets are chosen according to these criteria: (1) acceptable taste or smell, (2) easily farmed or produced, and (3) easily processed or cooked. As a result regular or familiar foods, such as beef, corn, apples, etc., have, in time, become a very small part of our total food territory. Most other plants, animals, and minerals have been forgotten. Lately, however, the world has taken a greater interest in these forgotten foods.

Examination of the present dietary situation has revealed three problems:

1. Since regular food represents only a small part of our food territory, it is possible for a human being to be deficient in some vitamins, minerals, amino acids, and other substances that nourish particular parts of the body and regenerate special cells or tissues

even though they eat the best of regular foods.

2. There is evidence that proves that human beings cannot assimilate capsules of concentrated vitamins or synthetic nutriments that were invented to supplement or replace the inadequate regular diet. Nutrients can only be assimilated in natural food form, because every nutrient is balanced with other nutrients and is accompanied by substances which increase its effectiveness and its assimilation.

3. Scientists, thus far, have not had the opportunity to test all of the forgotten foods. In other words, the properties in herbs are in some ways still a mystery and are not as familiar to us as proteins, vitamins, etc. Also, the chemical terms used to describe nutrients are inadequate for describing herbal properties. Nutritionalists must progress into the territory of the forgotten foods so that such limitations may be eliminated and so that their nutritional healing methods may be enhanced.

By studying the forgotten foods, we can promote health and prevent illness because we will know how to use them to improve the function of our internal organs and our entire body. The study of forgotten foods is divided into three sections: Herbology, Taoist Etiology, and Health Condition Determination.

II

Herbology

Herbology is a two-part study of herbs. The first part of Herbology is analysis of all plants, animals, and minerals to determine their nutritional values (proteins, vitamins, minerals, etc.), energy levels, and other chemical compositions. The second part is determining which parts of the human body each particular herb affects most, and how those parts are affected. This also involves preparation of the part of the herb most suited for utilization. For example, the magnolia tree's leaves and flowers are not of importance, whereas the outermost layer of the bark is of importance. The latter substance contains properties called *Tetrahydromanodolol, Isomagolol,* and *Ho-Curare,* which are very helpful in regenerating the stomach and uterus tissues. Another property called *Magnolol* is a gentle type of antibiotic and antitoxin.

Shen Nung, the founder of the Shen Nung Dynasty (3494 B.C.), and his administration researched the properties of herbs and their relation to mankind. Since the Shen Nung Dynasty thousands of different herbs have been researched and hundreds of formulas have been developed, due to the efforts of Taoists who regard herbal knowledge as most essential in the attainment of immortality.

For more than 6,000 years, the Taoists have kept written records of the herbs they used and their experiments with them. These written records are the basis upon which the theories and principles were developed to make possible the formulation of new herbal combinations with very little chance for error. These writings also explain how the herbal raw ingredients must be processed and prepared to obtain maximum healing results with minimum waste.

How do herbs work?

Herbs, like the regular foods, work by adjusting the flow of vital energy in the entire body of the human being. This is accomplished by increasing the energy where it is too low and decreasing the energy where it is too high. When human beings absorb the properties of the herbs, they also absorb the vitality of the herbs. The herbs' vitality passes through the pathways of energy (meridians) to reach the internal organs, to support and adjust them to their optimal efficiency . For example, the ginseng's electromagnetic field particularly circulates around the lung and spleen-pancreas meridians.

Herbs have been found to have tremendous energy levels. These energy levels were defined by two characteristics : Yin, which is negative, weak, sedative, and reducing; and Yang, which is positive, strong, tonifying, and increasing. Eventually the use of only these two characteristics was found to be unsatisfactory. In order to be more precise, the two characteristics were expanded to a scale of five, which are:

Hot	Strong positive energy
Warm	Medium positive energy
Neutral	Neutral energy
Cool	Medium negative energy
Cold	Strong negative energy

All herbs and regular foods belong to one of these five categories. As an example, dog meat is very energizing and is called Hot. Beef is Warm. Seafood, such as clams, is Cold. Pork is Cool. The whole egg is Neutral. If we are to effectively use our foods for better health, we must determine their energy levels; because our foods, if not properly balanced, can either over-energize or deplete us. Too much shellfish will deplete our energy, and too much dog meat will excessively energize us, encouraging hypertension, congestion, nervousness, etc. We can see, then, that it is very important to balance the energy by correctly combining the foods we eat.

For thousands of years it was known that every type of food affects our meridians in some way. Knowing this, Taoists spent an enormous amount of time in determining which foods and herbs affected which meridians. The Taoists found that ginseng, for example, affected the lung and spleen-pancreas meridians. Warm characteristics tonify and stimulate its related meridians (the lung and spleen-pancreas meridians). Besides the meridians, herbs directly affect the internal organs and supply the necessary materials to regenerate their particular cells or tissues.

Taoists determined the relationship of herbs and internal organs by matching their similar characteristics. Since there are five main internal organs, Taoists used five tastes to represent each organ.

Element	Taste	Organ
Wood	Acid	Liver (Nervous system and gallbladder)
Fire	Bitter	Heart (Small intestine and blood vessels)
Earth	Sweet	Spleen-pancreas (Stomach and muscles)
Metal	Piquant	Lungs (Skin and large intestine)
Water	Salty	Kidney (Bladder and bones)

Then the Taoists categorized every herb under these five tastes, after the taste of every herb was determined. For example, ginseng is sweet so it affects the spleen-pancreas. The herbs work like the Five Animal Exercises, that is, they support or degenerate the organs according to the Five Elements Theory and the Mother and Child Law.

Herbs contain many nutrients—ginseng contains Vitamins B_1, B_2, C, Calcium, minerals, amino acids, etc.—but they also harbor nutrients that are not found in regular food. These unique properties are called Effective Properties or Effective Composition. The Effective Properties of ginseng are Panaquilon ($C_{32}H_{56}O_{14}$), Panax Sapogenol ($C_{27}H_{48}O_2$), Panaxin ($C_{38}H_{66}O_{12}$), Panacin ($C_{15}H_{24}$), Ginsenin, and Amylase. We may call them "supernutrition."

Herbs are strong foods; nutrients are highly concentrated in natural, easily assimilable form. For example, the herb called Atractylodes has a high level of nutrients such as: Vitamins A and D (more than 20 times the amount in cod liver oil); Essential Oil, which can calm the overactivity of organ functioning; Atractylodes or Atractylons, which can lower blood sugar and relax heart muscles; Vitamins P, B_1, and B_{12}; several amino acids; and minerals. The intake of 1/4 ounce of Atractylodes equals 3 complete regular food meals—without extra fat, cholesterol, sugar, etc. It also costs less than a regular meal.

In laboratory studies, adrenalin was shot into the human body, resulting in raised blood sugar levels. After ginseng was administered, the blood sugar level returned to normal. This is an example of super-nutritional healing, a very important property found only in herbs. It is almost impossible to obtain such effective compositions in any daily, regular food diet, (which provides only simple nutrients).

Modern laboratory technology presently cannot identify all of the properties in all herbs because some unknown elements are lost in the analytical process. Nevertheless, these unknown elements still play important roles in helping and preventing illnesses.

An interesting fact about herbs is that they also purify the human body. We all know that the better we eat, the stronger our body becomes. Our bodies also contain parasites, such as germs and worms. As our foods make us stronger, it also makes these parasites stronger. If we like our foods, then the parasites must also like them. An example of this can be the corruption of an orange. If we place an orange on a table for a few weeks at room temperature, the orange will become covered with green-gray microorganisms. If we place a ginseng root in the same environmental conditions for many years, the root will remain unchanged, because the microorganisms hate its taste and will never consume it. Nutrients from regular foods nourish us and the parasites (which take away what is supposed to be ours). In contrast, nutrients from herbs nourish us only. In this way the parasites are naturally eliminated and we are allowed to enjoy the full value of our nutritional intake.

Every day we are poisoning our bodies with polluted air, preserved and chemicalized foods, drugs and alcohol. Some herbs are very effective in removing or neutralizing these toxins, because they improve the function of our internal organs.

To be most effective, herbs must be used in their natural, unrefined, and unchemicalized state. Most modern drugs have a common problem, negative side-effects. The side-effects occur because of the high concentrations of chemicals in them. If herbs were purified, chemicalized, and refined like many of the foods we have today, they too would lose much of their potential and natural balance. Thus, the most effective way to use herbs is to use the most potent portion of the plant in its natural state.

One very important principle of Herbology is that herbs must always be used in a combination or recipe. In the texts of Herbology it is stated that "There is not one thing in the world that is absolute." Everything, including herbs, has a positive side and a negative side. For example, ginseng energizes the body, especially the lungs and spleen-pancreas, slowly; but it also produces a strong side-effect if used alone. One of the properties of ginseng, called Ginsenin,

171

tightens the arteries. If the utilizer has a weakness in the vascular system, constant use of ginseng could lead to a stroke or heart attack. In order to offset or neutralize this possibly unpleasant side-effect, one must combine ginseng with another herbal ingredient, such as Astragalus. This herb is very effective in relaxing the blood vessels.

One principle used in developing herbal formulas is to use at least four ingredients. The Taoists use governmental terms when dealing with herbs: Emperor, Prime Minister, and at least two Ministers.

In order to produce an effective formula, it is necessary to correctly combine the herb's energy level (characteristics) and the specific organs (taste) they affect. For example, there is a very popular herb formula comprised of ginseng, atractylis, poria (a type of mushroom) and licorice. These four herbs, in combination, energize the lungs, spleen-pancreas, and stomach.

III

Taoist Etiology is the study of *Bing* and their causes. *Bing* means that one's health is not as it should be. The western equivalent of this term may be dis-ease. The word disease is not an appropriate translation of Bing because it connotes diagnostic procedures that result in the amassment of symptoms under a name, such as leprosy, bubonic plague, etc. Taoists do not invest time in following the progress of a disease or in naming a disease; for they prefer to pinpoint the cause of a disease and find ways to eliminate the cause. Taoists realize that it is fruitless to combat all the diseases on earth. They therefore sought for ways to fortify the human body against the onslaught of the diseases. Taoists gave all the dis-eases of the world only three names: Air Dis-ease, Water Dis-ease and Blood Dis-ease. This serves to indicate the chief sources of myriad problems. The Taoists also categorized all casual agents of dis-ease under seven titles: External Causes, Internal Causes, Non-External Causes, Non-Internal Causes, Blood poisoning, Water poisoning, and Food poisoning. An understanding of the logic behind these subjects is necessary for proper herb utilization.

Air Dis-ease

The accumulation of air in humans, according to the Taoist sages, can cause many kinds of diseases. When they spoke of the air within the body, they were referring to the amount of pressure therein. The internal pressure of the body must be balanced with the external pressure of the environment. If the internal pressure is low or weak, we have a condition which is much like that of a "vacuumized" can. A hissing sound is produced upon opening such a can. The sound is caused by external air rushing into the can because the can has no air inside. When the internal pressure of the body is weak, the external air (called "wind") will press into the body through the millions of tiny pores in the skin. The air naturally presses into the weakest and often the most exposed part of the body. When this "wind" gets into the tissues of the body, the tissues expand. This expansion causes the pores of the skin to be squeezed shut and the air to be trapped inside. Because the air is trapped by the closed pores, the local tissues are under pressure. This strain on the tissues causes pain, the first symptom of Air Dis-ease. The pain is usually felt in the areas of the upper back, shoulders, neck, and chest, because these are the main nerve areas and they are often exposed. The skin is often referred to as the "third lung" because Taoists believe the skin is closely related to all the organs of the respiratory tract. A series of second symptoms, occurring along the respiratory tract, immediately follow the first symptom of pain, because of this skin-respiratory tract relationship. The sinuses are affected, the nose becomes runny or stuffy, the throat becomes itchy and sore, the function of the lungs is impaired, and the energy of the lung meridian becomes depleted. Moreover, the germs and viruses brought in by the air penetrate deeply into the tissues and cause many problems. The third series of symptoms arising from this activity is usually a bowel or digestive dysfunction (upset stomach or diarrhea). These symptoms indicate that the body is working diligently to repel the attack of Air. Whether the Air Dis-ease will be the common cold, the flu, or other illnesses will be determined by the germs and viruses.

Moreover, accumulation of air in the body can be the cause of mental disorders, quick-temperedness, vertigo, or headaches. One knows that these problems are caused by accumulation of air when the problems are accompanied by these problems:

1. Shortness of breath—difficulty in doing deep breathing—and the sensation of an object fixed in the chest.

2. Inability to inhale—no matter how much air one breathes in, the lungs never feel full.

3. Inability to exhale—blockage of outcoming air. This is not to be confused with emphysema, which is the lack of lung flexibility.

4. Gastritis either in the stomach (belching) or in the intes-

tines (flatulence). This occurs because air is being released to relieve the high internal pressure.

5. Unnecessary sighing. This is an indication of excess pressure on the organs. This symptom is most accurately interpreted in younger individuals, because they should not feel the need to sigh from depression, as adults do. Sighing indicates an abnormality of the respiratory system.

The modern pathological terms used above are given to help the reader gain a greater understanding of Air Dis-ease. These terms were used by Kesetsu Otsuka, M.D., a famous and respected professor and physician, to interpret Air Dis-ease.

The transference of Air Dis-ease is not thought to occur through physical contact with an infected individual's body parts, but it is thought to occur through exposure to the same germ-ridden air. It is not possible to contract a virus by touching unless the body is already weak and the inside pressure is low. It is possible to receive germs through the air from an infected person, especially if they are using a mentholated substance, such as cough drops, lozenges, or syrup. The menthol has the effect of carrying germs out of the body and into the air through diffusion of its odor.

These germs and viruses can be expelled from the body through the usage of herbs and the encouragement of the natural eliminative processes of sweating, vomiting, and bowel movement. In the inducement of sweating, care must be taken not to expose the bare skin to the air because the internal pressure cannot prevent another influx of air. Sweating should take place with protective clothing in bed within the first three days of an illness. Vomiting and bowel movement are used to eliminate deeper infections by germs and viruses, and they are used after a period of sweating. Herbs are used to induce these eliminative processes, kill the germs and viruses, nourish and strengthen the weakened body, and help the body build up its weakened internal pressure. We must never try to suppress fevering, sweating, coughing, etc. because the germs and viruses will go deeper into the tissues . Serious problems will develop from latent germ or virus growth, causing permanent damage to the functions of the body.

Blood Dis-ease

There are five causes of Blood Dis-ease. Blood Dis-ease can occur when the bone marrow and spleen-pancreas become dysfunctional and produce inadequate amounts of blood cells. Blood Dis-ease is

174

also caused by blood corruption, blood clotting, and blood extravasation.

Corruption of the blood could be caused by bad air, by foods, or by physical contact with poisons. These poisons move through the body and damage enzymes, nutritional elements, and internal organs. If the quality of the blood is bad, such as unbalanced levels of iron or sugar, or if the quantity is insufficient, many problems such as low energy, migraine headaches, blood clots, and anemia will result.

Blood clotting is caused by sedimentation, poor circulation, low energy levels, high body temperature, pressure exerted on blood vessels by excess water in the tissues, accidents, heavy exercise, heavy labor or surgery. These result in three types of "dead blood" blood clots: those that form from heavy sedimentation; those that accumulate on the sides of the arteries; and those that settle to the bottom of the blood vessels.

Iron supplements, often recommended for women and older individuals, can be very dangerous, for the excess iron, being heavy, settles to the bottom of the vessels and attracts other sediments. If consumption of extra iron is continued over a long period of time, outpocketings in the blood vessels may be created. These pockets containing sediments may break and disperse the blood into the surrounding membranes, causing internal bleeding. This is sometimes indicated by blood in the stools. Blood clots occur in the areas of the lower stomach, the intestines and the sexual organs because of the gravitational pull of heavy sediment to the lower part of the body. Many autopsies reveal black-colored blood clots in these areas.

Another common cause of blood clotting is poor circulation caused by sitting and driving for long periods of time. Watching moving objects while being inactive depletes our energy, which is another cause of blood clotting. When blood circulates slowly, it is more likely to be "cooked" by body heat, especially when the temperature of the body is high. Heated blood coagulates and settles, usually, in the stomach area. Excessive pressure upon blood also causes it to coagulate and settle. Bruises are another form of blood clotting. Bruises result from accidents, heavy activity, and surgery.

Extravasated blood resulting from broken blood vessels can cause serious problems. Germs and viruses tend to settle in extravasated blood, and when the blood is absorbed, the germs and viruses are also absorbed into the bloodstream. Extravasated blood will settle in the abdominal area.

The major symptoms which indicate blood dis-ease are:

1. Dry and dark skin and nails. The skin appears very sooty, perhaps ashen, and the nails may be purple. The area around the eyes

and lips becomes dark.

2. Bruising easily or feeling cold because the circulation is blocked.

3. Abnormal menstruation. The timing, amount, color, cramps, headaches, etc. give a very good indication of the condition of the blood.

4. Frequent and/or sudden changes in body temperature.

5. Sudden loss of appetite, swollen stomach or a feeling of fullness in the abdomen.

6. Heavy-handedness, headaches, pain in the area of the shoulder blades, insomnia, somnolence, forgetfulness, light-headedness, blackouts, heart palpitation or a feeling of fear which is unfounded.

7. Chronic digestive disorders such as hyper-acidity or heartburn.

A further breakdown of the results of Blood Dis-ease includes:
1. Ulcers of the stomach or duodenum
2. Stomach cancer
3. Appendicitis
4. Chronic constipation, diarrhea, and hemorrhoids
5. Hardening arteries
6. Stroke
7. High or low blood pressure
8. Female organ disorder
9. Herpes
10. Shingles
11. Sciatica
12. Lumbago
13. Mental illness
14. Urinary problems—kidney or bladder infections or stones
15. Tuberculosis
16. Pneumonia or bronchitis
17. Cancer of all kinds, especially leukemia

Kesetsu Otsuka, M.D., also contributed these modern pathological terms.

Another Japanese physician, Dr. Nangahama, did extensive studies into the causes of Blood Dis-ease. These concerned inheritance from parents, abnormal menstruation, high temperature (inflammation), weak blood vessels, liver weakness, hormone imbalance, and imbalanced blood systems.

Water Dis-ease

The human body is essentially composed of water—it is 70%

176

water—so water is essential to our well-being. But water is also a source of many problems. The greatest percentage of water is in our blood. Water cools the blood temperature, thins the blood, and facilitates circulation of blood cells. Water cleans the blood of poisons or deposits and carries these to the kidneys to be eliminated in the urine. When the kidneys cannot filter all the water either because they are weak or because there is just too much water, the water goes back to the blood to circulate through the body. Usually, by this time, more water has accumulated in the blood. The blood vessels become enlarged, then they begin to contract spasmodically, squeezing the water into the tissues where it becomes trapped. Ballooning of the tissues and occasional pain are the results. Taoists call this water "dead water," and it gives rise to mucous, or phlegm.

One of the causes of water retention and mucous buildup is the chemicals in the water we drink. If we take an ordinary drinking glass full of water and leave it undisturbed, we may see for ourselves what happens to the stagnant water in our body. After only a few days our glass of pure drinking water begins to get cloudy and eventually it may turn green. After a few weeks, when most of the liquid has evaporated, we will have a green slime layer coating the bottom of the glass. In the body, this is called mucous, a gel-like substance which accumulates and harbors harmful microorganisms.

In America, approximately ninety percent of the population has a tendency to retain water. Many individuals who are overweight have an overabundant supply of fat *and* mucous. A test to determine the presence of mucous is to press hard on the upper arms or thighs for several seconds and then release. If an imprint remains from the pressure, water is definitely being retained. A woman is most susceptible to water accumulation because of the hormonal changes that she goes through every month and during the menopausal period. Water retention is also exceedingly common in men and children.

Besides kidney weakness or dysfunction, another cause of water retention is simply over-consumption of liquids. We are generally taught that we should drink at least eight glasses of water per day. The healthy, normally functioning kidneys should be able to filter out this much water. For those whose kidneys do not function at 100% efficiency, eight glasses of water per day can be extremely harmful. Taoist teaching suggests that water consumption should be limited to six cups of liquid per day, and that includes coffee, tea, fruits, vegetables, soups, etc.

Water accumulates in six areas, and it causes many problems. They are:

1. In all the major organs. Microorganisms contained in the

water cause inflammation of these organs.

2. In the tissues and under the skin—cellulite.

3. Between the membranes in the chest cavity surrounding the organs, muscles, and bones. We need a certain amount of water here to serve as lubrication; but when it is germ infested, it causes inflammation.

4. Underneath the heart area, causing a "floating" condition of the heart and fibrillation of the heart.

5. In the area of the diaphragm. Water can affect the liver and cause cancer.

6. In the brain.

The accumulation of mucous causes many kinds of Water Diseases, which are indicated by five groups of symptoms. And they are:

Group One
1. Heart palpitation
2. Fibrillation
3. Shortness of breath
4. Coughing
5. Fatigue
6. Constipation or diarrhea
7. Vomiting (especially vomiting of water)
8. Cold or chilly sensations
9. Phlegm

Group Two (excess or defiencies in internal secretions)
1. Hormones
2. Saliva
3. Semen
4. Vaginal secretion
5. Tears
6. Perspiration

Group Three
1. Dizziness
2. Tintinnitus (ringing ears)
3. Heavy headedness
4. Chest pain
5. Stomach pain
6. Shaking or trembling
7. Excessive thirst

Group Four
1. Gurgling, sloshing sounds from the stomach or abdomen
2. Neuritis
3. Swelling of the body, especially the ankles and legs
4. Female organ disturbances

5. Pleuritis
Group Five
1. Headaches
2. Interference with a locomotive function

The diseases resulting from water accumulation are:
1. Dropsy of the stomach or stomach ulcers
2. Bronchitis, asthma, pneumonia, and pleuritis
3. Cardiac problems and heart disease
4. Glaucoma, cataracts, myopia, and hyperopia
5. Nervousness, neuritis, epilepsy, and madness
6. Urinary problems—kidney or bladder infections, nephritis, and kidney atrophy
7. Arthritis and diabetes

The above modern pathological terms were supplied by Kesetsu Otsuka, M.D.

The body has three natural outlets for mucous, and they are:

1. Respiratory tract. The mucous is expelled naturally by coughing.

2. Skin. Water is eliminated either naturally through perspiration, or mechanically through the use of saunas, steam, hot baths, or herbs.

3. Bladder. Water is passed out in the urine.

In the expulsion of mucous, herbs are used to divert mucous from the respiratory and epidermal outlets to the bladder and to stimulate the natural diuresis function of the body to expel the mucous. The herbs are also capable of building the energy of the body, especially the kidneys.

Bringing the kidneys back to a healthy state is a difficult task. The practice of flushing the kidneys and taking diuretic pills extracts more work from the kidneys, but they also increase one's thirst. Drinking more water, although it defeats the purpose by making the kidneys work harder, is always recommended for alleviating thirst. The only effective way to treat the weakened, tired kidneys is to energize and nourish them to make them stronger. When a horse is tired, we must feed him and let him rest. Beating a horse to make him work will kill him. Diuretics have the effect of beating the kidneys, whereas herbs feed the kidneys with nutrients and energy. Along with herbs, mechanical methods for water expulsion, such as saunas, steam, hot baths, and massage, may be used to dislodge mucous and eliminate it.

External Causes

There are five types of climates which, after prolonged exposure, adversely affect the body. These are as follows: wind, which affects the liver, gallbladder, and nervous system; cold, which affects the kidneys, bladder, bones, and sexual organs; heat, which affects the heart , small intestine and circulatory system; dampness (dew, mist, fog), which affects the spleen-pancreas, digestive system, and muscles; and dryness, which affects the lungs, large intestine, skin, and breathing system.

Internal Causes

The internal emotional causes of dis-ease are excessive anger, which affects the liver; excessive worry and thinking, which affects the spleen-pancreas and stomach; excessive fear and fright (shock), which affects the kidneys; excessive joy, which affects the heart; and excessive sadness, which affects the lungs.

Non-External and Non-Internal Causes

Acute or chronic infirmities can be caused by aberrant lifestyle: over-eating, over-work, excessive drinking, excessive sexual activity, excessive fatigue, prolonged hunger, excessive talking, and excessive activity.

Blood Poisoning

Blood poisoning occurs within the blood. The blood poisons are the syphilis, tuberculosis, and gonorrhea bacteria. In this modern age, herpes and AIDS are also added to the blood poisons. These are passed from one generation to the next in either the semen of the father or in the blood of the mother. Once they are introduced into the human body, they are difficult to remove—even antibiotics are useless against them. Their interference with the genetic processes of the body cause unseen malfunctions of the internal organs and visible malformations of body parts. None of these abnormalities can be corrected entirely by surgery.

According to Taoism, interference by blood poisons with the genetic processes vital to prenatal development cause many problems. Sometimes they interfere with brain development and cause mental problems. Some individuals are born with weak hearts because a heart valve was malformed. Nerves are affected, livers are affected, all parts of the body are affected.

For millenniums, the misery and suffering caused by these blood poisons have conditioned mankind to think that life must be terrible. Actually, the miseries are caused by the ignorance of man's ancestors.

Through practising eugenics, an important part of Taoist Sexology, and utilization of herbs, the blood can be cleaned and we may be assured of having clean, healthy, intelligent, and complete children. According to Taoist teachings, when the blood is kept free from blood poisons for three generations, a genius may be born to that family.

This Taoistic teaching has been adopted by the originator of Homeopathy, a greatly esteemed German physician who gave up all of his honors to fight for these theories. Unlike the Taoists, this physician used Bach Flowers to treat these blood poisons.

Water Poisoning

Water poisoning is caused by the buildup of mucous, which arises from germ-infested water being retained in the body. This buildup of mucous first affects the nervous system, causing nervousness, spasms, or numbness. Nervousness is the first indication that poisoning from water has taken place. A second indication of water poisoning is sluggish or bizarre thinking processes, loss of locomotive functions, or headaches—all systems of brain damage. Other indications of water poisoning include water retention, heart problems, and kidney problems. Parkinson's disease is an example of water poisoning at its worst. Some herbal formulas have been created specifically to prevent or correct these undesirable situations.

Food Poisoning

Food poisoning is caused by eating incorrect combinations of foods, by the corruption of food in the body, and by food allergies.

Our foods must be acid-alkaline balanced in order to avoid corruption in our digestive system. Food improperly balanced, when mixed with saliva and other digestive juices, will go through a chemical change and will corrupt before completion of the digestive cycle. A very good indication of acid-alkaline imbalance is foul smelling breath, an indication of the presence of corrupted food in the stomach. Sometimes bad breath is caused by a disorder in the mouth itself. A sign of corruption in the intestines is foul smelling gas. Corrupted food is poisonous, and it can cause decay. We all know that tooth decay results from inadequate removal of food particles from the spaces between and around the teeth. The same type of decay occurs in the digestive system when food is not eliminated regularly and completely.

Some combinations of foods which become poisonous in the digestive system are beef and onions, sweet potatoes and bananas, pork and parsley, onions and honey.

Some types of foods are poisons within themselves, and overuse of these foods causes dis-ease. For example, garlic taken in abundance will cause damage to eyesight. Overuse of chili peppers as a condiment injures the digestive system. Oysters alone are poisonous, especially in the summertime because they harbor high levels of poisons. For this reason, oysters should be eaten only in the fall and winter seasons. Some people cannot eat these foods at all because of an extreme allergic reaction that results from their use. These allergies can cause great misery. Of course, a little of these foods can be helpful in combatting other poisons we may have accumulated—moderation is very important in eating foods.

No matter how well we think we eat, it is nearly impossible to avoid poisoning from food ingestion. Our regular food diet is classified as "weak" because of its short life span after harvesting. These "weak" foods cannot support life for long--they must corrupt. This is why we so urgently need herbs, the "strong" foods, to neutralize and combat the effects of food corruption and poisoning. Of course, the herbs we use must also be carefully balanced, because improper combinations of herbs can also become poisonous.

IV

Determination of Health Conditions

Many techniques determine the cause of a dis-ease, the organ(s) or bowel(s) that are most affected, the state of energy flow in the meridians—in other words, the health condition of an individual. The techniques include observation, interrogation, careful listening, face reading, abdomen reading, tongue reading, and pulse reading.

A
OBSERVATION

Observation consists of examining the person's physical appearance including the walk, stature, degree of composure, alertness, general cleanliness, color, and any physical malformations or mental incapabilities. These are basic conditions by which even a less experienced cultivator may judge the general state of health. Other conditions to look for in the following are:

The hair—abundance, texture, sheen, dryness, oiliness.

The nails—pinkness, flexibility, and smoothness.

The muscles and bones—tone and flexibility

The eyes—clearness, brightness, quickness (but no wandering or rolling).

The hearing—ability to hear the normal speaking voice. Deafness may be the first indication of a kidney disorder as the ears are the opening of the kidneys.

Generally, the skin coloring indicates balance or imbalance within specific organs, bowels, and/or body systems. The five colors show problems and their related viscera.

1. Pale coloring is related to problems of the lungs, skin, and respiratory system.

2. Redness is related to problems of the heart, brain, and blood vessel system.

3. Yellowish coloring is related to problems of the stomach, spleen-pancreas, digestive system, and muscles.

4. Blue coloring relates to problems of the liver, gallbladder, and nervous system.

5. Blackness or sooty coloring relates to problems of the bladder, internal glands, kidneys, and hormones.

The experienced cultivator is observant of all aspects of a person's character : whether or not they are on time, or if they always seem to be in a hurry; if the person exhibits excessive emotion or a lack of emotion (which generally reflects the condition of the lungs), and also the person's basic mental attitude about life. This may be discovered either through careful listening, or by interrogation. Each of the five organs governs a mental process. According to Taoism, the brain serves only as a processor of information and as a computor center.

The lungs govern sensitivity and are likewise affected by any imbalance or fluctuation of the emotional process.

The kidneys govern the will and decision-making. You may be sure that a person who exhibits weakness of will power (have difficulty in making decisions) will have deficient kidneys.

The process of analytical thought (pondering) is governed by the spleen-pancreas. Excessive worry indicates a troubled spleen-pancreas.

The liver governs thought and ideas. Those with degenerative liver conditions often have bizarre thoughts or grandiose, unrealistic ideas and great depressions.

The fifth organ, the heart, does not govern a single mental process, but is the ruler of the spirit. Feeling comes from the heart. When we are "heart-broken," the spirit is dampened and when our spirit soars, our hearts are open. When the heart is open, the spirit is set free.

B
LISTENING

This is done from a careful distance of three or four feet. The factors to be considered in listening are:

1. The quality of the voice. Unclear speech could indicate a throat or heart problem, or psychological disturbance. Vocal qualities are also linked with the organs and these qualities disclose imbalances within the organs. A shouting or calling-out quality shows a bad liver, a laughing vocal quality shows bad heart, a singing quality shows bad spleen-pancreas, a crying quality shows bad lungs, and a sighing quality shows bad kidneys.

2. The breath. Gasping could indicate water poisoning. A cough may be a respiratory illness—we listen for wetness (mucous), or dryness in the cough. If there is mucous, we may inquire as to its nature and thereby determine which of the viscera it is coming from.

3. The sound of gurgling water from the stomach or the bowels. This is an indication of digestive problems which could be either acute or chronic.

C
INTERROGATION

1. The bowel movement—regularity, colour, and consistency of the stools and the urine.

2. The diet—appetite and thirst, pH balance and energy level of foods consumed.

3. Symptoms—including pain, swelling, bleeding, vomiting, headache, dizziness, ringing in the ears, chills, fever, and sweating.

4. Menstrual cycle—timing, amount of blood, related symptoms such as cramps, headache.

5. Health history and eventual organ impairments from accidents or previous surgeries.

6. Body's dys-functions discovered by modern technologies.

D
ABDOMINAL READING

The basic considerations in abdominal reading are flexibility of the area felt, reactions of the nerves in the area, and the presence and direction of pain in the area.

At the onset of an abdominal reading, the person should be asked to lie on the back and relax. If there is tension in the abdomen from nervousness and/or apprehension, it may be mistaken for a symptom of distress in the body.

The first consideration of the cultivator is the degree of resistance or flexibility of the abdomen. If there is very little or no resistance, there is a lack of function. If there is a great deal of tension or hardness, there is congestion, excess of energy, overactivity and fighting within. The abdomen should have a little flexibility, it should spring back when pressed then released. This indicates a healthy level of energy and capability of the body to endure. For a person who has much subcutaneous fat, it may be difficult to feel the resistance, and it is more practical to look for pain instead.

The strength and tension of the abdominal muscles also give direct indication of trouble. For instance, in the case of inflammation, pressure on the corresponding area will create an immediate response in the form of muscle tension because of the natural reaction of the muscles to protect the inflammed area.

The area of the umbilicus is checked first as it is the center of the body's energy. This area should be relatively firm. If it is soft, the person is very weak. Next, the thickness and degree of tension in the abdominal muscles are evaluated. If flaccid, the person is of a weak constitution.

Swelling in the abdomen is the third consideration. If there is swelling and the abdomen is firm, the person is of a strong constitution, but if the swollen abdomen is also flaccid, the person is very weak.

The fourth area to consider is done by pressing the ribs and the lower area of the heart. There may also be pain along with the outward pressure.

There are several basic locations to consider in abdominal palpation which indicate specific internal conditions.

Organ Locations

The five organs can be read by applying pressure and by gentle tapping. If there is pain, or if the area is very soft, the organ lacks energy, indicating blockage. In tapping these locations, we listen for clarity of sound. If the sound is hollow there is a problem in the organs; if the sound is sharp and clear, this is normal.

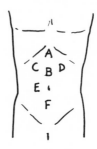

Figure 56

A. Center of the V-bone slightly to the left, relates to the heart.
B. One inch above the navel relates to the spleen-pancreas.
C. Underneath the V-bone to the right relates to the liver.
D. Underneath the V-bone to the left relates to the gallbladder.
E. Under the liver along the spleen relates to the lungs.
F. One inch below the navel relates to the kidneys, sexual organs and the bladder.

Other abdominal locations also reflects specific conditions as follows:

Location No. 1

If pressure in the area underneath the V-bones causes pain, the direction of the pain indicates the focus of the problem. If the pain shoots into the center and up, the focus is the heart. If the pain radiates upward, the lungs are afflicted. If pain shoots to the right, the liver is indicated; if the pain shoots to the left, the gallbladder is the focus. If the pain shoots inside, the stomach and spleen-pancreas are the focus of the problem, and if the pain shoots down and to the sides, the kidneys are indicated.

186

Location No. 2

This area gives an indication of the condition of the nerves. The technique is to apply pressure while moving the hands up and down along these areas. If the skin shows a jumping reaction immediately, the nerves are inflammed. If there is no reaction at all, the nerves have no energy and do not function properly. If the muscles in this area are very tight like a rope, the person has a nervous condition or possibly a digestive disorder related to the nerves such as over-acidity. The nerves are fed by the hormones so the latter will most likely be deficient.

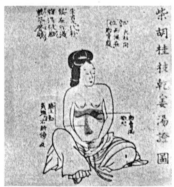

Location No. 3

If this area is either very soft and lacking flexibility or very hard, with a great deal of resistance but not necessarily pain, there could be ulcers or other digestive problems, blood clots or a problem with the colon. Also the diaphragm could be paralyzed which is an indication of a liver malfunction.

Location No. 4

Numbness in these areas over the pubic bone could be an indication of diabetes, impotence, urinary system problems such as infection, or lack of energy and function in the sexual organs.

Location No. 5

During the first stages of "air dis-ease", there is stiffness in the neck and back, headache, severe chills with fever, sweating, weakness and a floating pulse.

188

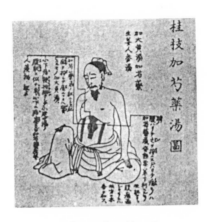

Location No. 6

Convulsions at the center of the upper abdomen and muscular tension of the lower abdomen (upper strong, lower weak), indicate fatigue, sexual weakness and tension.

Location No. 7

It may indicate acute abdominal palpitation above the umbilicus, distress under the heart, weak and flaccid abdomen, difficulty in stretching, sharp pain at the joints of upper limbs, sweating, severe chills and slight general water retention.

189

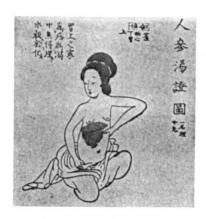

Location No. 8

It may indicate chest stagnancy, weak abdomen, suction sound under the heart, water stagnation in the stomach, cold limbs, soft stools or diarrhea, vomiting, dizziness, stomach ache, and feeble pulse.

Location No. 9

It may indicate lumbago, palpitation under the heart, chills inside the abdomen, suction sound caused by stagnant water in the gastrointestinal tract due to slow metabolism, stomach ache with diarrhea, and dizziness.

190

Location No. 10

It may indicate suction sound under the heart, asthma, coughing and rapid respiration due to influenza and stress, water in the
upper body.

Location No. 11

It may indicate accumulation of fluid in the upper body, fever,
asthmatic cough, sweating, dry throat, floating pulse and weakness
in the legs.

191

Location No. 12

It indicates a broad, distended upper abdomen. Also nausea, acute vomiting, serious chest distension, and constipation. And a sinking-strong pulse may result.

Location No. 13

Moisture and intense spasms above the umbilicus and below the heart indicate restlessness, insomnia, constipation, nervousness and mental instability.

192

Location No. 14

Hard lump below the umbilicus with acute pain in the lower left abdomen (in severe conditions, even the slightest touch of the abdomen brings unbearable pain), indicates blood dis-ease.

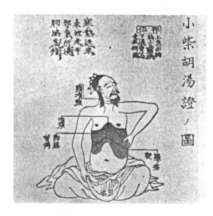

Location No. 15

Hardness and stagnancy under the heart, indicate fainting, chest swelling, nervousness, vomiting and acute headache, cold hands and feet, retching, excessive salivation, and a sinking-slow pulse.

E
FACIAL READING

In reading the face, there are five basic locations to consider: the eyes, eyebrows, nose, mouth, and ears. There are also one hundred and eight other facial locations that are used for character reading. (Please refer to Chapter 8.) Health problems are also indicated on the face. Taoists extensively researched the body's interconnections and found that facial locations corresponded to internal organs. From experience, the readings are 90% accurate. Beginning with the eyes, five locations will be examined in the following paragraphs.

There are five areas around the eye, each of which reflects the state of one of five organs.

1. The insides of the eyelid (top and bottom) reflect the stomach and spleen-pancreas. A reddish colour or white spots indicate trouble.

2. The whites of the eyes reflect the lungs. If they are red (not blood shot), the lungs are inflamed.

3. The inside of the iris generally reflects the condition of the liver.

4. Spots inside the pupil area of the eyes indicate kidney trouble.

5. The corners of the eyes reflect the heart. Swelling here indicates heart trouble.

Some other considerations concerning the eyes are:

A. Bulging eyes. Protruding eyes indicate a metabolic imbalance or calcium deficiency. The thyroid is implicated.

B. Three whites eyes. When the whites of the eyes can be seen above or below the iris, it is a sign of nervousness (perhaps hyperactivity). This person's sex drive is high and therefore is quite possibly depleted of hormones and also energy. This type of eye is usually found in one who never listens to anyone and who exhibits mercurial characteristics. This person is also very clever. Napoleon and Kaiser Wilhelm had this type of eyes.

C. Wolf eyes. The whites of the eyes are yellowish but not because of jaundice. These eyes are an indication of an extreme nervous condition— possibly nervous breakdown or mental disorder .

D. Watery eyes. This is an indication of a kidney and/or sexual organ imbalance, especially in women.

E. Cloudy eyes. This indicates a degenerated liver condition.

The eyes of a healthy person should be clear and clean—the whites should be very white and the iris clear without spots or variances in color .

THE NOSE

The nose generally reflects the spinal cord. If the nose is very strong, straight, and firm, the vertebrae are also straight and strong. Likewise, if the nose is weak and crooked, so is the spine. The character of the nose is also related to the sexual organs and the sexual glands as well. Because the nose is the opening for the lungs, blockage or obstruction indicates the lungs are or will become weak.

The tip of the nose, if firm, is a general indication of good health. If weak and soft, this person's general health is weak.

The personal characteristic of a person with a large or long nose is that of independence, financial motivation, and prosperity. The small-nosed person lacks self-confidence and is more easily confused or dependent.

The tip of the nose reflects the condition of the gallbladder and digestion. If this area is lacking firmness or strength, the gallbladder is weak.

The flanges over the nostrils can indicate the condition of the kidneys. The tip of the nose and the nostrils should be even in size. If the tip is larger, the kidneys are weak. The right nostril reflects the right kidney and the left nostril the left kidney.

The overall colour of the nose can show an illness that is just beginning to form in a particular organ. The colour code given previously applies to the nose—that is, whitish colour indicates the lungs; red, the heart; yellow, the spleen-pancreas; green or blue, the liver; and darkness, the kidneys.

If the tip of the nose always has a little drop of perspiration on it, the person is mentally depressed and possibly retarded.

THE MOUTH

The mouth generally reflects the spleen-pancreas and the brain. The characteristics of the brain are shown by the way the mouth is formed. A beautiful mouth will speak beautiful, kind words, and an ugly mouth will emit ugly words.

The natural shape of the mouth when it is closed reflects the mental condition. An upturned, smiling mouth shows a brain that is well balanced. A down-turned, sad mouth shows imbalance— hate and envy . A puckered mouth is a sign of a liver imbalance and also of hatred, jealousy, and isolation. (This person may also be very spoiled).

If the upper lip is thicker in the middle, this person is self-centered and nervous, indicating a liver problem or imbalance. If the upper lip is larger than the lower lip, there is a nervous condition, a liver disturbance, and/or menstrual problem (such as excessive bleeding).

If the lips are large and strong, so are the sexual organs, glands and ability. If the lips are thin and weak, so are the sexual organs and ability. If the color of the lips is abnormally dark, sexual depletion is indicated. If the lips are blue, there are internal toxins; if pale, there is a lack of blood, quality and quantity. If the lips or the surrounding areas are yellow, the person has indigestion. If they are very red, the person has a high sex drive and possibly sexual depletion.

Cracked tissue on the inside of the lips indicates a digestive disturbance ; on the outside , a nervous disorder. Cracked tissue at the corners of the mouth indicates food poisoning.

A very deep cleft just under the bottom lip indicates the possibility of addiction either to alcohol or drugs. This weakness could be inherited. The desire for alcohol or drugs can stem from excessive consumption of either one or both of the parents at the time of conception.

A cleft in the chin is said to be a sign of self-centeredness and secretiveness.

THE EARS

The shape of the ears tells us about a person's heritage because, when in the womb, the mother's thoughts and health directly affect the formation of the child. This includes the first organ to form, the kidneys, whose facial counterpart is the ears. The ears are the same shape and size as the kidneys.

If the ears are very meaty—that is, not dry or bony—this means the father and the mother of the child at the time of conception and during pregnancy were very clean, healthy, and well balanced.

If the ears are abnormally misshapen, the inheritance is very negative.

The ears also indicate the state of the nerves and the brain.

The ears should be placed relatively high—with the top level with the eyebrows. If placed too high, the person is very sensitive, possibly allergic. If very low, the gallbladder is small or weak (also, the person is very detail-oriented).

If the ear is dry and shriveled, the kidney function is very low. If the ear is thinly structured, the person is nervous, fearful, and shortlived. The mental function related to the kidneys is the

196

will, a lack of which causes fear. Large ears indicate self-confidence, and small ears show a tendency to be mentally depressed. Ears that are pointed indicate mischievous or worried nature and a tendency to get cancer (particularly cancer of the prostate in men, and cancer of the breasts or uterus in women).

The ears change in size, shape and color as the kidneys change. If the kidneys shrink, the ears will shrink also and become dry. Removal of a kidney can also bring on deafness.

The life span can be determined by the ear lobes: if they are very meaty and thick between the ages of one and five , the person will live a long life. If the lobes are small or non-existent, the person is not likely to live past seventy years of age.

EYEBROWS

Humans are the only creatures who have eyebrows. The eyebrows relate to the liver, gallbladder,and nervous system. Generally, if they are very short and sparse, they show that the person's constitution is weak . If the hairs are long, clean, and glossy , the constitution is strong. If the brows are dry and messy, general weakness is indicated.

High placed eyebrows show a tendency toward spiritual interests, kindness, and morality. Low placed brows show more practicality and materialism. If the hair of the eyebrows grows upward, the energy level is high, and if it falls downward, a deficiency of energy is shown. If it actually grows downward it shows depressive tendencies.

If the hair is very thin and sparse in the eyebrows, the person thinks a lot and may be depleting the liver. This person likes to scheme and play games and tricks.

The space between the eyebrows should be wide. This is a healthy state and shows intuition and intelligence. If the brows connect, the person will not be healthy and may also be very emotional, ill-tempered, and rushed. They could possibly develop high blood pressure and/or heart disease, culminating in heart attacks.

A mole inside the eyebrow near the nose indicates a liver problem.

A large and thick eyebrow is considered to indicate the male characteristics; a thin, weak brow , female characteristics . A man with thin eyebrows will have more feminine qualities—he may be an artist, and a woman with thick eyebrows will exhibit more masculine tendencies, such as a strong drive toward independence.

Very thick eyebrows also show great ambition which can lead to physical problems due to stress and competitive pressure.

197

If the brows appear thin and weak the person is nervous and thinks too much.

There are many more indications given by the face. Every mole, scar, discoloration or mark indicates something, depending on its position on the face. Please refer to Chapter 7.

F
TONGUE READING

The tongue can give very clear indications of the state of the health and should be considered along with facial, abdominal and pulse readings. There are basically two considerations relating to the tongue. One is the coating and the other is the quality. The coating on the tongue should be even, a little white and thin. A very thick white tongue coating is evidence of internal "coldness," or low energy in the organs. The associated pulse will be sinking and slow, indicating that the organs do not have enough energy to function properly.

If the tongue's coating is yellowish, either thick or not, there is internal inflammation, congestion and excessive energy or function.

If the tongue appears to be oily or dirty, there is a great deal of mucus present—a possible sign of water retention. There could be a condition of inflammation. This indicates dis-eases in the developing stages. An example might be water and inflammation in and around the lungs which could eventually cause pleuritis.

A white coating on the tongue indicates a chronic condition which may not show noticeable progression. If oily and white, the water in the body is blocked and becoming poisonous. A very white tongue coating indicates germ growth, which is secondary to the condition of low internal function. Allergies, extreme tiredness and excessive talking are also factors which can cause the tongue to turn white.

Black or very dark coating of the tongue is a sign of extreme degeneration—corruption of the internal organs. This person is close to death because the illness has reached the last or most yin stage.

If the back part of the tongue appears black and the front part yellow, serious corruption is taking place somewhere in the body. With pulse and/or abdominal reading, the exact location may be determined. If there are dark lines on the tongue with white or yellow spaces in between, there is internal poisoning from medication or internal corruption.

Purple coloring on the tongue in the form of lines, spots, circles or overall colour is a sign of blood clotting.

Red spots or pimple-like bumps on the tongue indicate air dis-

198

ease. The more spots there are, the worse the condition is. The internal pressure is imbalanced and there is probably inflammation.

If the center area of the tongue is red and the rest is white or yellow, there is corruption in the digestive system.

An entirely red tongue indicates not only inflammation and very high temperatures, but also depletion in the organs, which is unusual. This is a "false" inflammation—as the energy is extremely low. In this condition the activity has no root, just like a flower in a vase of—it will live for a while as if it were still in the ground, but it will soon die.

The tongue should be flexible, soft, moist, muscular, and long. These are the indications of good health.

If the tongue is pale, not pink or white but lacking color, there is a lack of blood, a shortage of energy, and general weakness. The mental condition also is very fuzzy: disorientation may occur, along with lack of intuition, and blank-mindedness.

A condition of dryness of the tongue indicates inflammation and disrupted functioning of the organs and also dryness and lack of secretions in the glands.

A stiff tongue that impedes the speech indicates tension within the body, stiffness of the organs, and/or nerve damage. A broken speech pattern such as stuttering indicates a nervous condition. The expression "tongue-tied" refers to a condition of extreme nervousness. Paralysis of the tongue also indicates nerve degeneration.

Some dentists recommend brushing the tongue, but this should not be necessary. If the tongue is healthy and strong, it will be clean.

G
PULSE READING

Pulse reading is the principal means of evaluation in the practice of the Forgotten Food Diet. It is the most thorough, all-encompassing technique yet established. It is also a vital link between Taoist Etiology and Herbology. The cultivator who has mastered this technique has the capability of sensing even the most subtle fluctuations of energy within the organs, bowels, meridians, and all other body systems. No mechanism has this ability; there is as yet no machine which can efficiently monitor the complete functioning of an organism in this or any other way. Pulse reading works because it enables the cultivator to gauge the energy level and the physical condition, hence the functioning of the entire body. The human body is a "lightning rod" for universal energy, and the successful cultivator is one who is able to call on this ability at will to sense these variances within others.

There are four places in the body where the pulse may be examined: the throat, wrist, ankles, and groin. The wrist is exceptional because six meridians travel through the wrist area and fifteen conjunctive channels or "lomo" run laterally through the area.

The pulse consists of six pulse locations: three on each wrist, each of which is related to a particular organ, bowel and body system. Each of the six pulses is subdivided into floating external and sinking internal pulses. The floating or yang pulse reflects the condition of the bowels, and the sinking, or yin, pulse give indication of the state of the organ systems.

The pulses will also indicate an impeded energy flow along any of the 12 main meridians in that a dysfunction of an organ or bowel correlates to the energy flow along its respective meridian. Light pressure is used to detect the surface pulses; strong pressure is used to detect the deep pulses.

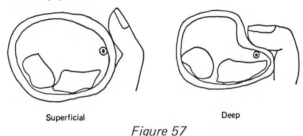

Superficial   Deep

Figure 57

A cultivator who after years of experience develops an expertise in reading the pulse deserves the utmost respect. A proficiency in pulse reading not only enables the cultivator to determine the most minute energy imbalance within the body at the time of the evaluation, but also supplies him with knowledge of disease suffered in the past. *He can therefore predict conditions which can be expected in the future, for they will be the outcome of the present conditions of the body which are the outcome of the past.*

Reading the pulses is still the most sensitive evaluation procedure in the world today. The series of clinical and laboratory tests administered to determine the cause or causes of pathological conditions can often yield no tangible results because they lack the sensitivity. Often a patient is obviously ill, but it may be impossible to determine the cause of his distress by modern medical procedures. In such cases reading the pulses is invaluable for it presents the entelechy of disease rather than the disease itself. The pulse sensitivity shows pre-clinical signs of imbalance, and it may be years before these imbalances are seen as an overt disease.

200

Following are the locations of the pulses on the wrists, and the organs and bowels they reflect:

Left Wrist (Yang)		Right Wrist (Yin)	
small intestine	heart	lungs	large intestine
gallbladder	liver	spleen-pancreas	stomach
bladder	kidneys	heart constrictor	triple heater

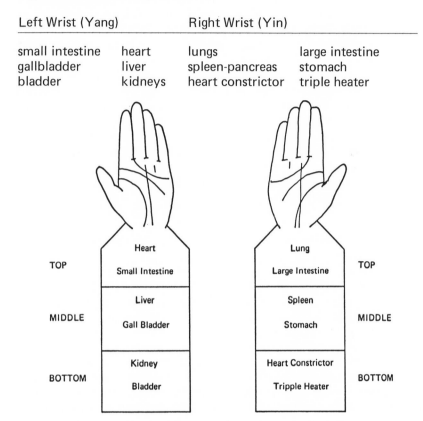

Figure 58

There are 27 pulse indications as expounded in *Chang Chung-Ching* (B.C. 180), but eight will usually suffice for the ordinary evaluation. The eight indications are fast, slow, vast, weak, slippery, astringent, tight but thin, tardy (irregular, often skipping a beat).

To determine the exact position of the puses, first locate the middle (or *kuan*) pulse which is at the level of the styloid protuberance, and place the third finger on it. Second, locate the top (or *tsun*) pulse which lies between the fold of the wrist and the styloid protuberance. Third, locate the bottom (or *ch'ih*) pulse beneath the kuan. The distance between the middle and the top pulse is equal to the distance between the middle and the bottom pulse.

201

An expertise of pulse reading is acquired only through practice of the techniques and may not be developed solely through book learning. To begin the pulse reading, the cultivator must maintain an even breathing pattern and be comfortable and calm. Of course, the ideal time is early in the morning when the mind is rested and clear and the senses acute. At any time, inner calm is essential to a good reading.

The first step in pulse reading is to check for either internal or external causes of the individual's condition. This is felt at a special location just above the middle location of each wrist. This location on the left wrist (*yen yin*), records external causes and, on the right wrist (*chih ko*), shows internal causes. The way this pulse is felt is by first placing the finger on the middle location and then rolling the finger about one eighth of an inch toward the person's hand. If a pulse is felt on the left wrist, the individual's problems are caused by external causes. If no pulse is felt here, or if the pulse disappears, there are no external causes. Likewise, if a pulse is felt at this special location on the right wrist, the person suffers from internal causes; and if no pulse is felt, or if the pulse disappears, there are no internal causes.

Once it is determined whether the individual's maladies are from either external or internal causes, the next step is to feel each of the six locations on both wrists, one at a time, beginning always with the middle (*kuan*) location of the right wrist which is the stomach and spleen-pancreas location. This pulse is felt first because the stomach gives the body life by processing the life-giving nutrients. If the digestion is good, the individual's condition can be helped, because the body can produce new cells from the nutrients supplied. If food cannot be digested, it is very difficult to effect a healing change in the body. If this pulse does not appear at all, the person is dying, and if it is weak, the healing process for that person will be slow. If the pulse is present and strong, healing will be fast and relatively easy, because the body will be able to heal itself.

Each pulse location is felt in three ways. First, the very superficial floating pulse, or yang pulse, is felt for by resting the finger lightly on the surface of the skin. Next, firm pressure is exerted to feel for the sinking, or yin pulse. Third, the fingers apply a degree of pressure that falls between light and firm pressure. The pulse felt is called middle pulse and it is used to gauge the resistance of the pulse. Lack of resistance indicates a lack of function and strong resistance indicates aggravation. If there is a floating pulse, the condition is superficial and mild. If there is no floating pulse, the condition is deep and serious. If there is neither a floating nor a sinking pulse, that organ/bowel group is either not all there or the

202

condition is extremely severe. There is a complete cessation of function.

In feeling for the quality of the pulse, there are a few considerations:

1. Timing. The timing of a pulse may be either fast or slow. This is measured by the timing of one breath—inhale and exhale—of the reader. A fast pulse is six or more beats per breath. A slow pulse is three or less beats per breath.

2. Area. The area is the space that the pulse occupies on the fingertip of the reader. A vast pulse covers a very large area of the fingertip but does not necessarily have strength. A small pulse feels like the tip of a nail and it may be either weak or strong.

3. Strength. The pulse may be either forceful or weak. A tight pulse beats very hard—it comes and goes with much force. The weak pulse may also be soft or small, but it lacks strength and resistance.

4. Depth. This quality is felt by pressing firmly. A collapsed pulse, also called hidden pulse, is not felt at all. No matter how hard one presses, one will be able to distinguish neither a floating nor a sinking pulse. A firm pulse is felt only when one presses with much pressure. The "onion" pulse is felt only at the floating and sinking levels. Nothing is felt in the middle.

5. Texture. A pulse has four textures: slippery, astringent, scattered and soft. A slippery pulse is likened unto pearls in a bowl of water. It feels round, small, mobile and fast. The astringent pulse feels "hairy," like the surface of velvet. The scattered pulse escapes the touch under pressure. The soft pulse is slow and rounded like a cottonball.

6. Resistance. This defines the degree of flexibility of the pulse when pressure is exerted on it. The "string" pulse feels like a tightly drawn violin string. It does not escape the touch. The "leather" pulse feels flat and somewhat strong, like the surface of a drum. The "marsh" pulse is small at the level just below the surface, where the floating pulse is felt, and round and soft at the level just above the area where the middle pulse is felt. And the "bog" pulse is small at the level just below the floating pulse and soft and round at the level of the middle pulse.

The five extraordinary pulses are found infrequently: skipping pulse, catching pulse, "bean" pulse, long pulse and short pulse. The skipping pulse is very irregular because it skips beats. It indicates palpitation or fibrillation, which are caused by nerves or clogged arteries. The catching pulse darts in and out and feels like a claw or hook. The bean pulse is round and hard. The long pulse is one continuous pulse because it is not separated into three locations.

The short pulse is felt at only one location; either the floating or sinking pulse is felt, but not both. The short pulse indicates either a complete lack of function or an absence of the related organ.

There are also nine death pulses. A cultivator must learn to distinguish a dying person from those who can be saved. If a person is dying, no efforts on the part of the cultivator can delay death. Following are the nine death pulses:

1. Strokes. If the pulse is vast, fast or tight, a great deal of damage has been done.

2. Bad colds, pneumonia, or infection accompanied by high fever. If the pulse is sinking, weak, small or astringent, the illness has reached the final stage.

3. Ulcers and tumors. If the pulse is skipping, the illnesses have reached the final stage.

4. Chronic diarrhea. If the pulse is firm, vast, floating, and fast, this is a very bad sign, but death may not be imminent.

5. Vomiting or nausea. If a pulse is tight, astringent or stringy, death is imminent.

6. Chronic coughing. Sinking, collapsed pulse indicates imminent death.

7. Asthma attack. Sinking and astringent pulses indicate an irreversible condition.

8. Internal bleeding or hemorrhage. A vast or fast pulse indicates death.

9. Death. A person who is dying has a pulse that is comparable to a fish swimming in water. This indicates that the spirit is leaving.

There are some general death pulses related to the various organ locations: a catching pulse at the heart location; a very hard and tight string pulse at the liver location; a pecking or dripping pulse at the spleen-pancreas location; a wispy pulse at the lung location; or a thumping pulse at the kidney location. These are all clear indications of impending death.

Another death pulse concerns the blood. An empty or onion pulse that is floating and not sinking indicates loss of blood, lack of blood (anemia), separated blood, blood clotting or menstrual problems. If the pulse occurs at all locations, blood dis-ease is indicated. If the pulse occurs at only one location, a hemorrhaging organ is indicated.

Moreover, any pulse that is contradictory to the condition of the individual indicates death. For example, when a person is extremely weak, or barely functioning, while the pulse beats strongly, death is imminent.

Pulse reading is also an important technique for locating the stores of mucous within the body. Lung mucous is indicated by a slippery pulse at the lung location. Spleen-pancreas mucous is indicated by a string pulse at the corresponding location. Liver mucous is indicated by a string pulse at the liver location. Heart mucous is indicated by vast and slippery pulses at the heart location. And kidney mucous is indicated by sinking and slippery pulses at the kidney location.

It is also possible to determine the age and sex of a child during pregnancy with the use of pulse reading. If the pulse at the bottom location has more strength than all others, conception has taken place. If the bottom pulse is slippery and fast (not scattered, but firm), the fetus is three months old. If the bottom pulse is slippery and scattered, the child is five months old. If the bottom location of the left wrist exhibits a pulse that is stronger than that on the right wrist, the baby is a boy. If the pulse at the bottom location of the right wrist is stronger than that on the left, the baby is a girl.

V

Herbal Combinations

When a cultivator has mastered Herbology, Taoist Etiology, and Health Assessment Condition Determination, he or she will be able to apply herbal combinations to help correct conditions.

About 1,000 years ago, during the Sung Dynasty, the Chinese government collected the most frequently used combinations for studies. After a thorough examination, the government found the combinations to be completely non-toxic and published approximately 2,000 combinations for public use. These combinations can correct abnormal conditions when they exist and strengthen the body when abnormal conditions do not exist. Forty-four main combinations will be given at the end of this section.

For thousands of years, Taoists have processed and prepared five types of herbal combinations: Tan, Kao, Wan, Shan and Jiu. The preparation of Tan involves highly technical alchemy. Considerable amounts of time — even entire lifetimes — were spent in preparing the Tan, because herbs for these must be collected when their potency peaks and must be processed by complicated alchemical processes. Every herb has a "peak profile," that is, their potency peaks only during specific seasons, dates and times. The alchemical processing of herbs involves specific months, dates and times and the appropriate orientation of the sun, moon, North Star, planets and stars. This kind of work is most delicate and highly complex. A tremendous amount of knowledge and wisdom is required for such work. The resulting Tan is the most effective of all forms of herbal combinations because it helps human beings immortalize their physical bodies.

The preparation of Kao involves only a simple extraction of the herbal combination. The resulting Kao is a liquid with a honey-like consistency. Certain herbal combinations can be made into a Wan, or tablet. Certain other herbal combinations may be made into powders, or Shan. Jiu is a preparation of certain herbal combinations in wine. The latter four forms are easier to prepare than Tan, and they are also less effective.

Sometimes all five forms of herbal combinations are substituted by another form, tea. Tea is used by most people because it is the easiest way to prepare herbs. Also the preparation of tea does not require a great deal of work or knowledge. That is why tea is rather ineffective in correcting abnormal conditions.

In the last twenty years, modern techniques have been implemented for the processing and preparation of herbs. When the herbal combinations are extracted and freeze-dried, powders and granules are produced. Powders and granules are convenient to take and are much more effective than herbal tea preparations.

Since herbal combinations do have certain healing value, some Japanese, German and Chinese research workers and medical doctors spend a tremendous amount of effort in studying and testing these combinations, using different methods. They have found very positive results and they have compiled lists of diseases that would be corrected by the herbal combinations. (Please refer to the list of herbal combinations under *Commentaries.)*

Although some practitioners of western medicine believe that herbal combinations are effective against diseases, their approach to treatment differs absolutely from the approach used by Taoists. Doctors mainly diagnose a disease, give a prescription and then concentrate on treating the area where symptoms occur. But Taoists believe that Forgotten Food Diet is a *diet* for daily living in order to balance and strengthen the entire body. The cultivator of Taoism may suggest an herbal combination that is completely different in meaning and approach from medical practice. For instance, he or she may study the energy imbalances detected on the pulse to choose a corrective combination.

Taoism has developed methods, including the Forgotten Food Diet, to strengthen the physical, mental and spiritual parts of an individual. In order to do that, they had to figure out the interrelationships between these three parts, as shown on the following table. They also incorporated the interactions of the Five Element

206

Theory (discussed in Chapter 2) to describe the dynamics of one's total condition.

Since the physical, mental and spiritual parts of an individual are all interconnected, there is no need for the psychiatric approach in Taoism. For instance, a mental condition or a nervous breakdown can be helped by strengthening the "wood" element at the physiological level, i.e., the liver and nervous system. (Refer to the line of the "wood" element in the Table 13 .) The person will then clarify his thinking process and appease his anger as well as strengthen the gall bladder and eyes. All of these physical and mental characteristics are listed on the line of the "wood" element in the table. (Alcoholics have confused thoughts and short tempers, while people with a strong liver possess clear thinking and a peaceful disposition.)

Clear thinking is necessary to trigger reliable intuition. According to the Five Element Theory, "wood" generates "fire." In other words, the thinking or thought process arouses the intuition. (Refer to the mental and spiritual parts of the "wood" and "fire" lines, respectively.) The healthier the heart, the clearer the intuitive response, as both are categorized on the same "fire" line.

Intuition represents our divine connection. In order to "walk with God," one has to follow the guidance of intuition or conscience in his or her daily life; this is also the purpose of Taoism. The Forfotten Food Diet helps us do that by strengthening our liver or heart, or any other imbalance which would affect the heart. From the Five Element Theory, it is easy to understand how another internal organ imbalance or abnormality will eventually cloud our intuition and conscience, if it will impair our heart's function. The previous liver and heart examples are only illustrations of causes for abnormality in our spiritual evolution. In Taoism, healing must be total in order to elevate the Cultivator to a greater spiritual evolution.

Careful Taoist research over the centuries has discarded any method with side-effects, as these cannot serve the same spiritual purpose. The consideration of side-effects as the least evil of two alternatives can only have a medical justification. From the Taoist viewpoint, the correction of one function at the expense of another does not reestablish the balance within the Five Elements, which is necessary to arouse our spiritual connection, including intuition and conscience. The scope and purpose of Taoist healing is consequently totally different from those of medical science.

The world's main religions also seek total healing like Taoism. But, their scriptures are not so complete in describing the practical methods to do that. The purpose of all the chapters of this book is to reveal these practical Taoist methods.

One should read carefully the examples following this table to appreciate these very valuable revelations.

Table 13

Element	Physical Part				Mental Part (exagerated by imbalances)		Spiritual Part
	Organ	Bowel	Superficial	Opening	Emotion	Trait	
Earth	Spleen-Pancreas	Stomach	Muscles	Mouth	Worry	Pondering	N/A
Metal	Lung	Large Intestine	Skin	Nose	Sadness	Sensitivity	N/A
Water	Kidney	Bladder	Bone	Ears	Fear	Willpower	N/A
Wood	Liver	Gall Bladder	Nerves	Eyes	Anger	Thinking	N/A
Fire	Heart, Sex Glands	Small Intestine	Blood Vessels	Tongue	Excitement	N/A	Spirit (Intuition, spiritual communication, conscience)

In the following examples of herbal combinations the reader must realize that when I list a few western pathological terms under *Commentaries,* it does not mean that I am prescribing herbal medicine for diseases, but that I am providing clear references to further the comprehension of the reader. This information under *Commentaries* was collected from the works of the famous and respected professor and physician, Kesitsu Otsuka, M.D., and other workers. For example:

WD-301: REGENERATION TEA

Profile:

Herb	Meridian	Characteristic	Taste
Rehmannia	Heart, Liver, Kidney	Cold	Sweet
Corus	Liver, Kidney	Warm	Acid
Dioscorea	Heart, Spleen-pancreas, Kidney	Neutral	Sweet
Alisma	Kidney, Bladder	Cold	Sweet
Poria	Heart, Lung, Spleen-pancreas Kidney	Neutral	Sweet
Peony (tree)	Heart, Liver, kidney	Cold	Bitter, piquant
Cinnamon	Lung, Heart, Bladder	Hot	Sweet, piquant
Aconite	Heart, Kidney, Spleen-pancreas	Hot	Sweet, piquant

Combination's Energy Level	Combination's Taste
Neutral	65% Sweet 30% Salty 5% Piquant

Commentaries:

This combination showed good results for adjusting blood sugar

208

level, regenerating the pancreas, kidney and bladder problems, stopping hemorrhage, resolving sexual and blood pressure problems.

1. Diabetes—builds up pancreas over a long period of time.
2. Sexual disorder, including impotence, testicle infection and premature ejaculation; builds up and cleans prostate gland.
3. Kidney and bladder infections; kidney stones.
4. Cataract, glaucoma.
5. Ringing ears.
6. Gout.
7. High blood pressure.
8. Water retention.
9. Stomach infections; helps digestion.
10. Can rebuild weak kidneys (Dialysis case: GT701 in conjunction).
11. Good against infections, including TB in the kidneys.
12. Pains in legs, swollen legs.
13. Helps regulate blood sugar.
14. Stops internal or external hemorrage.

Note: Can be used as a general tonic because it is rich in nutritive value. Stops bleeding in an emergency. Especially good for prostate problems.

Main Meridians: Rather balanced, but sedates the heart mainly and energizes the stomach, lung and kidney.

Nutritional Value and Effective Properties:
Iron, calcium, potassium, sodium, natrium, cerium, phosphorus, sugar, cellulose, glucose, ash, fructose, protein, starch, egg lipids, Mannite, Rehmanin, Tannic Acid, Resina, Tartaric Acid, Kuun, Bilinenrine, Argininin, Pachymos, Peonol ($C_9H_{10}O_3$), Benzoic Acid, Cinnamicaldehyde, Camphene, Cineol, Linalool, Enjenol, Aconite, Mesaconitine, Hypaconitine, and Jesconitine.

This herbal combination, used in the East today for the treatment of diabetes, was created 2,500 years ago when it was produced for Emperor Han Wu-Ti who contracted the disease. Diabetes was officially recorded in Chinese medical history in the seventh century approximately 1,000 years before its official discovery in the West.

The Japanese doctors have had magnificent results by using this formula to treat the disease of senile cataract. For example, in 1957, Sigenari Ogura, M.D., started to treat patients for senile cataracts with this formula. He compiled a report on 41 cases. Among the 82 separate eyes treated, the visual power of 68 (83%) improved. Eight (10%) remained unchanged and 6 (7%) decreased. Ken Fujihira, M.D., reported the complete data of 285 senile cataract cases treated with this formula at his clinic between January 1 and December 31, 1975. His results showed that 172 (60%) improved, 34 (12%) were unchanged, 29 (10%) were unstable (the vision in one eye improved and the vision in the other worsened), and 50 (18%) worsened.

Note: A non-Taoist who wishes to use herbal combinations should consult his physician first for his/her own protection.

The following instructions are to help you read the following herbal combinations easily and correctly:

1. Energy Level of the Combinations. Most combinations fall within the cool to warm range, as they are rather balanced energy-wise. These are the grades in energy levels:

Cold	Cool			Neutral			Warm	Hot
●	●			●			●	●

	Near Cool	Middle Cool	Low Cool		Low Warm	Middle Warm	Near Warm	
	●	●	●		●	●	●	

2. Taste Reminder:
        Sweet affects SP
        Piquant affects L
        Sour affects LV
        Salty affects K
        Bitter affects H

3. Abbreviations of Meridians:
        LV = Liver
        GB = Gallbladder
        H   = Heart
        HC = Heart Constrictor
        SI   = Small Intestine
        TH = Triple Heater
        SP = Spleen-Pancreas
        S   = Stomach
        L   = Lungs
        LI   = Large Intestine
        K   = Kidney
        B   = Bladder

4. Correlation to Dis-eases and Code Names:
        AD = Air Dis-ease
        BD = Blood Dis-ease
        WD = Water Dis-ease

BP = Blood Poison
WP = Water Poison
FP = Food Poison
GT = General Tonic

An herbal combination may be called AD-101, BD-204, etc.

5. Commentaries:

These are references to Western pathological terms derived from experiments by many contemporary specialists with these herbal combinations. As the reader will see, each herbal combination has been associated with benefits for a series of symptoms which may be totally unrelated to each other by medical science. This illustrates the Taoist emphasis on promoting the body's ability to repair itself and prevent or correct an abnormal state rather than focusing on symptoms and diseases.

Each combination has its own "profile": taste, distribution, energy level, meridians, combined attitudes, etc., and should be matched to one's nutritional needs as determined by pulse reading and the other Taoist techniques discussed before. This is the way for the Taoist cultivator to strengthen his physical, mental and spiritual body. However, the reader may be more familiar with the medical pathology and the provided commentaries are intended to further his or her comprehension of the scope of each combination. As a matter of fact, the listed commentaries represent symptoms or diseases eventually associated with a certain abnormal state of the body's function.

HERBAL COMBINATION LIST
(used in freeze-dried form)

AD-101 — TRAVEL COMBINATION

Ingredients: Pueraria, Ephedra, Jujube, Cinnamon, Paeonia, Licorice, Ginger, Citrus
Combination's Energy Level: Middle Warm
Combination's Taste: 50% Sweet, 25% Bitter, 15% Piquant, 10% Sour
Main Meridians: Primarily: L,H and B; Secondarily: LV and K
Commentaries:
1. Adjusting to changing weather, food, water.
2. Common cold, flu (first stage—2 to 3 days—opens up tissues to expel trapped air).
3. Mild infections; bronchitis; small pox; chicken pox; tonsilitis; scarlet fever; inflammation of ears, nose, mouth, throat, thyroid, lymphatic system and brain.

4. Nerve tension; headache; toothache; stiff neck; acute polio; arthritis; rheumatism; shoulder pain.
5. Allergy; boils; sinus and gum infections.
6. Menstrual difficulties with water retention; dropped uterus.
7. Eye inflammation and glaucoma.
8. First stage of stomach ulcer, indigestion. Adjusting stomach acid. Gastroenteritis.
9. Children's problems including stomach ache, lack of appetite, headache. Bed wetting.
10. Alcohol hangover.
11. Dysfunction of thyroid gland.

Note: May increase occurrence of skin problems such as psoriasis and acne as it expels poisons.

AD-102 — RESISTANT COMBINATION
*(also called "Five Accumulations" or
"General Ailment" combination)*

Ingredients: Poria, Atractylodes, Citrus, Pinellia, Tang Kuei, Black atractylodes, Paeonia, Magnolia bark, Angelica Dahurica, Citrus Kotakan, Platycodon, Ginger, Cyperus, Cinnamon, Ephedra, Jujube, Licorice, Gardenia

Combination's Energy Level: Near Warm

Combination's Taste: 40% Piquant, 30% Bitter, 25% Sweet, 5% Sour

Main Meridians: Primarily: L,H; Secondarily: S,LV,K

Commentaries: Blood, water, air and food poisons. Pain, chronic colds, flu, migraine. Building and cleansing of the blood. Strengthening of energy and resistance.
1. Female problems—discharge, cramps, irregular periods, anemia, yeast infections, lack of sex drive or orgasm, difficult labor.
2. Pain: rheumatism, backache, rheumatoid arthritis, lumbago; headache (migraine); bursitis; sciatic nerve pain.
3. Esophagus infections; acid stomach; hiatal hernia; stomach or intestinal ulcers; increasing food absorption.
4. Long, drawn-out colds.
5. Sinus and food allergy.
6. Circulatory problems: poor circulation, acute fibrillation, skipped heart beats, cold hands and feet, trembling of hands and feet, numbness, weakness.
7. Water retention, mucous; acute diarrhea.
8. Cysts or tumors (especially in the liver).
9. Blood building; blood pressure regulating; low energy, anemia.

212

10. Acne and other skin problems.
11. Increased resistance and prevention of epidemic diseases, especially with older people.

AD-109 — BREATHING COMBINATION

Ingredients: Pinellia, Ephedra, Paeonia, Licorice, Cinnamon, Asarum, Ginger, Schizandre, Astragalus
Combination's Energy Level: Warm
Combination's Taste: 45% Piquant, 20% Bitter, 20% Sweet, 10% Sour, 5% Salty
Main Meridians: Primarily: L, then H and SP; Secondarily: S,K and B
Commentaries:
1. Acute cold concentrated on chest. Sinus allergy.
2. Pneumonia; chronic coughing, excessive saliva, drooling.
3. Asthma and asthma attack.
4. Emphysema; pleurisy; pain in the rib cage.
5. Swelling-type arthritis.
6. Asthma/emphysema combined with water retention.

BD-201 — REGULATING COMBINATION

Ingredients: Rhubarb, Scutellaria, Coptis
Combination's Energy Level: Cool
Combination's Taste: 65% Bitter, 17.5% Piquant, 17.5% Sweet
Main Meridians: HC, SP, S, LV, LI, SI (evenly)
Commentaries:
1. Reduction of inflammation. Natural antibiotic.
2. Severe burns.
3. Severe constipation.
4. High blood pressure; adjusting of blood pressure; reduction of LDL cholesterol and hardening of arteries.
5. Acute high fever.
6. Madness (even severe like schizophrenic, psychopathic); nervous breakdown; epilepsy; tinnitus; sleepwalking.
7. Stopping of blood hemmorhage internally and externally.
8. Infections in mouth, gums, teeth, nose (red nose), ears, throat.
9. Shingles; skin rashes; herpes (acute).
10. Acute polio; muteness from birth.
11. Poison from alcohol, drugs, chemicals, including overdose of sleeping pills.

12. Acute dizziness, lightheadedness, hot flashes.
13. Palpitation.
14. Hallucinations.
15. Acute bleeding from stroke.

Note: In ancient times this combination was used for strong-type person with no diarrhea tendency.

BD-202 — HEMORRHOID COMBINATION

Ingredients: Tang Kuei, Bupleurum, Scutellaria, Licorice, Cimicifuga, Rhubarb
Combination's Energy Level: Low Cool
Combination's Taste: 35% Bitter, 35% Sweet, 30% Piquant
Main Meridians: Sedates TH, L and GB; energizes H
Commentaries:
1. Internal and external hemorrhoids.
2. Rectal bleeding.
3. Rectal ulcers.
4. Boils in the anus.
5. External use to wash the rectal area. Benefits are enhanced by cleaning the inside of the rectum with water after each bowel movement and applying Royal Jade Cream thereafter in conjunction with internal intake of this combination.

BD-203 — REPRODUCTIVE TONIC COMBINATION

Ingredients: Tang Kuei, Cnidium, Paeonia, Poria, Atractylodes, Alisma, Sargentia
Combination's Energy Level: Neutral
Combination's Taste: 45% Sweet, 15% Piquant, 15% Sour, 15% Bitter, 10% Salty
Main Meridians: H and SP
Commentaries:
1. Easing of pregnancy and related problems: morning sickness, miscarriage, labor pains, production and quality of mother's milk. Rich nutritional value for the mother and baby during pregnancy, labor/delivery and breast feeding.
2. Female nutritional problems; anemia.
3. Dizziness, headache, heavy-headedness; shoulder pain; lower back pain; weak knees and/or legs; tinnitus.
4. Menstrual problems: cramps, irregular flow, pre-menstrual syndrome.

5. Rebuilding of damaged tissues of uterus after abortion, miscarriage, etc.
6. Depression, nervousness due to hormone imbalance.
7. Acne stemming from a hormonal problem.
8. Increase of blood circulation and immunity.
9. Lubrication of joints.
10. Adjusting of blood pressure (high or low).
11. Female hormonal imbalance.
12. Tipped or poorly positioned uterus.
13. Bladder, urethra infections; yeast infections; kidney infections.
14. Infertility.
15. Chronic infections (men and women).
16. Tense shoulders and neck in young women.
17. Cold hands and feet in young women.
18. Endrometriosis.

BD-204 – COMFORT COMBINATION

Ingredients: TangKuei, Paeonia, Atractylodes, Poria, Bupleurum, Ranunculaceae, Gardenia, Artemisia leaf, Licorice, Ginger, Mint
Combination's Energy Level: Low Warm
Combination's Taste: 40% Sweet, 25% Bitter, 20% Piquant, 15% Sour
Main Meridians: SP, LV and H
Commentaries:
1. Menopause discomforts.
2. After hysterectomy, to deal with hormonal imbalance.
3. Phobia.
4. Female hormone adjustment.
5. Menstrual problems (cramps, irregular low, irregular periods).
6. Hot flashes, heart palpitations.
7. Nervousness, anger, depression, fear, insomnia, perspiration.
8. Hypoglycemia; enlarged liver.
9. Pressure in chest.
10. Chronic athlete's foot.
11. Tiredness or restlessness; dizziness.
12. Building of blood and increase of circulation; anemic tendency.
13. Multiple sclerosis.
14. Kidney weakness.
15. Fertility.
16. Lower back pain.
17. Skin problems like cracks in hands and fingers. Dry skin and cold feeling in hands and feet.

18. Hair loss for women.
19. Men's "mid-life" symptoms such as anger, insomnia, stiffness, occasional depression, fibrillation, coughing.

BD-206 — RELAXING COMBINATION

Ingredients: Atractylodes, Poria, Tang Kuei, Morus, Makino, Gambir, Bupleurum, Licorice, Pinellia, Citrus
Combination's Energy Level: Middle Warm
Combination's Taste: 50% Sweet, 45% Piquant, 5% Bitter
Main Meridians: Primarily: SP and H; Secondarily: S, K and L
Commentaries:
1. Hyperactivity, restlessness, excited nerves.
2. Insomnia, tension.
3. Epilepsy.
4. Impotence (nervous type).
5. Nerves; muscular dystrophy.
6. Liver inflammation.
7. Assistance in remission of brain tumor.
8. Children's nightmares, teeth grinding, bedwetting.
9. Nerve spasm.
10. Nervous breakdown with sensation of electricity in the nerves.
11. Arthritis with neurogenic disturbances.

BD-208 — UNLOCK COMBINATION

Ingredients: Poria, Ranunculaceae, Persica, Paeonia, Cinnamon, Honey
Combination's Energy Level: Middle Warm
Combination's Taste: 40% Sweet, 40% Bitter, 10% Sour, 10% Piquant
Main Meridians: L, K, B, LV and H
Note: BD-203 or BD-204 used when triple heater pulse is weak, empty or string. BD-208 is related to fighting or astringent pulse.
Commentaries:
1. Inflammation in female organs; discharge; endometriosis.
2. Blood clots.
3. Blockage in small tubes.
4. Varicose veins. Hemophilia.
5. Infections or swelling in testicles, prostate, bladder, kidney and ovaries.
6. Phlebitis.
7. Skin problems, including acne, shingles, black and blue marks.

8. Slow-type appendicitis; hemorrhoids; swollen rectum.
9. Infertility; inability to conceive due to blockage in sexual tubes (men and women).
10. Reopening of scarred tubes after reversing tubal ligation or vasectomy.
11. Menstrual problems due to blockage.
12. Ovarian cysts.

BD-209 — INFECTION COMBINATION

Ingredients: Paeonia, Cnidium, Rhemannia, Coptis, Scutellaria, Phellodendron, Gardenia, Forsythia, Schizonepeta, Siler, Mentha
Combination's Energy Level: Medium Cool
Combination's Taste: 45% Bitter, 35% Piquant, 20% Sweet, 10% Sour
Main Meridians: H, K
Commentaries:
1. TB infection.
2. Staph infection.

BD-210 — STONE COMBINATION

Ingredients: Bupleurum, Pinellia, Cinnamon, Paeonia, Scutellaria, Chinese Ginseng, Jujube, Licorice, Zingiber
Combination's Energy Level: Low Warm
Combination's Taste: 30% Bitter, 30% Piquant, 30% Sweet, 10% Sour
Main Meridians: Energizes H primarily and L, K and B secondarily. Sedates LV and GB secondarily.
Commentaries:
1. Common cold, flu.
2. Pleurisy.
3. Stomach and intestinal ulcers.
4. Acute hepatitis (pain, fever).
5. Jaundice, malaria.
6. Gallbladder and kidney stones.
7. Pancreatitis.
8. Acute pneumonia.
9. Night sweating.
10. Bed wetting.
11. Epilepsy.
12. Glaucoma.
13. Skin rashes, itching and dry skin.
14. Various abdominal pains.

BD-212 – DISSOLVING COMBINATION

Ingredients: Laminaria, Sargassum, Phellodendron, Anemarrhena, Trichosanthes, Adenophora, Scirpus, Zedoaria, Forsythia, Coptis, Scutellaria, Gardenia, Pueraria, Bupleurum, Tang Kuei, Gentiana, Licorice, Cimicifuga, Ginger
Combination's Energy Level: Cool
Combination's Taste: 55% Bitter, 17.5% Piquant, 17.5% Sweet, 10% Salty
Main Meridians: Primarily: K; Secondarily: L, LI, GB, LV, H and HC
Commentaries:
1. Benign tumors of any kind, including brain tumor.
2. Malignant tumor: enhancement of this combination by GT-701.

Note: Fibroid tumor: clinical tests have shown shrinkage of 1 cm. per month.

BD-213 – CIRCULATION COMBINATION

Ingredients: Tang Kuei, Anemarrhena, Capillaris, Angelica, Polyporus, Alisma, Atractylodes, Siler, Pueraria, Ginseng, Zingiber, Sophora, Cimicifuga
Combination's Energy Level: Low Cool
Combination's Taste: 50% Sweet, 25% Bitter, 20% Piquant, 5% Salty
Main Meridians: Sedates K; Energizes H and L
Commentaries:
1. Arthritis, bursitis.
2. Nerve inflammation.
3. Tennis elbow.
4. Disc problems, including slipped disc.
5. Old injuries: dissolution of blood clots.
6. Pain: sciatic nerve and spinal.
7. Frostbite: in conjunction with Royal Jade Cream.
8. Charley horse and cramps.
9. Bone inflammation.
10. Injuries to joints, ligaments and cartilage.
11. Rheumatoid arthritis.

BD-216 – VITAL COMBINATION

Ingredients: Bupleurum, Pinellia, Zingiber, Scutellaria, Jujube,

218

Chinese Ginseng, Licorice, Rhemannia
Combination's Energy Level: Low Warm
Combination's Taste: 40% Piquant, 35% Bitter, 25% Sweet
Main Meridians: Rather neutral and balanced among many meridians, but sedates LV very much and energizes H, SP and L a little bit. It regulates wood to control earth, which gets rebuilt as does metal.
Commentaries:
1. Diarrhea (chronic).
2. Hypoglycemia.
3. Arteriosclerosis; heart tissue inflammation; angina, cardiac asthma; fibrillation.
4. Infections in stomach, intestines, liver, gallbladder, pancreas; amoebas.
5. Stuttering.
6. Colitis, including bleeding.
7. Bleeding ulcers.
8. Bronchitis, emphysema, pleurisy, pneumonia.
9. Kidney and bladder infections; shrunken kidney.
10. Rashes, skin problems.
11. Eye, nose and ear infections.
12. Nervous breakdown; depression.
13. Indigestion, gas.
14. Improvement of food absorption.
15. Fluctuating blood sugar levels.
Note: In ancient times this combination was used for weak-type or underweight persons.

WD-301 – REGENERATION COMBINATION

Ingredients: Rhemannia, Cornia, Dioscorea, Alisma, Poria, Suffructicosa, Cinnamon, Aconite
Combination's Energy Level: Neutral
Combination's Taste: 65% Sweet, 30% Salty, 5% Piquant
Main Meridians: Rather balanced, but sedates H mainly and also LV; Energizes S, L and K
Commentaries:
1. Diabetes: increase of pancreas function and regulation of blood sugar over a long period of time.
2. Sexual disorder, including impotence, testicle infection and premature ejaculation.
3. Kidney infections, kidney stones.
4. Cataract, glaucoma.

5. Ringing ears.
6. Gout.
7. High blood pressure.
8. Water retention.
9. Stomach infections; indigestion.
10. Revitalization of kidneys. (Enhanced benefits with GT-701 in dialysis cases.)
11. Pain or swelling in legs.
12. Stopping of internal or external hemorrhage.

WD-302 — WATER COMBINATION

Ingredients: Alisma, Polyporus, Poria, Atractylodes, Cinnamon, Gardenia
Combination's Energy Level: Low Warm
Combination's Taste: 50% Sweet, 20% Piquant, 15% Bitter, 15% Salty
Main Meridians: L, K, LV and SP
Commentaries:
1. Water retention. Natural diuretic; Building of kidney function.
2. Acute stomach infections causing diarrhea.
3. Water in stomach—gurgling.
4. Stomach dropsy.
5. Acute bladder or kidney infections.
6. Epilepsy—foaming at the mouth.
7. Water in scrotum.
8. High blood pressure due to water retention.
9. Pain on the face from puffiness.
10. Hernia.
11. Hair loss or premature gray.
12. Night blindness.
13. Sun allergy or severe sunburn.
14. Weak nails.
15. Blisters.
16. Female menstrual problems.
17. Cataract; myopia; discomfort from light or sun glare.
18. Overweight caused by water retention.
19. Hives.
20. Bladder, urinary tract, rectal ulcers.
21. Cellulite prevention.

WD-307 — REDUCING COMBINATION

Ingredients: Bupleurum, Pinellia, Scutellaria, Paeonia, Jujube, Poncirus, Ginger, Rhubarb, Jeffersonia

Combination's Energy Level: Middle Cool

Combination's Taste: 55% Bitter, 25% Piquant, 10% Sour, 10% Sweet

Main Meridians: Primarily: LV; Secondarily: TH, HC, L and LI

Commentaries:

1. Overweight: regulating of appetite and reduction of weight.
2. Revitalization of liver and pancreas.
3. Nervousness; hardened arteries; high blood pressure; reduction of LDL cholesterol.
4. Strep throat.
5. Cardiovascular problems.
6. Bronchitis, emphysema, pleurisy.
7. Hepatitis; pancreatitis; gall stones; hardening of liver.
8. Stuttering.
9. Kidney infections; kidney stones.
10. Disorders of nervous system.
11. Bleeding or infection of eyes, nose, ears and throat; toothache; ringing ears.
12. Female problems.
13. Syphilis; shingles.
14. Hyperactivity, restlessness (including children).
15. Hypo- or hyperglycemia.
16. Aches and pains.
17. Insomnia, headaches from nervous tension.
18. Encephalitis.
19. Cardiac asthma (not other types).
20. Digestive system inflammation: intestines, stomach, liver, gallbladder, chronic bad breath and gas.
21. Obesity.
22. Skin problems, acne.

Note: This combination was used in the ancient times for strong-type overweight people.

BP-401 — CLEANSING (1) COMBINATION

Ingredients: Tang Kuei, Rhemannia, Akebia, Scutellaria, Alisma, Plantago, Gentiana, Gardenia, Nepeta

Combination's Energy Level: Cool

Combination's Taste: 50% Sweet, 30% Piquant, 15% Bitter, 5% Salty

221

Main Meridians: Primarily: LV and GB; Secondarily: SP; L and K; then LI, H and SI slightly.

Commentaries:

1. Genital herpes.
2. Gonorrhea or non-specific urethra infections.
3. Vaginal infections, yeast infections, discharge, including chronic.
4. Bladder infections; uterus infections.
5. Low-grade prostate infections.
6. Infection and discharge in rectum.
7. Various infections in lower part of the abdomen.

BP-402 — CLEANSING (2) COMBINATION

Ingredients: Tang Kuei, Paeonia, Cnidium, Lithospermum, Rhubarb, Cimicifuga, Astragalus, Gigas, Licorice, Lonicera

Combination's Energy Level: Low Cool

Combination's Taste: 30% Sweet, 25% Bitter, 20% Piquant, 15% Salty, 10% Sour

Main Meridians: K and HC

Commentaries:

1. Cancer and lumps in female system (breasts, uterus, etc.).
2. Cancer in lymphatic system.
3. Lupus.
4. Syphilis.
5. Herpes; shingles.
6. AIDS.
7. Body damage from exposure to radiation.

Note: Used for increased protection against veneral disease in ancient times.

BP-404 — DETOXIFYING COMBINATION

Ingredients: Bupleurum, Pinellia, Poria, Cinnamon, Scutellaria, Jujube, Chinese Ginseng, Dragon bone, Gigas, Ginger, Rhubarb

Combination's Energy Level: Low Warm

Combination's Taste: 40% Sweet, 30% Piquant, 25% Bitter, 5% Salty

Main Meridians: Rather neutral and balanced between the meridians, except energizes H (which therefore eases up the liver's work), while sedating LV and GB.

Commentaries:

1. Liver damage, recovery from hepatitis.

222

2. Cardiovascular diseases; coronary artery problems.
3. Adjustment of blood pressure (high or low).
4. Chronic prostate problems.
5. Nervous breakdown, depression, anger.
6. Forgetfulness, confused thinking.
7. Chest pain (inside or outside).
8. Gallbladder disorder.
9. Weight control.
10. Addictions: Assistance in quitting smoking, drinking and drug taking as well as lessening of withdrawal problems.
11. Hair loss.
12. Weak will power. Kidney weakness and infection.
13. Sexual disorders.
14. Epilepsy.
15. Mental disorders: improvement in brain function.
16. Improvement of food absorption.
17. Heartburn.
18. Fatigue.
19. Alzheimer's disease.

BP-407 — RETEXTURIZING COMBINATION

Ingredients: Tang Kuei, Rhemannia, Gypsos, Siler, Atractylodes, Akebia, Anemarrhena, Cicada, Sophora, Schizonepeta, Sesame, Licorice
Combination's Energy Level: Low Cool
Combination's Taste: 45% Sweet, 40% Piquant, 10% Bitter, 5% Salty
Main Meridians: Sedates SP, L and TH and energizes S
Commentaries:
1. Skin disorders, such as psoriasis, eczema, boils, sores, ring worm, dry skin, athlete's foot, fungus, shingles, herpes (not genital), over-all itchiness.
2. Poison oak.
3. Benefits enhanced when on a diet excluding butter, margarine, refined sugar and shellfish.
4. Benefits enhanced when used in conjunction with Royal Jade Cream.
Note: In rare observations, improvement in psoriasis was preceeded by a temporary worsening of the condition.

BP-408 — FACIAL COMBINATION

Ingredients: Siler, Forsythia, Platycodon, Angelica, Scutellaria, Cnidium, Schizonepeta, Gardenia, Coptis, Mentha, Rutaceae Peel, Licorice
Combination's Energy Level: Neutral
Combination's Taste: 55% Piquant, 35% Bitter, 10% Sweet
Main Meridians: Energizes L and LV, but rather neutral on the other meridians.
Commentaries: In some observations acne improvement was preceeded by a temporary worsening of the condition.

BP-409 — BLOOD PURIFYING COMBINATION

Ingredients: Ginseng, Bupleurum, Adenophora, Angelica, Laxiflora, Poria, Dahurica, Cnidium, Honeysuckle, Gladitschia
Combination's Energy Level: Low Warm
Combination's Taste: 55% Sweet, 30% Piquant, 15% Bitter
Main Meridians: LV, H and S
Commentaries:
1. Lupus.
2. Genital herpes; certain skin rashes.
3. Various infections in lymphatic system; ear leaking; ulcers and pussy sores on the body.
4. Rectal infections, such as infected hemorrhoids.
5. Poison oak.

WD-502 — BOWEL COMBINATION

Ingredients: Rhubarb, Mouten, Persica, Mirabilitum, Tricosanthes seed
Combination's Energy Level: Low Cool
Combination's Taste: 35% Bitter, 35% Sweet, 10% Piquant, 10% Sour, 10% Salty
Main Meridians: S and LI
Commentaries:
1. Prostatitis.
2. Various infections in the lower part of the body: rectum, testicles, prostate, bladder, ovaries, kidneys, urinary tract, vagina, intestines.
3. Appendicitis.
4. Bone marrow inflammation; lymph gland inflammation in woman's breast; skin sores.

5. Constipation and cleansing of intestinal walls.

FP-601 — OCEAN COMBINATION

Ingredients: Cyperus, Perilla, Citrus, Ginger, Licorice
Combination's Energy Level: Warm
Combination's Taste: 40% Bitter, 50% Piquant, 10% Sweet
Main Meridians: L, LV and SP
Commentaries:
1. Food poisoning, including shellfish reaction.
2. Stomach ache.
3. Stiff neck; shoulder pain, headache from indigestion.
4. Food allergy including sinus congestion.
5. Inability to smell things.

FP-604 — ACIDITY COMBINATION

Ingredients: Cinnamon, Corydalis, Ostrea, Fennel, Cardamon, Licorice, Ginger, Poria
Combination's Energy Level: Middle Warm
Combination's Taste: 40% Piquant, 35% Sweet, 25% Salty
Main Meridians: Primarily: Energizes LV; Secondarily: Energizes H, B and L. (From the Five Element Theory one can see that one result is to ease the functioning of earth, or acidity.)
Commentaries:
1. Stomach ulcer (including bleeding); stomach cancer.
2. Stomach acid imbalance.
3. Indigestion.
4. Morning sickness.
5. Fermentation.
6. Food allergy.
7. Food poisoning.
8. Hangover.
9. Hiatal hernia.

FP-605 — SWEET ORAL COMBINATION

Ingredients: Eriobotrya, Rhemannia, Asparagus, Ophiopogon, Chih shih, Capillaris, Dendrobium, Licorice, Scutellaria, Gardenia, Phellodendron
Combination's Energy Level: Cool

Combination's Taste: 55% Sweet, 35% Bitter, 10% Piquant
Main Meridians: H, SP and K
Commentaries:
1. Infections in the mouth.
2. Canker sores.
3. Gum infections and/or corruption.
4. Toothache.
5. Cancer on tongue, in the mouth or throat.
6. Throat ulcer.
7. Tooth decay.
8. Dry mouth (lack of saliva).
9. Throat irritation and mucous created by excessive talking.

GT-701 — BODY BUILDING COMBINATION

Ingredients: Chinese Ginseng, Astragalus, Atractylodes, Poria, Tang Kuei, Paeonia, Rhemannia, Cnidium, Cinnamon, Coix
Combination's Energy Level: Warm
Combination's Taste: 65% Sweet, 25% Piquant, 10% Sour, 10% Bitter
Main Meridians: Energizes all meridians with emphasis on H, TH, LV, SP and L.
Commentaries:
1. Increased immunity and anti-bodies.
2. Revitalization of all internal organs; tonifies the entire body; blood building.
3. Recovery from surgery.
4. Cancer: benefits enhanced when used in conjunction with other combinations. For example, colon cancer: GT-701 plus BD-216; liver cancer: GT-701 plus BD-404; stomach cancer: GT-701 plus FP-604, etc.
5. Leukemia and multiple sclerosis.
6. AIDS.
7. Anemia, low blood count, low energy.
8. Body building following depletion from excessive use of anti-biotics, exposure to radiation (including radiation therapy), chemotherapy and cobalt treatments.
9. Exhaustion in athletes.
10. Benefits enhanced with anti-biotics for chronic infections.
11. Blurry eyesight in conjunction with weak, depleted body.
12. Improvement of blood circulation.
13. Increase of appetite.
14. Improvement of lung function.

226

Note: In ancient times this combination was for the weak and elderly.

GT-703 – CENTRAL TONIC COMBINATION

Ingredients: Licorice (specially treated), Zingiber, Cinnamon, Jujube, Ginseng, Rhemannia, Ophiopogon, Sesame, Gelatin
Combination's Energy Level: Neutral
Combination's Taste: 65% Sweet, 20% Salty, 15% Piquant
Main Meridians: Sedates H and SP primarily. (Energizes L a lot, and TH secondarily.) The remaining overall impact on other meridians is rather balanced. Therefore, this combination has a strong concentration on sedating the heart directly and indirectly, while revitalizing the sexual glands. This combination is a heart specialty.
Commentaries:
1. Myocarditis.
2. Fibrillation.
3. Rhythmic disorder.
4. Heart failure, heart attack.
5. Shortness of breath; soothing of the lungs.
6. Chest pain.
7. Cardiac asthma.
8. Hypertension.
9. Edema.
10. Coughing caused by heart trouble.
11. Lack of energy, constant fatigue.
12. Impotence.
13. Angina.
14. Fainting because of blockage of neck artery.

GT-704 – BRIGHT COMBINATION

Ingredients: Tang Kuei, Paeonia, Cnidium, Rhemannia, Platycodon, Ginseng, Gardenia, Coptis, Angelica, Vitex, Chrysanthemum, Licorice, Juncus, Theaceae
Combination's Energy Level: Low Cool
Combination's Taste: 30% Piquant, 30% Sweet, 30% Bitter, 10% Sour
Main Meridians: Energizes LV, but sedates H, L, LI and SI slightly.
Commentaries: Eye disorders: peraplenitis, eye infections, etc.
1. Older people with deteriorating eyes.

2. Cataract; near- and far-sightedness.
3. Glaucoma.
4. Unfocused vision or uncoordinated eye focus.
5. Eye weakness and degenerative vision.

GT-705 — CHEST STRENGTHEN COMBINATION

Ingredients: Astragalus, Ginseng, Atractylodes, Tang Kuei, Bupleurum, Ginger, Jujube, Citrus, Licorice, Cimicifuga
Combination's Energy Level: Near Warm
Combination's Taste: 50% Sweet, 25% Piquant, 25% Bitter
Main Meridians: Primarily: SP, then L; Secondarily: S, TH, H and LI
Commentaries:
1. Chronic lung problems: chronic TB, asthma and emphysema.
2. Lung cancer.
3. Over-perspiration in weak people.
4. Shortness of breath.
5. Heart and spleen pancreas dysfunctions, including hypoglycemia.
6. Lung recovery, such as after impairment from injury.
7. Fungus in lungs.

GT-706 — ENERGY COMBINATION

Ingredients: Ginseng, Atractylodes (white), Poria, Licorice, Tang
Kuei, Paeonia, Cnidium, Rhemannia
Combination's Energy Level: Middle Warm
Combination's Taste: 60% Sweet, 20% Piquant, 10% Sour, 10%
Bitter
Main Meridians: LV, H, TH, HC, SI, SP, S and L
Commentaries:
1. Blood building, especially for women with low energy,
anemia, pale color, slow pulse, etc.
2. Fast overall tonic.
3. Dry skin, unhealthy hair; nerve inflammation; rheumatism,
congested lungs; irregular menstruation; food absorption;
nervousness; blood circulation; anemia.

GT-707 — GLANDS COMBINATION

Ingredients: Zanthoxylum, Cinnamon, Ginger, Jujube, Paeonia,

Licorice, Maltose

Combination's Energy Level: Middle Warm

Combination's Taste: 65% Sweet, 15% Piquant, 10% Sour, 10% Bitter

Main Meridians: Primarily: L, K and B; Secondarily: SP, S, LI, TH and GB

Commentaries:

1. Children bedwetting, nightmares, excessive crying.
2. Low metabolism, slow growth; growing disorders.
3. Headache.
4. Tonsilitis.
5. Lymph nodes, lymphatic system inflammation.
6. Weak liver, jaundice, gallbladder problem.
7. Indigestion; hypo- or hyper-acidity. Improvement of food absorption.
8. Intestinal disorder.
9. Spinal problems.
10. Asthma, chronic bronchitis.
11. Acute hepatitis; enlarged or hardened liver.
12. Coronary disease, short breath, chest pain.
13. Stomach pain.
14. Impotence, enlarged prostate.
15. Wet dreams.
16. Thymus and thyroid deficiencies.
17. Body building for children, including premature babies.
18. Acute angina.

GT-708 — GUM COMBINATION

Ingredients: Cinnamon, Scutellaria, Platycodon, Poria, Almond

Combination's Energy Level: Low Warm

Combination's Taste: 35% Piquant, 45% Sweet, 20% Bitter

Main Meridian: L

Commentaries:

1. Loose teeth, inflammation and infection in gums and teeth.
2. Cavities.

GT-710 — REBUILDING COMBINATION

Ingredients: Bitter almond, Ephedra, Cinnamon, Ginseng, Tang Kuei, Cnidium, Zingiber, Licorice, Gypsos, Acorus

Combination's Energy Level: Middle Warm

Combination's Taste: 50% Sweet, 30% Piquant, 20% Bitter
Main Meridians: Primarily: LV, H, SP and L.
Commentaries:
1. Stroke recovery, including paralysis.
2. Revitalization of the brain cells and nerve cells and adjusted coordination between the brain and nervous system.
3. Adjusted blood pressure (high or low).
4. Parkinson's Disease.
5. Encephalitis.
6. Arthritis (cripple).
7. Nervous disorders in the face and eyes.

GT-711 – LIFE WHEEL COMBINATION

Ingredients: Zeltinum seed, Cuscuta seed, Lycium seed, Plantago seed, Elettaria seed, Scaizendra seed
Combination's Energy Level: Middle Warm
Combination's Taste: 50% Sweet, 20% Sour, 20% Bitter, 10% Piquant
Main Meridians: TH
Commentaries:
1. AIDS; strengthened immune system.
2. Overall "tune up" of glandular function.
3. Impotence and low sexual drive.
4. Encouragement of youthful abilities.
Note: In the ancient times this combination was used to strengthen the seven glands considered to be the wheels of the life of a human being. These glands are the sexual, adrenal, pancreas, thymus, thyroid, pituitary and pineal.

GT-712 – CREATIVE COMBINATION

Ingredients: Ginseng, Atractylodes, Poria, Zizyphus, Longan, Astragalus, Tang Kuei, Polygala, Licorice, Saussurea, Jujube, Ginger
Combination's Energy Level: Near Warm
Combination's Taste: 65% Sweet, 20% Piquant, 10% Sour, 5% Bitter
Main Meridians: Primarily: SP; Secondarily: TH and L.
Commentaries:
1. Anemia.
2. Internal bleeding in intestines, uterus, kidneys; blood in urine.
3. Forgetfulness, tiredness, overwork, mental exhaustion, sad disposition.

4. Chronic gonorrhea; wet dreams.
5. Nerve tension, weakness.
6. Blood building, stomach toning, aiding of digestion.
7. In leukemia cases this combination has been used to encourage remission.

GT-713 — THROAT COMBINATION

Ingredients: Peppermint, Gardenia, Cardamon, Catechu, Cnidium, Rhubarb, Forsythia
Combination's Energy Level: Middle Cool
Combination's Taste: 45% Bitter, 40% Piquant, 15% Sweet
Main Meridian: L
Commentaries:
1. Increased throat function.
2. Voice clarification.

Natural Herbal Facial and Skin Care System

An extraordinary herbal skin care system was developed for the royal families of China. The herbal combinations were so treasured that they were more precious than priceless gems. This skin care system includes many secret combinations:

Royal Vital Clean-Off
This formula contains these precious ingredients:

Sophora	Alumen	Nepeta
Kuta	Milk	

- It sloughs off dead tissue and cleans the skin and its pores deeply
- Its natural, healing herbal content penetrates and works to soften and revitalize the skin and prepare the skin for further conditioning
- It makes shaving easier and protects and heals the skin
- It contains no preservatives or chemicals because it is a powder, which forms a substrate that is hostile to the growth of microorganisms

Royal Nutri-Mask
This combination contains these costly ingredients:

Plum flowers	Ginseng	Angelica

231

Dryobalanops   Carmellia   Taraxacu
Cypress
- It stimulates and tightens the skin to help restore natural elasticity and vitality
- Its herbal contents provide building blocks for the production of new skin cells
- Wrinkles and lines will immediately disappear

Essence of Pearl (face conditioner)
This combination contains these precious ingredients:
Pearls   Ginseng   Gingko
Almond seed extract   Cotylegon
- Pearls have been known for centuries for their skin beautifying properties in the Orient
- The combination contains natural moisturizers that are immediately absorbed by the skin because of their similarity to natural skin fluids
- It beautifies skin tissue because of its herbal conditioners
- It makes the skin unbelievably soft, radiant and youthful
- It was considered unique to bring back vitality to the skin locally

Royal Jade Cream
This combination has been famous in the history of China. It contains these costly materials:
Jade   Lithospermum   Frankincense
Myrrh   Pearls   Sesame Oil
- It helps generate new, healthy skin tissues and repairs old, unhealthy cells
- It removes scars, wrinkles and blemishes
- It makes the skin healthy and radiant
- The physicians of the Royal Family of China have also reported a wide range of benefits from Royal Jade Cream for symptoms like (or resembling): joints deformed by arthritis, herpes, sprained ankles, psoriasis, breast lumps, vaginal infections, skin cancer, spinal dysfunction, hemorrhoids, cataracts, glaucoma and eczema. Its effectiveness has been continuously proven over the centuries
- It forms a protective barrier from the effects of the wind, cold and pollution

SAR Gold Lotion
It contains these precious ingredients:
Asparagus (herb)   Liquid Gold

232

Ginseng   Royal Jelly

- It smooths and refines the texture of the skin
- It prevents the formation of wrinkles
- It controls oiliness and dryness with special corrective ingredients
- It revitalizes tired skin and gives it life and health
- It is antiseptic

Royal Hair Ener-G

It is made of these precious ingredients:

Cypress	Elsha	Ginger
Sophora	Mint	Litzia

- It restores health and balance to the skin and hair cells with nutrients that especially benefit the hair
- It stimulates luxuriant hair growth naturally
- It gives hair shine, life, luster, and body
- It soothes itchiness of the scalp and skin

Chang Chung-Ching (張仲景, A.D. 142–220, known as "The Medical Sage," was the Hippocrates of China. My forefather, Dr. Chung-Ching Chang, wrote the first herbal formula book.

VI

In the Bible, Revelations 22:2, it is stated that "The leaves of the tree were for the healing of the nations." God intended for us to make use of all the bounty which the earth provides, including the more peculiar varieties of digestible substances, the herbs. But we have strayed from the Way of God and we are now starving in an era of abundant food crops. We are starving because most of these chemicalized foods are not providing our bodies with the nutrients our bodies need. In addition, these foods are poisoning us to death while providing us with no defense against the onslaught of germs, viruses, pollution, and radiation. To rediscover the "forgotten foods" is to give ourselves another chance. With herbs, the cycle of nourishment is continuous and complete, thereby enabling the cells and the tissues to regenerate constantly and be cleansed from poisons. The healing properties of herbs go directly to the areas of the body which are most in need of replenishment, rebuilding, or cleansing. These areas are determined mainly through pulse reading. Herbs work faster and more efficiently than regular foods to nourish and energize us and to prevent illness.

An unprecedented state of balance and health may be achieved in your body when a diet of herbs is combined along with our regular food diet. The results of regular consumption of herbs and application of knowledge concerning our bodily functions will manifest themselves immediately with concrete, tangible rewards. The entire metabolism of the body changes, as problems that have plagued us for generations are worked out. With the use of herbs, we will be one step closer to the attainment of immortality.

5

THE TAO OF HEALING ART

TUEI-NA

I

    The Tao of Healing Art introduces us to extraordinary vistas and levels of health.

    Another name for the Tao of Healing Art is Tuei-Na. The word

Tuei means "the pushing away of abnormality." The word *Na* means the "taking out of abnormality." Together these words represent manual or implemental manipulation of meridian points to encourage, adjust and balance the natural functions of the three folds of the body.

The techniques of Tuei-Na, described as the oldest of healing techniques by the Yellow Emperor, are the result of dilligent research by Taoists. After noticing that human beings naturally and immediately clasp themselves upon experiencing pain, Taoists began to research the effects of manual and implemental manipulation for pain and other problems. From their research, many theories and techniques of healing were developed.

Healing is an art and a gift of kindness. It is an art because the changes within the human body are infinite and only the healer can sense the type and degree of intervention required. A machine does not have the wisdom and sensitivity to deal with the endless variations and reactions of the human body. No machine, even if it is computerized, can equal the skill of the healer.

The healer's kindness toward mankind augments the efficacy of the healing techniques; the healer is willing to give a part of himself or herself to replace that which is wanting in the sick. Kindness and wisdom are mankind's God-given gifts, and there is no machine which can emit these qualities.

Unlike the Tao of Revitalization, which is an expression of the art of self-healing, Tuei-Na is an expression of the art of social healing, that is, the healing of others.

The body cannot be compelled into health by surgery, use of machinery or other such methods that focus only upon the ailing parts. One part of the body cannot and must not be isolated. The body is similar to intricate clockwork: if one part is not in good condition, all of the other parts are affected. Concentrated attention to or treatment of one part will cause that part to be out-of-step with the rest of the body and will upset the entire system. There must be balance among the three folds of the body: the physical, the mental, and the spiritual bodies.

Following are the five theories of the Tao of Healing Art, which can be used to balance and change the entire body.

1. The Skin Theory. The skin is very important to the circulation of energy and to the functioning of the whole body. When the skin is tense, the meridians, the flow of energy and the natural functions are blocked. This is why the result of tension is pain. Touching the skin stimulates the nerve endings and unleashes the related emotions. In this way the body can relax and return to normality. In Taoism, the skin is a breathing organ like the lungs and,

together, they are the center for sensitivity or emotions at the mental level. Emotions are the basis for tension and relaxation; therefore, touching the skin causes changes in the functioning of the body. The skin must be soothed and relaxed through the human touch (massage, Tuei-Na, etc.)

2. The Nerve Theory. The nervous system consists of the central nervous system, which includes the brain and the peripheral nervous system. Many people develop nerve weaknesses because of toxins in their environment and in their food. These toxins accumulate in the liver and the nerves, placing an unnecessary stress on them. This strain weakens the nerves and causes mental imbalance and mental illnesses, including depression and nervous breakdown. Psychiatric or psychological treatments are not employed by Taoists for the Taoists attribute all mental imbalances to nerve weakness, which is a physical imbalance. Once we strengthen the nervous system with Tuei-Na, the psychological disturbances will be relieved.

3. The Circulation Theory. The blood vessels are the pathways of blood circulation. When the vessels are blocked by accumulations, the blood flow is obstructed, causing many problems. If we do not use preventative measures to stop accumulations in the blood vessels surgery will become necessary. If a person retains water, which most heart patients do, the excess water puts pressure on the blood vessels, and the heart is forced to work harder.

When circulation is impeded, blood will not reach the capillaries at the outer extremities of the circulatory system, such as the skin. Subsequently the capillaries will atrophy, and the skin will suffer from the lack of nutrients. The skin will wrinkle, the hair will fall out and the person will age. Tuei-Na can be used to encourage blood circulation and reverse the aging process.

Exercise is one way to stimulate the circulation, but the side effect of over-exercising is that it speeds up the heart and could cause damage. Even if the heart pumps faster, circulation will not be improved, because blockages will still remain in the blood vessels. In addition, increasing the rate of the heartbeat could cause a heart attack or the deterioration of the heart.

The best way to encourage the circulation is through the use of internal exercises or Tuei-Na. Tuei-Na soothes and relaxes the vessels to open them, and stimulates and encourages the flow of blood to remove blockages.

Poor circulation is indicated by coldness in the extremities because when the heart is working very hard and the internal temperature is high a coldness is felt externally. When the internal temperature is low, the body feels hot. Hot flashes are caused by poor circulation of the blood. This is why most women who have had a hysterectomy suffer from hot flashes. After the utilization of Tuei-Na, the condition will be relieved and the woman may feel cooler because circulation will be improved and the heart will be relieved of the extra burden.

4. The Tissue Theory. Normally the tissues of the body are tight. When water accumulates, however, the tissues will expand and constrict the blood vessels and impede circulation. Without the eliminatory action of good blood circulation, toxins accumulate and poison many cells. Because these dead cells cannot be eliminated, they also accumulate in the body where they will then corrupt. The body will then try to fight this corruption and elimate the cells, but this will compress the dead cells into a tumor and then help to spread the tumor's poisonous discharge. More tumors will result and the body will become weakened. From the Taoist viewpoint, cancer results from the accumulation of dead cells.

We cannot kill something with antibiotics if it is already dead. In the laboratories, attempts have been made to feed cancer cells with nutrients to determine their method of growth, but dead substance cannot grow.

To prevent cancer, we must encourage the eliminatory processes by relaxing the lymphatic system and the circulatory system. The lymphatic system is the pathway for water movement in the body; removing blockages from this system will prevent the accumulation of water. Improving the blood circulation will remove the toxins and corrupt cells from the body. Both of these improvements can be achieved through the utilization of Tuei-Na.

Another very important cancer preventative is cleanliness. One of the most common forms of cancer is that of the colon and rectum. Inadequate removal of excrement leads to corruption and a preliminary sign of dysfunction in the area of the rectal tissues. Hemorrhoids can gradually lead to further deterioration. With Tuei-Na, one may clean and massage the rectum to encourage blood circulation in the area which will prevent the accumulation of toxins from the excrement.

5. The Vital Energy Theory. We may refer to the energy of the body as electro-magnetism, vital force or spirit. Whatever we choose to call it, we will all agree that we cannot live without it. It is the basic force that moves the entire body.

Energy circulates throughout the body along minute pathways called *meridians.* Dr. Kim Bong Han of the University of Pyongang in North Korea arrived at a conclusion regarding the actual existence of these pathways for energy, after conducting an extensive series of experiments. He reported that the meridians were actually composed of a type of histological tissue as yet unnoticed by scientists. Prior to Dr. Kim's experiments, science had believed that the meridians were simply *imaginary* lines. Dr. Kim discovered the structure and function of the meridian system to be totally different from that of the lymphatic, circulatory and nervous systems. He noted that the meridians are channels (diameter 20-50 millimicrons) that are symmetrical and bilateral and which exist beneath the surface of the skin. They have a thin membranous wall and are filled with a transparent, colorless fluid. Each of the main meridians intricately develops subsidiary branches, some of which supply adjacent areas with energy while others ultimately reach the surface of the skin.

Recently German scientists have proven with the use of electricity that the meridians are pathways for energy. Using the six major meridians that run through the hand, it was found that by charging a certain amount of electricity (0.005 volts) into the lung meridian on the hand, a similar amount of electricity could be detected in the lungs themselves. (Although energy levels in the meridians may be gauged by electricity, energy itself is not electricity.) They found that each of the six meridians of the hand carries a different amount of energy and each meridian has an energy correspondence to its organic counterpart. This study led to the invention of a machine called the Point-locator which indicates the points where the branches of the meridians reach the skin surface.

Although the first scientific proof of the existence of the meridian system is believed to be the result of Dr. Kim's efforts, conclusive evidence of the existence of the meridians was actually found in 1937, by Sir Thomas Lewis of England. His report, published in the *British Medical Journal* of February 1937, stated that he had discovered an "unknown nervous system" that was unrelated to either the sensory or the sympathetic nervous systems. Rather than being composed of a network of nerves, he reported, his newly discovered system was composed of a network of thin lines. Although his report went relatively unnoticed by his colleagues, it was the first concrete verification of the physiological system that Taoists had mapped out thousands of years ago.

There are 12 main meridians — one assigned to each of the five organs, the six bowels, and the pericardium (here referred to as the heart constrictor). Each of the main meridians has both a point of entry and a point of exit. Energy enters the meridian at the point of entry, circulates along the meridian, and flows through the point of exit and on through the point of entry of the succeeding meridian. The point of exit on a meridian is connected to the point of entry on the succeeding meridian by a secondary channel. Treating a point of entry will affect the entire length of the meridian, in that the direction of the flow of energy along a meridian remains constant and never vacillates after flowing through the point of entry.

Tuei-Na is used to encourage the energy flow in all the meridians, energize a specific area on the body, and disperse or augment the energy flow.

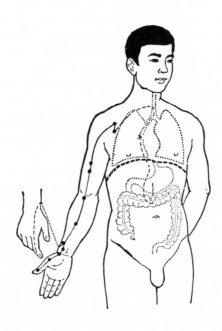

Figure 59
Lung Meridian — Main Points

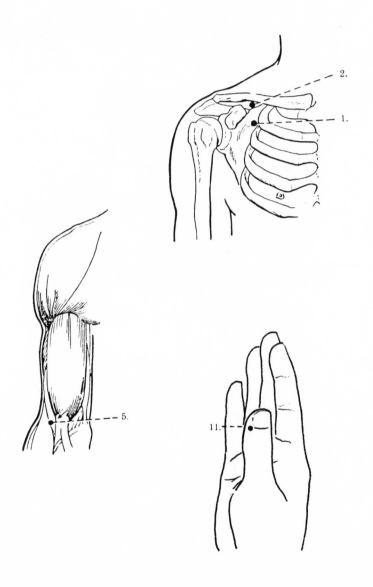

Lung Meridian — Main Points (cont'd.)

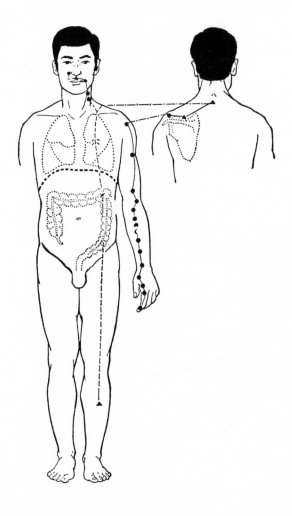

Figure 60

Large Intestine Meridian — Main Points

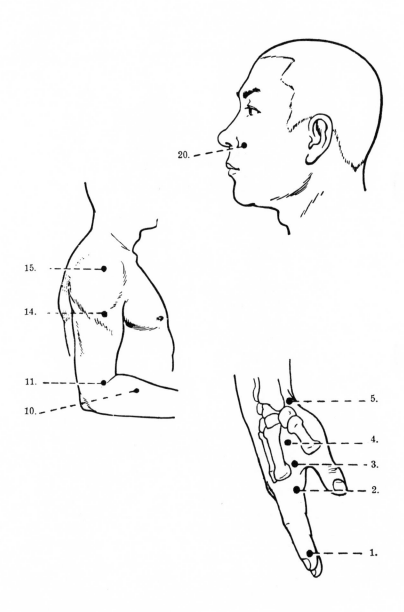

Large Intestine Meridian — Main Points (cont'd.)

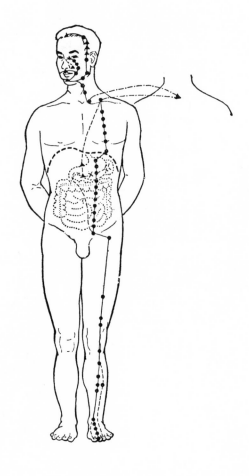

Figure 61

Stomach Meridian — Main Points

244

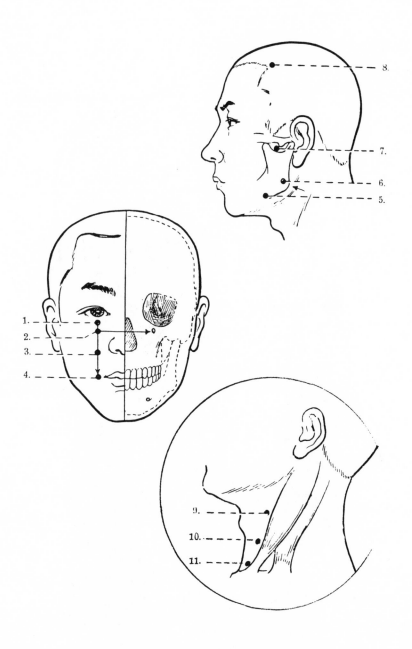

Stomach Meridian — Main Points (cont'd.)

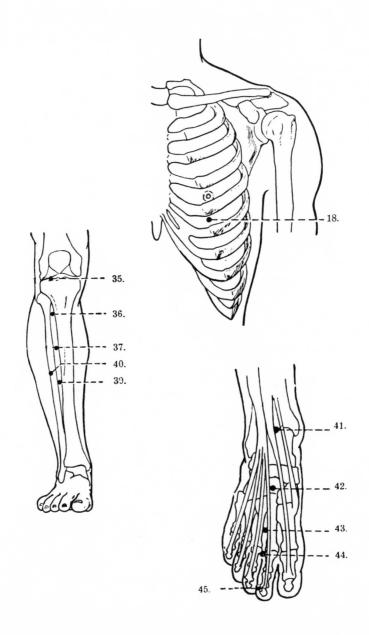

Stomach Meridian — Main Points (cont'd.)

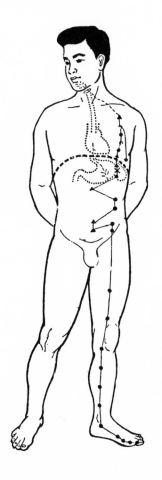

Figure 62

Spleen-Pancreas Meridian — Main Points

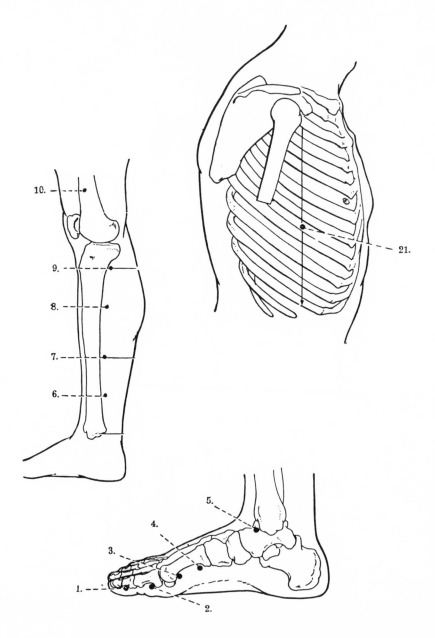

Spleen-Pancreas Meridian — Main Points (cont'd.)

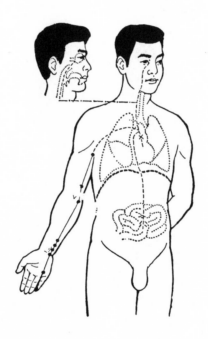

Figure 63

Heart Meridian — Main Points

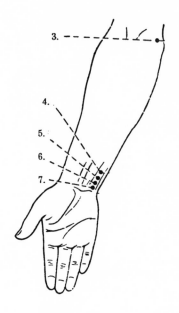

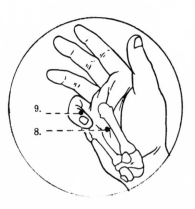

Heart Meridian — Main Points (cont'd.)

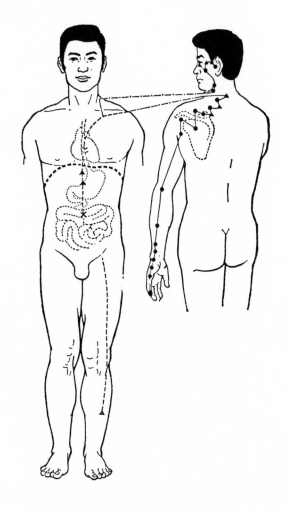

Figure 64

Small Intestine Meridian — Main Points

251

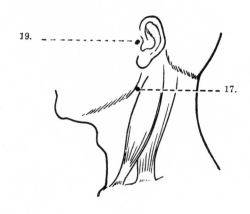

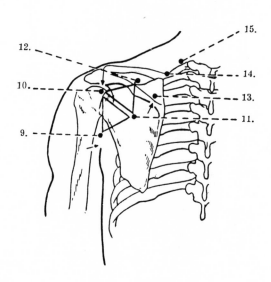

Small Intestine Meridian — Main Points (cont'd.)

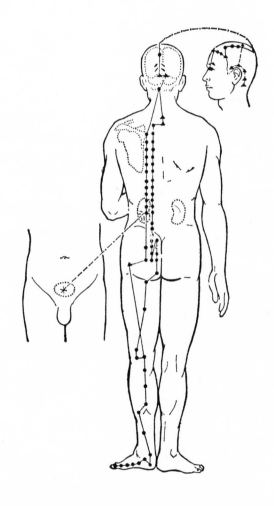

Figure 65

Bladder Meridian — Main Points

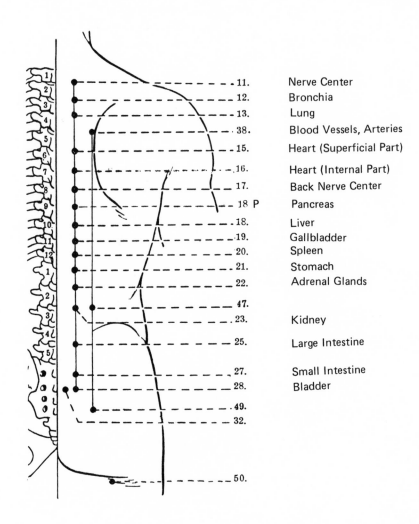

11.	Nerve Center
12.	Bronchia
13.	Lung
38.	Blood Vessels, Arteries
15.	Heart (Superficial Part)
16.	Heart (Internal Part)
17.	Back Nerve Center
18 P	Pancreas
18.	Liver
19.	Gallbladder
20.	Spleen
21.	Stomach
22.	Adrenal Glands
47.	
23.	Kidney
25.	Large Intestine
27.	Small Intestine
28.	Bladder
49.	
32.	
50.	

Bladder Meridian — Main Points (cont'd.)

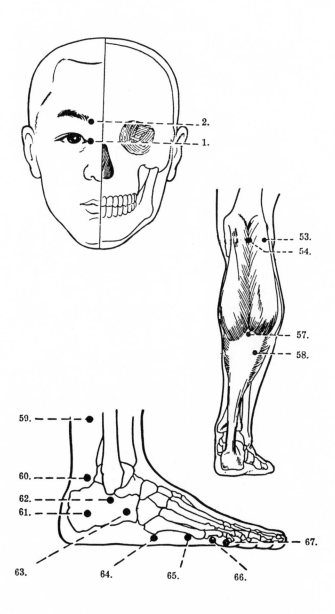

Bladder Meridian — Main Points (cont'd.)

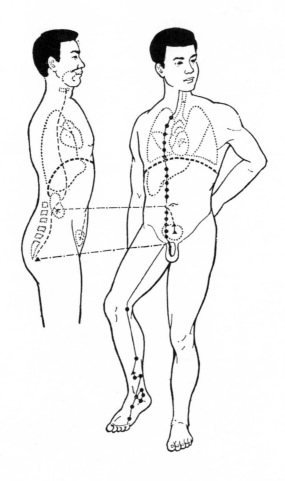

Figure 66

Kidney Meridian — Main Points

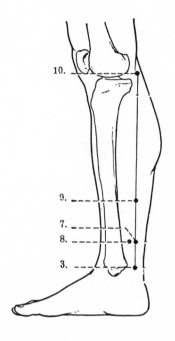

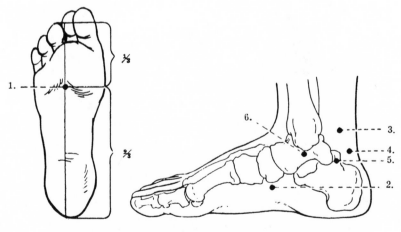

Kidney Meridian — Main Points (cont'd.)

257

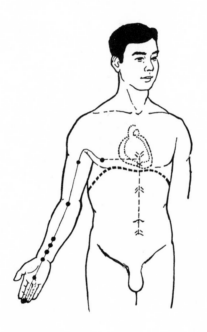

Figure 67
Heart Constrictor — Main Points

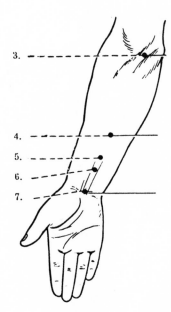

Heart Constrictor — Main Points (cont'd.)

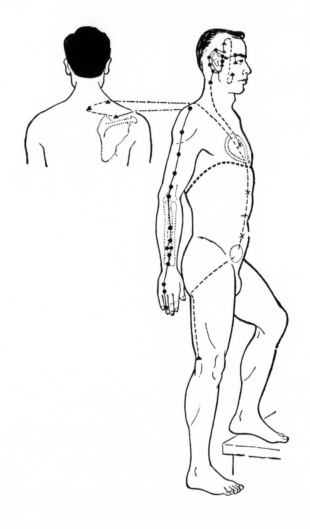

Figure 68
Triple Heater Meridian — Main Points

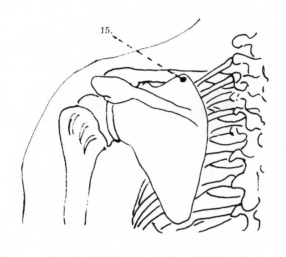

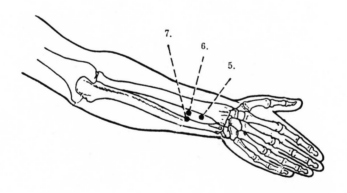

Triple Heater Meridian — Main Points (cont'd.)

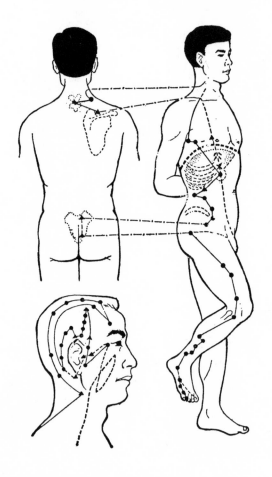

Figure 69

Gallbladder Meridian — Main Points

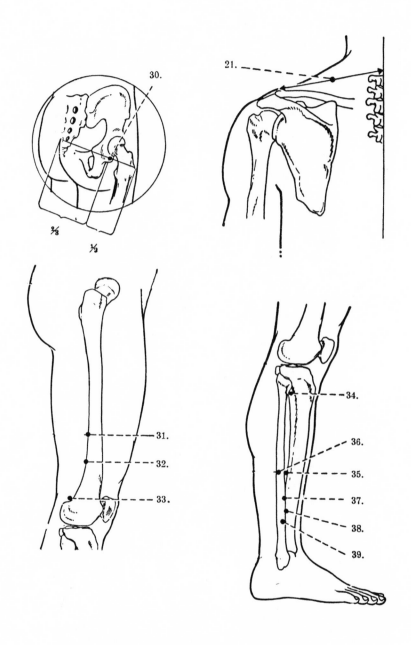

Gallbladder Meridian — Main Points (cont'd.)

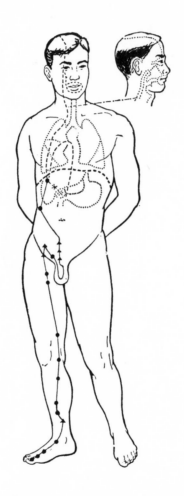

Liver Meridian — Main Points

Figure 70

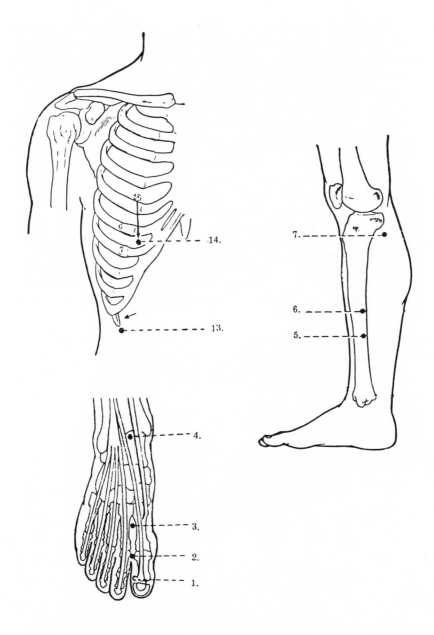

Liver Meridian — Main Points (cont'd.)

In addition to the twelve meridians, there are two extraordinary meridians. These meridians are justifiably called "life-savers" in that they provide for energy to continue its cycle of circulation regardless of whether any one of the organs or bowels becomes diseased and blocks the meridian circuit. Taoists explain the purpose of the two extraordinary meridians in an analogous manner by likening them to drainage ditches and dykes that exist alongside a major river. The river, of course, corresponds to the main or major meridians. If for any reason the river (main meridian) should become flooded and overflow its banks, the drainage ditches will accommodate the superfluous water (energy). Therefore the flow of energy along the two extraordinary meridians is not constant but is determined by the amount of excess energy in a main meridian.

The two extraordinary meridians are called Jen-Mo and Tu-Mo. Jen-Mo Meridian, or the meridian of conception, has 24 single points with an ascending flow of energy running up the front of the body from the perineum to the chin. Tu-Mo Meridian, or the governor meridian, has 27 single points with an ascending flow of energy running from the coccyx up along the back and atop the head, ending at the upper gum.

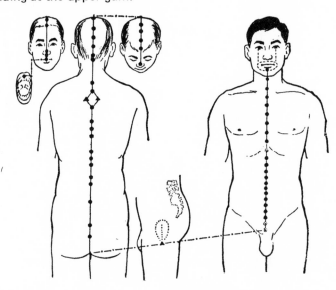

Figure 71

Tu-Mo Meridian — Main Points   *Jen-Mo Meridian -- Main Points*

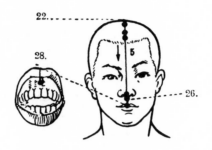

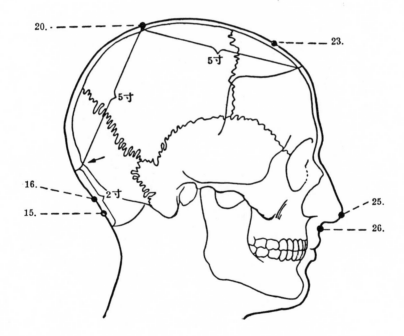

Tu-Mo Meridian — Main Points (cont'd.)

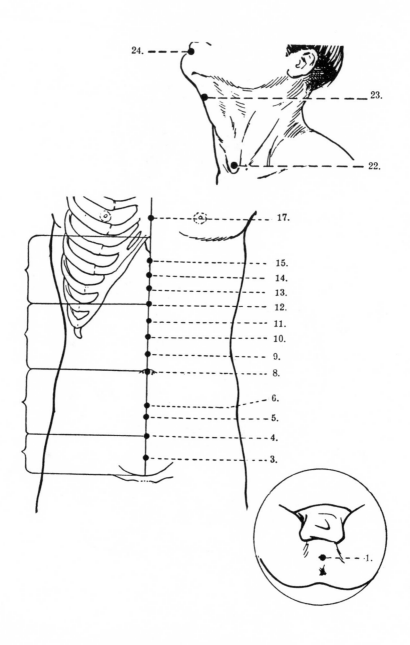

Jen-Mo Meridian — Main Points (cont'd.)

II

Tuei-Na consists of two types of approaches to healing. The first type contains sixteen hand and arm techniques, which are used to manipulate the body.

These sixteen techniques are divided into two groups: the Yang group containing eight techniques, and the Yin group which also contains eight.

YANG	YIN
Tuei	Na
Pai	Nieh
Tsa	Chue
An	Muo
Chieh	Guen
Dien	Rou
Tsuo	Jen
Zhe	Yun

The Eight Yang Techniques

1. Tuei—To push or smooth with palms or fingers to guide or encourage the energy flow.

Figure 72

2. Pai—To clap or cup with the palms.

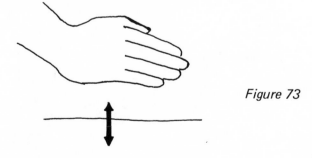

Figure 73

269

3. Tsa—To brush the meridians in the correct direction. (More pressure is applied than in Muo.)

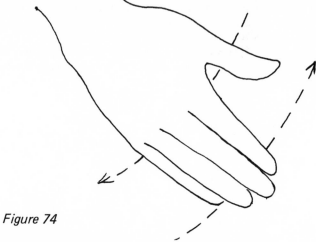

Figure 74

4. An—To apply pressure with the thumb, palm or elbow depending on the location of the meridian point.

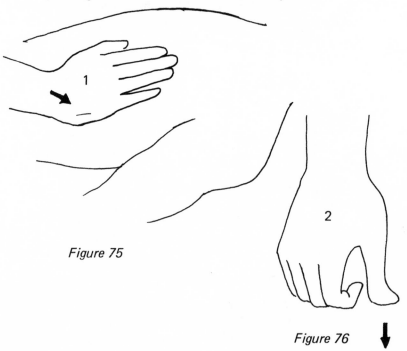

Figure 75

Figure 76

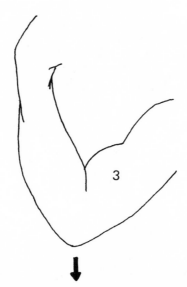

Figure 77

5. Chieh—To cut with the edge of the hand. This is used for the nerves and should be applied with caution, as it can cause pain.

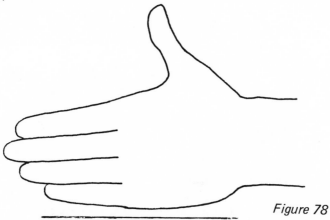

Figure 78

6. Dien—To point. This is rarely used as it can be very lethal.

Figure 79

271

7. Tsuo—To rotate or twist between the palms or fingers to loosen the blood vessels.

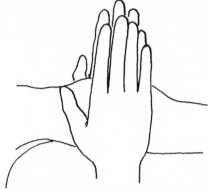

Figure 80

8. Zhe—To bend and stretch the arms, legs and fingers. Start slowly and then speed up, since most individuals do not exercise enough to keep muscles and tendons supple.

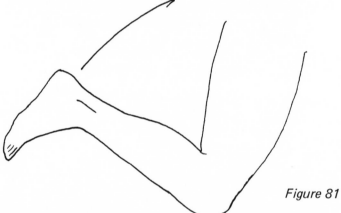

Figure 81

The Eight Yin Techniques

1. Na—To grab or take out abnormalities or negative accumulations with the use of visualization.

Figure 82

272

2. Nieh—To pinch or pick up between fingers.

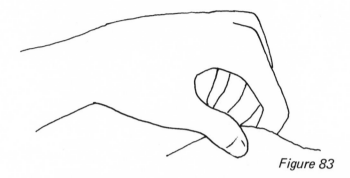

Figure 83

3. Chue—To beat or pound with the fist, palm, finger or sides of the hands to stimulate.

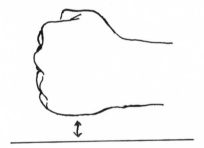

Figure 84

4. Muo—To massage, rub or stroke the meridians in the correct direction.

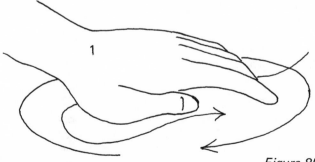

Figure 85

273

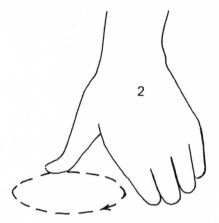

Figure 86

5. Guen—To rotate or roll the hands over the abdomen.

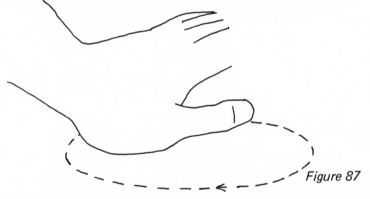

Figure 87

6. Rou—To rub or knead with the palms-over-palms or hand-over-hand technique.

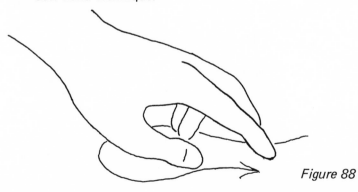

Figure 88

7. Jen—To shake or vibrate the arms, legs and head.

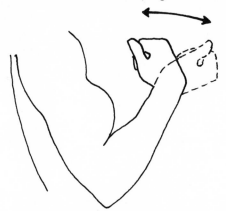

Figure 89 ·

8. Yun—To rub the palms together and apply the resulting heat or energy to the breasts, testes, penis and eyes.

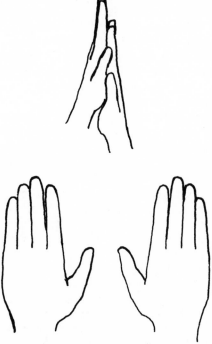

Figure 90

The second approach to healing with Tuei-Na consists of the utilization of five groups of tools which are used on the meridian locations and provide results similar to the sixteen techniques outlined above. These tools are identified with one of the elements of the Five Elements Theory in the following manner:

Fire	—	moxa	Earth	—	mud packs
		burning herbs			sand baths
		alcohol			creams
		sunlight			stone or jade
Metal	—	needles			(rubbing)
Water	—	salt water	Wood	—	small bamboo
		purified water			picks
		showers and			
		baths			

The use of needles for healing is called Acupuncture; therefore, Acupuncture is only one part of Tuei-Na.

I have developed a powder that is a composite of all the elements of the Five Elements Theory. Twelve years of research and five years of testing have gone into the development of this powder. The result is that the efficacy of the powder is greater than that of acupuncture needles or any other single tool. The powder generates heat and siphons energy and nutrients to the various points that lie along the meridian, to stop pain and correct other problems. The powder, unlike needles, will not cause any pain, tissue damage or transmission of germs. It also saves the energy of the healer, since manual manipulation is not required.

The procedure for using Acupowder is simple. Scoop a bit of powder with the sharp end of a nail file and transfer the powder to chosen points on the body. Use surgical tape to cover powder and surrounding area. The Acupowder will continue to work unceasingly for one or two weeks. At the end of this period, it can be removed or replaced easily. Since surgical tapes are waterproof, frequent baths or showers will not reduce the Acupowder's effectiveness.

Many people have benefited from the use of Acupowder. A couple from Washington came to see me because the wife was suffering from severe asthma attacks. They had found nothing that could help. I gave them some Acupowder and taught them where it should be placed for asthmatic conditions—along the bronchial points, the lung meridian and the spleen-pancreas meridian. The woman experienced relief, and the couple continued to use Acupowder for the next six months. She never suffered from asthma attacks again. A doctor wanted to study with me for a month, so he and his wife (five months pregnant) flew to San Francisco from Switzerland.

They arrived Thursday afternoon, and they were severely ill with jet lag and headaches. That evening I had a lecture at the University of California at Berkeley. They both wanted to attend but neither could move one step. So I placed some Acupowder on each of them. Fifteen minutes later they both felt well and refreshed. They attended the lecture and even gave a testimonial about the miraculousness of Acupowder at the close of the evening.

The sixteen techniques, the five groups of tools and Acupowder are used on points that lie along the meridians of the body, to pump energy into the meridians. These meridians and their points will be listed in the following pages.

The reader will encounter three words in the explanatory chart for the meridians. They are *High Point, Middle Point,* and *Low Point,* and they represent the different energy levels affecting all meridians. The high points, having greater energy levels, represent the most effective areas of the meridians. They are located at either elbow or knee level. Middle points, having medium energy levels, represent areas where meridians are only moderately effective; they are located at either wrist or ankle level. Low points have low energy levels and represent areas where the meridian is least effective. They are located at either the finger or toe level.

The reader should be aware that pumping energy into the High Points is not always wise. Sometimes only a little energy is necessary to bring a body back to health. This is best understood if the common household heater is used to explain it. The heater offers a variety of heat settings. During cold days more heat is needed, and during warmer days less heat is needed. We determine what amount of heat makes the environment most comfortable. In a similar way, we can also determine the amount of energy needed for healing.

III

To find the points on the meridians, the reader should refer to the appropriate charts of this book so that he or she may learn the positions of the points and meridians.

The meridian points and techniques are used together in many different ways. In the following pages, there will be several examples of how they are used.

When a child is sick and feverish because he or she has a cold, using the Tuei technique on points L5 through L7 brings the fever down naturally, without aspirin.

Another manipulation is the brushing (Tsa) of the lung meridian. Place five fingers of the right hand on the Chihtse (L5) point of the left arm (see fig. 91). Next find the point Liehchueh (L7) on the same arm. Starting from the Chihtse point, move the fingers downward along an imaginary line that connects points Chihtse and Liehchueh in a stroking motion. This is applied for problems in the thorax, lung, trachea, pharynx, etc.

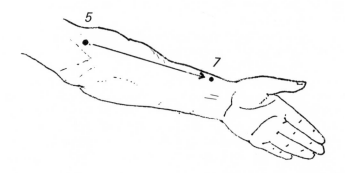

Figure 91

In any manipulation, the cultivator should use some Jade Cream (discussed in Chapter 4) to reduce friction, to form a barrier against too much energy loss and to speed up recovery of those who are suffering from abnormalities of the body.

During one of my lectures, a man in the audience stood up and related his experience to everybody in the audience. He had been suffering from severe coughing for three months. During that time, he had undergone all sorts of treatments, but nothing worked. What especially annoyed him was that the continuous coughing kept him and his wife awake every night. When he came to see me, I recommended stroking the lung meridian. He did not believe me, but that night, he tried that technique while reading a book — he did not want to waste too much time doing something he did not believe in. His wife, who was at his side, watched him for about four minutes and then fell into sound sleep. He continued for about one more minute and then fell into sound sleep. For the first time in three months, he and his wife slept like babies. For an entire night, he did not cough.

Dr. Grace Roesller once called me from Golden West College in Los Angeles to tell me about "a miracle." She was teaching class one day when the pollution was extremely bad. Her students suffered terribly from the allergies caused by the pollutants. They made so much coughing, sniffing and sneezing noises that she could not hear herself talk. She finally said, "Wait everybody! Roll up your sleeves and rub your arms like this . . ." The students did as they were told and she said that within one minute the room was so quiet one could hear a pin drop.

Another great manipulation involves the application of the Nieh technique (pinching) to the point Jenchung (see *Tu-Mo* 26). This involves placing the forefinger between the upper lip and teeth and the thumb outside the upper lip and pinching the flesh with these fingers. A few nurses have told me that they actually brought several dead patients back to life using this technique. These patients had been pronounced dead by the doctors. The whole hospital buzzed with excitement — everyone thought it was a miracle. Unfortunately, the doctors did not believe it and the event was shelved. About 3,000 years ago, a Taoist physician, Bien Chueh, brought a dead prince back to life with the same technique.

Another story concerning the efficacy of this technique was related to me after a lecture in Los Angeles. An acupuncturist came to me and shook my hand and then proceeded to tell me this story about his seven year old son. His son fell into a swimming pool and drowned. The father found the body floating face down on the water. He called the paramedics, who tried every technique to revive the boy. Nothing was working and precious time was passing. Suddenly, the father exclaimed, "Who am I? I am an acupuncturist. I should know . . ." So he took his son's lip between his fingers and pressed the Jenchung point so hard that his fingers penetrated through the tissue. A few seconds later, the boy opened his eyes! Upon physical examination it was determined that the boy had suffered neither brain damage nor any other physical damage.

MERIDIAN	GENERAL COMMENTS	IMPORTANT POINTS	LOCATION	INDICATIONS
Lung Meridian	The lung meridian has a descending flow of energy from the chest to the thumbs. It is used to disperse or sedate the energy of the lungs. The lung meridian may not be used to stimulate the lungs. It is used to relieve many problems associated with the respiratory organ.	L1	It is located in the depression below the center of the collar bone in front of the body.	L1 is the organ point of the lung meridian and it is used to disperse a great deal of energy from the lungs.
		L2	Same as above.	L2 may be depressed with L1 at the same time to relieve symptoms of asthma, bronchitis, sinus congestion and other congestions of the lungs.
	The lower part of the lung meridian from the elbow to the thumb is used for "lower level dispersal," and the upper part from the elbow to the chest is used for "higher level dispersal."	L5	It is located at the outer point of the bent elbow.	L5 is the high point of the lung meridian. It is used for acute coughing and/or congestion. The point disperses less energy than L1 and L2.
		L11	It is located on the outer side of the thumb near the bottom outer corner of the thumbnail.	It is the low point and it is used in emergencies during strokes. If this area is pierced and bleeding induced, the blood will reverse its path to the head, thus reversing the stroke and possibly preventing damage to the brain.
Large Intestine Meridian	The large intestine meridian has an ascending flow of energy, which flows from the tip of the index finger, up the outside of the arm, over the shoulder, crosses over the nose, and ends on the side of the nose. It has branches that cover the entire face and head. The large intestine meridian is used to tonify or stimulate the energy.	LI4	It is located in the web between the thumb and the index finger.	For most people, depression of this point produces pain. Pressure sends energy to the lungs, large intestine, head and arm. The energy revitalizes and nourishes the nerves, which is good for tennis elbow, nausea, headache, toothache, eye problems, nose problems, sinus congestion, spasm, and paralysis of the face. Use the point on the left hand for problems on the right side, and use the right point for the left side. Dentists have used this point as an anesthetic by rubbing this point for twenty minutes. No side effects result from this form of anesthesia.

MERIDIAN	GENERAL COMMENTS	IMPORTANT POINTS	LOCATION	INDICATIONS
Large Intestine Meridian (Cont'd.)		LI10	It is located on the outside of the arm, about two inches below the crease at the elbow.	If this point feels sore when pressed, it should be rubbed gently until pain is no longer felt; then use the fingers to brush up along the meridian. This increases the energy flow and blood flow, which increases metabolic functions. This point is used for arthritis, bursitis and nerve inflammation. LI10 can be used in conjunction with Stomach 36 (S36) to curb the appetite, which is increased by pressing LI10.
		LI14	It is located in the triangle of muscles on the back of the arm.	Depressing this point anesthetizes the back. Depressing the points on the right arm anesthetizes the right side of the back; the point on the left arm, the left side. Numbness is brought about by rubbing for 20 minutes. This point occupies the nerve center of the brain.
		LI20	It is located one eighth of an inch from either side of the flanges of the nose.	Gentle rubbing of this point will open the sinuses immediately.
Stomach Meridian	The stomach meridian has a descending flow of energy. The meridian runs from a position directly under the eye, down to the jaw, branches up in front of the ear, down the sides of the throat, down the chest, down the abdomen, down the middle of the front of the leg, and ends at the end of the second toe. Because it is descending, it disperses the energy flow (except in the eye to stomach interval where energy and the stomach may be stimulated).	S1	It is located under the center of the eye socket of both eyes.	It is used for cleaning the eyes. Used with LI20, which energizes, it will reduce energy circulation and refresh the function of the eyes. It is used for cataracts, which indicate an internal problem, possibly a liver problem.
		S4	It is located directly below S1, at the corners of the mouth.	It is used to energize the mouth, which is the opening of the spleen-pancreas and the stomach. It is a point for numbing toothaches and calming facial spasms.

MERIDIAN	GENERAL COMMENTS	IMPORTANT POINTS	LOCATION	INDICATIONS
Stomach Meridian (Cont'd.)		S6	It is located on the side of the face in the depression of the jaw when it is open.	It is used for light-headedness, ringing ears, gums and mouth.
		S9 through S11	These points run down the sides of the throat from the adam's apple to the top of the collar bone.	These should be used for self-treatment especially in the morning to cause a little coughing, which cleans the lungs. These energize the thyroid and the tonsils; relieve coughing, inflammation and allergic coughing; and encourage metabolism to rejuvenate old cells (a beauty asset).
		S18	It is located in an area 1 inch below the nipple for a man and in the fold marking the end of the breast for a woman.	It is used to determine if there are any problems or accumulations in the breast. If pain results from depressing the point, there are problems or accumulations. It is also a reading point for determining the condition of the breast.
		S30 A	It is located at the fold or meeting point of the thigh and the trunk of the body. The point is located in the middle of the fold in the front part of the body.	Pain detected from pressing this point may indicate nerve inflammation in the joints, sciatic nerve or leg. This area is the nerve center and the intersection of the stomach and spleen-pancreas meridians. Lymph nodes are contained here. So are the main arteries and nerve intersection.
		S36	It is located between the bones at the top of the shin.	This point is a stomach high point. It is used to decrease the appetite. It drains energy from the stomach meridian and decreases the rate of function. This spot may be sore for four different reasons: 1. Incorrect digestion. Cont'd.

MERIDIAN	GENERAL COMMENTS	IMPORTANT POINTS	LOCATION	INDICATIONS
Stomach Meridian (Cont'd.)				2. Water retention. 3. Tension or blockage in legs. 4. Inflammation of blood vessels (causing varicose veins and phlebitis). This point can be used to drain energy from the entire body—it is a point for cleansing, so it is used to relieve problems resulting from congestion: headache, sinus or nasal blockage, inflammation in the mouth, ulcers, acute congestion, indigestion caused by over-acidity or food corruption, thigh problems, cellulite, impotence caused by congestion or nervousness, premature ejaculation caused by anxiety, menstrual cramps and menstrual problems caused by accumulations, and tension.
		S40	It is located between S36 and S41	It is used to dissolve phlegm and remove leg cramps.
		S41	It is located over the dorsum of the foot in the middle of the cruciate crural ligament.	It is a middle point. It energizes the feet and dissolves pain, especially in the feet.
Spleen-Pancreas Meridian	The spleen-pancreas meridian has an ascending flow of energy. It runs from the end of the large toe and up the sides of the trunk. This is the best meridian for sending energy to all the internal organs at once. It is generally used along with the liver and the kidney meridians, which are in the same area and which are also ascending in energy flow.	SP4	It is located behind the front end of the proximal phalange on the inner side of the foot.	This point is usually a little tender. It is used to send energy to the joints, to relieve weakness or pain in the ankles, to relieve the symptoms of diabetes (especially in the lower lymph area), and send energy to the pancreas.
		SP6	It is located four fingers up from the top of the ankle bone on the inside	This is a middle point, which is always Cont'd.

MERIDIAN	GENERAL COMMENTS	IMPORTANT POINTS	LOCATION	INDICATIONS
Spleen-Pancreas Meridian (Cont'd.)			of the leg.	used in Tuei-Na, because three meridians converge at its location: the liver, kidney, and spleen-pancreas meridians. It is used to tonify the body. Pain from depression of this point indicates water retention, menstrual problems and liver imbalance. Use with S36, which drains energy, to create a balance. This point can be used to encourage the liver and spleen to produce more blood which is replenishing and nourishing.
		SP9	It is located on the inside of the leg at the bottom of the knee.	It is used for energizing the entire body. It is a powerful point. It does not connect with the liver and kidney meridians. This is a high point.
		SP10	It is located at the top of the knee on the inner side of the knee.	It is used for varicose veins, hardened arteries, and it energizes the blood vessels.
		SP21	It is located on both sides of the rib cage.	This point is usually tender when depressed. It leads directly to the heart, and if this point is blocked, no energy will go to the heart. It is used to energize the heart.
Heart Meridian	The heart meridian has a descending flow of energy. It runs from the middle of the armpit to the end of the little finger. It is generally used to disperse energy from the heart or the small intestine.	H3	It is located at the inner side of the arm in the crease when the elbow is flexed.	It drains energy from the heart to slow it down. It is the high point of the heart meridian.
	Stroking downward on the heart meridian to relax the heart (especially during palpitation to avoid heart attack.)	H9	It is located on the inner corner of the fingernail of the little finger.	It is used during emergencies, such as heart attacks, because it releases the heart, blood, and energy. It is a low point.

MERIDIAN	GENERAL COMMENTS	IMPORTANT POINTS	LOCATION	INDICATIONS
Small Intestine Meridian	The small intestine meridian has an ascending flow of energy. It runs from the hand to the upper back to the head and is used to augment the energy of the small intestine, the heart, and the arm.	SI9	It is located under the arm where the arm meets the back.	When we are tired we cannot absorb the nutrients in your food and the small intestine becomes corrupt. This point is used to augment the energy of the small intestine to prevent such problems.
		SI13	Located midway on the back torso, towards the inner edge of the shoulder blade.	It follows a straight line along with TH15 and GB21. Application of Nieh technique is recommended for relief of tension and stress.
		SI17 and SI19	These points are located behind and in front of the ear.	These points are used for energizing the ear. They are also used for ear problems such as deafness or ringing in the ears. With the thumb on SI17 and the index finger on SI19, tap on the index finger with the middle finger.
Bladder Meridian	This meridian has a descending flow of energy. It runs from the head to the foot. The lower part of the meridian is used for sedating, and the upper part is used for determining the condition of the internal organs.	B1 and B2	They are located at the inside corner of the eye and the eyebrow.	They are used to drain energy from the eyes.
		B10	This is located behind the head on the edge of scalp bone.	This point is used for draining energy from the head to temporarily relieve tension and headaches (including migraine headaches). Use the thumbs to rotate, apply pressure and vibrate the point. Do this ten times and repeat.
		B11 through B30 / B36 through B49	These points are located beside the mid-dorsal line. They are found all along the spine.	These points are used to determine the condition of the internal organs. If pain is felt when these points are depressed, problems are indicated and these points should be rubbed until the pain goes away.

MERIDIAN	GENERAL COMMENTS	IMPORTANT POINTS	LOCATION	INDICATIONS
Bladder Meridian (Cont'd.)		B50	It is located under the fold of the buttocks in the center of the leg.	It is used to relieve acute pain or congestion in the legs.
		B54	It is located in the middle of the back of the knee.	It is used to relieve arthritis pain in the knees. This is a high point.
		B58	It is located in the small depression in the middle of the calf.	It is used to relieve leg pain and cramps.
		B60	It is located behind the ankle bone at the achilles tendon.	It is used with kidney points 4, 5 and 6 to drain and tonify. It is also used to benefit the sexual organs and refresh the kidneys. It is the middle point.
Kidney Meridian	The kidney meridian has an ascending flow of energy. It runs from the middle of the sole of the foot to the chest. It is used to energize the feet, legs, bladder, kidneys, sexual organs, and the entire body because the kidneys and the feet are the roots of the body.	K1	It is located in the middle of the sole of the feet.	It is used to energize the feet, the kidney and the entire body. It is low point.
		K4, K5, and K6	These are located around the protruding ankle bone.	These are used to tonify the sexual organs and refresh the kidneys. K5 is a middle point.
		K9	It is located at the bottom of the calf on the inside of the leg.	If soreness is felt when this point is depressed, sexual depletion is indicated. This point is used to tonify. It is a high point.
Heart Constrictor Meridian	This meridian is covered when stroking the arm. It has a descending flow of energy. This meridian is used to sedate the heart and relax the blood vessels.	HC5	It is located 1 inch above the wrist, in the middle of the inner side of the arm.	Relax the blood vessels by pressing this point. Very effective for hardening of the arteries. It is a middle point.
Triple Heater Meridian	This meridian ascends from the fourth finger to the outer edge of the eyebrow. Some points on this meridian can be used to remove neck tension. Cont'd.	TH6	It is located in the same position as HC5, except it is on the outer side of the arm.	It stimulates the entire endocrine glands system, encourages sexual ability. It is a middle point.

MERIDIAN	GENERAL COMMENTS	IMPORTANT POINTS	LOCATION	INDICATIONS
Triple Heater Meridian (Cont'd.)	Some can be used to soothe the eyes. Eye weakness is associated with low levels of hormones in the triple heater.			
Gallbladder Meridian	This meridian has a descending flow of energy. It runs from the head to the foot. It is used for soothing the area of the ribs, which is very sensitive.	GB30	It is located in the center of the buttocks.	Pressure should be applied to this point with the elbow to relieve hip pain.
		GB31	It is located on the lateral part of the thigh, 7 inches above the patella.	It is used for anesthesia and for pain in legs.
		GB37	It is located five inches above the ankle bone in front of the fibula.	It is used for cleansing and stimulating the eyes. It is used especially for cataracts.
Liver Meridian	There are no particular points to be used on the liver meridian. The entire meridian is soothed by brushing upward along the kidney and spleen-pancreas meridians. The liver meridian ascends from the large toe to the liver area.			
Governing Vessel (Tu-Mo)	This meridian runs from the tail bone to a point directly under the nose.	Every point along the spine	There is a point on every vertebra.	Picking the spine tissues from bottom to top is great enjoyment. Tonifying every part of the body.
		TU26	Located in the middle of the upper lip.	An emergency point. Pressing it may bring a dead person back to life.
Conception Vessel (J'en-Mo)	This meridian runs from the point be-tween the scrotum (or vagina) and the anus to a point under the bottom lip.	JEN 4	It is located on the mid-abdominal line, 3 inches below the umbilicus.	It is a very important point in the treat-ment of kidneys and sexual organs.
		JEN 12	It is located on the mid-abdominal line, 4 inches above the umbilicus.	It is used for indigestion or any stomach trouble.
		JEN 22	It is located in the depression at the throat.	It is used for coughing, scratchy throat, and prevention of colds.

MERIDIAN	ASSOCIATED PROBLEMS
Lung Meridian	Fullness or pressure in chest; Urge to protect the chest with the arms; Fuzzy vision; Coughing; Wheezing; Shortness of breath; Pain in the L1 and L2 areas; Susceptibility to colds; Painful; Pulling sensation in the back half of the shoulder area; Pain along the lung meridian on the arm; Weakness in the thumb; Urge to urinate (only minimal amounts of urine are excreted); Variation in the coloration of the urine; Afternoon fever (a serious lung problem); Wet dreams; Diarrhea; Insomnia; Overwhelming sexual drive; and Irrational emotional involvement.
Large Intestine Meridian	Gum, jaw, and tooth problems; Swelling of the entire neck (not lymph nodes); Sensation of dryness in the mouth; Sore throat; Sinus or eye allergies; Dryness; Bleeding; Constipation; Diarrhea; Cracking or growth in the nose tissues; Pain in the front half of the shoulder area; Problems in the index finger; Pain in the areas 3 inches to the sides of the navel; Pain and chilly sensation in the lower back area; and Feelings of cold and exhaustion in the entire body.
Stomach Meridian	Chills; Sighing; Yawning; Temporary dark patching on the face; Light sensitivity of the eyes; Disgust for people; Sensitivity to wooden sounds (sounds produced by knocking on doors, etc.); Nosebleeds; Canker sores or cracks in mouth tissues; Heart palpitation; Blue-colored lips; Paralysis and swelling of the esophagus (causes pain when swallowing); Severe stomach pain; Kneecap pain and swelling; Hardness in the stomach area; Constant hunger and heartburn; Severe pain in S36 area (pressing on point shoots pain to the knee); Pain, spasm, and numbness in the second toe; Yellow-colored urine; Indigestion; Feeling of coldness in the stomach area; and Gurgling noises in the stomach.
Spleen- Pancreas Meridian	Nausea after meals; Paleness of the skin; Pain that shoots from the left to the right sides of the body; Relief after flatulence; Heavy feeling in the limbs; Gummy feces; Pain or stiffness in the base of the tongue; Yellowish tint of the skin; Infrequent urination; Problems in the big toe; Unnecessary worrying; Hypoglycemia; Imagining that one is never getting enough sleep; and Pain in the inner sides of the thighs.
Heart Meridian	Deep chest pain; Problems in the small finger; Pain and dryness of the tip of the tongue; Pain on the inner side of the arm; Palpitation; Redness of the face; Dull, radiating pain near the area of the nipple (women mistake this pain for breast cancer); High blood pressure; Hot flashes; Iris becoming yellow; and Sensitivity and pain in the area of the 5th and 6th vertebrae.
Small Intestine Meridian	Internal pain and swelling at both sides of the throat; Inability to turn the neck; Pain in the back side of the shoulder; Exhaustion; Inability to gain weight; Problems in the little finger; Pain in the area around the navel; Bursitis on the outer side of the arm; Ringing in the ears; Delay in menses; Looseness in abdominal skin; and Unprocessed food in the feces.
Bladder Meridian	Throbbing pain at the top of the head; Pain in the eyes; Feeling of dryness in the eyes; Pulling pain at the back of the head and neck; Any spine problem; Inability to bend at the waist; Pain at the back part of the knees; Charleyhorse; Hemorrhoids; Madness; Tearing whenever the wind blows into the eyes; Dripping nose; Problems in the small toe; Burning sensation in the bladder area; and Frequent, infrequent, or uncontrolled urination.

MERIDIAN	ASSOCIATED PROBLEMS
Kidney Meridian	Tired expression or darkness in the center of the face; Blood in the phlegm; Hoarseness of voice; Fuzzy or floating vision; Floating sensation of the heart; Feeling hungry without an appetite for food; Unfounded fears; Dryness and pain in the throat and mouth; Diarrhea; Irritability (sometimes combined with chest pressure); Pain along the inner side of the leg or sciatic nerve pain; Severe pain due to kidney stones (may be mistaken for stomach pain); Great amounts of urine or blood in urine; Swelling or edema of leg or foot; Pain in the sole of the foot (at point K1); Low or no sexual drive or impotence; Disturbed sleep and Weakness in the legs.
Heart Constrictor Meridian	Tingling or pulling pain at the inner side of the elbow; Burning or hot sensation in the palms; Pressure in the chest; Skipping heartbeat; High blood pressure and red face; Easily excitable; Chest pain (it shoots to the collar bone); Coughing or spitting of blood; Problems in the middle finger; and Encephalitis.
Triple Heater Meridian	Deafness, memory loss, and weak eyesight; Throat infection; Lower back pain; Metabolism slowdown; High or low blood sugar levels; Trouble in the sexual glands; Infection of the urethra; Problems in the ring finger; Tiredness; Emotional highs or lows; and Cold feet and hands.
Gallbladder Meridian	Bitterness in the mouth; Sighing; Pain in the ribcage; Dull complexion; Pain on the outer side of the foot; Softness of the bones; Migraine headache; Whites of the eyes becoming yellow-green or pain on the outer corner of the eye; Tumor in the thyroid or armpit areas; Perspiration; Pain shooting from the right to the left side of the knee; Colorless stools; and Problems in the small toe.
Liver Meridian	Pain in the entire side of the body; Water retention; Whites of the eyes becoming yellow-grey; Pain in the liver area; Vomiting; Fever; Gurgling of the stomach followed by diarrhea; Over-acidity; Pain in the testicles; Menstrual cramps; Bedwetting or constant dripping of urine; Extreme depression; Irrationality; Pulling pain in the inner side of the thigh; Problems in the big toe; and Pressure on the lower chest.

IV

Realizing that all human beings share similar organic structures, Taoists designed a general healing program to energize and balance the entire body. The general healing program utilizes all of the sixteen Tuei-Na techniques and most of the meridian points. This program, called Tune Up, will serve as a guideline for the design of treatment programs by healers.

The Tune Up can be completed in an hour. When specific problems are worked on in addition, more time is needed. In the Tune Up, selected points on the entire body must be manipulated in the order described below. The techniques to be used on the points are also described below: An, Nieh, Zhe, etc.

One final note: Jade Cream should be used during the Tune Up.

Step by Step Procedure for "Tune Up"
of the body or Taoist massage

I. **THE BACK OF THE BODY** (patient on stomach)
   A. The Legs
      1. Both legs at the same time
         a. K1 (An) with thumbs
         b. B60, K4, K5, and K6 (Nieh)
         c. SP6 (An) with thumbs
         d. GB37 (An) with thumbs
         e. B58 and B54 (An) with thumbs
      2.. One leg at a time
         f. Knees and ankles (Zhe)
         g. Repeat steps (a) through (e) for one leg and then the other leg
         h. B51 (An with palms, then Chue, then Pai and then Rou)
         i. Muo upward along the inside of the leg with the palm. Then Muo downward along the GB and B meridians on the outside of the leg with the thumb and index finger
      3. Both legs at the same time
         j. Chue thighs with the fist, palm and sides of the hands
         k. K1 (An) with thumbs
         l. Repeat step (i) except do so for both legs at once
   B. Buttocks and Lower Back

m. GB30 (An) with the elbow

n. B30 through B25. (An) with thumbs

C. The Back
1. B11 through B25 (An with the thumb and index finger to find deficiency in the organs of the body)
2. Muo up the spine and down the B meridian. Do this several times
3. Lower back and kidney area (Nieh)
4. Stroke back and forth across the small of the back with both hands 36 times
5. Nieh sharply with the thumb and index fingers up the lower spine and down the upper spine. Do this three to five times
6. Nieh downward along the B meridian, for chronic problems
7. GB21, SI13, TH15 (Rou and Yun). Any pain indicates a blockage
8. S19 (gentle pressure)

II. **THE FRONT OF THE BODY** (person is lying on his back)
A. The Legs
1. S41 (An) with thumbs simultaneously on both legs
2. SP6 and GB37 (An) with thumbs simultaneously on both legs
3. S36 through S41 (Tuei three times)
4. Muo downward along the S meridian with the thumb. Then Muo upward along the L, SP and K meridians to the knee with the palm of the hand
5. Repeat steps 3 through 4 for the other leg
6. Thighs (Pai up and down)
7. Rou and Nieh the K meridian from the knees to the pelvic bone. Repeat for the other leg
8. Muo upward along the inside of the legs and downward along the outside of the legs. Repeat for the other leg
9. Grasp points K4, K5, K6, B54 and B60 with both hands and Jen (shake) both legs
10. Then Zhe (bend) legs after shaking them
11. Standing in between both legs, Muo upward along the entire length of the inner sides of both legs. Then Muo downward along the entire length of the outer sides of both legs

B. The Arms
1. L14 (Nieh)
2. Tsa downward from L5, then Tsa upward along the outside of the entire arm

3. Shake arm
4. Repeat steps 1 through 3 for the other arm
5. LI10 (Rou) for bursitis or tennis elbow
6. LI14 (An) with thumb
7. Repeat steps 5 and 6 for the other arm

C. The Neck
   1. An L1 and L2 with the thumb. An GB21, SI13 and TH15 with four fingers
   2. B10 (An) with thumb
   3. Repeat step 1

D. The Face
   1. B1, B2, S1, GB1, LI20 and S4 (An) with thumb
   2. An SI17 with the thumb and SI 19 with the index fingers
   3. Rub across the forehead with the thumbs. Then press the temple very hard. Release. Then repeat
   4. Rub the third eye. Then Tsa up the forehead

E. The Breasts (female)
   1. Rub around the nipples. Rub outward in case of water retention and rub inward for stimulation

F. The Abdomen
   1. Using the palm of either hand, rub in a clockwise motion starting at the navel and rub in increasingly larger circles. Move slowly with no pressure. Reverse the motion

G. The Stomach
   1. Muo downard over the S meridian. Muo upward with the thumb over the K meridian and the fingers on the SP meridian. Do this while standing on one side. Repeat the entire procedure while standing on the other side
   2. Repeat circular rubbing of the abdomen described under F

H. The Final Movements
   1. Stroke upward along the K, Liver and SP meridians. Avoid the S meridian on the chest. Stroke downward along the L, H and HC meridians on the arms. Stroke upward along the LI, SI and TH meridians to the S meridian. Stroke downward along the S meridian to the toes
   2. Stroke the K meridian starting from the K1 point up to the pelvic bone
   3. With the person sitting up, vibrate and then Chue the shoulders and neck

The Tune Up also includes a complete healing facial massage. It uses facial preparations composed with Taoist principles. Although these preparations were reserved for the Royal family of China during a long period of history, they are now used by Taoist cultivators. Their composition is disclosed at the end of Chapter 4; they include only precious and natural ingredients known since ancient times for their fabulous healing properties, such as gold, frankincense, myrrh, jade, pearl, queen bee royal jelly and ginseng.

It was a great honor to receive such healing facial massage, which could be granted as an official "Royal Treat" to special guests. These preparations earned a great reputation for solving skin problems and promoting lasting beauty. They were also sought for their health and life enhancing benefits. The Ancient Taoists analyzed in great detail how the face reflects one's health and life circumstances as described under "Facial Reading" in Chapter 4 and "Personology" in Chapter 7. Since the whole body is interconnected, one can work on facial locations to relieve the related internal organs and improve life. This approach would not surprise the readers familiar with foot reflexology although this facial system is of course different.

Readers interested in more information about this healing facial massage can request it from the publisher of this book. In addition, they can also refer to my manual, *The Complete Book of Acupuncture*, for acupressure points specialized for facial beauty.

To give someone this healing facial massage, follow the instructions below:

1. Assemble these items:
    Washcloth (with a slit cut in the middle)
    Facial Steaming Machine (if you have one)
    Royal Vital Clean-Off
    S.A.R. Gold Lotion
    Royal Nutri-Mask
    Essence of Pearl
    Royal Jade Cream
2. Have the person who will receive the facial lie on his or her back. Roll up the washcloth and immerse it in hot water. Squeeze out the water and unroll the cloth on the face, positioning it so that the nose can breath through the slit. Then clean the face with Royal Vital Clean-Off mixed with a little water. Repeat the procedure described for the washcloth several times. This relaxes the tissues, gets rid of surface dirt and opens the pores.
3. Apply a very thin layer of S.A.R. Gold Lotion to the wet face with the fingertips. Then steam for 10 minutes. This procedure allows the S.A.R. Gold Lotion to penetrate deeply into the pores to loosen dirt deposits, nourish the skin cells and repair damaged or unhealthy cells.

4. Pat on the mask with fingertips (the mask should be made into a paste by mixing it with water first). Wait until the mask is dry and then wash it off. This removes dead skin particles and helps generate new cells.
5. Then re-apply S.A.R. Gold Lotion to tighten the skin and prevent bacterial growth.
6. Next apply a thin layer of Essence of Pearl for long-term moisturizing of the skin.
7. Follow with Royal Jade Cream. The cream should be applied to the whole face. A greater amount of cream should be placed on the following points:

 *Figure 92*

Massage the areas around the eyes gently by moving the fingertips lightly in a circle around the eyes. Follow the direction of the arrows. Then rub the palms together to generate heat. Place the palms on the eyes. This procedure prevents the formation of wrinkles and it gives the skin a natural tan. The cream also preserves the youth of the skin cells and makes the skin glow with life.

People with extra-oily skin should not be given this final treatment. They should be treated with Essence of Pearl, to correct their condition. When the condition is corrected, the final step can be included in their treatment.

Tuei-Na is a healing art: the healer must design programs to suit individual needs. By knowing the meridian points, the techniques, the tools, the Five Elements Theory, and the basic theories of Tuei-Na, one can easily construct a healing program for any kind of physical problem. No two Tui-Na sessions are completely alike, with the exception of the Tune Up program. Everlasting health can be attained by applying the principles of Tuei-Na.

The healer is most important. In tests using Kirlian photography, it was found that people who heal or have the ability to heal emit greater amounts of energy from their fingertips than other people. Healers are people who love humanity enough to want to help by sharing their energy. To accomplish this, the healer must have extensive knowledge of the workings of the human body and must prevent depletion of his own energy. The healer must be rich in spirit, mind and body to build up abundant energy reserves. Otherwise the healer will soon be ill. There is a saying which expresses the healer's responsibility clearly: "Healer, heal thyself."

If you are interested in Acupuncture, please refer to *The Complete Book of Acupuncture* by Stephen T. Chang (Celestial Art).

6

THE TAO OF SEX WISDOM

I

The conquest of death has been the goal of people in all cultures, in all times. The Tao of Sex Wisdom is the answer to mankind's search for eternal youth, happiness, health and wisdom.

Taoists realize from the reproductive process that the sexual glands are endowed with God's power to create and God's intelligence to organize life. In fact, God is also called energy. He is the life force which animates all living things and the motor of the creative process. He is the intelligence which engineers life and gives healing ability to the body to repair itself.

Since the sexual glands are themselves the source of life, the Taoists felt that these glands could also be used as a source of vitality or life force for their own bodies and discovered the methods of the Tao of Sex Wisdom for that purpose. By using these methods, we can revitalize ourselves with this living energy and promote self-healing to its full power. By energizing the whole physical body we can eventually incarnate God's nature to its fullest. All together, this is the process of longevity and eventually immortality.

The Tao of Sex Wisdom is quite different from the clinical or behavioral sexology that many people currently study and practice. The Tao of Sex Wisdom is a series of techniques that harmonize with the natural inclinations of the body and awaken the intuitive and spiritual centers. It does not stop at the stage of ordinary orgasm, which is the only focus of many people today.

Many negative beliefs have arisen around sex. Many people think that sex is dirty or sinful because they have no understanding of how sex relates to spirituality. Some religions set aside sex and advocate celibacy to heighten spiritual awareness. But guilt and celibacy result in the atrophy of the sexual glands. Taoists teach that exercising the sexual glands as if they were another part of the body — which they are—will preserve the hormone, nutrition and energy levels and bring direct benefit to the body thereby protecting it from disease and deterioration and opening the doors to higher levels of spirituality.

Most religions only worship God. They provide beautiful words, pictures or statues, but they do not provide a direct, tangible experience of God. God is everywhere and can be experienced everywhere. If one has always been blind, one cannot fully understand the meaning of the word *light*. Without experienceing love, you cannot fully understand the meaning of God. To experience love is to experience God. Experiencing love brings mankind closer to God.

The Tao of Sex Wisdom is a refreshing solution to reconcile people's common dilemma between their sexual instincts and their spiritual aspirations. On one hand, some social influences promote the sexual instincts at the animalistic level only. On the other hand, many religions ban or debase sexual activity hoping to promote a spiritual orientation away from the animalistic instincts. Neither approach fulfills people's needs, since human beings have both

296

physical instincts and spiritual aspirations. Tao of Sex Wisdom eliminates this dilemma by allowing the sexual instincts to serve a spiritual purpose.

The basic text of the Tao of Sex Wisdom is the *Shu Nu Ching,* or *The Classic of the White Madame.* The text was written at the time of the Yellow Emperor. It is based on the conversations between the emperor and his two wives, one dark and one light. The unity of these three—the Black Madame, the White Madame, and the Yellow Emperor—is intended as a spiritual symbol of the universal nature of Taoism. These conversations, which form the basis of the Tao of Sex Wisdom, are about the relationship between spirituality and sexuality.

Throughout its 6,000-year history, the book was regarded as a priceless jewel of knowledge. For thousands of years, most people were forbidden from reading it, since it contained genetic secrets .

About 1,500 years ago, during the Sui Dynasty, the book mysteriously disappeared. Luckily its name and contents were recorded in the pages of history.

Somehow the book reappeared in the Japanese imperial court about 100 years ago, during the period of the Meji Modernization. When Emperor Meji instituted a democratic form of government, the populace urged the royal family to reveal the book's secrets. The book was then translated into Japanese. The Chinese recovered the original copy from the Japanese Royal Family and reproduced it in many editions.

During its 1,400-year disappearance, the Chinese became even more secretive about the information contained within the *Shu Nu Ching.* The information, then transferred orally, was revealed only after performing elaborate rituals that insured secrecy and after a great price was paid. Although a great deal of money and effort was invested in the hopes of obtaining the information, there was no guarantee that the information was revealed in whole.

The *Shu Nu Ching* was written in classical Chinese, and vital information was hidden within the verses. If a person did not have the key, the treasure room could not be opened. Not everyone was able to read or understand the book.

People have told me — after following some of the Tao of Sex Wisdom techniques — that they finally understand what it is to enjoy not just sex, but life itself. They say they have received a lifetime of benefits from what they have learned.

Longer, happier, healthier and wiser lives can be attained through the practice of the Tao of Sex Wisdom. This is so because the Ancient Taoists were not ethereal, abstract philosophers. They were very practical people who discarded a technique when it did not work and who only developed and used techniques that did work.

People die from two things: disease and deterioration of cells.

To prevent disease, one must protect the immune system. A Taoist aphorism succinctly states that immunity is a natural gift of life:

When one does not incur small diseases,
one will not incur moderate diseases.
When one does not incur moderate diseases,
one will not incur serious diseases.
When one incurs no serious diseases,
one will never die.

In other words, if one keeps the resistance of one's body high, one will not be affected by germs or viruses. A person who is weak and lacks resistence can be killed by one germ.

To prevent deterioration, one must be "reborn." Jesus said that one cannot get into the Kingdom of God without rebirth.

Rebirth is based on the theory that sexual energy, capable of producing life, can also be used for rejuvenating old cells. Rebirth is called Abstract Pregnancy by Taoists. If one can make oneself "pregnant," one can give old cells new life.

Aging is the result of deterioration, death, or non-replacement of cells. A newborn baby is fresh because every cell in the baby's body is fresh. If our cells are always fresh, we will not age, and we will not die.

Both prevention of disease and prevention of deterioration can be achieved through the practice of the Tao of Sex Wisdom teachings. Why the Tao of Sex Wisdom is effective against disease and deterioration will be explained in the following pages.

II

The Tao of Sex Wisdom
as a Preventative of Disease

Medical science concentrates on one approach to healing which is more a classical approach to warfare than it is to healing. It finds the germs and kills them. That is why we have antibiotics and other medicines.

Taoists say it is best to prevent disease in the beginning. Taoists do not study disease, they study life and health and how to maintain them. This is the basic difference in approach between Taoism and medicine. Certainly, Taoists know how to heal. It is necessary that they do. But, their major concern is to prevent disease, to prevent their students from ever contracting a disease in the first place.

This is why Taoists have developed other methods of healing. The purpose is to increase longevity, not to get bogged down in fighting disease.

The ancient Taoists knew there were hundreds of millions of different kinds of germs, bacteria and viruses and that it was pointless to try to develop ways to kill them all. They realized that the only sensible approach is to keep the body healthy so it can resist all of its intruders. As a result, a very detailed and complete preventative method emerged thousands of years ago which is still very practical for our use today.

The human body is like an electric battery: it needs energy to function. At its functional best, it needs a maximum amount of energy. What happens if you, a human battery, do not have enough energy in your system? If you have only 70% of your full energy capacity, you will feel miserable. If you are only 50% full, you will end up in the hospital. If only 20% energy is left, you are under intensive care. At 0% the battery is empty and you are dead.

If you were to go to a funeral and pay your last respects to the deceased, he might look just the same as always. The only difference between him and you would be that his battery was dead. His body would lay unanimated. His spirit or life or energy would be gone. He would have no juice, no electricity left. That is why the Taoist principle is to keep your battery full always — to keep recharging yourself continually. You have heard the comment, "My resistance is down." This statement indicates that the person has less than 100% of his charge of energy. He is tired, run-down and susceptible to colds, illness, etc.

As soon as we open our eyes in the morning, we begin depleting energy. Every daily activity we ordinarily do will deplete our battery, weaken the immune system, and finally lower our resistence.

We receive much of the energy we need from the food we eat and the air we breathe. However, the body, much like an expensive automobile, must be finely tuned if it is to run properly and utilize this energy to the maximum.

Throughout the centuries, Taoists have understood that the body's seven glands are the energy centers which are responsible for regulating the flow of energy within the various systems of the body.

These seven glands, in descending order within the body, are:

1. The pineal gland, which directly affects the other glands through its secretions and allows one to communicate on the spiritual level. Intuition and conscience are also associated with this gland.
2. The pituitary gland, which governs the mind, i.e., memory, intelligence, wisdom and thought.
3. The thyroid gland, which maintains the metabolism of the cells in the body, governs growth and is also associated with the breathing system.
4. The thymus, which governs the heart and circulatory system.
5. The pancreas, which helps maintain control over digestion, blood sugar level and body temperature.
6. The adrenals, which support the functioning of the kidneys, bones and spine.
7. The sexual glands—the prostate and testes in the male, and the ovaries, uterus, vagina and breasts in the female—which are responsible for hormone secretions, sexual energy and response, and reproduction.

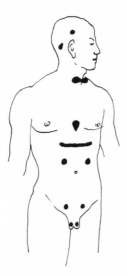

Figure 93

These seven glands may be visualized as vessels which are attached to one another by a series of arteries or tubes. Each vessel (gland) is dependent upon all the others for its supply of liquid (energy). If Vessel A (the sexual glands) is supplied with liquid,

300

this fluid will slowly disperse through the arteries to the remaining six vessels. Similarly, if Vessel C (the pancreas) were to be drained excessively of its fluid through a leakage of some kind, each of the other vessels would give up a portion of its supply to re-establish an equilibrium within the system.

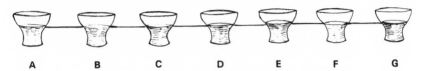

A   B   C   D   E   F   G

Figure 94

This is similar to the way energy flows within our bodies. A state of weakness or susceptibility to disease arises when one system, or in this case one gland, is deprived of energy for some reason. Our task then becomes to re-establish the balanced flow of energy so that we raise the level of energy within our body to its maximum.

Balancing the energy to its proper level is the Taoist way to re-establish the immune system. Through this increase of energy, we can then reverse our existing weakness and heal ourselves, as well as utilize the higher order of energy to open up our spiritual centers.

The sexual glands form the base of the glandular complex. The energy which supports the pineal, pituitary, thyroid, thymus, pancreas and adrenal glands is generated in the sex organs. When the sexual glands are not kept healthy through the practice of Tao of Sex Wisdom techniques, the entire body suffers.

The Tao of Sex Wisdom
as a Preventative of Deterioration

Taoists refer to the sexual glands as the "stove." A stove must have fire inside. Without fire, the stove will be useless to mankind because life will terminate when no food is cooked. The sexual hormones, or sexual fluids, are the body's "fire." These terms, "stove" and "fire," are ancient alchemical terms, from the days when this information was kept very secret. But they still provide a good metaphor to show how the process of rebirth works.

Another ancient alchemical term is "water." This term includes all the body's secretions from the kidneys, bladder, adrenals and sexual organs.

Jesus said that one has to be born of water and spirit. This may sound very confusing, but from the Taoist point of view it is very

301

clear. Because the "water" he was speaking of refers to the sexual organs. The sexual organs and kidneys, considered to be sister organs in Taoism, are related to the water element and have a mutual effect on each other. It is through the sexual organs, sexual function, and the process called rebirth that you can enter the Kingdom of God. In reality, the Kingdom of God is already within you. You merely have to help it surface.

Rebirth is a means of recharging one's "battery," to raise one's energy level and prevent aging. Aging occurs throughout the course of daily living. Aging occurs when sleep, the regular means of energy elevation, is hindered by insomnia or blockages in the body. (Sleep allows the universal energy to penetrate the points of entry and exit, also called acupuncture points, travel through all the meridians, and permeate and recharge every cell. This allows a person to wake up refreshed.) Aging occurs when non-Taoist methods of intercourse deplete the body's energy and cause a great deal of tension. (This tension blocks the body's ability to receive energy.) Also if one of the partners has a very low energy level, he or she will drain energy from the other person, since energy travels from areas of higher concentration to areas at lower concentration. Even if a couple is on the same energy level, an energy loss can still result.

III

Practical Techniques

The following pages contain important teachings of the Tao of Sex Wisdom.

Ejaculation

The physiological function of the prostate gland is ejaculation. When the penis is stimulated, the prostate swells with secretions. These secretions contain nutrients, hormones and vital energy. They constitute the semen which is the substance that serves as carrier for the sperm. (Sperm is produced in the testicles.)

When the average male ejaculates, he loses about one tablespoon of semen. According to research, the nutritional value of this amount of semen is equal to two pieces of New York steak, ten eggs, six oranges and two lemons combined! That includes proteins, vitamins, minerals, amino acids, etc.

An ejaculation also represents a great deal of lost vital energy. This is demonstrated by how tired a man feels after ejaculation. A popular expression for this is "coming." The word for it should be "going," because everything goes away: energy, hormones, nutrients, even a little of his personality! It is a great sacrifice for a man. He gives much away spiritually, mentally, emotionally and physically.

When the prostate gland swells to its maximum capacity, it begins a rapid series of contractions until it shrinks to its normal size. These contractions squeeze the secretions from the prostate through the urethra, into the penis and then out the tip of the penis. This is the process of ejaculation. Orgasm is an outcome of ejaculation.

Each time the prostate contracts and relaxes it draws sperm from the testicles. It is possible for a man to experience as many as twenty-one contractions. Since ejaculation is a function of the prostate gland, someone with prostate problems may experience only five contractions within an orgasm, or even only one. If there is a problem in the prostate, there will be a problem with ejaculation.

In a man, the sexual glands consist of the prostate and the testicles. The penis itself is not considered part of the sexual glands since it doesn't produce anything. It is simply a tube or channel through which the glandular secretions can pass, an instrument to be used by the sexual glands for procreation. The testicles produce the sperm and the prostate produces the semen with all its nutrients, hormones and vital energy.

The semen itself represents a great deal of vital energy in addition to its nutritional value. The ejaculation of the semen includes several hundred million live sperm. The loss of vital energy after ejaculation results in a lost erection. As the man "injaculates" as explained next, he retains this precious vital energy and is able to maintain his erection. This facilitates his taking the woman up through the nine levels of complete Taoist orgasm. What people commonly think of as orgasm in a woman actually only represents the fourth level in this nine-level sequence.

After ejaculation, all of the seven glands are depleted, particularly the sexual glands. According to Taoism, if you go in this direction — moving the energy down through the seven glands and out of the body — you are moving in the direction of the human being, and all human beings eventually die. However, by going in the other direction — moving the energy upward through the seven glands in the body — you can live an immortal life, a Divine life. For this reason, the ancient Taoists searched and uncovered a way for a man to have even more enjoyable orgasms without ejaculation, thereby retaining and utilizing his own vital energy.

The "Million Dollar Point": Injaculation vs. Ejaculation; Prolongation of Arousal: Natural Birth Control; Longevity

In Taoist Sexology, the man has his orgasm *without* ejaculating. Instead, he "injaculates." By pressing an acupuncture point located halfway between the anus and scrotum, the ejaculation can be reversed into an improved orgasm and the semen is recycled from the full prostate into the blood. This point is known as the "Jen Mo" (Conception Meridian) acupuncture point. When pressed with a finger, this point feels as if there is a small indentation or hole on the location.

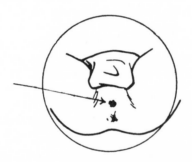

Figure 95

When the "Jen-Mo" point is pressed just prior to an anticipated ejaculation, the energy goes up into the body through the meridians which originate at this point, instead of going out of the body as it does during ordinary ejaculation. Done in this way, the man still has the pleasurable sensations which come with the contractions of the prostate and he still experiences an orgasm. He continues to press this point until the orgasm, or "injaculation," is complete.

This "Jen-Mo" point was nicknamed "the million dollar point" by one of my students. He said that he felt like a million dollars after he began using this technique. Everyone who has tried it has felt it deserved, the name. Other students have told me that before learning this method they felt like "lions" before orgasm, but took a nose dive just after! With the "million dollar point" there are no more nose dives, just soaring lions. One of the important benefits of this technique is that the man will dramatically increase his ability to maintain an erection. This will allow him to carry out all the steps of Taoist intercourse, and bring the woman to an orgasm as she has never experienced before.

Pressing the "million dollar point" is easy, and with a little practice you can do it quite discreetly without your partner ever knowing it. At the moment just before you are ready to ejaculate, simply reach around behind your buttocks and locate the point. Press it hard enough so that the semen is not allowed to travel out of the prostate and through the urethra.

Some practice may be necessary to learn exactly where to press and how much. You may wish to practice alone to master the technique. The pressure should be neither too heavy nor too light. If you press too close to the anus, you will not stop the ejaculation. If you press too close to the scrotum, the semen will enter the bladder and be lost when you urinate. In either case, you will have lost the benefit of the exercise. The pressure must close the channels right at the base of the prostate gland for the semen not to be lost through ejaculation or into the bladder. Only then is the semen recycled into the blood. See figure 95 for a better understanding. (While learning this technique, you might press with three fingers just to be safe. Also, don't become discouraged. Much practice may be required for perfect mastery.)

A word of caution here: if you have a prostate infection, it must be cleared up before you begin using the "million dollar point." It is perfectly fine, however, to use the anal contraction technique from the Deer Exercise or to massage the prostate gland directly to assist in the healing process. When the problem has been taken care of, then go ahead and begin pressing this point.

If you have pressed the point and prevented ejaculation, there is a way to tell if the semen has gone into the blood steam or the bladder. Urinate into a glass. If the urine is cloudy, you will know that the semen passed into the bladder. If you set the glass aside for an hour or two, you will see that the semen has settled to the bottom, leaving clear urine at the top.

People whose diet is very alkaline will tend to have bubbly urine, but it will be much more so if semen has become mixed in with the urine. During ordinary ejaculation—that is, when *not* using the "million dollar point"—about one third of the semen goes into the bladder.

305

Taoism is not theoretical. It gives you immediate results. When you press this point you will begin to experience the creative energy being drawn up from your sexual glands.

For a woman, the equivalent of this is achieved through discontinuing the menstrual period, which can be achieved by practicing the women's Deer Exercise. When a woman no longer menstruates she no longer loses vital energy contained in the blood. Of course, this happens naturally anyway with the menopause, which is a great blessing despite the way many people view it. However, through the use of the Deer Exercise, this can occur earlier and a woman can reverse this energy loss sooner.

During the first forty years of life, men and women die at about an equivalent rate, according to actuarial figures. This is because men are losing energy through ejaculation and women through menstruation. Men ejaculate, women bleed. By the age of fifty, many women have already passed through menopause. As a result the death rate becomes 25% higher for men, as most of them continue to ejaculate. At the age of sixty, men die at even a higher rate differential than women, for almost all women have passed menopause by that time. By the age of seventy, the difference in death rates is even more dramatic as men keep depleting themselves. This is a much-overlooked reason why there are so many widows and so few widowers.

Some people might feel that it is unnatural to stop the ejaculation, that the natural thing is to *have* one. This is true on one level. It is natural for *human beings,* the highest level of animal life on this planet, to have ejaculations. It is also natural for them to die. God has given us the opportunity to achieve Divine life, but it can be accomplished only if ejaculation is prevented in the Taoist way, or in the case of women, only if they cease their menstruation according to Taoist principles. It is a question of choice. So, what might be considered unnatural on the human level is totally natural and necessary on the level of Divine living.

During ordinary orgasm and ejaculation the prostate contracts and expands, pumping its secretions out of the body, until it is depleted. However, when the "million dollar point" is pressed, the prostate does not get depleted as quickly. The semen does not enter the penis. It remains in the prostate where it is absorbed into the blood steam and carried to the rest of the body. The prostate still becomes emptied, but much more slowly. This can take as long as five minutes and is part of the Taoist orgasm.

Even more important than the longer and more intense orgasm is the fact that the semen, with all its energy and nutrients, is not lost through ejaculation. It remains in the body to travel to all of

306

the seven glands and energize them. The semen further benefits the body by providing nutrients, lubricating the skin and joints, and lubricating and coating the nerves, thus preventing such disorders as multiple sclerosis, and energizing the entire body.

In Acupuncture the "million dollar point" is referred to as Number One Conception Vessel, or "Jen-Mo #1." It is an "energy gate," and our bodies always leak energy from here even when we are not having sex. So, when you press this point during sexual intercourse, not only do you prevent the semen from leaving the body, you prevent your vital energy from leaving as well. This is why the Taoist sitting position for both men and women includes the placement of the heel of one foot against this point to keep it closed. (The tip of the tongue is another point of energy leakage. In Taoist methods of meditation it is recommended that you have the tip of your tongue touching the roof of your mouth in order to retain the energy in your body.)

The "million dollar point" technique is particularly useful to athletes before a game or competition. Many of them like to use sex as a way of relaxing, and yet they are concerned about becoming tired before their competition. By using this point they will not have to worry. They will feel energized instead.

It is also useful for a woman to know about the "million dollar point." With it she can help her husband or lover obtain greater satisfaction from intercourse and avoid depletion. A student of mine said that she uses the technique by reaching over and pressing the point before her mate's ejaculation. She reported that a new partner is always impressed by his orgasmic experience. Unfortunately, she keeps the credit rather than educating him about what she is doing.

If a man suffers from premature ejaculation, pressing the "million dollar point" would prevent this occurence. However, this would be dealing only with the symptom of premature ejaculation, for the problem is actually caused by a weak prostate. For complete correction of the problem, Parts 1 and 2 of the Deer Exercise for men are recommended. These will strengthen the prostate. Prostate massage is also valuable, particularly with Royal Jade Cream. Lotus seeds in the diet will benefit the prostate, as will absorbing the secretions from the woman's vagina through the penis during intercourse. The Forgotten Foods Diet is also very valuable.

As valuable and pleasurable as the use of the "million dollar point" is — and it *is* an immediate way to begin the rejuvenation process or be "reborn" — it is still only a technique for beginners and for the prevention of possible pregnancy. The Deer Exercise, which we will now discuss, is the main technique for the prevention of ejaculation in Taoist Sexology. After sufficient practice it will replace the need to use the "million dollar point."

The Deer Exercise for Men: Rejuvenation; Natural Birth
Control; Increased Arousal
Period

The Deer Exercise achieves four important objectives. First of all, it builds up the tissues of the sexual organs. Secondly, it draws energy up through the seven glands of the body, all the way up into the pineal gland, thereby leading to a spiritual life and enlightenment. (There is an actual hormone pathway leading from the prostate, connecting with the adrenal glands and continuing on to the other glands.) Also the blood circulation in the abdominal area is increased at this time and this blood helps to transport the nutrition from the semen to the rest of the body.

Bringing the energy up into the pineal gland feels like a chill or tingling sensation going up the spine to the head. It feels a little bit like an orgasm. If you feel a sensation in the area of the pineal gland, but didn't feel the tingling go up your back, don't worry. You just didn't notice it. It *has* to go up your back to get to the top.

Self-determination is the third benefit derived from the Deer Exercise. If one gland in the seven gland system is functioning at a low level, the energy shooting up the spine will stop there. This is an indication that there is some weakness in the area that needs attention. For example, if the thymus gland is functioning poorly, the energy will stop there. The energy will continue to stop there until the thymus gland is replenished. When the thymus is again functioning at a normal level, the energy will then move further along up the spine toward the pineal gland.

If the energy moves all the way to your head during the Deer Exercise, this is an indication that all seven glands are functioning well and that there is no energy blockage in the body. If you don't feel anything during the Deer Exercise, this indicates a blockage. Everyone has the ability to experience the sensation if their body is functioning at a normal level.

The fourth benefit of the Deer Exercise is that it builds up sexual ability and enables the man to prolong sexual intercourse. During normal intercourse the prostate swells to maximum size before ejaculation, becoming full of semen mixed with sperm which has come up from the testes. During ejaculation the prostate shrinks back and empties, then refills and empties again a few times. After this, the man has completed his sexual intercourse and cannot continue to thrust. All the energy is drained out of his body as well. If, however, he uses the Deer Exercise to pump some of the semen

308

out of the prostate when it is full, pumping it in the other direction into the glands, he can empty out his prostate to perhaps eighty percent. Then the prostate can fill again, thereby maintaining sexual energy and prolonging intercourse.

Without the Deer Exercise it would be harmful to interrupt orgasm or prolong intercourse. This is because the prostate is somewhat like a rubber band: in order to retain its elasticity it needs to be released. In this case, the prostate could become enlarged, and instead of being relieved by the pumping action of ejaculation, it would remain enlarged for a long time until the semen was carried away by the blood stream. This is not a problem with the Deer Exercise because the prostate is relieved.

Figure 96

Instructions for the Man's Deer Exercise

This exercise may be done standing, sitting or lying on your back.

First Stage (The purpose of this stage is to produce the semen.)

1. Rub the palms of your hands together vigorously. This creates heat in your hands by bringing the energy of your body into your hands and palms.
2. With your right hand, cup your testicles so that the palm of

309

your hand completely covers them. (This exercise is best done without clothing.) Do not squeeze. Just a slight pressure should be felt, as well as the heat from your hand.

3. Place the palm of your left hand on the area of your pubis, one inch below your navel.
4. Move your hand in clockwise or counter-clockwise circles eighty-one times, with a slight pressure so that a gentle warmth begins to build in the area of your pubis.
5. Rub your hands together vigorously again.
6. Reverse the position of your hands so that your left hand cups your testicles and your right hand is on your pubis. Repeat the circular rubbing in the opposite direction another eighty-one times.

When the hands are doing the circling motion, concentrate on the sensation of growing warmth within the sexual organs, which are the stove for the body's energy. In all Taoist exercises it is very important, even necessary, to concentrate the mind on the purpose of the physical motions, for this will enhance the results. It will unify the body and mind to bring full power to our purpose.

Second Stage

1. Tighten the muscles around your anus and drawn them up and in. When done properly it will feel as if air is being drawn up your rectum, or as if your entire anal area is being drawn in and upward. Tighten as hard as you can and hold as long as your are able to do so comfortably.
2. Stop and relax a moment.
3. Repeat the anal contractions. Do this as many times as you can without discomfort.

As you do this second stage of the exercise, picture in your mind the sexual energy as a light or flame rising up the spine to the head.

Note: A) The ancient Chinese said to rub eighty-one times because that is equal to 9 x 9, nine being the "yang" number. Actually, it doesn't matter if you rub eighty times, eighty-two times or even one hundred times. The more the better, but the ancients liked to be precise.

B) At first you may find that you are able to hold the sphincter muscles tight for only a few seconds. Please persist, and after several weeks you will be able to hold the muscles tight for quite a while without experiencing tiredness or strain. When done properly, a pleasant feeling will be felt to travel from the base of the anus, through the spinal column, to the top of the head. This is due to pressure being placed on the prostate gland as it is gently massaged by the tightening action of the anal muscles. (The anus can be thought of as a little motor used to pump the prostate gland. It has nothing to do with the seven glands, but we can use it to work indirectly on the prostate. When the prostate goes into spasms we have an orgasm. By alternately squeezing and relaxing the anus during the Deer Exercise, the prostate is massaged and we get a high feeling.)

C) Do this exercise in the morning upon rising and before retiring at night.

Impotence

Impotence in men means there is no longer any sexual feeling. This is the result of prostate failure. If this condition persists long enough, a man finally loses normal sexual interest altogether. Medical science says that most men over the age of fifty are likely to have prostate problems, and treats this as part of the normal sequence of events in a man's life. Taoists Sexology says it is definitely *not* normal for the prostate to wear out. It happens through ignorance and misuse.

The prostate gland can be maintained in a state of health and proper functioning through regular practice of the Deer Exercise, by regular prostate massage, and through the use of special herbs formulated for the purpose of nurturing and regenerating the prostate tissues and functions. These formulas include such prostate "food" as lotus seeds, ginseng, pumpkin seeds (which contain zinc) and others. Royal Jade Cream, which is discussed in Chapter 4 is an excellent treatment for the prostate when combined with prostate massage.

The Deer Exercise for Women: Healing, Rejuvenation and Natural Birth Control

Taoist Sexology provides a way for a young, fertile woman to eliminate her menstrual period in a safe way. If the Deer Exercise, parts one and two, is used over a period of time it is effective in stopping menstruation, and is an excellent and completely safe form of birth control.

Normally during the monthly cycle, the uterus creates a lining of blood vessels to prepare a home for the anticipated fertilized egg. This fertilized egg acts like a suction cup: it sucks on the wall of the uterus and attaches itself there, draining the nutrition it needs from the mother's blood. There it continues to grow into a fully developed baby.

311

At first, some women are reluctant to stop their menstrual period. They think it is "unnatural." On the contrary, there is no need to worry. The monthly cycle is Nature's way to provide repeated opportunities to conceive. When the woman is pregnant, the body instinctively knows that there is no need for preparing the uterus with blood to nourish another egg. This is why the menstruation stops. The blood and energy normally lost in menstruation is then used in the body and by the sexual glands in particular to benefit them as they are to feed the fetus.

Likewise, in stopping the menstruation with the Deer Exercise, the woman triggers the body's inner intelligence or instinct not to feed a future egg but instead to nourish and strengthen the sexual glands. In other words, it is a way for the woman to communicate to her body that she does not need to be pregnant at this time.

Should she later wish to become pregnant, she just interrupts the Deer Exercise and the menstruation will resume shortly thereafter, with the benefit of a prospect for a healthier pregnancy. Should she change her mind again and decide to cease her periods, she will be able to do so much more quickly than the first time.

Incidentally, it is not necessary to continue the hand rotation 360 times in the exercise, twice a day, once a woman has succeeded in stopping her period. Less than 100 rotations, twice a day, will suffice to maintain the interruption of her menstruation once it has stopped. She will be the judge by testing how many times seem to be the threshold beyond which the period resumes again.

The Deer Exercise has other benefits. It stimulates the production of the female hormone estrogen in the vagina, uterus, breasts and ovaries. This is very rejuvenating for the woman and can greatly relieve the symptoms of menopause. In this case, the Deer Exercise naturally increases the secretion of estrogen and the body naturally balances the increased estrogen with other substances.

The body knows what amount of estrogen it needs at any time. Man-made estrogen is a drug which is not balanced. A doctor adminstering estrogen cannot know what level of the hormone is needed in the bloodstream because every hour the hormone level in the blood changes and is impossible to measure. Also, man-made estrogen is just a chemical by itself, and eventually it will cause problems either from over- or under-stimulation.

The Deer Exercise also eliminates the problems related to the menstrual period, even when the period itself has not stopped yet. These problems include emotional ups and downs, water retention, hormone blockages, cramps and abnormal flow, either too heavy or too light. (A light menstrual flow indicates a blockage and body poisoning. If the period stops under usual circumstances and without
312

the Deer Exercise, this indicates disease.)

The vagina also benefits from the Deer Exercise. It becomes tighter, more flexible and more meaty, which increases the man's pleasure during intercourse. A woman who has had children can greatly benefit from the Deer Exercise. Her vagina will be loose and enlarged which means a great loss of penile sensation for her partner during intercourse. With the Deer Exercise the vagina is automatically exercised and energized, which results in a youthful tightening of the vaginal tissues.

Instructions for the Woman's Deer Exercise

As you do the two steps of this exercise, visualize the fire or energy coming from your lower sexual gland and rising upward along the spine into the breast and to the head. The mind is used as it influences and facilitates the movement of blood and energy. Linking mind and body at the same focus is a prerequisite to the harmonious and powerful function of vital energy. Bringing this energy to the pineal gland in the head is the Divine purpose.

First Stage

This exercise can be done sitting on the floor or on a bed.

1. Sit so that you can place the heel of one foot so that it presses into and up against the opening of your vagina. You will want a steady and fairly firm pressure so that the heel presses tightly against the clitoris. If it is not possible to place your foot in this position, then use a fairly hard, round object such as a baseball. (You may experience a pleasant sensation due to the stimulation of the genital area and the subsequent release of sexual energy.)
2. Rub your hands together vigorously. This will create heat in your hands by bringing the energy of your body into your palms and fingers.
3. Place your hands on your breasts so that you feel the heat from your hands enter into the skin.
4. Rub your breasts in an outward, circular motion, moving very slowly. Your right hand will turn counter-clockwise and your left hand clockwise.
5. Rub in this circular manner for a minimum of thirty-six times or a maximum of three hundred and sixty times.

Second Stage

1. First, tighten the muscles of your vagina and anus as if you were trying to close both openings, and then try to draw your rectum upward inside the body, further contracting the anal muscles. When done properly this will feel as if air is

313

being drawn up into your rectum and vagina. Hold these muscles tight for as long as you can comfortably.

2. Relax and repeat the anal and vaginal contractions. Do this as many times as feels comfortable.

Figure 97

IV

Healing Positions

These positions use the different reflexology zones of the penis and vagina for healing. Each of the healing positions applies pressure to certain parts of the sexual organs, depending on which part of the body requires healing. By stimulating certain parts of the penis or vagina, corresponding organs are stimulated and energized. These are ancient techniques which have been tested and proven over thousands of years.

The Eight Healing Positions for Men

For these healing positions the man does the work and the woman is the tool for healing. The man receives specific healing benefits, but the woman benefits at the same time. All eight of these are good for the woman's sexual organ problems. They will stimulate the production of sexual hormones and help correct menstrual problems. In these positions the man should continue and prolong intercourse for as long as it is comfortable, without ejaculation, using the anal contractions of the Deer Exercise. (Taoist intercourse, i.e., the Sets of Nines, greatly enhances the benefits of these exercises.)

Position 1 — For sex-related problems, including impotence, premature ejaculation and difficulty in achieving orgasm

The woman lies on her side with her hips twisted so that her pelvis is facing upward as far as possible. The man is on top and penetrates with his penis. In this position, follow the preceeding general instructions, or do up to two Sets of Nine each day for fifteen days.

This position heals all sex-related problems such as impotence. You have to work very slowly to gain self-confidence. In the beginning just insert the penis and work from there at your own pace. Most men have some sexual ability. It is unusual to be completely impotent. Usually the erection is lost either half-way into the vagina or partway through intercourse.

If a man has trouble reaching orgasm, it is generally because he is not totally present. His mind wanders and he fantasizes. In reality, he is *two* different personalities — one is having sex and the other is off somewhere else. Because this position is somewhat awkward for the man, it forces him to concentrate on what he is doing, thus preventing his mind from wandering or fantasizing.

The important thing is for the man to work up to the point where he can do the two Sets of Nine each day. In fifteen days he should be completely healed of any sex-related problem. It is a very enjoyable way to spend your time, and much more effective for sexual problems than hormones, vitamins or surgery. I recommend that for vacations you stay at home and heal yourselves this way. Conventional vacations are usually very stressful and expensive and seldom provide the relaxation people hope for.

Figure 98

Position 2 — For energizing the body

The woman lies on her back with her head and shoulders supported by a big, high pillow, and bends forward at the neck. This position slightly curves the vagina, allowing the penis to be massaged where it is needed. The man comes in front of her and penetrates with his penis. In this position follow the preceeding general instructions, or do up to three Sets of Nine three times a day. In twenty days the body will be completely energized.

This position also benefits the woman by drawing air up into the vagina which stimulates certain internal organs.

Figure 99

Position 3 — For strengthening the internal organs, including the liver and kidneys

Both the man and woman lie on their sides (either side), facing each other. The woman keeps her lower leg straight and bends her upper leg backward, while the man penetrates with his penis. In this position, follow the preceeding general instructions, or do up to four Sets of Nine a maximum of four times a day for twenty days.

Figure 100

Position 4 — For bone weakness

The woman lies on her left side with her left leg bent as far as possible toward the back. Her right leg is kept straight. The man comes face to face with her, finding the angle where he can insert his penis. He may be either a little bit on top of her or directly face-to-face. In this position do up to five Sets of Nine a maximum of five times a day for ten days or follow the preceeding general instructions.

This position is good for healing arthritis, lukemia, bone marrow disease and for speeding up the healing of broken bones.

Figure 101

Position 5 — For blood vessel problems

The position for this is exactly like Position 4 except that the woman lies on her *right* side and her *right* leg is bent. The man enters

316

the same way, facing her but a little bit on the top. In this position follow the preceeding general instructions, or do six Sets of Nine a maximum of six times a day for twenty days.

This position is good for all types of blood vessel problems, including varicose veins and hardening of the arteries. It also helps high or low blood pressure *if* the arteries are causing the problem.

Figure 102

Position 6 — For blood problems, including blood pressure

The position for this is with the man on his back relaxed. The woman faces him on her knees and the man penetrates. The woman does not move, but the man moves up and down from underneath. In this position do up to seven Sets of Nine a maximum of seven times a day for ten days, or follow the preceeding general instructions.

This position is good for anemia, low blood pressure, poor blood quality and "blood clots." (A large number of physical problems can be caused by clotted blood.) Blood clots form in the body much in the same way as milk curdles when it is cooked. When the body is drained of its energy, this lack of energy causes a slowdown of blood circulation. This slowing of the circulation causes the body temperature to rise, and this heats up the blood. The blood forms a skim layer just as milk does when it is cooked. This thickened portion of the blood remains in the body and accumulates in certain areas, causing a good deal of pain. X-ray equipment does not pick up the presence of these blood clots in the body, but they become a habitat for all kinds of germs.

Figure 103

Position 7 — For lymphatic system problems

For this the man lies relaxed on his back and the woman kneels over him on her hands and knees. The woman faces the man and can

317

do a little movement, but basically the man moves after penetration. In this position do up to eight Sets of Nine a maximum of eight times a day for approximately fifteen days, or follow the preceeding general instructions.

Figure 104

Position 8 — For all-purpose healing

This one is difficult for the woman because the position is hard to assume. The woman gets on her knees and then bends all the way back with her feet under her buttocks until her head and back rest on the floor. The man penetrates from the top front. (A pillow in back may help the woman.) In this position do up to nine Sets of Nine a maximum of nine times a day for ten days.

Figure 105

By changing the woman's position in the above methods, the shape of the vagina is changed and the friction from the penile thrusts affects different areas of the penis. Through the process of reflexology this affects different parts of the body, providing healing stimulation to these areas. The man works to heal himself and the woman serves as his tool. In the woman's healing positions, which I will cover next, the woman works to heal herself and the *man* is the tool.

The Seven Healing Positions for Women

In these positions the man completely serves the woman. Unlike the benefits the woman derives from the man's healing positions, there is no real healing benefit here for him.

The degree of penile penetration is important in the woman's healing positions because the various Zones of Reflexology are located along the length of the vagina. Therefore, different portions of the vagina require massage, and penetration is shallow or deep depending on the different requirements.

Once the penis is inserted in these positions, the woman rotates

318

her pelvis for the purpose of massaging and stimulating the vagina. The man does holdbacks when necessary and must communicate with the woman when he needs to slow down. He should not ejaculate or have an orgasm while in these positions.

Each of the following positions require the same amount of repetition: they should be done up to nine times a day for a maximum of ten days.

Position 1 — For lack of energy as indicated by blurred vision, excessive perspiration, weakness, fainting, rapid heartbeat and weak, shallow and rapid breathing

For this position the woman lies flat on her back. The man is on top of her and penetrates as deeply as possible. The woman rotates in circles underneath him, moving both clockwise and counterclockwise. The man lets the woman work and remains in this position until she feels she has had enough. She may or may not have an orgasm, this is not the object of these healing exercises.

Figure 106

Position 2 — For the pancreas and liver, especially diabetes; for hot flashes, weak knees and painful feet and knees when standing for long periods

For this position the woman lies on her back and wraps her legs around the man's thighs — not his back or shoulders. The man is on top on his hands and knees and only penetrates with the head of his penis, or about one and one-half to two inches. Again, the woman rotates in both directions for as long as she can continue comfortably. The man's position on his hands and knees enables shallow penetration, and the penis only touches the lung, pancreas and heart zones of the vagina. (Note: this position is also good for all the joints of the body.)

Figure 107

319

Position 3 — For the stomach, spleen and female organs; all digestive problems

Here the woman lies on her back with her legs locked around the man's waist and with her arms around him. The man is on his hands and knees and penetrates her halfway. The woman rotates in both directions for as long as she can continue comfortably.

Figure 108

Position 4 — For water retention, kidney and bladder problems, constant high fever, water poisoning, dried blood, pituitary gland problems

For this position the man lies on his back. The woman is on her knees facing the man's feet. Only the head of the penis penetrates—the woman can hold the penis for more control—and she rotates in both directions for as long as she can continue comfortably.

(Water retention slows down the blood circulation by pressing on the blood vessels. This raises the body temperature and creates what the Taoists called blood clots as explained before. Water retention is generally a woman's problem—few men have it.)

Figure 109

Position 5 — For the nervous system, liver, ulcers and eyesight

In this position the man lies on his back and the woman is on her knees facing him. The penetration of the vagina goes from shallow to deep as the woman moves up and down on the penis, while at the same time rotating. This method gives the vagina a thorough massage.

Nervous problems are generally women's problems. The female organs often have some problems with such things as menstruation and blockages and the resulting hormonal imbalance affects the nervous system. As a matter of fact, women in general have more physical problems than men and they are more difficult to treat

320

because the female body is more complicated than the male. Child-bearing depletes a woman's body even further.

Figure 110

Position 6 — For energy blockages in the meridians, headaches, poor blood circulation, menstrual problems (i.e., cramping, abnormally heavy or light flow or no period at all)

For this position the man lies on his back relaxed. The woman is on her knees and supporting herself with one elbow, a little to one side of the man. She holds his penis with one hand and his head with the other, and allows the penis to penetrate halfway, holding it all the while. The woman rotates in this position for as long as she can continue comfortably. (It is very hard for the penis to penetrate in this position, and that is why the woman has to hold it.)

Figure 111

Position 7 — For blood shortage and anemia, poor circulation and pale, dry skin

This is an easy position. The woman lies on her back with her knees up to her chest and her feet in the air. The man kneels on his knees in front of her and penetrates very deeply. The woman rotates while the man holds steady. This position shortens the vagina, allowing for very deep penetration. If the penis is too long, the man can wrap the base of the shaft with a handkerchief to prevent it from going too far into the vagina. (He should *always* do this if his penis is longer than his partner's vagina.) Also, the use of a handkerchief makes the penis more erect and helps maintain the erection longer. It works the same as a "cock ring"—by blocking the blood vessels, the blood cannot flow back out of the penis as easily.

Figure 112

You will have to arrange your time for these exercises. It is possible that the women's exercises take less time than the men's. In five minutes she may have had enough, whereas the Sets of Nine require a certain amount of time to complete.

Remember, all the healing positions are to be done without the man ejaculating, so that he can continue to be the instrument for the healing as long as necessary. He probably will need to do the Holdbacks to accomplish this.

V

Morning or Evening Prayer

Love plus Truth equals True Love. Of course the word "love" has different meanings. True Love means two hearts united with no gap between them, not a social love. The love you have for your wife or husband is different than the love you have for a friend. Even close friends still have a distance between them.

Neither man nor woman should live alone. Not necessarily in the sense of physically living together, but in the sense of a sexual relationship. Men and women need each other for satisfaction and to heal, balance and adjust their physical bodies.

Taoism teaches us that every part of the body is holy. And, if we are enjoying a full life as human beings with the use of Sexology, this is equal to a Divine Life. Suffering is *not* divine. When you reach a certain level of existence you become spiritual. Suffering to become spiritual is an idea of the ego. Man has not been forced to suffer. God gave him a choice.

Without will power or choice, man is only a machine. God told Adam not to eat from the Tree of Knowledge, giving him a choice. ("Knowledge" in this case is synonymous with religion.) God told Adam he would "die" if he ate from this Tree, death meaning separation from God. Man chose to have the knowledge and then became ashamed and tried to cover himself. Before this, man felt pure. We have to go back to this purity.

To please God we have to please ourselves first, because God is in us. If we live a Divine Life, we are already in the Kingdom of God. We don't have to pay any duty to God. He can do whatever He needs for Himself.

322

God's will was to have one perfect person. Because man is part of woman and she part of him, it pleases God that they live together. During what is known as the Morning and Evening Prayer, man and woman are united together and become one perfect person. To perform the Morning Prayer, the man first does the Sets of Nine and brings the woman to orgasm. But if time is limited, you may completely ignore the "orgasm" and proceed directly to the Missionary Position.

The Bible always refers to the Spirit, the Soul and the Body, not just the Soul and the Body. In illustration 15, the spirit is represented by the circle. It is surrounded by a triangle representing the soul or mind and by an outer square representing the mortal body.

The Nine Levels of Orgasm and the counting involved with the Sets of Nine require considerable discipline on the part of the man so that he does not succumb to lust. The man serves the woman with his body. With the morning and evening prayers people will start and end the day in peace away from worries and conflicts.

Since we have our bodies, we must use them and discipline them. They should be used as a tool for the Soul-Mind to follow the Spirit. When we let our Spirit lead us and follow our intuition, conscience and communication with God, our thinking, emotions and decisions follow. (Please refer to Chapter 1, Section I.)

As human beings, we cannot get rid of our bodies. We have to satisfy them. The Morning and Evening Prayer satisfies and disciplines the body at the same time. When approaching the Prayer, we should ask our bodies to listen to our Spirit. We should make a decision to please God. The feeling should be one of Pure Love.

When two people meet, they become like a square. During the Morning Prayer they are locked together and share a meeting point. The square then becomes a triangle. The woman is completely opened up and receiving, completely yin. The man is at his Taoist orgasm and is in the position of complete giving, which is complete yang. Her complete yin state and his complete yang state constitute a perfect yin-yang balance. This balance becomes a circle with no beginning and no end.

There is no gap and no sharpness in the circle because no criticism exists between the man and woman. For the couple there is only feeling, no judgement or thinking. They have their eyes closed and are feeling each other. This feeling is complete love, pure unification.

This unification represents the yin-yang, the microcosm and the macrocosm of the universe and is everlasting. At that moment the couple is beyond space and time. Even if the prayer lasts only for two minutes, that in itself is infinity.

The woman's orgasm during the Morning Prayer can last from two to ten to twenty minutes. She is completely relaxed during this time and has no more physical desire. The Morning Prayer is thus a form of meditation. The body's trembling and vaginal secretions are a *part* of the orgasm and can occur a few times before the woman is completely opened up.

For the man, the Morning Prayer is the same as the Ten Holdbacks, in the Sets of Nines, except that when he gets to that point he stays there and holds it, using only feeling and no knowledge. This is the Tree of Life.

The man requires more than an erection for the Morning Prayer. The prostate needs to be swollen to around 98% to keep the man's interest up. If he needs relief, he can do the Deer Exercise.

When you have trained yourself to the level of the Morning and Evening Prayer you will no longer need to proceed through the Nine Levels of Orgasm or the Sets of Nine. The woman will open up right away and reach the meditation stage in two minutes.

The purpose of meditation is sometimes misunderstood: it is often confused with "thinking." When confronted with a problem people are often heard to say, "I'll have to meditate on it," meaning that they will think about it. The real purpose of meditation is to tune into God.

The Morning and Evening Prayer is the best meditation of all. It combines communication with God together with internal exercise and healing. This is the level of complete oneness, or "no mind," and once you reach this level you will find yourself so fulfilled that you will have no desire left for common human sex.

Love cannot be studied or taught. It comes from the heart and is truly spiritual in origin. Love is giving. In the Morning Prayer the man gives himself to the woman; the woman's gift is her surrender to the man. The two melt together, exchanging energy and healing. In this way, sex can be used by human beings to experience the Divine.

The Morning and Evening Prayer gives you complete love automatically, which is not the same as the mental picture of romantic love we carry in our minds. It can be said that it is the culmination of Taoist Sexology. Just as you start the day with the Morning Prayer, conclude the day with the Evening Prayer, which is performed in the same way as the Morning Prayer. The experience is beautiful, and you will go to sleep relaxed and peaceful. The next day when you wake up you will be ready for the Morning Prayer.

You can pray to God for the right partner to come to you. God is always with you, so there is no need to go out looking for Him. Nor do you have to beg Him for anything. He is always present and He is all-knowing. With His power working through you, you can create the right person for yourself.

What you need to know is that your thoughts form your reality. The mind's idea is *basic* reality and it comes way before the materialization. The material thing you can touch or see is a phenomenon created by the mind.

You can materialize anything with the right thoughts. In this case, just concentrate your thoughts on the right partner for you and visualize what you want in your mind. You will create the right person for yourself.

VI

Eugenics

The Taoists say that if someone is born with a physical, mental or psychological defect it is the responsibility of the individual's parents, and that the problem was created through careless conception. If a couple plans to have a child it is absolutely essential that they take great care at the time of conception and throughout pregnancy in order to ensure that the child will be totally healthy. There are a number of rules which a couple must follow in order to bring this about:

1. Do not conceive a child if one or both of the parents are drunk or an alcoholic at the time of conception. A child conceived under these conditions will be born with a liver condition which will result in a nervous condition and some kind of mental problem.

2. Do not conceive a child when one or both of the parents are extremely tired. The child will always be weak and sickly, with little resistance to disease.

3. If the couple conceives a child during a battle in wartime, it will be very hyperactive and have a violent nature. This can also apply to different types of battles, such as a struggle for power within a large corporation, a great upheaval or struggle within a society or even during intense competition for daily survival.

325

4. If the parents conceive during a hurricane or other violent storm, it will lead to a child with low resistance to disease.
5. If the parents conceive at the time of sunset, the child's eyesight will be poor.
6. If one or both parents are under the influence of drugs or medication, the child will have nervous and mental problems. This includes long term medication for chronic conditions.

It is the responsibility of the parents to guarantee that the succeeding generation is strong and healthy to ensure the health of the human race. Conceiving a child is a serious responsibility about which we should give great thought. Considering all the juvenile delinquency and the problems and difficulties with youth there is a strong possibility that much of this is a result of parents who were not aware of such information as is presented here. How can humanity as a group be strong if the people involved are weak? This is not something to be taken lightly.

Parenthood is and always has been a serious matter. People simply cannot procreate like animals, with little or no concern for the results. Today we are recognizing that we must take responsibility for our lives and our environment. Certainly nothing is more important than our children and the health of the future generation. The rules listed above are not intended as helpful suggestions. They are solid facts, known and recorded by Taoists for thousands of years.

A few general conditions are necessary in order to conceive a healthy child. It is vital that the parents eat well, be of good health, think positively and have a very peaceful environment. It is also important that they get along well with each other.

When they feel the timing is right, they should first take a relaxing bath and provide themselves with pleasant, restful surroundings: comfortable room temperature, a candle or two burning, a little incense and some soothing background music. Then, 30 minutes after their bath, they can proceed to make love.

VII

Other Topics

Tao of Sex Wisdom is an enormous subject. I have had clinical and behavorial sexologists attend many of my lectures. Afterwards, they have come up and said such things as, "You covered in the first five minutes of your lecture what I have just spent six years studying in the university. The rest of what you discussed was never even mentioned in my courses. And it's the most helpful information of all." Because Tao of Sex Wisdom is such an enormous subject, the rest of the topics cannot be adequately explained in the few pages of this chapter. However, a list of the topics can be given and it is as follows:

Theory of Rhythm (sexual rhythm)

Improvement of the Tools (improvement of penile shape and size; vaginal tone and the shape and size of the breasts)

Sexual reflexology: merging two people completely

Social Diseases

Men's Holdback Technique

"Sets of Nine" — technique offering the most enjoyable inter-course, as well as reversal of frigidity.

The Nine Steps to Orgasm (women)

The Nine Healing Positions for Men and Women

Benefits of the Ten Holdbacks for Men

Problems caused by Improper Sex

Forbidden Sexual Practices

Circumstances Favorable for Lovemaking

Foods that Help Lovemaking

Face Reading (for finding suitable partners)

Masturbation

Homosexuality

Sex Determination (choosing the baby's sex)

For more details and the complete knowledge of sex wisdom, please refer to the book, *The Tao of Sexology* (Stephen Chang, Tao Publishing).

7

THE TAO OF MASTERY

The Seventh Pillar of Toaism, the Tao of Mastery, is invaluable in the understanding of humanity and the purpose of one's own existence. It can also serve as a priceless guide for the achievement of lifelong goals and harmony between oneself and the universe. The Tao of Mastery is an amalgam of six systems: Personology (shape study), Fingerprint System, Numerology, Astrology, Directionology and Symbology (spiritual communication).

I

Personology

Human beings possess three bodies. The most tangible body is the superficial physical body. The mental and spiritual bodies are intangible and are merged with the physical body. The matter that builds up the physical body occupies space and time. Therefore, all physical bodies possess shapes. The building of organic shapes and forms is guided by genes as is the determination of intelligence, temperament, reaction patterns and personality. Therefore shape, form, intelligence, personality, etc. have a common origin in the genes.

When something interferes with the genes, everything is affected. For instance, when parents contract syphilis, they will produce a child who harbors many detectable abnormalities, because the syphilis germ interferes with the genetic guidance of infant development. From the outer appearance of the child, one can accurately infer that the intelligence, behavior, etc. are also abnormal, since everything is intimately related via the genes. There is a definite bridge between the physical and mental bodies.

Beside the genes, there are the nerves, which begin at the brain and end in the face and the extremities. The nerve endings are the reservoirs of the brain's electrical impulses, or messages. So the three folds of the human body are not distinct, separate entities. They are merged together and they function together.

The face is the show-window of the entire body. The face is the yardstick whereby one determines the inner or true person. Through face reading one acquires insight into a person's personality and his past, present, and future, since past and recent studies have shown that the mind possesses powers that determine a person's destiny.

Personology was originally utilized for diagnostic purposes. It is based on the fact that all conditions of the entire body could be properly gauged by the face. (All nerve impulses of the body travel to the brain, and all nerve impulses from the brain travel to the face). Many of us are able to detect an individual's state of mind by reading the facial expressions (worry, happiness, etc.) and many of us have used touching the forehead as a gauge of the inflammation of bodily organs. One can detect such signs even if the subject tries to disguise them. (For details refer back to Chapter 4, Section III).

Gradually, Personology became a social scientific study of the relationship between two variables: facial features and individual fates. Each feature was studied one at a time, through the use of data from millions of individual cases. Direct correlations between facial features and specific fates were found after thousands of years of continuous statistical analysis.

The principles of Personology have withstood thousands of years of continuous application and have never been proven invalid. In the West, the association between the facial features and temperament is instinctively understood to be true: Corporations always conduct personal interviews and airport personnel use a "hijacker's profile," compiled by U.S. Marshalls, to screen passengers. Moreover, the work of a western scientist named W. H. Sheldon proved that there is a definite relationship between physical appearance and temperament.

Since the entire universe can be described in terms of the Five Elements, and since we are a microcosm of the universe, mankind can be described in terms of the Five Elements. Taoism divides mankind into five basic morphological types, each exhibiting different characteristics. They are as follows:

Morphological type	Characteristics
Metal	Bright, intelligent, comely, sharp-featured, confident, self-indulgent, selfish

Figure 113

Earth	Practical, business-oriented, frugal, thick-skinned, thick and tight in musculature

331

Figure 114

Wood

Stubborn, thin, deep-thinking, fastidious, unhurried

Figure 115

Water

Flexible, clever, unstabilized, easy-going, smooth-talking, soft and water retentive tissues

Figure 116

Fire   Quick-tempered, nervous, creative, bright, forward, talented

Figure 117

These morphological categories are further defined as strong or weak (Yang or Yin). When Metal, Earth, Wood, Water, and Fire are strong (Yang), their basic characteristics are strongly pronounced. So people who are obviously quick-tempered, nervous, etc. are easily typed as Yang Fire. When, for example, Metal is weak, its basic characteristics are masked by those of other elements. This person, therefore, is a meld of two morphological types. Thus, there are a minimum of ten morphological types.

The cycles of generation and destruction of the Five Elements Theory can be used to illustrate the interaction between individuals. For example, if a married couple consists of a Yang Fire husband and Yang Water wife, their marriage would be full of conflict and would eventually lead to a divorce. However, if a Yang Fire man were married to a Yang Earth wife, the marriage would last.

The determination of an individual's fate involves reading the facial features individually, judging the color, shape, and disfigurations of the many areas of the face. The face is divided into 108 areas.

Each area represents one facet of an individual's existence: spouse, children, wealth, etc. Also, each area represents how the individual fares at a particular age. The state of matters at the present time can be determined when blemishes suddenly occur in these areas.

An entire book is required for explaining the techniques of Personology, so the material in this section is incomplete.

108 FACIAL LOCATIONS

333

1, 2	=	Success, Boss
3	=	Business
4	=	Hope
5	=	Life, Jail, Frigidy, Adopted
6, 7	=	Legal
8	=	Family Affairs
9	=	Health
10	=	Business (up or down)
11,12,13	=	Money, Genital, Fate
14	=	Uterus, No Children
15,16	=	Wealth, Savings
17	=	Willpower
18	=	Poison, Diet, Accident
19	=	Resident, Room, Private Location
20	=	Self Awareness
21,22	=	Ancestor
23,24	=	Parents
25,26	=	Legal Affairs (Civil Law)
27,28	=	Inheritance
29,30	=	Spouse
31,32	=	Building, Helper
33,34	=	Order
35,36	=	Digestion
37,38	=	Under, House
39,40	=	Spirits
41,42	=	Creation, Invention
43,44	=	Friends
45,46	=	Living Room
47,48	=	Disease
49,50	=	Children
51,52	=	Travel
53,54	=	Order and Regulations
55,56	=	Employees
57,58	=	Neighbor
59	=	Working Attitude
60,61	=	Gain, Loss
62,63	=	Woods, Family Property
64,65	=	Happiness
66,67	=	Ranch, Field, Open Space you own
68,69	=	Mind
70,71	=	Car
72,73	=	Far Away Place
74,75	=	Travel Affair
76,77	=	Money (Gain, Loss)
78,79	=	Accident
80,81	=	Sex Affair, Relationship
82,83	=	Power Struggle
84,85	=	Writing, Letter
86,87	=	Parent's House
88	=	Publication Sales
89,90	=	On the Road
91,92	=	Secrets
93,94	=	Spouse Relationship
95,96	=	Strategy
97,98	=	Disease, Illness, Death
99,100	=	Relative
101,102	=	Epidemic, Emergency
103,104	=	Robbery
105,106	=	Pride
107,108	=	Ranch or Farm

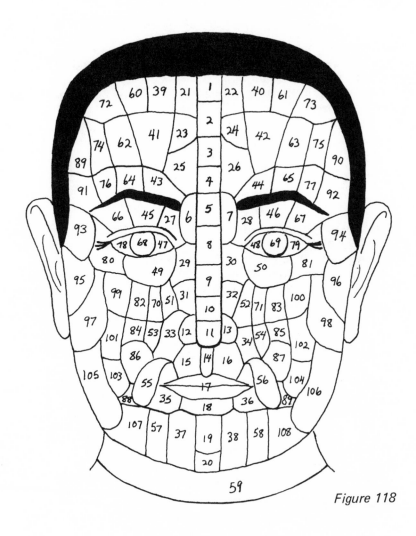

Figure 118

II

Fingerprint System

It is an indisputable fact that every individual possesses a unique set of fingerprints. Through Taoist studies, fingerprints have been tied to the I-Ching system, thus enabling the determination of the personality, aptitudes, interests and health of an individual, along with suitable choices for marriage and occupation. Fingerprints are much more than an aid to criminal investigations, and the finger-print system is another invaluable method for understanding oneself and others.

The Fingerprint System is a subject too complex to be explained within a few pages.

III

Numerology

Numerology is the science of numbers. In Chapter 1, we have traced the evolution of the universe: the progression from one atom to the solar system to the universe. The order of this progression can be expressed by the number one through nine inclusive. According to Taoist legend, these numbers arose on the back of a turtle from the Lo river 6,000 years ago.

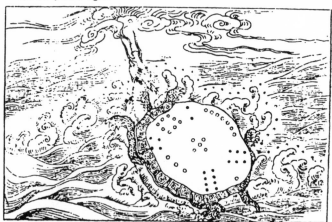

The numbers were represented by markings on the tortoise shell, and represent the universal principles that govern all manifestations of the universe. Therefore, they are the counterparts of the *Pa Kua*. These nine numbers correlate to the *Pa Kua* thustly:

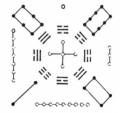

Figure 119

These numbers have special meanings, and they are:

1 — K'an — Water

This number represents difficulty, danger, challenge, harsh conditions, coldness, darkness, all the characteristics of winter. These harsh conditions cause the emergence of these characteristics: aggressiveness, independence, individualism, leadership and creativity. These latter characteristics are also very much part of the number 1.

2 — K'un — Earth

This number represents conflict, destruction, contention, bleeding, all the things that are likely to occur during a late summer. These characteristics must be neutralized by the following characteristics: tactfulness, cautiousness, weakness, understanding and peace. The number two, like all other numbers, is dualistic in nature.

3 — Chen — Thunder

This number represents all the characteristics of Spring, that is, renewal, regeneration, reawakening, lightness, hope. These conditions foster self-expression, sociableness, popularity, communicativeness and happiness.

4 — Sun — Wind

This number represents all the characteristics of the wind: instability, etherealness, changeability, capriciousness. These characteristics are balanced by the following characteristics: stability, order, practicality, endurance, discipline.

5 — Tai Chi — Yin-Yang

This number is a meld of characteristics from all the other eight numbers. It is characterized by completeness, adapability, change, vitality, constant activity and freedom.

6 — Tien — Heaven

This number represents all the characteristics attributed to heaven: dignity, creativity, strength, aloofness, progress, sovereignty and all the fulfillment derived from an autumn harvest. These characteristics

337

are balanced by the following: familial gatherings, sharing, caring, family matters, compassion, service and love.

7 — Tui — Lake

This number represents the outrageous gaiety of the time period after the harvest. There is entertainment, laughter, enjoyment and festivities. This light-heartedness is balanced by introspection, philosophizing, quietude and seclusion, all the characteristics of mystics and philosophers. The number seven is a complex meld of all these characteristics.

8 — Ken — Mountain

This number represents all the characteristics of the mountain, for example, its richness, quiescence, immovability, slowness, tolerance, stability and reclusion. These are balanced by the characteristics of city life: responsibility, hard work, finances, recognition, power, business and competition.

9 — Li — Fire

This number represents brightness, warmth, charm, beauty, superficiality, self-centeredness, materialism and cleverness. These characteristics are balanced by the following: selflessness, universality, compassion, love, tolerance and unending service.

Just as the trigrams are used in I-Ching to clarify the enigmas of life, these numbers are used in formulas to facilitate an understanding of one's earthly existence. Numerology is used to determine one's destiny, past life, compatibility with others and compatibility with one's vocation. One determines such enigmas by converting one's name into numbers.

It may appear simplistic to categorize people into nine destinies, or twenty-seven categories when we include appearance and past life as part of one's characteristics. However, the reader may judge for him or herself how valid or helpful these indications may be by following the methodology discussed below. Truly, precision or individualized details would require to incorporate in the analysis the impact of time, date and location of birth, as well as other methods of the Tao of Mastery. However, the general indications of Taoist Numerology shown below remain valid. In any case, the reader may be surprised to recognize the influence of his or her name on his or her life.

338

It may also reveal whether or not the reader has yet unfolded into his or her destiny. As a matter of fact, one may tend instead to live up to one's societal image or cling to one's past life, as one is unconsciously more familiar with it. However, one has to face one's destiny in this life eventually in order to live harmoniously with the Tao.

In the West, numbers are assigned to the alphabet as follows:

A/J/S	1
B/K/T	2
C/L/U	3
D/M/V	4
E/N/W	5
F/O/X	6
G/P/Y	7
H/Q/Z	8
I/R	9

To determine one's destiny, use the following procedure. The numbers that correlate to the name are added, like this:

KARL VINCE MONTPARNASSE

$$2+1+9+3+4+7+5+3+5+4+6+5+2+7+1+9+5+1+1+1+5 = 88 = 16 = 7$$

88 is reduced to 16 by adding the first digit to the second. Then 16 is reduced to 7 by adding 1 to 6. The example given shows the process of determining the number that corresponds to one's destiny, or what one was born to manifest. Adding the values of all the letters in your *full* name (at birth) in the same manner will reveal your destiny. Prefixes and suffixes (Mrs., Jr., etc.) are not part of one's name. Just as piecing together triagrams will produce a picture of a part of the universe, piecing together these numbers will achieve the same thing.

To find the meaning of your destiny number, study the delineation of that number below.

Destiny Number	Explanation
1	This number represents hardships, difficulties and negative circumstances. People having 1 as their destiny number will have a troubled childhood marked by problems in family and finances. But, they will have a more fortunate middle period. During these years, success may be achieved which will provide security throughout

this person's later years. Throughout life, this person will worry excessively.

2
This number represents accomplishment, receptivity, and supportiveness. People having 2 as their destiny number will play a secondary role in all undertakings. They have gentle, adaptable and amiable personalities and cannot be leaders since they are more suited to behind-the-scenes work. They gain satisfaction through supporting others. The most fortunate period of life is the middle years. The later years will be rather bland.

3
This number represents rebirth, happiness, rejuvenation and all the characteristics of Spring. People having 3 as their destiny number will have to carve an existence with their own efforts, as they will not receive much help from their parents. Some will attain great success, and some will lose it. They lead exciting lives, as they are vivacious and amiable. During the early years, funds should be set aside for a happy retirement.

4
This number represents the characteristics of the wind—transience, pervasiveness and change. Those having number 4 as their destiny number will have fortunate childhoods. They have logical minds, but they are weak-willed and indecisive. They work well under a strong superior, as they will produce the work expected of them. They are successful during the early years. They should set aside funds for their retirement, since they are generous with money.

5
This number represents all the characteristics of all the other eight numbers. For some people whose destiny number is 5, life in general may be very fortunate or unfortunate. Those who are fortunate will be ambitious, positive, moral, and will attain great success. Those who are unfortunate will be slow learners, immoral, negative and materialistic, and will have many enemies. Sometimes, they may be thrown in jail.

6
This number represents creation, wisdom and strength. Those with 6 as the destiny number may succeed early or late in life. The later years

are most propitious for these people. They possess a great deal of self-confidence and leadership qualities. They are ambitious and will work hard to get what they want. Nothing stands in their way. They are very materialistic, yet spiritual at the same time.

7   This number represents joyousness, ripening and harvesting. People with this destiny number will have exciting childhoods. They may be spoiled by their parents. As adults, they will be able to read people's moods. Because of this they are very popular. Their minds are sharp and they like to dress well. They like things their way. The middle years and the late years are the most propitious.

8   This number represents stability, immovability and peace—all the attributes of a mountain. Those having this destiny number will have childhoods characterized by wealth. As adults they will also be wealthy, since their business ventures are usually successful. They work hard to attain success. Although they have sharp minds, they tend to be very stubborn and dislike change.

9   This number represents charm, brightness and fire. Those with this destiny number have fortunate childhoods. They are always at the center of attention, so they place great importance on outer appearances. They act impulsively and emotionally. These people should establish themselves during the early years, since their later years are inauspicious.

The information derived from the ability to calculate Destiny Numbers can be used for business purposes. How one's product will fare on the market depends on the numerological value of its name. You can pre-determine how it will fare by giving it a name with the numerological number of your choice.

With Numerology, you can also help determine how other people see you. To do so, follow this procedure:

KARL VINCE MONTPARNASSE

2+9+3+4+5+3+4+5+2+7+5+1+1 = 51 = 6

Find the sum of the values for all the consonants in your full name. Reduce large numbers to a single digit by adding the digits of the large number together. Then check the meaning of your number in the following explanation of the Appearance Numbers.

Number	Appearance
1	You seem to display leadership, individuality, independence and assertiveness. People are naturally drawn to you by your charisma and they depend on you to take control of any situation. You seem to do things before they become fashionable. You always seem to be in the spotlight, whether at work or at play, and this may cause resentment.
2	You seem to be gentle, harmonious and amiable. You speak with tact, and you like to help those in need. Although you are not ambitious or aggressive, your monetary common sense prevents deep financial troubles. You are very concerned about details. You always seem to be working behind the scenes, so people may not notice you.
3	You seem to be gregarious, optimistic, charming and pleasing. You have a natural likability. You bring cheer into a world of gloom, and you always seem to be the life of the party. People may be a little envious of your popularity. And you seem to be very talkative. You may appear to be flighty.
4	You seem to be very practical, cautious and extremely stable. Iron-strong self-discipline makes you seem too work-oriented. Orderly environments seem important to you. People think you are reliable, honest and down-to-earth, but do not regard you as someone with a "fun" personality.
5	You always seem to be engaged in a variety of activities. People may judge you as restless and undependable, but you know that you have more abilities than many to overcome eventual hardships. You have good conversational skills, so you have much helpful interchange with groups of people.

6	You have maternal or paternal qualities. You seem to make any environment warm and comfortable, because you care about the welfare of others. Your home and family are very important to you. You always seem to be helping or serving others, and they may take advantage of you.
7	You seem to be serene. The serenity seems to be derived from vast learning and a penetrating mind. People think of you as mysterious, aristocratic and unreachable. They believe you have no petty concerns, and that you have an unvoiced understanding of the matters of the world. You may appear to be too aloof to those around you.
8	You seem to be very strong both mentally and physically. You are difficult to sway once your opinions have been formed. You also seem to be very wealthy and to occupy an important position in society. You have an authoritative air and you command respect. But sometimes you may seem dictatorial.
9	You seem to be selfless, tolerant and compassionate toward others. You seem to be generous and humanitarian. People think that you like to sacrifice yourself for humane causes. Some may resent your saintliness while others may respect your concern for humanity.

With Numerology, you can influence how others see you by de-emphasizing the negative aspects of your personality and emphasizing the positive aspects. Also you can eliminate the messages you have been sending out to people by altering your personality somewhat to suit the requirements of your job, family, etc.

Numerology can open doors to the past. With Numerology, one can determine the way one was in a past life.

To find the number for your past life follow this procedure:

KARL VINCE MONTPARNASSE

$$1 + 9 + 5 + 6 + 1 + 1 + 5 = 28 = 10 = 1$$

Add the values for all the vowels in your name. If necessary, reduce large numbers to a one digit number. Note: The letter Y is considered to be a vowel whenever it is the only letter among consonants that produces a vowel-like sound or whenever it is pronounced like a long E.

To find the meaning of your number read the following:

Number	Past Life
1	You were a leader with power and following. The ability to lead men requires a great deal of self conviction, independence, aggressiveness and wisdom. The memories of the glories or follies of a past life can easily spill over into the present life. You may still be preoccupied with leading others.
2	You were a follower who brought peace between warring factions or else escaped turmoil in search of peace. You could not bear any form of conflict partly because of an inability to deal with complex problems or partly because of your magnamimity. Your love for peace may still govern your present actions.
3	You have spent your previous life giving and receiving joy. Attaining happiness was your only goal in life. When others sought after money, you sought after happiness in every way possible. This tendency to drop everything that is a source of misery to you and seeking merriment may still govern your present actions.
4	You led a methodical life. Since you were extremely practical, you may not have experienced great vicissitudes in life. Life may have been bland, but it was rather secure. A desire for stability may still be the cause of your present actions.
5	You lived a life full of experiences. Restlessness may have carried you into many distant lands, through many jobs and many activities. You needed to experience all of what life has to offer. You could not have led a methodical life. This restlessness may still govern your present actions.
6	You lived a life that was deeply involved in the family. You gave and received love. You made the family your life, smothering family members with your love, opinions, ideas and rules.

You may have loved cooking, interior design-
ing, sewing, painting, etc. The memories of the
past may still govern your present-day actions.

7   In your past life, you searched for a greater
understanding of life. You wanted to learn the
secrets of the universe. You may have been a
mystic or a philosopher. Your obsession with
obtaining knowledge may have made you re-
clusive. You had great intellectual gifts and
great wisdom. Your present life may still be
influenced by the past.

8   Your past life was motivated by ambition, power,
and hard work. Because of your ambitions, you
would have had to endure more hardships than
other people. Also you would have had to use
your intellect more and learn more than other
people. Every minute of your life may have
been filled with decisions that would influence
many people. The amount of responsibility may
have exceeded normal levels, but the rewards
were great. In your present life, you may still
be goaded by ambition and the desire for success.

9   You lived a life devoted to selfless service to
others. Being too involved in the troubles of
others, you may not have had a life of your
own. This was due to a generous and expansive
personality. Your own troubles meant nothing
to you. This tendency to neglect your own
needs and help others may still govern your
present life.

Sometimes the strong memories of a past life may interfere with
the lessons you were born to learn in this life. The urges caused by
the memory of strong habits may pull you away from your present
duties. You should judge wisely the importance of these conflicting
impulses and then set one aside.

IV

Astrology

The North Star Astrological System is the means whereby the darkness of uncertainty is lifted from our lives. The North Star astrological chart is a blueprint of one's entire life. The chart reveals in detail one's financial and marital prospects. It can reveal the amount and kind of property one may own. It can reveal the appearance of one's spouse and the abilities of one's children. It can reveal all the potentials and pitfalls that life will unveil on a daily, monthly and yearly basis. With foreknowledge of life's potentials and pitfalls, one can act harmoniously with the cosmic forces that govern our lives. One's personal relationships, health and business will improve, and life will no longer be tormented by tension and stress.

From my point of view, the North Star Astrological System is the most accurate in existence. It is the only system which utilizes the North Star and the Big and Little Dippers as the major or primary stars, and the stars of the middle sky as the minor or secondary stars. In total, one hundred and eight stars are utilized.

These stars are unlike those of the twelve constellations of the zodiac which are used in the other systems of astrology. Every second we are bombarded by electromagnetic waves emitted by the stars. Taoism traces the particular actions and reactions that characterize our lives to the electromagnetic influence of these stars. To govern every second, day, month or year of our lives, those stars must always be present, like the North Star, which is even more constant than the sun. The sun leaves our sight at night, but the North Star is forever present, regardless of the time of day. However, the stars of the zodiacal constellations are present only at specific times of the year and are absent for the rest of the year. For example, Cancer appears only during the summer months of every year.

The Big Dipper is very important in the North Star Astrological System. From earth, the "handle" of the Big Dipper is seen to rotate 360 degrees clockwise. Completion of the handle's rotation indicates the passage of one year. The moon, which traces the progression of the month, and the sun, which traces the progression of the day, are also very important in the astrological system.

The position of these stars during one's birth influences the outcome of one's life. They also serve the function of recording one's every action in life, to determine how we must repay for our actions in the next life.

In 1964, the year I researched the Han Dynasty astronomical findings, I found further validations of the correlation between

346

celestial and earthly phenomena. In the year of Jesus' birth, astronomers of the Han imperial court recorded the appearance of an enormous, bright star. The star was seen both at night and during the day. It moved slowly from the east to the west.

During Jesus' birth, three wise men appeared from the east bearing gifts of gold, frankincense and myrrh. Since the Bible mentioned that the wise men came from the east and followed a star to find Jesus, they could have come from Persia, India or China, where astrology and astronomy flourished at the time.

To determine the nationality of the three wise men, one must examine the nature of their gifts. In China, there was a tradition of giving infants presents made of pure gold. The tradition is still alive today. And there was a tradition of giving mothers frankincense and myrrh, as these are the best herbs for healing the wounds of childbirth. Only in China are frankincense and myrrh used for healing wounds. Therefore, it appears that the three wise men may have come from China. The Han court may have sent three envoys to follow the star, find the infant Jesus, give him and his mother their gifts, and prove the validity of the astronomers' proclamations.

During the Han Dynasty, astrology was extremely popular. Everyone believed in it. Everyone also believed that each person on earth is represented by a star in the heavens. They believed that when a great man is born, a great star appears and rises and that when he dies, his star fades and falls. Astronomers were assigned to watch the skies twenty-four hours a day. The star that appeared upon Jesus' birth would have been looked upon as the birth of a great man.

An event recorded by the Han Dynasty historians tell of the indisputable accuracy of the observations made by those astronomers. One night, an astronomer sat watching the stars of the Emperor Kuang Wu and his visiting friend Yan Tse-Ling, who was sleeping with the Emperor that night. The astronomer was shocked to find that the brightness of Yan Tse-Ling's star covered that of the Emperor's. Suspecting that Yan Tse-Ling was an assassin, the astronomer ran through the halls of the palace in a panic to report that the Emperor was in danger. Just then another astronomer who had taken over the vigil of the heavens observed that the stars had separated and the brightness of Yan's star had diminished, and he reported this. Throughout the halls of the palace, the panic lessened to uneasiness, since the stars indicated that the danger had passed. As it was already nearing daylight, everybody waited until the Emperor arose from sleep. When the Emperor emerged from his chamber, the incidence of the stars was related to him. The Emperor laughed and said that Yan Tse-Ling, while asleep, had accidentally placed his leg over him.

The various aspects of life, work, marriage, money, etc., are divided into twelve categories, called the Twelve Houses. The position of a star within the Twelve Houses reflects the position of that star during one's birth. And how one fares in a particular aspect of life is determined by determining the effect the star has upon a particular house.

This is a simplified view of the North Star Astrological System. This summary was given because a complete explanation of the astrological system would fill volumes.

V

Directionology

Anything that occupies space and time is directional and has sides that face North, Northwest, Northeast, South, Southwest and Southeast directions. Directionality arises when North and South are defined. North and South poles are defined only when there is magnetism. All magnetic phenomena are essentially electrical in nature and ultimately can be described as arising from interactions between the moving and spinning electrons of the atomic nucleus. We are composed of atoms, so essentially our bodies are magnets. Like the lodestone, we are subject to the forces of attractions and repulsion. And, like the lodestone, we exert magnetic forces upon other matter which are attractive or repulsive in nature. There are also short-range electric forces, as well as many others, that one matter exerts upon another.

When we expand our point of view from the microcosmic to the macrocosmic, we find that these forces are the attractive or repulsive forces between one human being and another, and between a human being and money, property, and so on.

It is the purpose of Directionology to guide us in directing these forces so that our ventures or undertakings will be more propitious. Directionology is the science of selecting the most auspicious direction for achieving success in any undertaking whether through action or inaction.

Directionology can be applied to all areas of life, from birth to death. One major area of application is housing, because we spend the majority of our lives within buildings. Buildings, as well as their furnishings, occupy space and time and possess eight exposures to the eight directions. They emit forces that affect their owners.

Therefore, the placement of buildings and furnishings must correlate with an individual's directionality. When the placement is inauspicious, there is interference with the individual's brain waves, and creativity, logical thinking and emotional balance are disrupted.

A company is maintained by division of labor among its employees. That is why a company is divided into many departmental units, such as marketing, accounting and manufacturing. The employees of a particular department think, act and dress similarly — they are one entity. The forces emitted by these people as a unit should be directed in such a way that the unit's undertakings are successful. This is why Directionology can be tremendously beneficial in business.

When the principles of Directionology are applied to companies, the various departments are arranged accordingly:

Direction	Departmental unit
Center	Board of Directors, Boardroom
N	Personnel, Research, Reception
NW	President, Vice President
NE	Accounting, Environment, Real Estate
E	Planning, Development, Advertisement, Young male employees
SE	Board of Directors, Information, Inspection, Business, Manufacturing
S	Ideas, Management, Study, Communication
SW	Secretaries, Labor, Products, Management
W	Financial Planning, Entertainment, Bookkeeping, Young female employees

Japan's economic success is based on the thorough study and application of the principles of Directionology. Understandably directionology is extremely popular there.

Western businessmen who have utilized the principles of Directionology in Hong Kong have reaped immediate and great benefits. Recently, U.S. magazines reported that a few famous American firms have also gotten wonderful results from applying the principles of Directionology. Benefits range from successful business mergers, new businesses, robbery prevention, improved cooperation between workers and increased productivity for company members to marital bliss, health improvement and successful careers to individuals.

The services of a Directionologist can be bought for a certain amount of money per square foot of office space in Japan and Hong Kong. The services of the Directionologist can also be bought for determining proper burial sites. Directionology can affect the welfare

349

of the descendents of the deceased, as well as business.

Directionology is also the science of correct color usage. To each direction, the ancients have assigned a corresponding color.

These colors can be utilized in the office or home to enhance the effectiveness of Directionology.

Directionology can also be utilized for crop rotation and travel.

With Directionology, one can live in harmony with the higher influences that govern our lives. Life will cease to be a series of struggles that result in few rewards.

(Sometimes Directionology is abused and reduced to a superstition. One must be cautious of a false Directionologist.)

Directionology is a complicated subject that can only be explained in the space provided in an entire book.

VI

Symbology (Spiritual Communication)

Symbology is the use of spiritual codes to facilitate daily activities, bring mankind closer to the Tao, and hasten mankind's evolutionary progress.

This is possible because symbols, or multi-formed artistic embodiments of the concepts of Taoism, influence the workings of the forces of the universe and of one's own body for one's benefit. And these are accomplished without black magic or witchcraft, since the effectiveness of the symbols has a logical basis.

The workings of the universal forces are influenced through telepathic dialogues with those who are in a higher evolutionary level. The vocabulary of these dialogues are calligraphic symbols which are developed under the hands of the Taoist, who is guided by these higher beings. Certain wishes are projected from the mortal world to the otherworld by painting these calligraphic symbols on a piece of paper and then burning it, or by embedding these symbols in permanent forms of art, such as carvings and paintings. For example the figure on page 360 is a portrait that was painted in the Sung Dynasty. It is of a uniformed spaceman with constellation dots. (Tao-Tsang 853: 166.)

Symbols play a crucial role in influencing the workings of one's own body for one's benefit. Realizing that many problems have a psychological basis, Taoists began using symbols to correct the state of the mind. Taoists made symbols to remind people of the Tao in their daily activities, to prevent them from hurting themselves and others. Having symbols to project people's wishes will provide them with a psychological support for their daily activities and endeavors. People will feel that they have the support of the omnipresent, higher beings. Thus, faith, trust, hope and a positive outlook on life are strengthened.

The effect a symbol can have on a person is exemplified by this story about a fighting couple. Having irreconcilable differences, the husband and wife fought every minute, everyday. One day both husband and wife consulted a Taoist master. The master drew a symbol and instructed the couple to place it under their pillows. Then the master told the couple to stop fighting for fourteen days, otherwise the symbol would not work. During the fourteen-day truce, the couple managed to devise a method for preventing an argument. This method maintained the peace even after the fourteen-day truce. The symbol was actually a psychological remedy for the couple.

Other uses for symbols include:
> Making the atmosphere peaceful, hospitable, clean and holy, anyplace, anywhere
> Improving health
> Increasing wealth
> Increasing happiness
> Reminding a person to do good deeds
> Aiding in meditation
> Decorating the home
> Protecting against evil
> Sending prayers (by focusing your concentration on your wishes)
> Healing
> Helping in one's evolution
> Gifting

The *Pa-Kua* sign is the basic symbol of Taoism. It can be produced in any size and it can be hung in any place. It is hung to provide protection, peace, balance, success, power and righteousness.

One college professor told me the following story. His office was in between two other offices which belonged to two ladies who fought bitterly and constantly. He was always dragged into their fights, which occurred without any good reason. They all realized this and tried everything to stop the insanity. They tried seeing psychologists and psychiatrists, but nothing worked. The man even contemplated resignation.

So, I recommended that he hang a *Pa-Kua* sign from the Foundation of Tao in a place where everyone would notice it. Immediately he came back to tell me that he felt the vibration change when he hung up the sign. He also told me that no one had fought again.

A student of mine had a friend who was both an accountant and an investment advisor. This friend, confident of his abilities, ran expensive advertisements, which brought only very few clients to his door. For years his business was extremely slow, and he considered changing locations. Then my student purchased a sign from the Foundation and gave it to his friend as a gift. In that same week, his friend's office was crowded with people and his phone rang unceasingly. His friend did not have to move to another office. Both thought the sign was responsible for the sudden change in luck.

I myself have personally experienced the power of the sign. A young woman brought her mother to my office to seek my help. Her mother had been possessed for twelve years. Her mother had been placed in mental institutions, treated by psychiatrists, and had been the subject of several exorcisms performed by several ministers. Nothing worked. When the mother came in, guided by her daughter, I was slightly taken aback — I had never seen anyone who looked like her. Her mother had a green face. Some areas of her face bulged out and some sank in. Her lips were blue. Her dark brown hair, cut short,

352

stood up by itself. She tried to say something but no words came out. She suffered from shortness of breath and she did not have the strength to walk or stand.

After the young woman helped her mother to sit down, she asked me for my help again. I sat down behind my desk and lowered my head to ponder the problem. I had never seen someone possessed, and I had to think of another way to help the woman because I do not favor exorcisms. Just then I heard a sharp scream. I looked up quickly. The screams came from the daughter, who was exclaiming, "Look at my mother! Look at my mother!" My eyes rested on her mother, who looked beautiful! Her face was no longer green! Her cheeks were pink, her complexion was smooth, and her lips were red! Her hair lay flat on her head and it was blonde! The woman stood up crying and walked toward me, saying, "Doctor Chang. Thank you! Thank you! That thing has left me!" She hugged me. But I had to tell her the truth. "Dear lady," I said, "I do not deserve your thanks. This wonderful miracle you so much deserve is none of my doing. From where you sat you faced the *Pa-Kua* symbol directly. The evil spirit cannot withstand the power of the symbol. That must be the answer . . ."

Symbols come in many forms. Some are drawn with red or black ink on papers that are of the colors of the eight directions. These can be placed in silk bags and carried on the person. (Taoist masters always made symbols for their students to remind them of the Tao). Wood, stone, glass windows, pottery, and lacquers can be carved also.

Symbol to bring assistance from the Sovereign

353

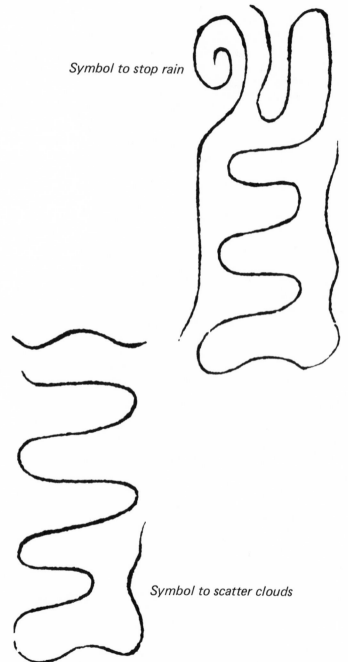

Symbol to stop rain

Symbol to scatter clouds

354

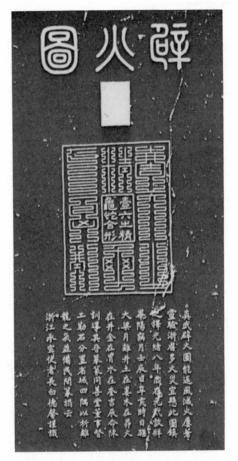

Symbol engraved on stone to prevent fire

Symbol to stop fog

355

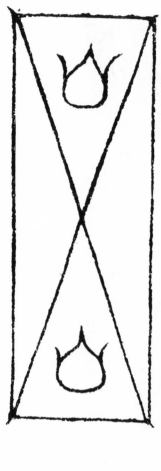

Symbol to protect the body from evil

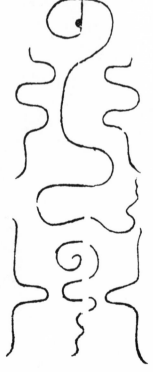

Symbol for purifying the body

356

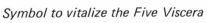

Symbol to vitalize the Five Viscera

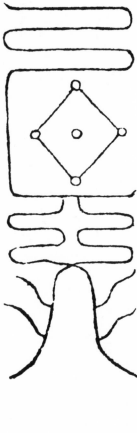

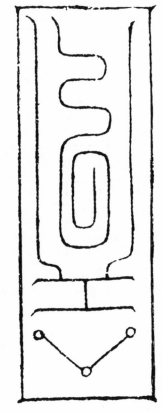

Symbol to prolong life

357

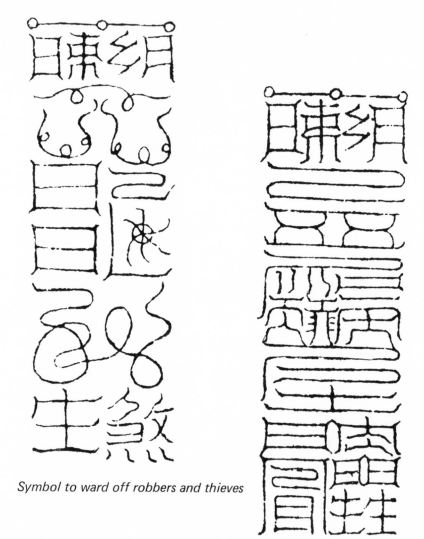

Symbol to ward off robbers and thieves

Symbol to protect against wrangling

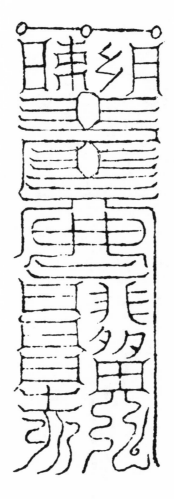

Symbol to ward off disaster

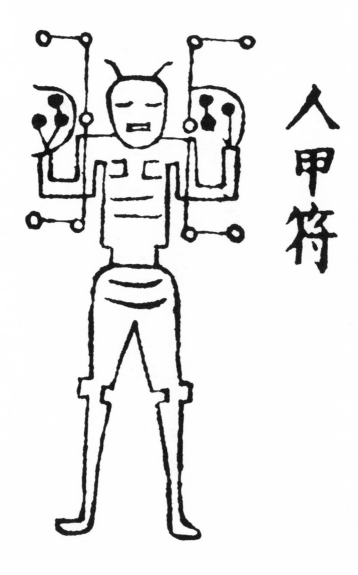

Symbol of universal figure, 1300 years ago

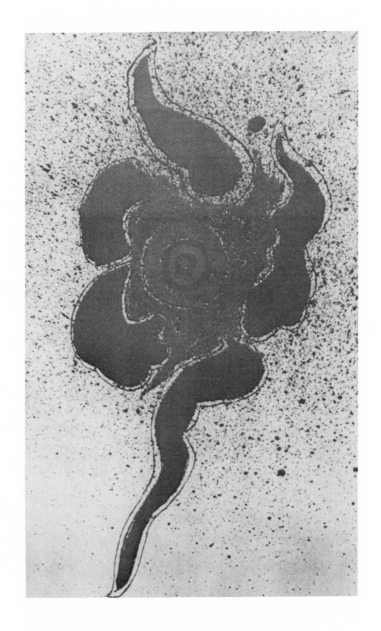

Symbol means abundancy — wall picture
Color: Gold, red, yellow and black

*Symbol for energy — wall picture
in red and black*

8

THE TAO OF SUCCESS

I-CHING

I

    I-Ching is the secret of all success—financial, political, marital, or any other. It reflects the changes that are constantly operating throughout all levels of the universe—the cycles and tides of fortune which we must learn to know and ride if we are to achieve success. It enables us to glimpse something of these mysterious rhythms, and to re-align our lives so that we can live more in harmony with the laws of nature. This is the key to success.

I-Ching is divided into two systems of wisdom, the Space and Time I-Ching System and the Taoist Methodology or the Tao of Change. The Space and Time I-Ching System enables us to forecast events through the use of the date, time, and Five Elements. Unlike many other methods of divination, the Space and Time I-Ching System does not simply fortell future events and then leave you to cope with them as best you may. It offers sound advice on what should be done, best time to do it, which direction one should proceed in, how to start and maintain that direction, and with whom one will have to deal. Taoist Methodology is the study of social philosophy, transactional psychology, and the nature of the universe, as represented by the 64 hexagrams. Each hexagram is composed of six lines, each of which represents a developing stage in individual, group or universal transactions. No questions about the nature of the universe or the life contained within it are left unanswered.

Success cannot be attained if either one of the two systems of wisdom is neglected. I-Ching Strategy provides many insights into every human or universal transaction and is therefore vital to a person's preparation, which determines how one uses one's judgement. When a person's judgement fails because his mind is limited by space and time, (normally a human being does not know about the opportunities in his future), the Space and Time I-Ching System can help a person turn unforeseen opportunities to his advantage. According to Taoism the formula for success is as follows:

$$S = P + O$$

Success is the sum of preparation and opportunity.

The I-Ching resulted from centuries of research by scholars and sages who sought to integrate the artistic, scientific, and practical elements of life. The foundation of the I-Ching, the *Pa-Kua*, was laid down by Emperor Fu-Shi. Further enlargements and embroideries on this subject were made by the scholars and sages of the Chou Dynasty, a dynasty famed for its I-Ching research work.

The founder of the Chou Dynasty, King Wu, was himself a Taoist. His father, King Wen, was a famous I-Ching scholar. His prime minister and commander in chief, Chiang Shan (also known as Chiang Tse Ya or Chiang Tai-Kung), was also a famous Taoist. This man helped King Wu establish the solid foundations of an 800-year empire by utilizing the teachings of Taoism.

Confucius was also an I-Ching scholar; he wrote the commentaries on the I-Ching. At forty-six years of age, Confucius sent a prayer. He said, "If I may have a few more years, I will begin the study of the I-Ching when I am fifty, and then I shall make fewer transgressions in the remainder of my life." Confucius studied the I-Ching until his death at 73 years of age. In the last 23 years of his life, he devoted so much time to the study and interpretation of the I-Ching that the leather thongs binding his copy wore out and had to be replaced three times. A significant part of the Book of Change was written by this I-Ching scholar.

The I-Ching has retained its eminent reputation through subsequent centuries. In every age its guidance has been sought by Chinese philosophers, statesmen, warriors and ordinary people when faced with an important decision or major undertaking.

The tradition is still maintained today. It is widely studied in the modern universities and employed in business negotiations in many parts of Asia.

The I-Ching is reserved for the use of the true cultivator, someone who will refrain from using this wisdom for petty, evil or blind purposes. Those who abuse the wisdom have unfailingly met with disasterous ends. Historical records have proven this to be true.

The Space and Time I-Ching System will not be discussed in this book because it is a complex subject which can only be thoroughly explained in the space provided by an entire volume.

II

Taoist Methodology, or the Tao of Change, consists of many sets of guiding principles that help us understand the universal laws which we cannot escape. Knowledge about these universal laws can help us find the answers to our problems in order to accomplish our "preparation."

The Tao of Change reveals that nothing stands still. That nothing lasts forever and that for everything there is a proper time. He who does not strive to hasten good fortune prematurely, he who can accept inevitable decline, achieves true contentment. Treading the middle path of balanced progress, he avoids all conflicts by aligning himself with steady rhythms of the universe and finally becomes one with Tao, or walks with God.

The Tao of Change is as timeless and as limitless as the changes in this universe. The universe is in essence a manifestation of change. All that exists must change. If nothing changes, there would be no life, and if there is no life, there would be only emptiness. The universal changes follow many complex sets of rules, and there is a pattern to these rules. The Tao of Change is about these rules and their patterns. As the pattern of change is repetitious, the Tao of Change will never be obsolete. The timeless and limitless teachings of the Tao of Change direct man through the maze of universal changes.

Everything, including success and decline, follows a specific pattern of succession and occupies a specific period in time. Understanding and following this pattern insures true contentment. Doing otherwise, fighting decline or fighting any other changes, will result in abject misery, because the way of the universe cannot be changed. The person who fights the universe always loses. The Tao of Change helps people live with the way of the universe, reap many rewards in the process, plan for what is inevitable in order to meet all challenges and adversities with confidence, and become wise masters of their fates.

The ultimate purpose of the Tao of Change is to raise the caliber of human beings, so that they may enter the Kingdom of God. By living correctly, according to the way of the universe, people will dissolve their past Karma and then lead productive lives. The Tao of Change presents abstruse evaluations of all sides of an issue, and this encourages people to sharpen their intellect while solving their problems. The Tao of Change helps people climb the ladder of society, success and evolution so that, in the end, all may enter into the Kingdom of God.

The teachings of the Tao of Change are encoded in hexagrams. To extract the teachings, these hexagrams must be deciphered. But before deciphered messages can be presented to the reader, he or she should achieve an understanding of the Yin and Yang digram, as it forms the content of the hexagrams.

366

The Yin and Yang digram symbolizes the many aspects of change. The digram represents all the pairs of opposites in the universe, from the most trivial (two faces of a paper) to the most vital (God and Satan). The digram also presents the pairs of opposites as single entities — the two faces of the paper together make one piece of paper. One half without the other results in nothingness. So, according to the Yin and Yang theory, God and Satan are one, and one cannot condemn one without condemning the other.

How is this so?

In older versions of the Bible, the first book of the Old Testament was Job, not Genesis. A story about Job was told in this first book. In a dialogue between God and Satan, God praised Job for his faithfulness and righteousness. Satan challenged God, saying that Job's faith, a result of God's gifts, would disappear when the gifts disappeared. God allowed Satan to test Job and Job suffered many adversities. Seeing that Job's faith was unfaltering, Satan challenged God again, saying that harm inflicted upon Job's person would end his faith. God accepted the challenge and permitted Satan to do his work. Still Job was unremitting. In this book, God and Satan work together and counsel each other. The trials of Job seem to be caused by Satan, but Satan has God's permission.

The Yin and Yang digram represents another aspect of change, of interaction such as the interaction between God and Satan. There are two types of interactions, one generating and one degenerating. They are as follows:

Generating: 1) Yang generates Yang   3) Yin generates Yang
              2) Yin generates Yin   4) Yang generates Yin

Degenerating: 1) Yang destroys Yang   3) Yin destroys Yang
               2) Yin destroys Yin   4) Yang destroys Yin

The generating interaction can be understood in terms of the following example. Rampaging criminals cause people to establish a police force to protect themselves. So Yin (criminals) generates Yang (police force) because the police force would not exist if criminals did not exist. Gradually the police force grows (Yang generates Yang) and soon it becomes burdensome to support. (Taxes are raised.) Meanwhile, criminal forces grow, also. (Yin generates Yin). Corruption in the police force results in its participation in crimes (Yang generates Yin).

The degenerating interaction can be understood in terms of the following example. When a police force captures a criminal, a Yang-

367

destroys-Yin interaction is taking place. When the government cuts the force's funds, a Yang-destroys-Yang interaction is taking place. When its funds are reduced, the force is overcome by criminals, a Yin-destroy-Yang interaction. While criminals kill each other a Yin-destroys-Yin interaction is taking place.

The third aspect of change indicated by the Yin and Yang digram is that Yin in its most acute form becomes Yang and vice versa. This nature is exemplified in a poor person's rise to wealth (Yin becomes Yang).

The fourth aspect of change is that anything and everything has both Yin and Yang natures. Taoists never encourage celebration because hidden within a happy situation is the seed of sadness. Hidden disasters develop under fortunate circumstances and good fortune develops under disastrous circumstances.

The fifth aspect of change involves a reciprocal Yin and Yang relationship. An example of this would be the mutual attraction of the positive and negative poles of a magnet.

The digram capsulizes the many aspects of change between Yin and Yang forces: how Yin and Yang generate or degenerate each other, how Yin and Yang push against each other, how Yin and Yang fight against each other, how Yin and Yang help each other, how Yin and Yang penetrate each other, how Yin and Yang melt each other, and so on.

When one digram is placed beside others, the changes can be endless. There are, however, rules governing change and they are as follows:

1. There is a specific pattern of change. Following this pattern retains normality. Disregarding this pattern results in abnormality.
2. Anything undergoing a change must be transformed completely.
3. Change itself must not change. If change becomes something else, the universe will no longer exist. Everything changes except change.

These rules dictate that there must be six lines of Yin or Yang in a hexagram, and these lines determine how a hexagram is to be read.

A hexagram is read in an upward direction, beginning from the bottom. The bottom-most sign is given the name Line 1. The top-most sign is called Line 6. The signs in the middle are Lines 2, 3, 4 and 5. The sign for Yin is ▬ ▬ and the sign for Yang is ▬▬▬ .

Next, the hexagram is divided into Yin and Yang positions. Lines 1, 3 and 5 are defined as being in Yang Positions. Lines 2, 4 and 6 are defined as being in Yin Positions. A sign in a Yin Position can be either Yin or Yang. A sign in a Yang Position can be either Yin or Yang. A Yin sign in a Yin Position, or a Yang sign in a Yang Position purports advantage or normality, and a Yang sign in a Yin Position, or a Yin sign in a Yang Position purports disadvantage or abnormality.

Lines 1, 2 and 3 of the hexagram are called Inner Lines. Lines 4, 5 and 6 are called Outer Lines. Lines 2 and 5 must be read with care, since these are critical areas called Valleys. Line 2, bound on both sides by Lines 1 and 3, is likened unto a valley being bounded on both sides by mountains. The same can be said of Line 5. Lines 2 and 5 are areas of importance since these sinking areas are traps for the unwise.

After this, the rank of each of the lines is considered. The rank increases as one moves upward through the lines. Beyond Line 5, the peak, everything plummets downhill.

The next area of examination concerns the implications of sign and position compatibility or incompatibility. Yang denotes rigidity, strength, nobility, respect, high position and fullness. Yin denotes softness, flexibility, weakness, commonality, dishonor, poverty, emptiness and reception. When a sign falls into a position of the opposite nature, compromise is suggested. When the natures of the sign and position are the same, conditions are accentuated.

Another way to interpret the hexagram is as follows. Line 1 represents a beginning, Lines 2, 3 and 4 represent second, third, and fourth stages of development, Line 5 represents the highest stage of development, and Line 6 represents an ending.

Then one examines the Self and Response Lines. When one looks at Line 1, one must also look at Line 4. In looking at Line 2, one must look at the response in Line 5. In looking at Line 3, one must look at the response in Line 6. Consequently, Lines 1, 2 and 3 are called Self Lines and Lines 4, 5 and 6 are called Response Lines. Self and Response Lines aid each other.

Another aspect of the hexagram is Neighbor Lines. Neighbor Lines are Lines 1 and 2, 2 and 3, 3 and 4, 4 and 5, 5 and 6 and Lines 1, 2 and 3; 2, 3 and 4; 3, 4, and 5; and 4, 5 and 6. Lines 1 and 6 have one Neighbor Line and Lines 2, 3, 4 and 5 have two Neighbor Lines. Neighbor Lines are for making comparisons.

The next thing considered is seniority. Line 2, located above Line 1, is superior to Line 1. Line 3 is superior to Lines 2 and 1. Line 4 is superior to Lines 3, 2, and 1. And so on up the hexagram.

The last thing considered is the three folds of the body. Lines 1 and 2 represent the physical body. Lines 3 and 4 represent the mental body. Lines 5 and 6 represent the spiritual body.

FIRST GROUP: SUCCESS

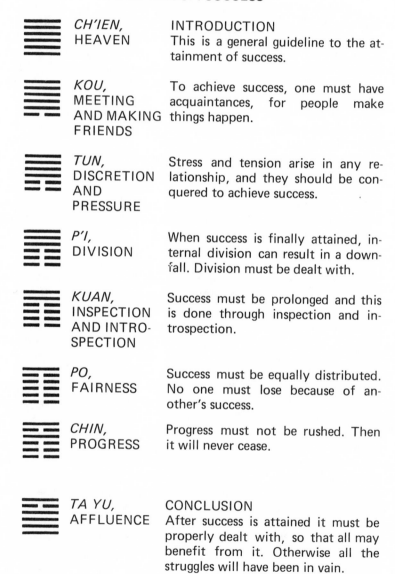

CH'IEN,
HEAVEN

INTRODUCTION
This is a general guideline to the attainment of success.

KOU,
MEETING
AND MAKING
FRIENDS

To achieve success, one must have acquaintances, for people make things happen.

TUN,
DISCRETION
AND
PRESSURE

Stress and tension arise in any relationship, and they should be conquered to achieve success.

P'I,
DIVISION

When success is finally attained, internal division can result in a downfall. Division must be dealt with.

KUAN,
INSPECTION
AND INTRO-
SPECTION

Success must be prolonged and this is done through inspection and introspection.

PO,
FAIRNESS

Success must be equally distributed. No one must lose because of another's success.

CHIN,
PROGRESS

Progress must not be rushed. Then it will never cease.

TA YU,
AFFLUENCE

CONCLUSION
After success is attained it must be properly dealt with, so that all may benefit from it. Otherwise all the struggles will have been in vain.

CH'IEN

The Image

This hexagram is called *Ch'ien,* meaning heaven. Heaven is represented by six Yang signs, since the Yang sign symbolizes the attributes of God, the ruler of heaven. The attributes are as follows: leadership, bravery, bliss, longevity, benefits,and constancy. This is the image of success.

The Lines of This Image

Line 1, where Yang sign falls into Yang position, represents mankind's raw creativity, ambition, aggressiveness and positiveness. These raw gifts must be refined through education by elders and teachers. At this stage, everyone must be receptive to all forms of education, because everyone is still unrecognized by society. At this stage, a person needs patience, learning, humility and a desire for self-improvement. Everybody's duty at this stage is to build a broad and tall base of knowledge so that it will lift everyone to the second stage. You cannot automatically upgrade your station in life, because no outside assistance is indicated in the Response Line 4 (Yang sign in Yin position). If you do not work hard at accumulating knowledge, you will never improve your station in society, evolution, and so on.

Line 2, where Yang sign falls into Yin position (or a valley), represents a critical stage where abnormality, disadvantage and compromise are numerous. These present themselves whenever or wherever a new idea, plan, situation,or position falls upon a person. These are unavoidable since a superior will always notice you when you are qualified and will lift you into a higher station in life. In this critical stage, your knowledge will be put to the test. Inadequate learning will force you back to the first stage. Adequate knowledge will buoy you to a higher stage. At this critical point, you also must continue self-education, in order to make friends with those below you and to please your superiors. Do not let jealousy or dissatisfaction bring about your fall. Do not be afraid of trouble, but use knowledge and wisdom to do everything right. If everything is as it should be, promotion is inevitable, indicated by a helpful Response Line 5.

Line 3, a Yang sign in a Yang position, represents success. Success is the sum of past preparation and opportunity. Although you have reached this stage, you cannot stop; stopping means the end. Although you have reached the top of your present circle, you must look elsewhere for a foothold to continue your climb. (You have reached the end of the Inner Lines or Inner Trigram.) There are many people below you, but you are alone at the top. Although plagued by many problems, you cannot seek the help of those below you, and there are not many people at your position in life who can help you. This is an awkward stage. To overcome this, share your riches with those below and induce them to work together to help you solve problems. Also you may seek help from outside your organization, i.e. merge your organization with another. Always seek more knowledge, in order to make every move a wise one.

Line 4, a Yang sign in a Yin position, indicates that one is a beginner again, but at a different level. You have expanded your organization (opened a new branch in another city, merged with another organization, etc.) and you must build it into a successful new establishment. You, a Yang sign in a Yin position, must give generously to meet the needs of those around you. This is exemplified by American foreign business dealings and by Japanese business dealings in America. Both supply the other countries' needs. To understand the needs of others, one must accumulate more knowledge.

Line 5, a Yang sign in a Yang position, represents national and international success, since most of the world's population is below you (represented by Lines 1 through 4 being under Line 5). But this is also a dangerous stage since everyone below you desires your possessions. To avoid being overthrown, you must retire. The world's most respected figures are those who retire and allow those below to move up. Continue to accumulate knowledge in order to retire wisely.

Line 6, a Yang sign in a Yin position, represents sharing. A person at this stage in life must share his wisdom and knowledge to help others below him acquire success. One retires to help the people of the world.

KOU

372

The Image

The *Chien* has changed to the *Kou* hexagram, with a Heaven trigram above and a Wind trigram below. The wind is the first materialization from the abstractness of heaven, and it is represented by the movement in the first line. Wind can be felt and it is the first universal element affecting a person directly. It meets and soothes the person. It can stimulate and it can destroy. The wind is the harbinger of the seasons; it delivers a message to the people. Because the wind meets people and stirs the calm, it has come to symbolize the meetings between people. These meetings are categorized as follows:

1. Meetings at physical levels (brief sexual liaisons, for example)
2. Meetings at mental levels (marriage, business partnerships, etc.)
3. Meetings at spiritual levels (carrying out a divine mission)
4. Meetings that benefit all parties involved
5. Meetings that destroy all parties involved

The Lines of This Image

Line 1, a Yin sign in a Yang position, represents attraction as the means of making friends. This is also a warning against unselective friendships, such as the relationship between a prostitute and her client (represented by one Yin sign among five Yang signs). There is an unhealthy addiction associated with this kind of relationship, once a person has indulged in it. This kind of relationship is useless since no evolutionary progress is made from it. It can even be destructive. Friends must be carefully selected and friendship must be carefully nurtured. Only the unenlightened masses engage in friendship at the physical level. Attraction must be used carefully for beneficial purposes. One can cultivate a friendship with lawyers for legal purposes, for example. People who are silent, even-tempered, decisive, and hard-working make excellent friends.

Line 2, a Yang sign in a Yin position, represents a testing period for a recently-made friendship. Many doubts and troubles result from this period when two people from different backgrounds, with different personalities, or with different thinking try to make their friendship last in the wrong way. To make a friendship last, do not let friendship (Yang) become too overwhelming (Yin). Enthusiasm must be tamed and distance must be maintained. Revealing too much to each other too soon can result in envy of each other's possessions or intelligence, because a Yang sign in a Yin position indicates conflict. Maintaining distance and silence show that both people respect each other's ego and opinions.

Line 3, a Yang sign in a Yang position, represents progress in friendships. But caution must be exercised. A friendship that lasts through Stage 2 progresses and grows, and both parties progress and grow with it. Both parties gain from teamwork but both parties must remain uninvolved. A person must not become involved in a friend's questionable business activity. A person should not be brought down by participating in a friend's business venture that is morally or legally questionable. Never respond to those who approach you with an offer to fill your rooms with gold, silver, and jewels, for this can endanger your success. Choose to engage only in legal business ventures.

Line 4, a Yang sign in a Yin position, represents a betrayal. You cannot rely on your friend or spouse forever; you must prepare for their betrayal. Circumstances change overnight and a close friend or spouse can become one's worst enemy. This is exemplified by the betrayal and denial of Jesus by Judas Iscariot and Simon Peter. (Simon Peter was supposed to be as solid as a rock.) People cannot be relied upon entirely and one should not be hurt when betrayal happens. You must prepare for this, so that when it comes you will not lose much. If you continue positively, you will win them back, and then their hearts will be truly yours. When you have won the hearts of men, you will have passed a great test: that of becoming a leader of men.

Line 5, a Yang sign in a Yang position, represents spirituality. Having conquered the hearts of others, you must turn to conquering the self. You must achieve a complete understanding about the physical, mental and spiritual aspects of yourself. Others regard a person at this level as a sage. Only that person knows that he or she can be his or her own worst enemy and best friend, and that he or she has great inadequacies. At this stage, a person must do Internal Exercises to control the self completely to spiritualize the body.

Line 6, a Yang sign in a Yin position, represents the perpetuation. Friends do not last forever, so one must build a spiritual friendship that lasts forever. Jesus founded a religion that would last forever, winning him the love of generations of human beings.

TUN

The Image

The *Tun* hexagram is composed of a mountain trigram below and a heaven trigram above. Originally the universe was evenly divided between the earth and heavens. However, the earth began to build up, forming the mountains, and began to push back the heavens. The Yin began to invade the Yang. The competition between the mountains and the heavens symbolize the stress and tension resulting from the competition between people. The heavens withdraw, but they will never be blotted out by the mountains. Heaven will always remain infinitely great.

The Lines of This Image

Line 1, a Yin sign in a Yang position, symbolizes withdrawal and weakness on our part. When stress comes you should not lose your life and hope in drugs or alcohol. Stress is caused by hiding our inadequacies (Yin) when we face a great challenge (Yang). Stress begins when you do not come to terms with your inadequacies and blame others for your mistakes. To fight stress, withdraw. Do not cover up your inadequacies, but humble yourself and seek information and learn. People will help you only if you let them know you need it. Make friends, but do not bare one's heart to them, just get vital information from them. Always be aware of your shortcomings. Thank others for detecting your errors and encourage them to find others, so that you will learn more. Doing otherwise — boasting of your talents when you have none — will make you unpopular. Your position is weak and you cannot afford to make mistakes. You are your only saviour (no help is detected in the Response Line).

Line 2 (Yin sign in Yin position). The two Yins stabilize each other, but the Response line offers no help. When you are promoted to a higher level, stress and obstacles become greater, and the best way to cope with these is to maintain your position. Do not seek fast remedies such as change of jobs or selling or buying property. Move slowly and never lose your footing. Use what you have learned and establish a reputation of reliability. Stability will reduce stress and help you survive until the next promotion.

375

Line 3 (Yang sign in Yang position) represents greater stress. In this position, you must reduce the likelihood of being replaced by newly-trained people by studying hard and putting in extra hours. Strengthening your qualifications will reduce your inadequacies, and therefore, reduce your stress. When the stress becomes too great, it can become a deadly disease. In this case, you must leave voluntarily. There is no point in trading your life for possessions that can be accumulated in many other ways. Adopt a spiritual attitude and prepare to go into another business and let the people below you take your place. Not fighting them may save your life.

Line 4 (Yang sign in Yin position). You (Yang) must learn to give generously and to give up prized possessions. To do so requires self control, something that can be learned through the practice of Internal Exercises. The purpose is to relinquish small gains to acquire great gains. When you are able to achieve such a level of self-discipline, you will be able to extricate yourself from conflicts with others over possessions. You will be able to free yourself from health-destroying entanglements and concentrate on making yourself a success.

Line 5 (Yang sign in Yang position) represents stress from loneliness (no comparable lines flanking Line 5). When you are very successful, you will have no real friends. Money opens a chasm between the affluent and the rest of society because people desire the possessions of the affluent. To eliminate the stress that comes from loneliness, retire from the position of power, so that those below may take the empty seat. You must donate your services to help those below you. Your retired life will be filled with purpose, you will gain many friends and you will be honored for your generosity.

Line 6 (Yang sign in Yin position) represents withdrawal for permanent gain. At this stage, a person must donate his or her knowledge and material possessions. By withdrawing from your possessions, you do good for the people of the world and you become closer to God. Not understanding withdrawal means you do not truly understand advance. Those who cannot give up a small piece will never get the large piece. Those who cannot bear temporary losses will never have permanent gains.

The Image

The *Pi* hexagram, composed of an earth trigram below a heaven trigram, symbolizes division. Heaven is forever ascending and earth is forever descending. This represents a breach of communication, and a polarization and division in an organization. After an organization has survived the hardships mentioned in the previous hexagrams and has finally achieved success, it will inevitably experience polarization and division. This is a very dangerous position, as the entire company can be destroyed by internal conflicts. An organization is divided into two halves: one composed of Little Men, the other composed of Gentlemen. The Little Men are represented by the earth trigram and the Gentlemen, by the heaven trigram. Little Men are distinguished by the following characteristics: selfishness, short-sightedness, negativity, and narrow-mindedness. Gentlemen are distinguished by these characteristics: broad-mindedness, kindness, unselfishness, positivism, and generosity. During the conflict between these two warring factions, the organization stops progressing.

The Lines of This Image

Line 1 (Yin sign in Yang position). In the beginning, when the enterprise is still young, the weeds are indistinguishable from the grass. The Yin and the Yang, or the Little Men and the Gentlemen, will remain hidden for the time being and will not reveal themselves.

Line 2 (Yin sign in Yin position). After awhile, the two groups will only tolerate each other superficially. The Little Men (Yin) are in a favorable position (Yin) for making headway. When the Little Men gain more power, the Gentlemen lose. Hostility between the two groups, though suppressed superficially, is growing deeper. The two groups can be distinguished, and the Little Men outnumber the Gentlemen.

Line 3 (Yin sign in Yang position). The Little Men, after making many gains, become complacent and neglect to cover up their schemes. Their evil deeds begin to surface and a person can correctly distinguish the Little Men from the Gentlemen.

Line 4 (Yang sign in Yin position). When the Little Men reveal

377

themselves, the Gentleman leader of the organization must make a list of the Little Men to be eliminated. This is still a dangerous period of time for the leader as the Little Men hold great power. The leader must secretly devise a plan for eliminating the Little Men.

Line 5 (Yang sign in Yang position). Now the leader has the support of powerful Gentlemen and is in a position to enact his plan. Now the weeds must be pulled. Spare no one and show no mercy, for the Little Men will only come back and destroy the Gentlemen. Vanquishing the Little Men is a difficult deed because the leader must first vocalize his or her loyalty to a carefully chosen faction and use his or her wisdom to protect his or her interests and eliminate the opposition. If a leader chooses the wrong group, he or she will go down with the defeated.

Line 6 (Yang sign in Yin position). Now the organization must be rebuilt. Although the storm has passed the victorious must not become complacent. Otherwise they will become Little Men themselves. Even the most righteous can become close-minded, selfish, and shortsighted. The most important thing to be done after the victory is to remind the Gentlemen of their moral standards. Gentlemen must keep their minds clean. Otherwise a new group of Little Men will emerge.

KUAN

The Image

The *Kuan* hexagram is composed of an earth trigram below a wind trigram. The wind never ceases to circulate, or travel, upon the surface of the earth. The wind also penetrates everywhere, brushes past everything and sweeps away dust. The wind represents unending inspection, introspection and trouble-shooting. In any endeavor, you must inspect all work to eliminate mistakes, in order to insure continuing success.

The Lines of This Image

Line 1 (Yin sign in Yang position) represents mistakes and shame.

378

Success means that many people are working under you. The greater the successes, the greater the number of people employed. The number of mistakes increases with the rise in the number of people employed. The only way to decrease the number of mistakes is to use constant reminders about close attention to detail. Lectures and training will encourage those below to pay close attention to their work.

Line 2 (Yin sign in Yin position) represents a person, sitting in a well, looking up to a limited view of the heavens. People in low positions have limited views, but they think they have a complete picture. Even though these people think they are right, they will harm others and themselves by their limited thinking. Those who are in high positions must not believe or be swayed by every word of those below and must check their statements. Those at the top must retain an open mind and must be receptive to valid new viewpoints. Those at the top must not neglect the fact that the universe is constantly changing and that people below do not have a complete perspective on these changes.

Line 3 (Yin sign in Yang position). At this stage, the leader must inspect him- or herself. The leader should meditate on his or her actions at least three times a day to learn the truth about him or herself. Introspection must be on the physical, mental, and spiritual levels. The leader disciplines him or herself strictly. A leader must set an example for those below, in order to insure continuing success.

Line 4 (Yin sign in Yin position). At this point, you are one step away from world-wide success. To pave the way for this you must go out and learn about the cultures of the world, so as to expand your viewpoint. You must learn how you may help the people of the world, in order to gain their acceptance. You are beginning anew, on a higher level.

Line 5 (Yang sign in Yang position). This is a critical position to be in. Many people (all the Yin signs) below you are depending on you. Introspection is even more important now, because every one of your actions imparts on everyone below you. You are representing an entire society and one mistake on your part will cause many people to suffer. At this stage, you must invite and accept criticism, which will improve you and help you benefit others below you.

Line 6 (Yang sign in Yin position). At this stage you must share your knowledge and wisdom with others. You must teach others the value of introspection. Teaching others to improve themselves is a never-ending work, since nobody on earth is perfect. You must teach others the virtue of retaining a wide viewpoint, since the universe is constantly changing.

PO

The Image

The *Po* hexagram is composed of a mountain trigram above an earth trigram. The mountain and earth are made of the same things, the only difference between the two being that the mountain contains more earth. This represents the rich and the poor. Both subsist by the use of money, but the rich have more money than the poor. The higher the mountains are, the lower the earth is. The higher the earth is, the lower the mountains are. The hexagram represents the contrary relationship between the privileged and the unprivileged. For example, management demands more work for less pay from workers. And workers want less work for more pay. There is constant fighting between the two factions. If management is victorious, then the economic system will be capitalistic (slavery). If workers are victorious, then the economic system will be socialistic (communism). Pure capitalism builds, through the deprivation of the earth, mountains that are too high. Pure socialism, through tearing down the mountains, builds high grounds. Neither capitalism nor socialism can solve the problems of the people. Under capitalism, people suffer most cruelly. Under socialism, everyone is poor. This hexagram shows how the world's problems can be solved by the Taoist economic system of social capitalism. Social capitalism benefits all groups of human beings and it maintains peace and fairness.

The Lines of This Image

Line 1 represents pure capitalism. The people are slaves who are not allowed to complain, who have no rights and who suffer every minute of the day. These people are unorganized, but there are futile attempts to rebel. Peace and order is destroyed when workers make demands to correct unfairness.

Line 2. Socialism is born. The workers begin to organize and fight

380

back. They begin to make demands. When these demands are not met, hostility grows.

Line 3 represents the growing strength of the socialistic movement. Bargaining begins and when demands are not met, violence results.

Line 4 represents the victorious workers. Society is on the verge of adopting communism. With each victory, the workers grow in power. But those on top are still fighting for their privileges. If life is conducted in this pattern, no problem is resolved. Fighting will be more intense, and society will fall behind. This is a great social disaster.

Line 5. Taoism begins. There are two alternatives: those on top can destroy themselves by continuing to be corrupt and mindless and suppress the rise of the workers, or those on top can invite the workers to join them (the Taoist solution). An example of sharing between the two groups is worker ownership of a company.

Line 6 represents peace and harmony. When the privileged allow the unprivileged to join them, there is unity among the people. This is a society of permanent peace and fairness.

CHIN

The Image

The *Chin* hexagram is composed of a fire trigram above an earth trigram. This represents the sun bathing the earth in light, which slowly increases in brightness, as during sunrise. If progress, advancement and success are to endure, they must be attained gradually. If they are attained suddenly, they will not last. This is a universal principle, and it applies to everything in life. You must progress slowly, surely and everlastingly.

The Lines of This Image

Line 1 represents darkness, or obstacles, in the beginning. Unknown to people, you are distrusted. The only way to break through the darkness is to be patient, maintain high moral standards, accumulate knowledge and work hard.

Line 2 represents patience in overcoming obstacles in work and in pleasing others. Any attempt to achieve explosive success can cause envy, which can bring about your downfall. Be humble and work hard to dissolve any likelihood of negative results.

Line 3. You have gotten to the top. In order to continue to grow, you must associate with a group of useful people, because they hold the key to your promotion. Share only good, new, and moral ideas with them.

Line 4 represents a dangerous position. Joining one group has made you an enemy of another. Those people will try to use your statements against you. If you have only presented your good side, they will not succeed. You also must overcome this situation by radiating a positive attitude, sharing your ideas and using your wisdom to win over the trust of the opposition.

Line 5 . You may be a weak leader who has inherited followers or a high position. Although you may have no ability, you can still survive by finding talented and skilled advisors (Yang neighbor lines). You must trust their advice.

Line 6 represents spirituality. Turning towards spirituality allows you to grow forever. Material possessions do not help a person grow.

TA YU

The Image

The hexagram is composed of a fire trigram above a heaven trigram. This represents the sun in the middle of the sky. Everything goes smoothly, everything is bright and shining. The sunshine embraces everything under the sky, so it symbolizes great success and great material possessions. Material possessions are symbols of financial success. This hexagram, which teaches the ways to deal with riches, is the conclusion of the Success Group.

The Lines of This Image

Line 1. A person, newly rich, will naturally adopt a haughty manner. He or she may display their wealth and look down on others.

This attitude endangers the newly rich, because no one will tolerate them, teach them or advise them. This is the seed of calamity. At this stage, the newly rich must remain humble and forget the fact that they are rich. Doing so will prevent them from losing their wealth.

Line 2. The affluent should reinvest their money in their business. The money should be used to benefit others. This way money will continue to come in. Not doing so — putting the money in a safe — will result in the loss of money.

Line 3. Having money and knowing how to use it is what is meant by being truly rich. The affluent deserve a luxurious life, but if they live such a life while others are living in abject poverty, they are in the wrong. If the affluent live a luxurious life while at the same time actively help others to live a luxurious life, they are in the right. Not helping others will result in a great calamity.

Line 4. The affluent tend to use their money to cover up the corruption or scandal caused by their mistakes. Most of the affluent find it hard not to cover up their mistakes. They are, however, using the money to buy privileges, which is to gain advantage over others. If they do this, their wealth will perish even while they are asleep. Money should not and cannot be used effectively for corrupt purposes.

Line 5. The affluent must share their wealth with others. They must give their money away. If they do not do this, the most important things to them (health, life, reputation, etc.) will be lost. This is guaranteed to happen.

Line 6. If the tight-fisted manage to live, their suffering will be greater than anyone else's on earth. Money will be of no use to them. They will have no children, or their children will meet with disastrous ends. This is guaranteed.

SECOND GROUP: RISK

 K'AN,
WATER

INTRODUCTION. To be successful, risk must be taken.

 *CHIEH,* DIS-
CIPLINE AND
RELIGION

Discipline and religion are forms of risk. One's life can be destroyed when too much or too little emphasis is placed on discipline.

 *CHUN,*
BEGINNING
AN
ENTERPRISE

It is a great challenge to begin an enterprise. There are many uncertainties.

 *CHI CHI,*
POLITICS

Politics involve many risks. Most politicians drown in the political river.

 *KŌ,*
REVOLUTION

The risk involved in subverting a government is very great.

 *FĒNG,*
MONEY AND
POWER

Money and power are sources of greater risk. The rich who do not share their money with the poor will see their houses crumble and the deaths of their beloved.

 *MING I,*
INJUSTICE

Those who injure others will injure themselves.

 *SHIH,*
MILITARY

CONCLUSION. Warfare is riskier than any other activity. Warfare is the Tao of abnormality.

384

The Image

This hexagram is composed of two water trigrams. There are many kinds of water: sea water, river water, lake water, etc. Sea water is intimidating, because of its immenseness and unpredictability. The sea hides organisms that are still shrouded in mystery. Undersea pressures, undersea caverns, the dark depths of the sea, the mercilessness of its storms and its blue tranquilness hold us in a state of awe. River water is never stagnant. It flows continuously and swiftly. Lake water is calm, unchanging and beautiful. Because water sustains life, it is the source of man's wealth. Where there is life, there is activity and excitement. Dealing with water involves a great deal of risk and difficulty. Although water is the softest of all things, it is also the most powerful. In summary, water symbolizes intimidation, unpredictability, change, mercilessness, wealth, excitement, risk, difficulty, and power.

The Lines of This Image

Line 1 represents weakness and powerlessness. Those just starting their climb in society or at work have unpredictable futures . Starting out can be exciting and dangerous.

Line 2. You must depend on your knowledge to overcome risk and danger. Nothing can be overcome without knowledge. You must educate and train yourself.

Line 3. Ambition must be accompanied by talent. If ambition exceeds talent, then danger lies ahead. Too much ambition causes a person to move ahead too fast, and he or she can be drowned by his or her mistakes.

Line 4. If you realize that your knowledge is inadequate, you can suppress your ambition, humble yourself and work with others to overcome a period of danger. You must be honest with yourself and others and gradually work toward your goal.

Line 5. To overcome extremely dangerous situations, you must not be over-confident of your talents. You need the combined talents of many people, and you must carefully plan and investigate before you tackle the problems. You must remain patient in order to overcome adversities.

Line 6. When danger has passed, do not think that the worst is over. Man is in danger every minute of the day. You must always be honest with yourself, lead a stable life, and be cautious. If you do not do so, the second wave of danger will drown you.

CHIEH

The Image

This hexagram is composed of a water trigram over a lake trigram. The lake serves as a reservoir for water. When water levels are exceedingly high, the extra water is stored in the lake. When water levels are exceedingly low, water is drawn from the lake for use. This hexagram represents mankind's reliance on religion and self-discipline. Because human beings do not know their fate, they have devised religion to give themselves moral or psychological support. Is religion helpful? Used correctly, it can help. Used incorrectly, it can make matters worse.

The Lines of This Image

Line 1. Most orthodox religious teachings teach people to be virtuous, moral, cautious and hopeful. They also teach people to learn the wisdom of the universe. Church members actively help one another. At first glance, this seems to be good for mankind.

Line 2. Then things go wrong. The churchgoers become very confused and seek help from the church. Soon they seek the church's help for every problem that occurs in their life, and they become "addicted" to the church. Chou Dynasty scholars likened religious fanatics to people who are addicted to wine behind closed doors. The people appear to be faithful followers, but they are in fact anesthetized by the teachings, and they no longer understand the real world. They believe they are shielded from advertisities by the church. These people can no longer function in the real world.

386

Line 3. The addiction worsens. The drunkenness is no longer confined behind closed doors; it is spreading to the homes of innocent people. The fanatics begin to pull outsiders into the vortex of fanaticism, and religious cults are born. These people make others useless to society and they give religion a bad name.

Line 4. A person who can discipline himself, that is, overcome egoism, refrain from provoking trouble, maintain courtesy and peace through kindness and tact, and remember his goals, will have a more promising future than others. One's life is in one's own hands. You must ride the vicissitudes of life yourself, because fanaticism cannot overcome them.

Line 5. You must never overdo self-discipline or become an ascetic. Asceticism is another form of religious fanaticism. Asceticism may be attractive to those who like to control their bodies, but ascetics benefit neither themselves nor the world. It is wise to be moderate.

Line 6. You must not use self-discipline as an excuse to escape your duties. The monk who goes to practice self-discipline in the mountains is escaping the challenges of the world. The millionaire should not behave like a beggar in order to escape the problems brought about by wealth. Everyone is here to evolve and everyone must learn to overcome adversity.

CHUN

The Image

The hexagram is composed of a water trigram above a thunder trigram. Water in the sky is in the form of clouds. Thunder announces a rainstorm. In the darkness, there is a flash of light, and then there is creation. The rain nourishes the organisms on the earth and triggers their creation and growth. This hexagram represents the starting of a new business and the challenges and uncertainties with fear or failure associated with it.

The Lines of This Image

Line 1. When a person is driving in the rain at night, he cannot see what is ahead. The driver must continue although he is anxious. Slowly he moves toward his destination. Without a destination, the driver can get lost and suffer serious consequences. At this stage, a person must have a goal, a destination.

Line 2. Yin sign responds to Yang line number 5. At this stage, a person is like a young lady waiting for a lover who is far away. Men are constantly at her side, courting her, but she does not respond. She has the willpower and patience to wait for her lover. To build up a business, a person must have patience, persistence and goals.

Line 3 represents a hunting trip into the mountains. In this dangerous situation you must have hunting skills. Otherwise you could be killed. Without goals, persistence or skills, you cannot succeed.

Line 4. Although a person has fulfilled the foregoing requirements, success will not arrive automatically. A person must be given an opportunity to become successful. Opportunity cannot be controlled by mortals, but we should always be prepared to accept opportunity when it is given to us. How do you know whether an opportunity lies in your future? You know, because you have faith.

Line 5. Even though you have goals, persistence, patience and opportunity, you must associate with people. Without the help of a group of people, you cannot succeed. To get their help, you must share your wealth with them. When there are 100 miles to cover, the last ten miles are the longest miles, because near the end egotism causes you to treat other people cruelly.

Line 6. The successful founder of a business will suffer from a terrible disease: the fear of losing. Fear can cause a person to become too cautious and too narrow-minded. Soon all progress stops because people distrust each other. To lose the product of your life work to fear is very unfortunate.

CHI CHI

The Image
388

The hexagram is composed of a water trigram above a fire trigram. Water is heated for cooking. A high degree of uncertainty is associated with cooking. Heating, timing and results are difficult to control. In the Chou Dynasty Old Text, this hexagram symbolized the challenges associated with the crossing of a river. In crossing a river, one cannot accurately determine the depth or speed of the water. To live the life of a politician is to cross a river.

The Lines of This Image

Line 1. The river crossing begins when a wagon is guided cautiously into the water by its owners. The water covers the wheels and everyone inside the wagon is anxious. The wagon moves slowly—its driver does not dare guide it faster. When a person goes into politics, he or she must be extremely cautious. Everything can be lost and there is no turning back. Going into politics, like gambling, provides a great deal of excitement.

Line 2. Yin sign in between two Yang signs, like one woman in between two men. Politicians used to be very practical. Regular politicians have no moral standards — they are only concerned about benefits and harm, in order to preserve their positions.

Line 3. Even though a politician has prostituted himself mentally, he will not get all that he deserves. The best politicians are those who are not always practical. The politician who does not forget his policies, ideals and talents is more dependable. In the end, honesty surpasses mental prostitution.

Line 4. The water soaks the clothes of the people inside the wagon. Politicians are beset by many hard-to-solve problems. Those who cannot remove the clinging cloak of problems will suffer great defeats. Those who have the ability and the fortune to solve the problems will be hailed as heroes. Problems are solved only by those who have great fortunes, since no mortal can control all the causes.

Line 5. The greatest vice of the politician is egotism. The politician who attributes his success to his own abilities rather than his fortune will make great mistakes. He will reward himself with luxuries and indulge in corruption. He will be removed quickly, no matter how much the public loves him.

Line 6. The head is covered by the water. Most politicians do not make it to the other side of the river. Most of them drown. The few

389

who get to the other side succeed.

KÔ

The Image
This hexagram is composed of a lake trigram over a fire trigram. The lake is a limited body of water. It is similar to water in a pot. Fire under a pot of water will cause the water to dry up, just as a revolution eliminates the privileged class. This hexagram is the guiding principle of revolution, which develops in six stages.

The Lines of This Image

Line 1. Without a noble and compelling idea (any "-ism"), there can be no revolution. This idea must attract many people. The revolutionary leader must have the ability to attract people also. He must be resourceful, talented, virtuous and charismatic.

Line 2. The idea must absorb many people and unite them into a powerful group. That group must have a party theme, such as helping the unprivileged solve their problems or attacking a corrupt government.

Line 3. Now the group is ready to revolt publicly. They must use propaganda effectively to broadcast their party theme over and over and over again, until it is permanently fixed in people's minds.

Line 4. The enemy will try to suppress the revolt through violent or covert actions. The revolutionaries should take this opportunity to broadcast their plight and win the hearts of the people. The revolutionaries can also use their enemies' actions as an excuse to protect themselves by taking up arms. Engaging in warfare with the opposition must be the last alternative. If a military solution is used too soon, it can result in a great loss for the revolutionaries. Propaganda must be used to loosen the hold of the existing government, and then the military should be brought in to topple the government in one stroke.

Line 5. Once the revolutionaries seize power, they must first elim-

390

inate the old injustices completely. The revolutionaries must avoid the temptation of becoming the oppressors, otherwise they will incur the wrath of the people and human resources will be wasted.

Line 6. A new system must be instituted. Then everyone must rest. Everyone must share the resources and be treated kindly. People cannot continue to fight indefinitely, or else they will be driven to rise up against the new government.

FÊNG

The Image

The hexagram is composed of a thunder trigram over a fire trigram. The clash of thunder and fire symbolizes power, abundance and financial success. Money and power are difficult to contend with.

The Lines of This Image

Line 1. In the quest for money and power, people have committed sins against others and have had sins committed against themselves. Contention is best eliminated by compromise. You should not allow yourself to ruin the lives of others, and you should prevent others from harming yourself. Compromising requires great wisdom and talent.

Line 2. Most people think money and power provide security. Nothing can be farther from the truth. Those carrying nothing on their person are freed from sins. Those carrying one piece of jade become the victims of intrigues. The day becomes so dark that stars can be seen. There is no limit to the intrigues and trouble, created by money and power or the uselessness of money and power.

Line 3. Those who do not share their wealth will be harmed irreversibly. The wealthy must choose between money and health. Without health money is useless.

Line 4. Most of the wealthy bury or hide their money. Doing so

391

will only result in rotting money. Again money is made useless to those who earned it. The minute money touches the ground, it becomes someone else's.

Line 5. Those who are intelligent find ways to give their money away. The more one gives, the more one receives.

Line 6. If, at this stage, a person still clings to his money, he will see his house crumble down upon him and he will witness the death of those who are dearest to him. With no one to inherit the money, the money will go into some else's hands.

MING I

The Image
   This hexagram is composed of an earth trigram above a fire trigram. When the sun does not rise over the earth, there is no light. Sin and injustice lurk within the darkness.

The Lines of This Image

Line 1. If strength cannot prevail over the sins and correct them, escape must be immediate. Like a wounded bird who flies away in terror, one must escape the stronghold of sin.

Line 2. The darkness is alluring. Many people participate in illegal activity because they are lured by the prospect of earning money quickly. Those who do so injure themselves greatly, because they are sacrificing evolutionary progress for a few dollars. The wound is greater than that of the bird's.

Line 3. If safety cannot be found, then you must fight back. To correct evil is to do a good deed.

Line 4. The war against evil is a long one. You must have patience, willpower and wisdom. Any weakness in your willpower will cause evil to prevail over good.

Line 5. When the strength of evil forces exceeds that of the good, it
392

is wise for the good to escape to a place where evil cannot reach it. On earth there will always be a place with sunlight.

Line 6. Although sinners do injure others, they also injure themselves. Evil cannot last forever. When evil reaches a climax, it must then decline.

SHIH

The Image
The hexagram is composed of an earth trigram over a water trigram. A most unpredictable danger (water) is hidden underneath a facade of calm. On the surface, the military seems calm and quiet, but underneath, the military has the power to cause untold miseries and destruction. This is the hexagram of warfare.

The Lines of This Image

Line 1. When an army goes to war, superior weapons alone will not guarantee a victory. Victory is the sum of planning and discipline. Without a good plan, the army fights blindly. Without discipline, good plans will not be carried out and the army will still fight blindly.

Line 2. The army must have an excellent general. A good general not only possesses military knowledge, but also love and loyalty for his country. Because the general embodies patriotism, he must imbue his soldiers with patriotism. The general provides his army with a compelling cause for going to war and guides the army toward victory.

Line 3. Half the battle is done covertly. Good spies help win the war.

Line 4. Some people go to war to occupy others' cities. Some people engage in wars to win over people's hearts. The second alternative is the wisest. If you can win the hearts of your enemies, you gain their cities without any bloodshed or suffering. When you are righteous, you will win the heart of the enemy.

Line 5. If a good army is used for invading another land, it will

393

always lose. The good army is used for protecting the homeland. When the army is used for a righteous cause, it will always win.

Line 6. When the war is over, you must deal with the army wisely. You must promote those who justly deserve rewards. If not, the army will be used by your enemies to hasten your fall. That is why Sun-tse called warfare the Tao of Abnormality.

THIRD GROUP: STABILITY

 KÊN, MOUNTAIN — INTRODUCTION. To be successful, one must learn how to stop activity. The most beautiful music has periods of silence.

 PI, BEAUTY — Inner and outer beauty play a great role in the stabilizing of success.

 TA CH'U, TOLERANCE — Tolerance of shortcomings is a vital part of maintaining or stabilizing a high position in society.

 SUN, LOSS — There is no perfect gain or loss. Knowing how to lose is knowing how to gain greatly.

 K'UEI, DIFFERENCE — Differences must be pushed aside and people must be brought together to bring about success.

LÜ, COURTESY — Good manners demonstrate discipline and respect for others. Other people will be willing to help a well-mannered person maintain a high social position.

394

 *CHUNG FU,* FAITH — Having faith will move mountains. It is better to trust and fail than to distrust and always fail.

 *CHIEN,* GROWTH — CONCLUSION. One should understand that growth is incremental. Stabilized growth appears to be slow.

KÊN

The Image

This hexagram is composed of two mountain trigrams. A mountain is a kind of fence, a limitation. A mountain is rich because it contains a wealth of animal, vegetable and mineral resources. A mountain is extremely stable. A mountain protects refugees during wartime and it is a retreat to meditators, businessmen, etc. who are lured by its stillness. A retreat into the mountains indicates a temporary withdrawal from any activity and a period of intense spiritualization. One withdraws from intense outer activity to engage in the inner activities of the body. During the Chou Dynasty, this hexagram symbolized the human body. The first line represents the toes; the second, the legs; the third, the torso and pubic area; the fourth, the chest area; the fifth, the mouth; and the sixth, the head. The underlying message is that Internal Exercises must be practiced to control the body's inner activity. This hexagram teaches the virtues of stopping: how stopping can prevent many aggravations and how stopping can be used to further one's progress.

The Lines of This Image

Line 1. There is no virtue in holding on to something tenaciously and hoping success will result from it. There is virtue in stopping and analyzing your situation, and then moving in another direction. Stopping allows you to save yourself from committing transgressions against others and yourself. Stopping saves a person from a great deal of pain and aggravation.

Line 2 represents the difficulty of stopping. Many people are unable to willfully stop their activities. Although you must stop, you continue because you follow those who are not stopping. Although you have made a mistake, you do not stop for fear of losing face. The only way to save yourself from disaster is to ignore the opinions of others and to stop and proceed in the right direction.

Line 3 is about the inability to stop sexual desire. The inability to conquer sexual desire has resulted in the fall of many great men, because their reputation, health, and life suffered. Too much energy and time are lost in this pursuit, so wise people must suppress and control sexual desire. For further information regarding the principles of sex, refer to Chapter 6.

Line 4 represents the achievement of inner peace in the heart and mind, through the practice of Internal Exercises. Inner peace cannot be achieved by limiting physical movement. A person, ill and lying still, can still have a heart that is beating 160 beats per minute.

Line 5 represents cessation of oral activity. All disasters are caused by indiscreet remarks, and considerable harm can be done to your health if you eat unwisely and ingest wrong substances through the mouth. For information regarding the correct way to eat, please refer to Chapter 3.

Line 6. At this stage you will have the ability to stop (control) yourself. You understand the virtues of limitation. The most beautiful music has periods of silence. So do human beings.

PI

The Image

This hexagram is composed of a mountain trigram above a fire trigram. This hexagram represents the molten lava within a volcano. The lava bursting from the volcano is a beautiful sight to behold. This hexagram symbolizes beauty. The fire, or lava, in the mountains or volcano, decorates the mountain and brings it to life. The fire attracts people's attention. Inner and outer beauty play an important part in a person's evolution, and beauty must be correctly dealt with. This hexagram explains the philosophy of beauty.

The Lines of This Image

Line 1 represents outer beauty. The eyes play an important role in the outer beauty of any person. The beauty of the eyes can make a plain person beautiful. This beauty does not rest in the eyes' color or shape; it is the glitter and sparkle of the eyes that attract people's attention. Eye Exercises give the eyes the glitter. You must also decorate yourself. Clothing is especially important. You must not be careless of your clothing. You must find a style and a color that suits your personality perfectly. A person who belongs to the fire element must wear a certain color. A person belonging to the water element must wear another color. A person must be discouraged from wearing too much make-up. The objective is to draw people towards a person, not to frighten them away.

Line 2 represents beauty attained through associations. You must decorate yourself with the proper possessions. You must then decorate yourself through associating with people who will enhance your self-esteem, because you will be enhanced in another's eyes.

Line 3 represents inner beauty. You must decorate yourself with high moral standards and actions. You should not change your mind often, you should keep your word and you should not hurt others.

Line 4 represents enhancement through patience. A person must be pure at heart to be patient. Patience attracts innumerable blessings.

Line 5 represents enhancement through your services. Being selfish pushes people away. Giving attracts people.

Line 6 represents moderation. Too much decoration frightens people away. In this position, you must withdraw. Otherwise over-decoration creates distrust. Over-decoration symbolizes affectation. There is a proper time, place and way to decorate and you must master it.

TA CH'U

397

The Image

This hexagram is composed of a mountain trigram over a heaven trigram. This represents a limiting of heaven. Heaven, representing riches and success, inside a mountain also becomes a mine. Hidden riches are useless. The riches must be mined and utilized so that all may benefit from them. The wisdom of the leader must embrace all of his people, as the mountain embraces the expanse of the heavens. If he cannot do this, the society will fail. As the expanse of the heavens is infinite, the mountain, or wisdom, must also be infinite. The mountain "contains" money, success, people, friends, talent, and virtue. A leader's path to power is at first blocked by many obstacles. But a leader must overcome these and acquire riches to gain power. The leader must have infinite wisdom to become a leader and rule well those below him.

The Lines of This Image

Line 1. At the beginning everything is at a standstill. No amount of talent or aggressiveness can extricate a person out of this position. You must appreciate the state of matters and use this opportunity to train your patience and tolerance and enrich your knowledge. Losing your temper with superiors is a sign that you need more training.

Line 2. Problems must be dissolved wisely. Enemies must be removed secretly. You must not engage your enemies directly. Dissolving trouble requires tolerance and patience. You must wait for a favorable moment, and then take action. Sometimes, when you wait long enough, the problem will have already been dissolved.

Line 3. At this stage, you must acquire many riches: money, people, talent, virtue, etc. Your wealth gives you power. You must win your enemies over by indirect ways instead of conquering them the hard way (you get to the other side of the mountain through curving roads that go *around* the mountain).

Line 4. You must learn to make use of these riches. You must make use of money by sharing it with others. You make use of people's talents by being tolerant of their shortcomings. Being tolerant does not mean that you have to be completely insensitive. You should be insensitive to shortcomings but sensitive to the causes of obstacles in order to dissolve them.

Line 5. At this stage, you must deal with great doses of anger. Anger can destroy a person's health. You must learn to be able to see the purpose behind negative occurances. Every negative or positive force merges together for a good purpose. Anger will be quickly dissolved.

Line 6. Having accumulated so much richness within you (money, tolerance, friends, etc.), you can become the most powerful and indestructible person in the world. You can become the wisest leader of mankind.

SUN

The Image

This hexagram is composed of a mountain trigram over a lake trigram. The higher the mountain is, the lower the lake appears to be. The higher the lake is, the lower the mountain appears. When one gains, the other loses. This is the state of affairs for human beings. When one class gains the next class must lose. This is because the amount of resources in the universe is limited. This fact is unalterable because it is a universal law. So one person's gain must be based on another person's loss. The contentions that result over the possession of resources will always be bloody and endless. The only way to overcome such a sad state of affairs is to distribute the resources as evenly as possible to all human beings.

The Lines of This Image

Line 1. At first there is an active effort to gain. But you should know that there is no perfect gain or perfect loss. To win is to take away from others. To avoid committing a transgression while trying to win over some resources, we must try to let everyone else win too. If we do not wish to lose, we must not let others lose.

Line 2. The people of the world are categorized as A or B. When A gains, B loses. The world would be perfect if A equaled B. But wanting this is to be too idealistic. Bloodshed over the limited resources of this world could be reduced if everyone voluntarily stepped back and allowed others to have a little more. Little sacrifices do add up and the result would be peace. Once sacrificing begins, it spreads like a contagion.

Line 3. Contrariness involves only two parties (Yin and Yang). A third party cannot exist. Everything boils down to two parties which contend with each other until one party prevails over the other. If A, B, and C exist, then A and B will team up against C. C will lose and will gradually be reduced to zero. Then A and B will contend. To eliminate B, A must split B into opposing forces E and D. If E is eliminated, D is left. To eliminate D, A must split D apart. When all opposition is eliminated, A itself will split into two opposing forces. Contention goes on forever. The dialectical materialism follows this pattern of contention. This theory of unending contention is a negative view of the universe.

Line 4. A positive view of the universe is as follows. Anything that exists must have Yin and Yang sides. Yin cannot exist without Yang. For example, we will not understand what life (Yang) is if death (Yin) does not exist. And one side cannot be eliminated so that only one side exists. For example, if you wanted only Yang, you must get rid of Yin. The only way you can do this is to replace Yin with another Yin. If you wanted to preserve life, you must eliminate disease (Yin) with herbs (Yin). You are replacing Yin with Yin so that Yang can continue. (Positives result from double negatives.) After all the trouble you have gone through, Yin still exists. So any thought of contention should be eliminated. Only thoughts of even sharing between Yin and Yang should exist.

Line 5. When contrariness reaches its most serious level, a leader who uses the *Sun* Strategy will overcome it. When a leader can sacrifice himself, he will gain a million benefits. Pride incurs the hatred of others. Losing earns the respect of others. If Jesus did not sacrifice himself on the cross, he would not have become the king of kings.

Line 6. Those who fight for temporary gains by hurting others will suffer and lose greatly. Those who sacrifice a little will receive permanent gains. You can live a long, happy life and help many people by suppressing ambitions. This will result in the elimination of anger, tension, and stress. This is using the wisdom of loss.

K'UEI

400

The Image

This hexagram is composed of a fire trigram above a water trigram. The more powerful the fire (sun) is, the faster the lake is dried. When water is heated it rises and the resulting mists reduce the radiance of the sunlight. This means that no one can get along perfectly with another person, because everyone has different backgrounds, viewpoints and thoughts. When no one agrees with anyone else, the group or society falls apart.

The Lines of This Image

Line 1. To bring people together, you must isolate similarities from differences and unite them under their similarities.

Line 2. In a society polarized over complex differences, the contrariness never gets better. The wise leader must use his own honesty and righteousness to attract Gentlemen to his side.

Line 3. If the state of contrariness in a group or organization worsens and you can no longer handle it, you must bring in an outside party to help you. Friends, lawyers and relatives who are willing to step in will resolve the problem.

Line 4. If you cannot resolve the problem by attracting people to your side or bringing in outside parties, you must wait and let time solve the problem. Stay away from the conflict while you wait.

Line 5. While waiting, you must actively search for people with your viewpoint and win them over to your side and make them a part of the team. At this point, you feel disheartened by your previous failures, but you should try positively to find comrades.

Line 6. When one has many helpers, one tends to doubt them, since nobody is perfect. This must never happen. You must never become too critical of people's shortcomings, since your position is still weak. Because every bit of talent is needed, you must be tolerant of all the shortcomings. A statesman's tolerance is as great as the sea.

LÜ

The Image

This hexagram is composed of a heaven trigram above a lake trigram. The sky and the lake compliment each other. When the lake is closed off from the sky by trees, the sky is not reflected in the lake. The lake loses its beauty and the sky is not complimented by its reflection in the lake. We must do as they do, that is, we must please each other and help one another by being courteous.

The Lines of This Image

Line 1. You must learn etiquette in order to be pleasing to others. By being pleasing in manner and appearance, you will be well-liked. Discipline is involved in the learning of good manners.

Line 2. You must be a Gentleman on the outside and on the inside. The hypocrite's practice of putting up a facade of good manners only when necessary is useless — the roughness of character always shows through. Good manners must come from a real desire to please.

Line 3. There are many pretenders among Gentlemen. These people are *often too nice.* Why? Because these people are very ambitious and their ambition surpasses their talents. These people, unable to attain success through honest means, will satisfy their ambitions in devious ways. They must not be trusted.

Line 4. Fire is used to test gold. Adversity separates the pretenders from the Gentlemen. During calm periods, everyone is pleasant. But when adversity comes, the resulting pressures strip away the facades and the pretenders will hurt others to preserve themselves.

Line 5. People in high positions must have manners. From their eating habits, you can determine whether they are Gentlemen. Those who show selfishness, by eating too much too quickly, must not be trusted. Those who are well-mannered must refrain from criticizing or insulting those who are not. It is not wise to incur the wrath of the Little Men, who can bring about your downfall. You must not use your standards to judge others.

Line 6. Manners are useless when they are not used to solve problems. There are six things that are truly important: You must devise a plan for accomplishing a good deed; you must enforce the plan by actively following it; you must review what you have done; you must determine whether you have spoken correctly; you must determine whether you have treated others correctly; and you must

402

be disciplined.

CHUNG FU

The Image

The hexagram is composed of a wind trigram over a lake trigram. *Chung Fu* means emptiness in the middle. A boat floats because it has no inner core. To remain afloat, we must always remain "empty," so that we will always be receptive to new ideas. In order to accept new ideas, you must have faith and trust. Religion requires that you trust in the existence of God, even when you do not see Him. To live happily, you must trust people. If everyone had to see the outcome of their trust before they gave it, the universe would come to a halt. This hexagram is about faith and trust.

The Lines of This Image

Line 1. It is better to trust and fail than to distrust and always fail. Trust is a subjective power. It is the power a person has over others. Subjective power is similar to objective power. The difference between the two is that subjective power is positive in nature and allows a person to convert others while objective power is based on coercion. Subjective power allows you to concentrate your efforts on one thing, to bring it to completion and achieve success. Without trust or faith in something, one will never succeed in anything. Faith and trust push doubt aside.

Line 2. Faith can move the sea, the wind, and the mountains. That is how great the power of faith is. Having it you can accomplish great deeds, because everything in the universe will come to your aid.

Line 3. Being too untrustful will result in failure. You are too busy calculating everything right and left, and nothing is accomplished because you think nothing will succeed.

Line 4. To succeed, loyalty must exist between the members of any group or organization. Without trust there is no loyalty. A family is successful only if there is trust among the family members. Everyone, from couples to government officials, must have trust.

Line 5. Faith involves giving your energy, money, etc. to build

403

something. But you must refrain from counting the immediate returns. Counting the returns is not faith. If you do not risk this much, you will have nothing. Those in high positions must give first. Giving first creates a bond of trust between those in high and low positions. Trust makes an organization successful and everybody will benefit because of it.

Line 6. Those who take advantage of their high position and the faith of those in lower positions for selfish gains will cause those in lower positions to rebel. Good or bad deeds are determined by a quick flash in the mind — they are mankind's creations. Faith gives mankind unique creative power. Because nothing exists without faith, faith must not be misused.

<h2 style="text-align:center">CHIEN</h2>

The Image

This hexagram is composed of a wind trigram above a mountain trigram. The wind represents the trees on top of a mountain. Many years are needed for a tree to mature completely. Trees make a mountain seem rich and beautiful. All the organisms that populate a mountain depend on trees. Although the rate of growth is slow, it is steady and constant.

The Lines of This Image

Line 1. A mountain contains millions of hidden seeds. The seeds are the source of the mountain's richness. Success, like the seeds, is unseen in the beginning. Like the seeds, success will someday burst forth.

Line 2. When a person first ventures out into the world, he or she is like a sprout. That person, like the sprout growing next to a pine tree, will not be noticed. At this stage, he or she must remain humble, be patient, work hard, and refrain from bragging. Given enough time, the sprout will become a tree. But if the sprout calls attention to itself prematurely, people will regard the sprout as a nuisance and pluck it out. On the other hand, attempting to help the sprout grow faster by pulling on it will only kill it. Nothing is obtained immediately. Because the mountain lasts forever, there is no need to be hasty to save a few minutes.

Line 3. Those who have never encountered any hardships will think that everything comes easily. These people will not take the events in life seriously. These are the seeds of failure. On the other hand, those who take life too seriously and try to do everything to succeed will also fail. Their inflated ambitions are also the seeds of failure.

Line 4. Under some circumstances, no matter how hard you work, you will never gain recognition. The only way to overcome this situation is to humble yourself and work until a solution presents itself.

Line 5. Any successful person succeeds for four reasons: 1. They have goals; 2. They work hard; 3. They are not anxious, but are patient and tolerant; 4. They move up step by step. When a person fulfills these four criteria, he or she will be successful automatically and will gain the respect of other people.

Line 6. Adjoining the highest peak of success is a decline. After attaining full success, a person should give retirement full consideration. Retirement is carried out in four steps. 1. Retirement must first be planned; a person must prepare for retirement. 2. A person must step down at a proper time — good timing is important. 3. A person must step down in an orderly, organized manner. 4. A person should leave people with an everlasting memory. Thus diefied, a person will forever be successful. Retirement must be stable and successfully executed.

FOURTH GROUP: FORCE

CHÊN,
THUNDER

INTRODUCTION. One must deal with all kinds of forces. These forces are dangerous.

YÜ,
ENTERTAIN-
MENT

Entertainment is a force no one can resist. Overindulging in entertainment causes deadly diseases.

HSIEH,
RELIEF

People should always be alert. If people are too relaxed or complacent, calamity results.

HÊNG,
HELP

Human beings will always need help. That is why they must study the principles of giving and receiving help, a natural force inborn in human beings.

 *SHÊNG,* PROMOTION — The force that pulls a person up the ladder of success must be used and understood.

 *CHING,* WELL — One must make oneself beneficial to others. When one is needed, one is valuable to society.

 *TA KUO,* ABNORMALITY — Abnormality exists because normality exists. Normality exists because abnormality exists. One must tolerate the force of abnormality.

 SUI, FOLLOWING — CONCLUSION. The force that induces people to follow each other cannot be avoided. Mankind cannot live alone; man is a social animal.

CHÊN

The Image

The hexagram is composed of two thunder trigrams. When two strong forces strike each other, something is stimulated by the generated energy. A thunderclap causes fear to spring up in the hearts of men. Thunder announces a rainstorm, which will nourish the earth and cause organisms to grow. Life and activity follow the rain. Because lightening flashes across the sky continuously, it symbolizes consistency. Lightening is dangerous.

The Lines of This Image

Line 1. When your life is threatened by a disease or any other calamity, you must not fight back forcefully, although fighting is a basic

406

human instinct. Instead of engaging a threat directly, you should painstakingly prevent such threats from developing. When you wait until calamity is near to deal with it, many losses will be suffered. You must be wise.

Line 2. When there is no time for prevention and the strength of the threat is too great, you should temporarily avoid it. If you do not avoid it, you will unwisely expose yourself to an onslaught. After time reduces the strength of the threat, you can deal with it directly.

Line 3. If there is no time for prevention or hiding, you must deal with the threat indirectly. Fighting the threat from an indirect angle saves a person from bearing the brunt of the onslaught.

Line 4. Yang sign in between two Yin signs, represents a talented person being trapped by unfavorable circumstances. It is very difficult for even the most talented person to escape this situation. You must therefore be tolerant. No matter how much you suffer, you must not fight back.

Line 5. You should retaliate with softness, because softness conquers hardness. When two forces charge at each other blindly, both will suffer enormous damage. By using a soft approach, you can use the enemy's momentum to destroy him.

Line 6. At this stage, you will be able to present a soft outer personality while maintaining a hard inner personality. You will be ridiculed for your weakness, but you should be patient and tolerant, so that you will not strike back. You should not be afraid of losing face when you must save yourself from danger. For example, you should not pretend that you are not sick when you should be seeking medical help. When a threat is near, you should escape. And if you can deal with the threat, you should do it well.

YÜ

The Image

The hexagram is composed of a thunder trigram over an earth trigram. Thunder stimulates growth on earth and brings the earth to life. When the earth comes to life, it is a time for entertainment, re-

407

joicing, enjoyment and happiness. Entertainment is a basic, instinctive need of human beings. But only Little Men devote their lives to fulfilling this need. The purpose of life is to evolve. Your evolutionary progress depends on how well you learn your lessons. Every minute of life is precious in that lessons can be learned. With any waste of time, you sacrifice a chance to learn a lesson.

The Lines of This Image

Line 1. Some people never understand the purpose of life. They live only for entertainment. Their lives are completely wasted. In the end, these people will suffer bitterly because of poverty.

Line 2. Those who can discipline themselves—not seek entertainment or stimulation—truly have time to enjoy life. These people will also be successful in life.

Line 3. Those who use entertainment to gain something are doing bad deeds. They are wasting not only their lives, but also the lives of others. They make others lose their chance to learn and evolve.

Line 4. More than half the members of any group live for fun. These people do not understand Gentlemen, who do not play. These people also ridicule Gentlemen. Gentlemen must therefore ignore their ridicule and live wisely.

Line 5. Those who occupy important positions in society must never waste time on entertainment. Many great men have caused their own downfall by indulging in entertainment.

Line 6. Overindulging in entertainment can result in the contraction of social diseases, including venereal disease. These diseases will not cause immediate death, but they will cause much suffering. You will pay a high price for a few seconds of pleasure. These diseases also serve as warnings against pointless merrymaking. You must learn to enjoy your work. When you are able to find joy in work, you have reached a higher level of spirituality.

HSIEH

The Image
408

This hexagram is composed of a thunder trigram above a water trigram. Clouds are composed of condensed water vapor. Clouds accumulate but no rain is released. Thunder signals the release of rain. Periods of calm and accumulation are followed by periods of turmoil and release. This wave-like pattern directs all manner of activities occuring within the universe. These vicissitudes provide a natural form of entertainment.

The Lines of This Image

Line 1. A person who has just overcome adversity will feel comfortable and happy. The feeling of accomplishment surpasses any feeling resulting from indulgence in entertainment.

Line 2. After you have overcome an obstacle, you must abstain from celebrating, which is a form of entertainment. When you indulge in entertainment, you forget to be cautious, and then you will plant a seed of calamity.

Line 3. When a society becomes complacent during times of peace, problems will arise. People will have to struggle in order to keep up with other progressive societies.

Line 4. You must stay away from evil activities. If you must cut off a finger to save the entire body, you must do so.

Line 5. You should form constructive relationships with those who have wisdom. Wise people will help each other use time constructively, prevent calamities from happening and entertain each other by sharing wise thoughts. Wise people are distinguished by three characteristics: they are able to plan ahead to prevent mistakes or calamities, they are able to analyze situations sharply, and they are industrious.

Line 6. Calamities, once they are detected, must be eliminated immediately. You should not wait for calamities to develop or to engulf you. When problems are not solved immediately, they will grow until they become too difficult to handle.

HÊNG

The Image

This hexagram is composed of a thunder trigram above a wind trigram. The sound of thunder is loud, but if thunder is accompanied by wind, its sound is amplified. Without the wind, thunder would not have a terrifying quality. This hexagram is about help. Help is always needed when something happens.

The Lines of This Image

Line 1. This line deals with the method of asking for help. You must ask for help directly and honestly. Asking for help indirectly delays action and discourages people from helping. When you ask for help, you must plainly state everything including how you will repay your helpers.

Line 2. This line deals with the methods of giving help. You should help people overcome their problems permanently by teaching them the universal principles. Do not offer the kind of help that keeps people dependent upon you. Doing so will earn you many enemies. By helping people stand on their own, you are helping them learn difficult lessons. Nothing in this world is obtained easily.

Line 3. People who are always waiting for miracles are those who do not look for help in the conventional way. These people are too anxious to succeed. Needless to say, they never will. They must learn how to place their "eggs" in the correct "basket."

Line 4. A hunter may spend a great deal of energy trying to hunt down animals in a forest where animals do not exist. When you have expended a great amount of energy without getting any results, you must look for another "forest." You must analyze your situation and look for other alternatives. You should not be stubborn.

Line 5. Those who repeat the same mistakes are people who do not know themselves well. Because they do not know their own strengths and weaknesses, they are unable to place their "eggs" in a specific "basket." These people tend to blame others for their failure. Friendship is the best medicine for these people. They must accept criticism from their friends and correct themselves.

Line 6. Those who do not know what direction to take are too selfish. They are protecting themselves from adversity because they love themselves too much. They also do not listen to the advice of wise friends, because they think they know what is best for themselves.

These people must listen to their friends.

SHÊNG

The Image
The hexagram is composed of an earth trigram over a wind trigram. The wind, blowing upon the earth, represents trees that are growing out of the earth. Trees emerge from the earth and grow upward. This is about the climb to success.

The Lines of This Image

Line 1. To make him or herself attractive and likeable, a person just beginning the climb up the ladder of success must make him- or herself pleasing in manner and appearance. People help people who are pleasing.

Line 2. You must be honest, loyal, and industrious. When people find that your services are indispensable, you automatically will be promoted to a higher position in society.

Line 3. When you are promoted, you should not become haughty. Otherwise jealousy will take away your success. You should regard a retreat as an advance.

Line 4. To move up, you must find a good superior. You should help and please this superior, but you should not participate in his or her illegal matters. When this person is promoted, you are promoted also.

Line 5. People may overlook you, even if you are extremely talented. Some believe that talented people are restless. Therefore, they are not given posts that require patience and watchfulness. You must give others the impression that you are talented, patient, and watchful.

Line 6. When you have reached the top of the ladder of success, you must climb higher. You must develop your spirituality. You must first learn the lesson of success to become spiritual.

CHING

The Image

This hexagram is composed of a water trigram above a wind trigram. In the past, wood was used to drill and build wells, which produce water. Because water sustains life, cities or villages are erected around a well. A well is useful and beneficial and it provides many advantages.

The Lines of This Image

Line 1. A person's worth is determined by how much he benefits others. Those who contribute nothing to society are not welcomed. Those who are welcomed are valuable to society, and they are usually well-known.

Line 2. A person should not accuse others of using him when they really need him. When people need a person, that person is valuable to society. If you hold your services back, you are being selfish. You should be happy that you can benefit society.

Line 3. People who are moral and talented are, like pure spring water, treasures that sustain a society. If a country or society fails to tap this source of wealth, it will suffer greatly. If a country or society allows its enemies to use its treasure, it is doomed to be destroyed.

Line 4. The well that produces no water is useless. There is a problem and it must be corrected. When you are no longer needed, you must correct yourself immediately. You must train yourself, learn new technology, do anything to make yourself useful again.

Line 5. Water is judged by the amount of people drinking it. The best water is that preferred by many people. A leader must learn the wisdom of the best waters. He must forever improve himself, so that people will prefer him over others. A real leader is someone who is loved by the people. A real leader does not force people to follow him.

Line 6. When people use well water constantly, the emptying action

412

causes new water to flow into the well. The well is kept useful through continuous use. If well water is not used, it becomes stagnant. A person must serve other people constantly in order to remain valuable to society. The more useful a person is, the more useful he becomes. A person must also improve himself constantly.

TA KUO

The Image

This hexagram is composed of a lake trigram above a wind trigram. A lake contains many pockets of air. Bubbles arising from these air pockets make the lake water unclear. This signifies abnormality. Many things in the universe are abnormal. Normality exists because abnormality exists. Abnormality exists because normality exists. We must be tolerant of abnormalities.

The Lines of This Image

Line 1. During periods of abnormality, only a person with superior power can change or overcome the abnormality. When you do not have such power, you must work with other people to maintain peace.

Line 2. The abnormality is tolerable because it may offer a small hope.

Line 3. When people try to correct an abnormality with too much force, they cause the abnormality to worsen.

Line 4. When people try to correct an abnormality with too little force, they cause the abnormality to worsen.

Line 5. The abnormality is intolerable because there is no hope available.

Line 6. Many mistakes, or deaths, result from a lack of understanding of the abnormality.

SUI

The Image

This hexagram is composed of a lake trigram over a thunder trigram. Thunder can be described as powerful, and water can be described as weak. Thunder, smothered by a body of water, cannot express itself. Thunder submits to the lake. This hexagram is about compliance. You must follow other people even if you dislike doing so.

The Lines of This Image

Line 1. All things in the universe undergo change. You must follow these changes. Otherwise, you will have to leave civilization and become a hermit in the mountains.

Line 2. The stream of change flows in two directions. You must select one direction by calculating the benefits and harms associated with the streams of change. It is easy to select a direction which will yield many benefits and little harm. When you cannot decide upon a direction because the options are rather similar, you must weigh benefit against harm. You can choose the direction with greater benefits if you do not mind the harm, or you can choose the direction with less harm if you cannot handle any more problems.

Line 3. Human beings can choose only one direction—they cannot handle more than one. They should choose by first analyzing their situation. Then they must make a decision. Decision-making requires willpower.

Line 4. When a talented person climbs up the ladder of success, many people will follow him. He will not need to follow others. The position of a leader is more dangerous than that of a follower, because the leader must deal with the possibility of being deserted by his followers. To prevent desertion, the leader must be humble.

Line 5. Before they became leaders, true leaders were the best followers. True leaders are leaders because they remember how they felt as followers. They treat their followers fairly and they help their followers. That is why true leaders have a great following.

Line 6. To get other people to follow you, you must follow them.

To persuade others to satisfy your needs, you must satisfy the needs of others. When you fulfill the needs of others, you will never be alone.

FIFTH GROUP: FREEWILL

 SUN, WIND

INTRODUCTION. Willpower must be used constructively. Human beings must learn how to choose wisely. The only right human beings have is to do good.

 *HSIAO CH'U,* OPEN-MIND-EDNESS

Open-minded people will never fail. People must learn to keep an open mind in order to master new situations.

 *CHIA JÊN,* FAMILY

The family is a natural team. The family is also a basic unit of society. If the family is successful, the country and the world will be successful.

 *I,* GRATITUDE

A person must be thankful for help given by other people and heaven. Human beings have no control over success. Success is achieved through the help of others.

 *WU WANG,* ENDURANCE

The best scheme is not to use schemes, and the best lie is not to lie. Wise people often seem to be foolish.

 *SHIH HO,* JUSTICE

People who commit crimes for the first time in their lives may be given another chance. Those who commit crimes for the second time must be punished. Those who commit crimes for the third time must be removed.

 *I,* NEED AND SUPPLY

A system must be devised to put everyone to work. People must will themselves to work.

415

 *KU,* PRE-
VENTION

CONCLUSION. The best medicine is prevention. One must willfully prevent disease from undermining the most important aspect of free will. Without life, one has nothing.

SUN

The Image

The hexagram is composed of two wind trigrams. The wind penetrates everywhere, but it does not circulate randomly. The wind is composed of air and pressure, and its circulatory path is governed by pressure. The wind flows from areas of high pressure to areas of low pressure. This shows that there seems to be no true free will in the universe, especially in the Human Kingdom. People are governed by external and internal pressures. External pressure is caused by politics, religion, economics, the family and peer pressure. Internal pressure is caused by thoughts, knowledge, background and physical condition. There are also pressures which are neither external nor internal in nature. These pressures are uncontrollable circumstances. According to Buddhist teachings, there are eight uncontrollable circumstances that everyone must suffer through, and they are: birth, illness, aging, death, not getting what one wants, getting what one does not want, not getting the person one loves, and separation from one's beloved after one finally gets him or her.

The wind blows fairly. In spring, the winds are mostly from the east; in summer, the south; in autumn, the west; in winter, the north. Actually the degrees of freedom conferred upon the four kingdoms of the universe are these: the members of the Kingdom of Vegetation, possessing only physical bodies, have absolutely no free will. The members of the Kingdom of Animals have a limited degree of free will. The members of the Kingdom of Humankind, possessing physical, mental and spiritual bodies, can *exercise* their will. Gentlemen have more freedom than Little Men. Sages have more freedom than either. Immortals are absolutely free, because their bodies are not limited by space or time. By learning the wisdom of the winds, we can develop our spirituality. We can also be what we want, get what we want, and keep what we want.

416

The Lines of This Image

Line 1. At this stage, a person has no control over his four physical needs: fighting, entertainment, eating and sex. This person follows his basic instinctive needs. This inability to control the basic instincts is considered to be a disease, because there is no balance between the three folds of the body. The physical body is dominant.

Line 2. At this stage, a person has developed a little mental ability. But the person does not have enough knowledge to think clearly, form intelligent opinions or make decisions. As a result, he depresses himself and other people. Depression is contagious.

Line 3. A person must learn how to make wise choices. The *Sui* hexagram teaches a person how to make such a choice.

Line 4. Willpower will help a person emerge from any problem in triumph, like the sun emerging from behind the clouds. Willpower helps people make the right decisions, i.e., do only good deeds. The only absolute right a human being has is to do good.

Line 5. Leaders have a great following. Leaders have more responsibility than their followers, because a wrong decision made by the leader will hurt a great deal of people. A leader must encourage and accept advice, and he must make decisions that will benefit people. A leader must have a strong willpower to do so.

Line 6. A leader with a strong willpower, in the end, pushes his subjects too forcefully, and this creates fear. The subjects, unable to meet their leader's demands, may revolt and destroy everything. A leader must never push too forcefully. He must always be considerate of others.

HSIAO CH'U

The Image

This hexagram is composed of a wind trigram above a heaven trigram. Wind in the heavens blows away the clouds. The clouds are blown into various shapes. Because the clouds are dispersed, no rain will fall. The foregoing represents the dispersal of the members of a successful organization and the weakening of a politician's power. A politician must build up his power. This hexagram is about building up your abilities.

The Lines of This Image

Line 1. The universe is always changing. New ideas and situations are constantly materializing. You must build up your ability to be flexible.

Line 2. When people seek the same things, they become competitors. This is not good. If you do not lose, the other does. You must use strategy to win the other party over to your side. When you accumulate a great following, you build up your strength.

Line 3. You must build up your patience. If you wish to succeed, you must wait until the propitious moment. If you do not wait or analyze your position, you will lead your following in the wrong direction. Then you will be abandoned by everyone.

Line 4. A person must build up his abilities in secrecy. If your strengths are made known to your enemies, they will be able to work a strategy to cripple your power.

Line 5. After you have solved external problems, you must solve internal problems, which develop soon after external pressure is relieved. Using force to suppress internal problems will relieve the problems temporarily. The problems will only be resolved through peaceful resolutions.

Line 6. When you are very powerful, you must share your power with others. You will not last long if you become a dictator.

CHIA JÊN

The Image

The hexagram is composed of a wind trigram above a fire trigram. Fire produces wind and wind produces fire. One cannot do without the other. This reflects the unconditional assistence family members give to each other. The family is a source of power, because family

418

members help each other out of love for one another. The members of your family are unlike the people outside.

The Lines of This Image

Line 1. The members of a family *must abide* by certain regulations. These regulations divide the labor and make a family strong. When the family is governed by emotions, contention breaks out easily among the family members. When every member follows a certain set of rules, peace will be easily maintained.

Line 2. The family must *be* a family. The family members *must eat* together. The mother is very important. If she cooks for the family, the family will be ruled by her. People who eat together will not be indifferent to each other.

Line 3. For a family to be successful the family members *must* do everything together. Everyone must treat each other well. Do not let familiarity displace manners. This encourages closeness.

Line 4. The family that is a successful team will flourish. But there are three dangers every successful family must face, and they are: waste, haughtiness and corruption. The family that can overcome these evils will prosper.

Line 5. Every member must perform his duty and the family should not be dismantled by external influence. The father must act as a father; the mother, as a mother; and the children, as children. If so, it is a righteous family. If there will be righteous families there will be a righteous society. Then there will be a proud country.

Line 6. The family is the fundamental unit of society. If the family is successful, the country will be successful. If countries are successful, the world will be successful.

I

The Image
This hexagram is composed of a wind trigram over a thunder tri-

gram. Wind and thunder help each other. Society will be productive if unrelated people can trust and help each other.

The Lines of This Image

Line 1. When you are helped, you must express gratitude. When you borrow something, you must return it in good condition. This way you will not accumulate bad Karma.

Line 2. When you are successful, you must thank heaven. You must never think that success is the result of your own efforts. When you thank God, you will receive even more rewards. Remember we have no control over opportunity; we can, however, control preparation.

Line 3. You should express your gratitude in your actions. You must help others actively. You should donate your money.

Line 4. You must do things for other people. You are here today because of their support. You must listen to others' advice.

Line 5. When you are in a high position, you may try to hold on to your position by plotting against others. Intrigues are not necessary if you have been helpful and kind toward other people.

Line 6. Your advantage is another's disadvantage. You should give up special advantages to help others. You should voluntarily retire.

WU WANG

The Image
This hexagram is composed of a heaven trigram above a thunder trigram. Thunder calls attention to the infiniteness of heaven. Thunder accentuates the attributes of heaven: glory, honesty, power and prominence. Thunder tests the purity of human beings. Those who are frightened of the roar of thunder have done wrong. Those who are not afraid of thunder are pure at heart. Nothing lasts. Things are built up and then torn down. Things aggregate and then separate. This hexagram is about how you can stand firm and endure.

The Lines of This Image

Line 1. To stand firm, you must be honest. The best scheme is not to use schemes or not to lie.

Line 2. You must not be lazy. You must not take shortcuts. When you plant crops, you cannot skip one step of the planting procedure. Nothing will result from laziness.

Line 3. Honesty and industriousness are not panaceas for every problem. Unsolvable problems exist to test you. You must not become depressed. Even the best people will be unjustly accused of wrongs they did not do. You must stand firm.

Line 4. A person will incur the wrath of heaven when he blames heaven for his failure in an endeavor that would have resulted inevitably in failure. The depression that person suffers is the result of his own stupidity. You must never be too ambitious.

Line 5. You must never be too attentive about trivial details. Those who can fly do not care about being tripped by stones, rocks or even trees.

Line 6. People who stand firm are sometimes unjustly accused of being stubborn. People who stand firm are wise; stubborn people are not. Wise people also appear foolish.

SHIH HO

The Image

This hexagram is composed of a fire trigram above a thunder trigram. The combined power of thunder and fire is used to symbolize the power of justice. This hexagram is about criminals.

The Lines of This Image

Line 1. Evil Men and Little Men are always committing crimes and breaking laws. Human beings are not perfect. Those who commit petty crimes for the first time in their lives should be allowed to go free. They should be admonished for misdemeanors and they should be given another chance.

Line 2. The criminals who commit a second crime should be placed in jail. They should be punished and educated.

Line 3. Criminals who commit a third crime—those who do not change even after undergoing extensive education—should be eliminated. These people are useless to society, because they cannot be educated and they waste time and resources. To be kind to them is to be cruel to society.

Line 4. Society must be placed on the alert when a person who enforces the law commits a crime. Such people must be eliminated immediately.

Line 5. A judge must first listen to the arguments of both parties before making a decision.

Line 6. The judicial system must be strong, otherwise criminals will exploit it. You must not be kind to criminals, because being kind to them is being cruel to good people.

I

The Image

This hexagram is composed of a mountain trigram over a thunder trigram. There is no movement above, but there is movement below. This represents digestion. An abnormality occurs when there is movement above (food is expelled from the mouth). This is a hexagram about the need and supply of resources.

The Lines of This Image

Line 1. Everyone must work. Those who do not work cannot eat.

Line 2 . The upper classes should help support the lower classes. Children must be supported by their parents. Parents who give birth to children with the intention of making the children support themselves should not give birth.

Line 3. There are always Little Men who do not want to work. These

422

people are always looking for people to support them. A system must be devised to put everybody to work. A good system encourages people to work. A bad system encourages people to look for ways to earn money effortlessly.

Line 4. Taxes should not be used for supporting officials. Taxes should be used for paying officials to work. The official who does not work is a criminal.

Line 5. The government that depends on another government for support is the worst kind of government.

Line 6. When you are able to support people's mental and spiritual needs, you will be blessed. The more people you support, the greater you become.

KU

The Image

The hexagram is composed of a mountain trigram over a wind trigram. The winds at the foot of a mountain penetrate everywhere. This represents the penetration of germs into the body. Illnesses are caused by the germs. Light illness must be corrected with light medication. Serious illness must be corrected with heavy medication. Those who are wise will try to prevent illness rather than cure it.

The Lines of This Image

Line 1. The basic weaknesses and illnesses of human beings are inherited from their parents through the blood and genes.

Line 2. Ascertaining the cause of an illness is very difficult. A disease is like a weed in a forest. The healer must be thorough, persistent and pure of heart. Otherwise he will not be able to find the cause of a disease.

Line 3. To eliminate an illness, you must sacrifice some time, money, and freedom. Little losses result in great gains.

Line 4. Illness must be treated quickly. Allowing an illness to linger will result in more problems.

Line 5. The best treatment for all illnesses is to correct the mental body. Illness results when the mental body cannot control the physical body. Taoist teachings place great emphasis upon treating the physical, mental and spiritual bodies together.

Line 6. To survive a disease, one must follow the Taoist teachings diligently. When there are no minor illnesses, there will not be major illnesses.

SIXTH GROUP: PEOPLE

LI, FIRE

INTRODUCTION. A single flame cannot last. People must associate with other people. This hexagram shows how people can be grouped together.

LÜ, IM-MIGRATION

A successful immigrant is one who contributes to the new country. He must not always take.

TING, TALENT

People should learn how to use talent. One untalented person can ruin everything. A country's talent that is used by another country is a great misfortune.

WEI CHI, TIMING

Nothing can be done if timing is not right. To succeed, one must be able to pass a period of unfavorable timing.

MÊNG, EDUCATION

Education must be a priority. Children must be taught about themselves and other people. Then they may be taught technical knowledge.

HUAN, SEPARATION

Separation is death. It must be prevented. Rationality is more useful for preventing separation. Using emotion will achieve the opposite effect.

 *SUNG,* LAWSUIT — Lawsuits are just manifestations of egoism. Neither plaintiff nor defendant wins. One should stay away from lawsuits.

 *TUNG JÊN,* GROUPING — CONCLUSION. A person should learn how to deal with people. The flames are bright. People must work together to benefit each other. People who are of one mind can bend metal with the force of their minds.

LI

The Image

The hexagram is composed of two fire trigrams. Fire cannot burn by itself. It must be fueled by oil, wood, or coal. A single flame cannot last long. Fire represents a gathering of people. Because fire is bright, clear, hot and beautiful, it is used to symbolize emotion, passion, desire, relationships, contention, enjoyment, capriciousness, sex, birth, and the continuation of life. Fire fulfills mankind's needs, destroys mankind's creations, and enlightens mankind. Fire symbolizes challenge.

The Lines of This Image

Line 1. Human relationships are not always fair. A talented person is always placed beside a slow superior. Consequently, that person can neither display his talent nor his intelligence. He must also stifle his ambition.

Line 2. Moderation brings balance and peace to any activity or endeavor.

Line 3. The sun rises and sets. The seasons change. A person must do

425

as many good deeds as possible, because he can never recover wasted time.

Line 4. You must enjoy the things you want. If you do not do so, you will experience disaster. You must use your God-given talents. If you do not do so, you will be abandoned by your following.

Line 5. To attain success, you must think of the dangers that lie in your future. Sorrowful people are wiser than those who laugh. Rational people endure longer than emotional people. People who worry attain success earlier than those who do not worry.

Line 6. A person must be kind to others. When you go fishing, you must toss out a net with a hole in it. You must let some fish escape. When you go to war, you must kill only the leader of the opposing army. You must let the soldiers go.

LÜ

The Image

This hexagram is composed of a fire trigram above a mountain trigram. When a fire starts on a mountain, it is hard to stop. It travels widely and quickly. People must move to new places because their position in society is insecure. To move is to develop, and travel is a form of enjoyment. People might not remain in one place for their entire lives.

The Lines of This Image

Line 1. When immigrants arrive at a new land, they must suffer bitterly. Because they do not understand the language of their adopted country, they will be confined to menial labor. They will receive no assistence from the natives, because they will not know any of them.

Line 2. An immigrant must be patient and he must work hard. After a period of time, the natives will know and understand· him. An immigrant will slowly accumulate friends, and his business will grow.

Line 3. If an immigrant treats the natives haughtily, he will incur the natives' hatred.

426

Line 4. A wise immigrant will contribute to his adopted country. Then he will be allowed to become a permanent resident of that country.

Line 5. To establish a good reputation, the immigrant must *give* rather than *take.*

Line 6. When an immigrant becomes wealthier than the natives, he will be the object of envy. If he does not share his wealth, he will be forced to move.

TING

The Image

This hexagram is composed of a fire trigram above a wind trigram. The stove, or *Jing,* is very important to the family. A family without a stove would starve to death. In Taoist Sexology, the stove is the sexual organs. The stove is the source of energy. The stove also represents new blood or new talents, without which a country or corporation would collapse.

The Lines of This Image

Line 1. It takes only one untalented person within a group of people to ruin everything. You should use this opportunity to expel that person.

Line 2. A good organization must establish a good system for taking in talent and putting it to use to build up the organization.

Line 3. Talented people have two faults: being envious of others before they achieve success and being haughty after success is achieved. A talented person becomes a Little Man when he is envious. By being haughty, the person is belittling others. This is a great loss to himself and others.

Line 4. When an organization misuses its talented people, this is a great loss.

Line 5. Those who do not have special talents are talented if they

427

have tolerance and know how to use other's talents. This applies particularly to those who obtained a high position through luck.

Line 6. The world is always changing. Talents that are useful today are useless tomorrow. You must continue to bring in fresh talent. Otherwise there will be a great loss.

WEI CHI

The Image
This hexagram is composed of a fire trigram above a water trigram. Flames fly upward and water flows downward. This represents a contrary situation wherein people are uncooperative. Nothing can be successful.

The Lines of This Image

Line 1. When the timing is not right, a great deal of labor will be wasted. You cannot be successful no matter how hard you try. You must be wise and do things when the timing is correct.

Line 2. You should not idly wait until the timing is right. You should educate yourself and prepare yourself until an opportunity arrives.

Line 3. Sometimes you are forced to do something that requires skills that surpass your own. You must seek outside help. If you cannot find it, you will fail.

Line 4. In government, when timing prevents the solution of any domestic problem, a military campaign can be started outside the country. When timing prevents the solving of your problems, you should do some traveling.

Line 5. Upon detecting unfavorable timing, a leader must quickly find a talented staff to help him save his reputation.

Line 6. When an apple is unripe, it cannot be eaten. Talented people must learn to wait. If you can pass an unfavorable period of time, you will be successful, for not failing is one form of success. When timing is unfavorable, nothing turns out as expected.

428

MÊNG

The Image

This hexagram is composed of a mountain trigram over a water trigram. A natural fountain on top of a mountain provides pure and clean water. When this water flows down the mountainside, it becomes dirty. When an innocent child grows up, he will encounter many things. If the child receives a good education, he will be a good person. If the child receives a bad education, he will be a bad person. This hexagram is about education.

The Lines of This Image

Line 1. In any country, education must be a priority. Everything else is secondary. Education exists because of everyone's desire for betterment. The educator is responsible for stirring up a desire for self-improvement in people's hearts. Without this desire, a successful educational system cannot be built.

Line 2. Children must not be taught "dead" knowledge at the beginning. Dead knowledge bores the children and it discourages them from wanting an education. In the beginning, children should learn about people, and they should learn how to be good human beings. The educators must be the most knowledgeable people in the country. Their wages should reflect the fact that they are the nation's most revered people. Without these people, there will be no second generation.

Line 3. Next, students should be taught how to protect the three folds of the body. Only after this should they be taught technical knowledge. With a background in Taoism, students will not abuse the technical knowledge for selfish purposes. No "monsters" will be created.

Line 4. Unfortunately, educators are not respected enough. This is a great misfortune for mankind. As long as incorrect education prevents people from becoming Gentlemen, the world will never be at peace.

429

Line 5. Information about the three folds of the body should be presented in this order: physical, mental, and finally, spiritual. This is the highest form of education. Education, when presented in this form, will be exciting and helpful to students. When they cannot apply the knowledge obtained from school to their daily lives, they will regard their school as torturous experiences.

Line 6. Education, like the water flowing downward along the mountainside, is continuous. Everyone is here to learn lessons. If everyone receives the wrong education, the progress of the universe is delayed.

HUAN

The Image

This hexagram is composed of a wind trigram above a water trigram. The wind scatters the water. Unification is the principle of life, and separation is the principle of death. Anything that is failing will first fall apart. We must prevent separation.

The Lines of This Image

Line 1. The seed of separation and death is everywhere. The seed of death lies buried in every new project. By being aware of this seed, a person can prevent the seed's germination. A person will avoid mistakes that can start the separation process. A person can also remove the seeds of separation.

Line 2. When signs of separation are detected, do not try to forcefully hold the separating parts together. One should wait for the cause to surface and then remove it.

Line 3. Communication can cement the separating parts together. Many separations are caused by a lack of communication. When communication ceases, doubt springs up. Doubt causes many problems. You should spare no trouble in keeping the channels of communication open.

Line 4. Another way to prevent separation is to unite everyone under a leader. An aura of respectability must be created around this leader, otherwise he will not attract a following.

430

Line 5. During a separation, the leader must remain calm. When the opportunity presents itself, the leader must use rationale to pull people together. Using emotion will achieve the opposite effect.

Line 6. When a separation cannot be prevented, one should escape.

SUNG

The Image
The hexagram is composed of a heaven trigram above a water trigram. Heaven is stable and constant. Water is changeable. In the courtroom, the role of heaven is assumed by the judge, and the role of water is assumed by the other members of the court. The restless people below the bench must obtain the permission of the judge before they act.

The Lines of This Image

Line 1. Contention has already started before the contending parties appear before the court. The more the opposing parties fight, the more anger and hatred is created. It would be wise if, during a quarrel, both parties could contain their anger and quietly and slowly discuss ways to resolve the problem. When emotion is removed from the discussions, lawsuits can be prevented. Lawsuits are simply methods of healing fractured egos.

Line 2. Before you become involved in a lawsuit, you should sit down and analyze your situation. Are you bringing suit for the right reasons? Can your arguments persuade the court? And so on. Then analyze your opponent. Compare yourself with him. If you feel that you cannot win, you can retract and prevent a great loss.

Line 3. You should avoid involvement in a lawsuit, unless you are protecting yourself from intrigues. Even then, lawsuits should be used only as a last resort. You should try to communicate with the opposition first.

Line 4. No one wins in a lawsuit, not even the winner. Everyone loses his time, money, and health. If one party yields a little, a great deal of stress and tension can be prevented.

Line 5. In lawsuits there are no guaranteed victories, unless a person bribes the court. A person can cheat the court but he cannot cheat the universe or heaven. You should never get involved in something you cannot win.

Line 6. The person who sues others to generate excitement or display his power is the most despicable person on earth. No one will want to associate with this person.

T'UNG JÊN

The Image
The hexagram is composed of a heaven trigram above a fire trigram. Flames fly upwards toward the sky. Both heaven and fire share the same goals. People should work toward the same goal as their group.

The Lines of This Image

Line 1. The flames are bright. You must participate only in those group activities which benefit humanity.

Line 2. The person who tries to destroy a group's unity has evil intentions. This person will try to split an organization or gathering into fragments.

Line 3. To unite people, you must find one shared value or goal between them.

Line 4. Similarities are not enough to unite people. People must work toward a similar goal, an ideal.

Line 5. Ideals are not enough. People must also derive some benefits from their work. The leader of the group must be different—he cannot take any of the benefits that are available. The leader must share the problems. The leader must earn the respect of his following.

Line 6. When two people can be of one mind, the power of their minds can bend metal. If a group of people can be of one mind, great things can be accomplished. History has shown that three people

432

with the same goals can change history. Separation is easy. Coming together is hard.

SEVENTH GROUP: PEACE

 *K'UN,* EARTH

INTRODUCTION. The earth is peaceful, motionless, and quiet. Learning the wisdom of the earth can help a person overcome any disaster.

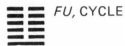 *FU,* CYCLE

People need salvation. But those who are fanatical about helping others become an obstacle to the progress of humanity.

 *LIN,* GOVERNING

The best governor is one whose existence is only known. The secondary governor is one who is loved by the people. The worst governor is one who is hated and feared by the people.

 *T'AI,* BALANCE

Peace does not last forever. It is succeeded by turmoil, which is then succeeded by peace. A government will always degenerate and then collapse.

 *TA CHUANG,* POWERFUL PEOPLE

Powerful people must never overestimate their power. Heaven will never give powerful people an easy life.

 *KUAI,* REBELLION

One must show no mercy when dealing with rebels. The leader is the basic cause of a rebellion. Unless the leader corrects himself, there will always be rebels.

 *HSÜ,* DEADLOCK

Patience must be learned. In a cruel society, many traps are set for the innocent. Patience and waiting are the best weapons against these traps.

 *PI,* COOPERA-TION

CONCLUSION. People must co-operate with each other. Equality must be maintained if cooperation is to be maintained. Equality is fairness of distribution of resources.

K'UN

The Image

This hexagram is composed of two earth trigrams. Earth, being completely Yin in nature is the direct opposite of heaven. The earth represents passiveness, acceptance, sorrow, contention, competition, intrigue and death. On the other hand, earth also represents solidity, richness (hidden mines), enjoyment, peace and quiet. It also supports many forms of life.

The Lines of This Image

Line 1. Disasters do not occur without a reason. Disasters are accumulations of many wrongs. For example, a son will kill his father because he wants to end the many years of torment his father has inflicted upon him.

Line 2. The earth displays three virtues: it supports every organism; it is peaceful, motionless, and quiet; and it tolerates all substances. You must learn the wisdom of the earth.

Line 3. Being quiet is the same as being " productive . " The wisest people are quiet and unassuming, because they do not want to belittle others by displaying their talents. Those who are superficial—exhibitionists—will retard their own progress, because they are disliked by others. Being peaceful is a form of cultivation.

Line 4. In times of turmoil, only those who are unassuming will survive. The exhibitionists will be eliminated.

Line 5. Wise people prefer to remain hidden from the public eye.

434

The highly educated will be humble. The highly talented will be unaffected.

Line 6. Death is the end. It swallows up honor and shame, wealth and poverty, happiness and sadness. All of life's struggles become meaningless at death. People should learn how to live meaningfully and die meaningfully. A meaningful death is greater than a meaningless life. Death is the end of life. Life is the end of death. And death is the beginning of a new life.

FU

The Image

This hexagram is composed of an earth trigram above a thunder trigram. A new cycle begins. The universe is cyclic. Things are born, things develop, things reach a climax, and then things fall. This is followed by another beginning.

The Lines of This Image

Line 1. Negativity ascends until it reaches an apex, and then it descends. As negativity descends, positiveness ascends. When positiveness reaches an apex, it also descends. And the cycle continues. When a thoroughly evil person is penitent, evil wanes and goodness waxes. Although penitence is only a flash in the mind, it has far-reaching consequences.

Line 2. When a person is penitent, that person will become a humanitarian. He will help an ever-widening circle of people until he has helped an entire society.

Line 3. When a person helps people on such a grand scale, he will meet people he does not like. When he begins to dislike, he will become unsocial. He must willfully suppress the urge to become unsocial.

Line 4. Although your kindliness surpasses that of others, your kindliness will not hasten the arrival of success. To be kind, you must be patient and persistent. You must continue to help others, even if you receive no rewards for your serivces. True devotion earns

435

the love of the people. Your kindliness can earn the love of a country.

Line 5. When you reach a peak in your career, you are respected and tremendously successful. However, you must not become haughty. The greater you become, the more humble you must be. True greatness comes from serving people.

Line 6. People can easily become fanatical about humanitarianism. Those who become addicted to humanitarianism become so narrow-minded that they become an obstacle to humanity. These people are most corrupt in that they will not allow other people to think differently than they.

LIN

The Image

The hexagram is composed of an earth trigram above a lake trigram. The lake is bounded by the earth. It is controlled by the earth. This hexagram symbolizes the philosophy of control.

The Lines of This Image

Line 1. The person who is above all others must be just and righteous. Those who are not will not be able to control the people below them. They cannot govern worldly affairs.

Line 2. The best governor is one who's existence is only known. The second best governor is one who is loved by the people. The worst kind of governor is one who is hated and feared.

Line 3. Those who want to govern must not use speeches to govern their subjects. Rather, they must control their subjects with actions. Speeches should at least be equal to actions. When speeches outnumber actions, harm is done.

Line 4. A good governor uses talented people to help him think and work. The worst kind of governor is one who over-estimates his own worth—he thinks he is always right and does not listen to advisors.

436

Line 5. The highest governor (kings, emperors, etc.) must have three virtues: no wisdom, no ability, and no activity. What does this mean? It means that the highest governor must not use his wisdom, ability, or actions to govern others. He must use talented and capable people instead. And he must use these others' ideas and actions to govern people.

Line 6. The most successful—unforgettable—governors must have three virtues: kindness, mercy, and self-control.

T'AI

The Image

This hexagram is composed of a heaven trigram above an earth trigram. Earth is oriented downward and inward. Heaven is oriented upward and outward. These natures circulate and balance. Where there is balance, there is peace. When peace passes, turmoil arrives. There is a time for peace and a time for turmoil. There is a time for unification and a time for separation. Mankind must see through things: neither peace nor turmoil will last forever, since one succeeds the other constantly.

The Lines of This Image

Line 1. A country or society that has just passed through a period of turmoil will experience peace. All that has been destroyed during the period of turmoil must be built anew. During the period of rebuilding, everyone is enthusiastic, happy, helpful, and generous.

Line 2. When the rebuilding is nearly complete and a new society appears out of the ashes, dreams are fulfilled. But then greed motivates people to desire more than they need. They begin to hurt each other and to form divergent groups. These groups cannot co-exist peacefully. At this stage, the society can still be prolonged if its leader is righteous, just, and farsighted.

Line 3. The sun has reached the highest position. The seemingly good and peaceful society has reached a climax. Now you can see many symptoms of incurable corruption. People are selfish. They

437

have forgotten past sufferings. This society can still be prolonged if its leader can mend some of the corruption. With a good leader, it can still maintain a facade of greatness and strength.

Line 4. At this stage, you can see many poor people. There are many who are unemployed. Immorality is rampant. There is corruption in government. The good hide in the mountains, because they are discriminated against.

Line 5. Corruption has reached a climax. Most politicians are not statesmen. They are unwise, uneducated, shortsighted, cheap politicians. They are, according to an old saying, a bunch of devils dancing and splitting the spoils. The country can still remain unified if there is a threatening outside force waiting to fight. The corrupt government can still point a finger at the outside force to buy time.

Line 6. The lamp is empty of oil. The country collapses. No one can save it. Then a new period will begin.

TA CHUANG

The Image
This hexagram is composed of a thunder trigram above a heaven trigram. There is nothing to inhibit thunder from expressing itself. There is plenty of space to accommodate such power. This hexagram is about power.

The Lines of This Image

Line 1. The powerful person who is haughty will never be successful. He will eventually fail.

Line 2. A person who is talented, wise, and humble will have infinite power.

Line 3. In the universe, nothing is absolutely perfect. The most intelligent person can think about a problem 1,000 times and will always miss one thing. A fool who can think about a problem 1,000 times will get at least one idea. A person with power must not be too trusting of his ability.

438

Line 4. If heaven confers upon powerful people ease and good fortune, they will cause great calamities and hurt many people. Heaven rarely confers upon powerful people ease or freedom, because limiting their power protects their subjects.

Line 5. When you meet a very powerful person, you should not fight him directly, if you think you are not as powerful as he. Even the most powerful person has one weakness. If you can secretly ferret out his weakness, you can control him.

Line 6. The most rigid things can never overcome the softest things. For example, the most rigid sword is useless against water, because water cannot be broken by a slashing sword. Some of the most powerful people are slain by the most stupid people.

KUAI

The Image

This hexagram is composed of a lake trigram over a heaven trigram. Lake water does not usually rise above ground level. When it does overflow the banks of the lake, it is described to be at the level of heaven. Floods symbolize rebellion of the subjects. This hexagram deals with rebellion.

The Lines of This Image

Line 1. Rebellion, like overflowing lake water, cannot be contained by a few people. Rebellion is a result of timing and many other causes that have been building up over a period of time. Rebellion should not be covered up or ignored. Covering up a rebellion will only fuel its process. In the beginning, people tend to cover up a rebellion because they do not like to face it.

Line 2. You must publicize a rebellion. You must explain as clearly as possible that rebellion hurts everyone. Everyone should learn that rebellion is always subdued and that siding with rebels is a fatal mistake.

Line 3. To destroy rebel forces, you must first ferret out the rebel sympathizers from one's own following. There are many rebels outside because there are many rebels inside.

439

Line 4. You must be merciless when you are destroying the rebels. Being kind to them is the same thing as being cruel to oneself. Rebels will use words like humanity, benevolence and kindness to soften their opposition and to make their opposition lose critical timing.

Line 5. You should take a good hard look at yourself. Your past actions are the causes of the rebellion. If you do not correct yourself, rebels will always spring up.

Line 6. To destroy rebels, you must eliminate as much of your weaknesses as possible. Then you must ferret out the weaknesses of the rebels. You must not strike blindly. Instead, wait until a weakness presents itself and then strike. To wait one day is to live one day.

HSÜ

The Image

This hexagram is composed of a water trigram above a heaven trigram. When one sees that the clouds are accumulating in the skies, one must prepare oneself for the rain. Although the skies darken steadily from the monstrous clouds, no rain falls. You are held in suspense. Because you cannot control the rain, you must wait patiently for it to fall. When things are at a deadlock, you must wait until opportunity arrives.

The Lines of This Image

Line 1. People's needs are so excessive that resources cannot satisfy them. When the supply does not meet the demand, competition arises. Difficulties that arise from competition are objective problems, not a product of your fate. If you are to survive in such a cruel society, you must meet certain conditions. Patience is a basic condition of success. A patient person will get what they want in the quickest way possible.

Line 2. Every minute, irritating things occur. If you cannot learn to be patient, anger and frustration will cause poisons to build up within the body and your health will be sacrificed for trivial reasons. You can train your patience by learning Internal Exercises.

440

Line 3. The formula for success is as follows:

Preparation + Opportunity = Success

Time is needed for building up skills, intelligence, etc. Opportunity arrives after considerable waiting. Preparation and Opportunity involve patience and waiting.

Line 4. Life is full of traps set by other people. This is especially true in a competitive society. Those who are impatient will run too fast, overlook the traps and fall into them. Those who are patient will be able to see the traps clearly. Patience is the best weapon against the inevitable pitfalls.

Line 5. What is real patience? Is it passivity, evasion and drinking wine every day? No. True patience is being stable, unhurried, and calm. Patience is displayed by a predator, when it is about to attack a prey.

Line 6. Patient people can endure bitterness better than others. Patient people can tolerate heavy labor— the kind others could not tolerate—and they can accomplish things that other people could never accomplish. If you know that you can be patient, you know that you can surpass everyone else in greatness.

PI

The Image

This hexagram is composed of a water trigram above an earth trigram. Water wants to inundate the earth, but earth will not allow it to do so. Water and earth are so close together that they are constantly pushing each other back and forth (as is most evident on a beach). This hexagram is about competition.

The Lines of This Image

Line 1. The most basic nature of mankind is doubt. It is the most potent poison in man's relationships. But people cannot and should not live and work without other people. This is a difficult situation, because you must be with people you distrust.

Line 2. Doubt must be diminished through a system which assures

441

equal distribution of resources. Elimination of competition results in the elimination of doubt. When people no longer doubt each other, they will be more cooperative when working together.

Line 3. Competition can also be eliminated by having everyone think of himself as a part of the group. You should always think about how you can benefit everyone. Competition causes people to hurt each other. It causes people to think about how much society owes them. Since people will always need other people, even during periods of intense competition, it would be wise if they could remove the element of competition voluntarily from their relations with others.

Line 4. To accomplish something, you must find a partner who has the same goals. A partner must also be able to keep his word. A partner must also care about fairness. Partners who fit the above description will contribute to a lasting partnership.

Line 5. To maintain a high level of cooperation among people, everyone must be honest. Nothing can last if anyone cheats.

Line 6. You must never be greedy, as it will cause a breach in fairness. Where there is no fairness, there will be no cooperation among people. Fairness must be strictly maintained. The distribution of resources between your spouse and children must be fair. Fairness must not be thrown aside for the sake of love. Fairness cannot be replaced by anything in the world.

EIGHTH GROUP: RELATIONSHIPS

 *TUI,* LAKE INTRODUCTION. People's relationships can be summarized as follows: Those who benefit others are called good. Those who do not benefit others are called bad. Those who are too good have special motives. True friends are those who criticize.

 *K'UN,* POVERTY The greatest cause of poverty is laziness. There are many other kinds of poor people.

 *TS'UI,* ECONOMICS — Capital must be used to make the economy flourish. People must learn marketing strategy.

 *HSIEN,* PASSION — Love is different from lust. Love is sacrificial in nature. Love that is conditional is not pure.

 *CHIEN,* STOPPAGE — Stoppage occurs because of people's selfishness.

 *CH'IEN,* HUMILITY — People must be humble to each other. True humility causes people to yield. Those who are most humble are the rich people on earth. They are happy with themselves and other people are happy with them. Humility is very important in diplomatic policy.

 *HSIAO KUO,* OVER THE LIMIT — Ambitions that excel talents cause problems. One should practice moderation.

 *KUEI MEI,* MARRIAGE — CONCLUSION. Marriage represents the peak of happiness. It is the sweetest form of relationship between people. Conditional marriages are time-bombs. Marriage is the hardest thing to succeed in. One who can succeed in marriage can succeed in anything.

TUI

443

The Image

This hexagram is composed of two lake trigrams. The lake, unlike the sea, is a limited body of water. A lake is beautiful and peaceful. People, especially lovers, are attracted to a lake. The lake symbolizes affection, emotion and conviviality. Because a lake is a limited body of water, there is no communication between lakes. This is the hexagram of friendship.

The Lines of This Image

Line 1. The basis for love or hate, like or dislike are benefit and harm. The person who benefits people is liked or loved. The person who harms people is disliked or hated. People who benefit others are called good. People who harm others are called bad. You can be called a good person by one and a bad person by another.

Line 2. Most friendships are based on favorable first impressions. People trust or rely on first impressions too much. This is unfortunate. Many enemies are made when friends are not selected after deep consideration.

Line 3. People like to be beneficiaries. Some people will exploit this state of mind in order to obtain something, and will say extremely pleasant words or send too many gifts. Their motives are suspect.

Line 4. A person who has no friends will never be successful. Friends can lift a person to great heights, or they can destroy him. Therefore, one should cultivate only true friends. True friendships are based on sharing of knowledge, talent, ethics, etc. Do not have too many acquaintances.

Line 5. A leader's following is very important. He or she should be able to distinguish the good from the bad. Good followers are those who criticize. Bad followers are those who use pleasant words.

Line 6. Little Men have many friends. Gentlemen have few friends.

K'UN

The Image

This hexagram is composed of a lake trigram over a water trigram. The lake is almost completely dry and the little bit of water remaining is useless. No longer productive or beautiful, the lake symbolizes poverty. The causes of poverty are divided into two groups: subjective and objective. Objective causes are uncontrollable causes of poverty, and they include political or social injustices and natural disasters. This hexagram is about subjective causes of poverty, which can be controlled. People who follow the philosophy of this hexagram will no longer be poor.

The Lines of This Image

Line 1. One major cause of poverty is laziness. Lazy people will make many excuses to avoid work.

Line 2. Another cause of poverty is addiction. When a person is addicted to something, he will use all of his money to support his habit.

Line 3. The lack of intelligence also causes poverty. Work cannot be done without an orderly mind. When a person's ambitions surpass his talents, he will not get what he desires most. Honor becomes shame and gain becomes loss.

Line 4. The talented and the wise will temporarily experience poverty. These people look upon poverty as a lesson which will increase their wisdom. Mental richness will someday transform into material richness.

Line 5. The rich who are never satisfied are also poor. These miserly people always want more money and hide it. They are not capable of spending it. Not spending money is the same as not having money.

Line 6. A person who fears everything is also poor. This person is suffering from mental illness. Because he is too afraid to do anything, he will remain poor forever.

TS'UI

The Image

The hexagram is composed of a lake trigram above an earth trigram. Earth that is permeated with water is very rich. It can support many forms of life. This hexagram is about economics.

The Lines of This Image

Line 1. A business is successful for three reasons: interest, capital, and time. The owner must be interested in his business and he must be highly *skilled.* The owner must invest a great deal of capital in his business. The more he invests, the more successful the business will become. The owner must also invest a great deal of time in the business. The longer the business lasts, the greater its credibility will be.

Line 2. A business must fulfill a need, and it must fulfill it well, in order to be successful. One should investigate the needs of the people.

Line 3. To become wealthy, one must earn money and save it.

Line 4. Businesses that make good use of the earth's resources are the best kind to get involved in.

Line 5. When one's business becomes successful, one must maintain a steady level of success by helping others. Do not monopolize, as monopolization will dry up the lake—causing a depression. Everyone will suffer.

Line 6. Do not expand one's business too rapidly. Depression sets in whenever too many businesses expand too quickly. Expanding slowly delays or prevents depression.

HSIEN

The Image

This hexagram is composed of a lake trigram above a mountain trigram. A lake in a mountain is very beautiful. It symbolizes attraction, love, and emotion.

The Lines of This Image

Line 1. Great limitations are imposed upon love. Love will be limited by different environments, families, habits, society, religion, and politics. True love will overcome these odds slowly. When these limitations are overcome too quickly or forcefully, the relationship will not last. Similarities can make a relationship last longer.

Line 2. Love is different from lust. Real love is silent. Real love causes a person to sacrifice himself for his beloved. Lust is active. Lust causes a person to seduce someone else. One can distinguish love from lust by carefully watching another person's movements.

Line 3. True love is expressed when both partners think in the same way and feel in the same way. True love causes one partner to sadden when the other partner is sad.

Line 4. One should not decorate oneself with symbols of wealth, position, or power. True love is not influenced by these things. Loving the true person will bring happiness.

Line 5. The highest form of love is love for humanity.

Line 6. The enemy of love is selfishness. One will never love another when one is selfish. People who are incapable of love are the most unhappy people in the world.

CHIEN

The Image

The hexagram is composed of a water trigram above a mountain trigram. The mountain forms a block between the water and ourselves. People frequently encounter obstacles. The philosophy of this hexagram teaches people how to deal with these obstacles.

The Lines of This Image

Line 1. When one encounters an obstacle, one should not rush forward. One should analyze the situation in order to overcome the obstacle.

Line 2. Obstacles are caused by selfishness. Everyone should compromise and sacrifice a little to remove obstacles.

Line 3. If the obstacles cannot be removed by the foregoing methods, one should cease progress in one's direction of endeavor and then one should eliminate the Little Men. You will never solve the problem if you do not do so.

Line 4. One must teach Little Men to put aside their selfishness for the good of all.

Line 5. To remove an obstacle, one must wait for a propitious moment. When that moment arrives, you must quickly remove the obstacle. You must not give the obstacle a chance to recover.

Line 6. If one still cannot succeed in removing an obstacle, one should obtain the help of others.

CH'IEN

The Image

This hexagram is composed of an earth trigram over a mountain trigram. The mountain that is lower than the ground is humbling itself. This hexagram is about humility.   a

The Lines of This Image

Line 1. The person who humbly does his work makes himself and others happy. Everything will be pleasant and success will be attained easily.

Line 2. Pretending to be humble is a disgusting activity. A person is not humble when he is cheating others. The cheater is like a wolf in sheep's clothing. Humility must come from the heart.

Line 3. True humbleness is a willingness to learn from others, accept new ideas and advice, and serve others. The person who is humble is truly happy.

Line 4. Humility begins with respecting one's parents and learning from them.

448

Line 5. Humble people are the richest people on earth. They are rich mentally and materially. They also have true friends.

Line 6. A country's diplomatic policy should utilize humility to make peace with other countries. Modest countries last the longest. The countries that are bent upon conquering others never last. Humility attracts friends.

HSIAO KUO

The Image

The hexagram is composed of a thunder trigram above a mountain trigram. The sound of thunder will be amplified when it bounces off the walls of the mountain. Thus thunder is made more frightening. This hexagram is about coping with enormous problems.

The Lines of This Image

Line 1. Many people have high standards. When their talents cannot satisfy their desire and ambition, they become miserable. Their goals are too big and they tear themselves apart with stress and tension.

Line 2. A person should concentrate only on his duties. He should not be over-enthusiastic and do the work of others. Otherwise he will cause many needless problems.

Line 3. It is not wise to do too much work or to do too little work. Doing just enough is proper and wise. Those who are moderate are the sages.

Line 4. All calamities arise from overdoing. The country that goes out of its territory to vex other countries will cause many problems.

Line 5. One should never set goals that are too easily obtained. Those who leave things halfway finished have health problems. They will not live long.

Line 6. This line represents the dangers of amplifying the physiological processes. Over-stimulation or inflammation of the body results from imbalance. Anything that causes imbalance creates illness and illness causes death.

KUEI MEI

The Image

This hexagram is composed of a thunder trigram above a lake trigram. Thunder above a lake causes waves to form on the lake. One stimulates the other. This hexagram is about male and female relationships. When two people decide to live together forever, they get married. Marriage is an occasion for rejoicing and it is the highest form of entertainment.

The Lines of This Image

Line 1. The completion of one's marriage vows is dependent upon and governed by fate. Marriage is an unpredictable as warfare.

Line 2. Two people entering into a marriage should realize that helping and balancing each other can be a form of torture and that they may argue constantly.

Line 3. Marriage should not be forced. It should not be used for business purposes and it should not be used as a payment for a favor. A marriage that is forced is like a time-bomb.

Line 4. A person should not rush into a marriage. As much time as possible should be taken to find a good spouse. One cannot find a good mate when one is in a hurry. Never having married is not as bad as regretting a bad marriage. Many people are hurt when a marriage does not work.

Line 5. Marriage must be a pure and unconditional act. When a person enters into a conditional marriage, he or she is fooling him- or herself. The losses will outnumber the gains.

Line 6. A marriage is extremely difficult to maintain. Like the eye, it cannot tolerate one speck of dirt. A conditional marriage always ends unhappily. Any problem that may arise during marriage must be resolved by the couple. Intermediation by a third party, including counselors cannot replace this and will make problems worse. The marriage is the foundation of the family. The family is the foun-

450

dation of the society. The society is the foundation of the country. And the country is the foundation of the world. Very few people are able to make something as vital as a marriage successful. They never follow the five foregoing principles.

III

Conclusion

Eight thoughts are represented by each of the groups of hexagrams. From one thought, 48 variations of that thought are derived, through logical reasoning. The hexagrams form a system of logic which explains the universal law. The hexagrams are mankind's guide to the universe.

During the Sung Dynasty, a famous scholar named Chu Shi studied the I-Ching in depth and frequently gave lectures on it. His lectures were attended by thousands of government ministers, nobility, scholars, etc. For months, the mountains would become his lecture hall, since several months' time was needed to explain one hexagram fully. The hexagrams are rich with meaning.

I have given only a summary of the philosophies contained within the hexagrams. The deepest meanings of the 384 lines of the 64 hexagrams are explained in simplest terms. Even though the teachings are abbreviated, the reader who follows these teachings will obtain infinite blessings from them.

The first group is the introduction to the entire 64 hexagrams. The last group is the conclusion to the entire 64 hexagrams. The first hexagram, *CHIEN*, introduces success. The last hexagram, *KUEI MEI,* is the conclusion of success, for marriage is the hardest thing to succeed in. Most people who are successful in other areas could have terrible marriages. The person who can succeed in marriage can succeed in anything.

The method for forecasting is not given. Please do not throw some coins and then read the fortune from a hexagram. These hexagrams should not be used as a method of fortune telling. You should prepare, enlighten, develop, and improve yourself, because you are your own key to success.

9

FLOW WITH THE TAO

I

Lao Tse said, ''People of highest caliber, upon hearing about Taoism, follow and practice it immediately. People of average caliber, upon hearing about Taoism, reflect for some time and then experiment. People of lowest caliber, upon hearing about Taoism, turn and let out a great laugh. If people do not laugh, it will not be Taoism." "My words," he said, "are simple and easy, but few people can do as I say."

Those of lowest caliber are legion and those of highest caliber— those who truly possess the Tao—are few. Most people have neither the fortune nor the ability to understand the Tao, or the Truth. This is why human evolution seems to progress so very slowly.

The word "fortune" bears great significance to Taoists, not only because Taoism is worth a gold mine to those who find it, but because people must have the fortune to find it. Throughout the centuries, the richness of Taoism has never been flaunted in public, just as the riches of the truly rich are never flaunted in public. Taoism awards its cultivators immediately. It is too valuable to be the subject of preaching.

Who has the fortune to meet with Tao?

The Tao is actually everywhere and it is forever awaiting obtainment by anyone with sincere devotion and discipline. The Tao is formless, nameless, and undiscriminating. Therefore, to practice Taoism, the cultivator need not leave family, friends, work, or belongings. Pao Piao Tse said, "Preeminent scholars can obtain Tao in the battlefield. Secondary scholars can obtain Tao in urban areas. Lower scholars can obtain Tao only in the mountains." No matter who or where you are, no sacrifice is demanded of you. You need not become a monk or a nun or hide in the mountains. You need only devotion and discipline. Therefore, whoever has true devotion and discipline has the fortune. To whomever has the fortune, the doors to Taoism will be thrown open.

Taoists called the unthinking masses the *Regular People,* the researchers of the truths of life the *Scholars,* the devoted and disciplined the *Cultivators,* and the possessor of the Great Tao a *Truer.* Truers understand the nature of the universe and possess its wisdom. The god-like beings are called *Immortals.*

The Law of Cause and Effect also determines who is fortunate enough to cultivate Taoism in his present lifetime. Those who have done many good deeds in the past will have the fortune to cultivate Taoism. Knowing this, the cultivator must revere his or her fortune and do more good deeds to safeguard his or her future.

This is not an easy task, for Taoism has powerful tools that can be easily abused. Through the practice of Taoism, people's respect can be won and enormous material profits can be made. However, these gains can tempt and lead cultivators astray, harming others for short-sighted gains. People may also be tempted to make a living from utilizing only one part of Taoism. Thus many people

454

lose sight of the original purpose of Taoism.

According to Taoism, the cultivators who stray are wasting themselves, their fortunes and their future. They will suffer, sicken, and die like Regular People. So there are ample motives for doing many good deeds.

One should not erroneously call oneself a cultivator, because one will waste oneself and others. A true cultivator of Taoism must study the entire teaching of Taoism. Many people who call themselves cultivators concentrate on only one of the eight departments of Taoism, thinking that the benefits derived from that particular department is enough. This is a great waste. Unfortunately, some self-proclaimed Taoists pass this unsound approach of Taoist study on to their students, which creates even more waste and leads to death.

Waste is the cause of calamities and death is the greatest punishment, according to Taoism. People who promise or guarantee results without asking for hard work create waste. These people, who claim that only prayers or rituals will save you, waste your life by leading you away from the cultivation of Taoism.

If people walk with God today, they will have a tomorrow. If people do a good deed today, they will receive rewards tomorrow. Results are guaranteed by your own hard work.

According to Pao Piao Tse, the Taoist cultivator must make longevity, happiness, health, and wisdom his or her primary reasons for cultivating Taoism. The second priority is to help other people find the Tao.

In order to help us live longer, healthier, happier, and wiser, Pao Piao Tse gave us this advice: "Never depend on diseases not to attack you. Only depend on your invulnerability to attack." He also said, "To become a Taoist, one shall never hurt oneself. There are many things that hurt people greatly. Unfortunately, people never pay attention to these."

Almost two thousand years ago, Pao Piao Tse wrote that as a cultivator you should avoid these destructive influences, which are:

Forcing yourself to think too much—trying to solve a problem you will never be able to solve

Forcing yourself to lift weights far beyond your capability

Worrying until depression sets in

Too much entertainment, joy or excitement

Fulfilling endless desires and ambitions—becoming over-enthusiastic

Talking or laughing too much

Insufficient rest or sleep

Too much exercise or participation in martial arts or sports

Drinking too much
Lying down immediately after stomach is full from eating
Running too much
Crying or shouting too loudly
Celibacy
Too much sex
Allowing yourself to become too cold before adding clothing
Allowing yourself to become too warm before removing cloth-
ing
Spitting
Dirtiness
Walking too quickly
Reading too much
Listening to loud music or too much noise
Sitting for great lengths of time
Sleeping for great lengths of time
Allowing yourself to become too hungry before eating
Over-eating
Drinking too much water
Rising too early
Perspiring too profusely
Racing horses (or cars today)
Being in crowds
Allowing the cold wind to contact the body after consuming
alcohol
Eating too many raw foods
Bathing too often and too long
Sleeping without covers or camping out too often
Studying or researching too intensely
Overuse of the heater during the winter and overuse of the
cooler during the summer
Going out on extremely cold, hot, windy or foggy days
Over-consumption of sour, spicy, sweet, bitter or salty foods

All of these activities reduce the body's resistence, which leads
to disease. Pao Piao Tse said, "Accumulating these destructive influences unawares reduces the term of life."

Moreover, Pao Piao Tse advised people to study Taoism. He advised people to begin with Herbology, Tuei-Na or Internal Exercises, as these confer upon the student everlasting health. And health
buys time for the completion of all the departments of Taoism.

II

A true cultivator of Taoism will automatically gain the following powers:

1. The power to see through things. All things in the universe emit electromagnetic waves. Television and radio were created to receive these waves sent from thousands of miles away. This ability to receive electromagnetic waves and reconstruct an image from them is innate in human beings. Because of desires of the physical body and self-centeredness, this ability has been covered over and humanity has become powerless. Through the cultivation of the Eight Pillars of Taoism, people will automatically rediscover their powers. They will not need to open a box to see its contents. The image of the object will have already been constructed in the brain before the box is opened. People will be able to see through others both physically and mentally. Physical problems, emotional states, etc., will all be apparent to the true cultivator. This power eliminates distance from space.

2. Intuitive or psychic power. A true cultivator will be able to read someone else's mind and forsee events before they occur. Things evolve under definite patterns and history repeats itself. The true cultivator will have gained insight and recognize the warning signals. This power eliminates distance from time.

3. Healing power. All true cultivators will automatically have the ability to heal.

4. The power to project an image from the body. All true cultivators will be able to be in several places at the same time.

5. The power to transform into different forms or into nothingness.

6. The power to control circumstances and prevent various forms of violence from hurting people.

From the first day a person begins cultivating Taoism, these powers begin to increase. These powers are given to cultivators to insure that they will someday reach immortality. Those who cultivate Taoism will receive all the powers claimed in the New Testament and more.

Another principle of the Yin and Yang Theory applies to the cultivation of Taoism. There are true cultivators and there are imitators. Taoists derive their power from cultivation. But magicians can imitate Taoist powers. Sometimes the imitation of Taoist powers can look even more attractive than the real thing. Truth is truth, and imitators are only imitators.

Magicians imitate Taoist powers to flaunt their abilities. Taoists who have such powers do not flaunt them. Chuang Tse said, "It is not wonderful that Taoists can gain power. It is very wonderful that they do not flaunt their power."

Since Taoists possess powers, they are cautioned against abusing them. The abuse of power — using power for unrighteous gains — will be a great misdeed.

This book is the first in history that constitutes a compilation of all the departments of Taoism. From this book, readers can learn and practice true Taoism in the correct sequence and direction.

This book will not contain detailed information about Space and Time I-Ching System, Personology, Astrology, Directionology. Before these can be given to the reader, he or she must have a thorough understanding of the teachings given here. Otherwise these powerful systems can be misused and the cultivators will be induced to become egotistic, materialistic and ambitious. Those who misuse such vital heavenly secrets will meet with severe punishments. Blindness is an example of the lightest form of punishment; death, the severest. Also the reader may feel overwhelmed if the excluded information which is extremely technical, were included in this book. This volume already provides enough information to help a cultivator benefit from practicing Taoism.

Although the exclusion of certain information is done for the protection of mankind, a devoted cultivator will eventually have the fortune to learn the entire truth and become a Truer.

The Foundation of Tao offers lectures and courses on all levels of Taoism from time to time, in different countries and different cities.

Lao Tse said, "The highest excellence is like water. It benefits all things without striving. It stays in the lowest and the most abhorred places. Hence its way is near to that of the Tao . . .

"The excellence of a residence is in the suitability of the place, that of the mind is in abysmal stillness, that of association is in being with the virtuous, that of government is in its ability to secure good order, that of work is in its workers' capabilities, and that of any movement is in its timeliness . . .

"Favor and disgrace would seem equally to be feared; honor and great calamity, to be regarded as personal conditions of the same kind. What is meant by speaking thus of favor and disgrace? Disgrace is to be placed in a lower position after the enjoyment of favor.

458

The obtainment of favor leads to the apprehension of losing it, and the loss of it leads to the fear of calamity. This is what is meant by saying that favor and disgrace would seem equally to be feared. And what is meant by saying that honor and great calamity are to be regarded as personal conditions? What makes me liable to great calamity is my having the self. If I had not the self, what great calamity could come to me? Therefore, he who would administer the state, honoring it as he honors his own person, may be employed to govern it. And he who would administer it with care which he bears to his own person may be entrusted with it . . .

"Honest words are not beautiful. Beautiful words are not honest. Those who have perfect knowledge do not dispute. The disputants do not have the perfect knowledge. Dilettantes never have true wisdom. Those who do not have true wisdom are dilettantes . . .

"The Taoist does not possess. The more that he expends for others, the more he possesses. The more that he gives, the more does he have . . .

"The way of heaven: it benefits without hurting.
The way of a Taoist: he does without striving."

SO LET US FLOW WITH THE GREAT TAO!

INDEX